System Firmware

An Essential Guide to Open Source and Embedded Solutions

Subrata Banik
Vincent Zimmer

Apress®

System Firmware: An Essential Guide to Open Source and Embedded Solutions

Subrata Banik
Bangalore, Karnataka, India

Vincent Zimmer
Tacoma, WA, USA

ISBN-13 (pbk): 978-1-4842-7938-0
https://doi.org/10.1007/978-1-4842-7939-7

ISBN-13 (electronic): 978-1-4842-7939-7

Managing Director, Apress Media LLC: Welmoed Spahr
Acquisitions Editor: Susan McDermott
Development Editor: Laura Berendson
Coordinating Editor: Jessica Vakili
Copy Editor: Mary Behr

Distributed to the book trade worldwide by Springer Science+Business Media New York, 1 NY Plaza, New York, NY 10004. Phone 1-800-SPRINGER, fax (201) 348-4505, e-mail orders-ny@springer-sbm.com, or visit www.springeronline.com. Apress Media, LLC is a California LLC and the sole member (owner) is Springer Science + Business Media Finance Inc (SSBM Finance Inc). SSBM Finance Inc is a **Delaware** corporation.

For information on translations, please e-mail booktranslations@springernature.com; for reprint, paperback, or audio rights, please e-mail bookpermissions@springernature.com.

Apress titles may be purchased in bulk for academic, corporate, or promotional use. eBook versions and licenses are also available for most titles. For more information, reference our Print and eBook Bulk Sales web page at www.apress.com/bulk-sales.

Any source code or other supplementary material referenced by the author in this book is available to readers on the GitHub repository: https://github.com/Apress/System-Firmware. For more detailed information, please visit www.apress.com/source-code.

Printed on acid-free paper

Table of Contents

About the Authors

Subrata Banik is a firmware engineer with more than a decade in the computer industry. He has acquired experience in system firmware design, development, and debugging across various firmware architectures like UEFI, coreboot, and Slim Bootloader for x86 and ARM platforms. Subrata has profound experience with platform enablement, which had led to working on all leading PC makers' products. Subrata is an active member of open-source firmware (OSF) development across different projects like coreboot, oreboot, flashrom, and EDKII, where he is one of the leading contributors in open firmware (coreboot) development. Subrata has received multiple US patents and is very passionate about learning new technology and sharing knowledge among enthusiast engineers. Subrata has presented technical talks at industry events such as the Open Source Firmware conference, Institute for Security and Technology, and Intel Developer Forum.

When not writing or working, he enjoys watching sports (especially football) or spending time with his daughter. A fun fact about Subrata is he is a strong believer in time travel.

You can chat with Subrata on Twitter at @abarjodi or at www.linkedin.com/in/subrata-banik-268b3317/.

ABOUT THE AUTHORS

 **Vincent Zimmer** has been working on embedded firmware for the last 30 years. Vincent has contributed to or created firmware spanning various firmware initiatives, including the Extensible Firmware Interface, where Vincent presently leads the Security subteam in the UEFI Forum. Vincent has co-authored various papers and books. He is also a co-inventor on over 450 US patents.

About the Technical Reviewers

Stefan Reinauer is a Staff Engineer in the ChromeOS Group at Google Inc. He has been working on open source firmware solutions ever since he started the OpenBIOS project in 1997. He joined the LinuxBIOS project in 1999 and worked on the first x64 port for LinuxBIOS in 2003. In 2005, Stefan founded coresystems GmbH, the first company to ever provide commercial support and development around the coreboot project, working on ports to new chipsets and mainboards. In 2008, Stefan took over maintainership of the LinuxBIOS project and renamed it as coreboot. He was the original implementer of the project's ACPI and SMM implementations. Since 2010, Stefan has lead the coreboot efforts at Google and contributed significantly to what is the largest coreboot deployment in the history of the project. He currently lives in the San Francisco Bay area.

Zhixiong (Jonathan) Zhang has been working on system software and firmware for the last 20 years. Jonathan is passionate at achieving computer system solutions (such as CXL memory solution) through holistic designs of software/hardware, and of various software components. He is thrilled at collaborating with industry colleagues to form visions, and make them into reality.

Jonathan has been spearheading coreboot/LinuxBoot development for servers based on Intel Xeon server processors, through multiple generations from ground up. He initiated and has been leading an industry coalition on this journey. Prior to Meta, he led UEFI/ATF development for ARM servers and made it commercially viable from the ground up; he also led UEFI and windows/Linux driver development for smart phones.

Jonathan is a frequent speaker on firmware/software topics at industry conferences. He is an active participant of several industry standard organizations (such as CXL forum, OCP, UEFI forum) and made a number of specification changes.

Foreword by Jonathan Zhang

This book contains key aspects of an evolution that is about to happen for system firmware (a.k.a. the BIOS). The last similar scale change in system firmware happened in the late 90s, from BIOS to UEFI. While the birth of the BIOS (e.g., the separation of system firmware from the operating system) in the 70s led to the era of the PC, UEFI laid a solid foundation for the success of computer desktops and servers, which is the foundation of the modern Internet world.

Now, with the Internet moving toward cloud services and artificial intelligence, will the innovation of UEFI continue to meet needs or will there be an evolution in system firmware?

Thomas Khun described in his book *The Structure of Science Revolutions* the concepts of paradigms and revolutions. These concepts apply not only to scientific research but also to the computer industry. We normally operate in a paradigm. A well-established paradigm is very useful and powerful, and thus we tend to neglect stuff outside of the paradigm. As time goes by, the anomalies pile up and then a paradigm shift happens, which is called a revolution.

In the world of system firmware, the transition from BIOS to UEFI was a revolution. Now the transition from UEFI to OSF (open system firmware) will be another revolution. Even though there are several variants, a typical OSF stack includes following components:

- Silicon initialization binary. The silicon vendor owns this.

- coreboot. It does platform initialization. It adopts the Linux kernel design philosophy and it has a Linux kernel style development community/process.

- LinuxBoot. As the bootloader, its main responsibility is to find the target kernel/OS and jump-start it. LinuxBoot has the Linux kernel as-is, and u-root as its initramfs.

UEFI, as the current paradigm, is

- Deployed in the majority of servers

- Supported by most modern operating systems

- Worked on by the majority of the system firmware community

One anomaly is the shift to cloud computing. Hyperscalers need to manage servers at scale, and in the meantime they often have feature differentiation and shortened time to production (TTP) needs.

OSF allows hyperscalers to own the system firmware more easily, since a smaller engineering team will be capable of developing and managing it at scale, enabled by industry collaboration. With Linux playing an instrumental role in OSF, Linux engineers are turned into system firmware engineers, therefore system firmware can be managed at scale just like Linux. In addition, new feature support and bug fixes in Linux can be leveraged in system firmware directly, leading to improved stability and reduced security vulnerability.

Another anomaly is the arrival of the computer architecture golden age. David Patterson declared that, like the 1980s, the next decade will be exciting for computer architects in academia and in industries. Not only scientific research but also societal advancements (such as Web 3.0 and the metaverse) demand exponential growth in computational power. On top of that, the focus on computation is shifting from general purpose computing to artificial intelligence workloads. However, Moore's Law is not supported by chip process technological improvements alone any longer. All of these changes require a new generation of server processors and server systems. New technologies and design philosophies beyond the von Neumann architecture have been springing up. Other examples include heterogeneous processor design enabled by chiplet and UCIe, and new interconnect technologies such as CXL, to name a few. All of these new technologies require timely development of system firmware as part of holistic solutions.

In the meantime, another event that happened in the industry was the maturation of Linux into the de-facto standard of the OS industry. Linux answers computer technology advancements gracefully and manages versatility effectively. Why should we develop software for the same technology twice–once for Linux, and another time for system firmware? Why should we stabilize and harden software for the same technology twice? Why should we require two vastly different skill sets for system firmware engineers and kernel/OS engineers?

You might ask whether OSF is mature enough for prime time. This is an important question. After all, technology alone is not good enough; we see too many cases where a good technology does not gain traction in the industry.

With over 10 years of technology accumulation, FSP (Firmware Support Package) technology, as Intel's silicon initialization binary, matured. FSP is a Plan-Of-Record for Intel server processors, starting with Intel's Sapphire Rapids Scalable Processor. In addition, as part of Intel's OneAPI initiative, Vincent Zimmer coined Universal Scalable Firmware (USF) architecture, which supports OSF.

On the other hand, coreboot has been shipped in hundreds of millions of devices, notably chromebook, among other products. LinuxBoot has been running at-scale at some of the world's largest data centers.

Those components together, as open system firmware for servers, have seen great progress in the last several years. In 2021, OCP (Open Compute Project) accepted OSF for OCP DeltaLake server (based on Intel Copper Lake Scalable Processor) and is available for the community. An OCP community lab is being built to enable access to OCP gears, with DeltaLake servers included, for the community. OSF is planned to be deployed in production in ByteDance's data centers.

In addition to technology maturity, the OSF for servers also benefits from a growing ecosystem and open source community. Subsequently, a company can spend a minimum amount of resources to get OSF for servers into production. The majority of system firmware features are the same among the server developers, so why would they not work together? In other words, some server developers may not want to hire 30 system firmware engineers; instead, they want to have 3 system firmware engineers that work with partners and communities to achieve the results traditionally done by 30 engineers.

coreboot and LinuxBoot are fully open source, and each participant benefits from community resources for new features and bug fixes. Silicon vendor company binary blobs are not open source (yet), but silicon vendor companies have been allowing their customers to engineer the solutions together. Such a new collaboration model is actually one of the key factors that OSF for servers has been advancing at a fast pace in the last few years.

We are fortunate to have the firmware industry's best minds to author and review this book, to enable the industry to rethink system firmware. Even though the groundwork has been going on for some years, the actual paradigm shift has just begun. The benefits of such a paradigm shift to the computer industry at large has just started to show up.

I hope you are as excited as we are to benefit from and contribute to this paradigm shift. Some years later, once we live in a world where a new processor (and/or technology) has system firmware support in a fraction of the time that it takes today, where system firmware is not a black box to owners and the computer industry at large, and where firmware engineers' productivity has dramatically increased compared to today, we can proudly say that we did it together!

Preface

Firmware is an essential part of any computing system, be it a device that creates content like a personal computer, a workstation or consumer electronics device like a smartphone, a smart home device, a wearable, or a powerful server that stores user data. Similarly, a course on system firmware is also an essential part of any computer-centric education for the following reasons:

- Firmware is capable of providing consistent behavior across different architectures.

- It empowers the system integrator with its flexible nature to configure the hardware interface and also to communicate with the operating system.

- It is the key to optimizing the platform resources to maximize power and performance efficiency.

- We must try to avoid bugs or detects during product development but providing workarounds or fixing the bugs inside firmware is comparatively easier than other layers because changing hardware is costly and modifying operating systems is time consuming.

- Firmware has the uniqueness to focus on security, both SoC-based security and platform security.

Also, this field is undergoing rapid changes as underlying hardware is more open now, more and more new computing devices are coming to market to reduce redundant tasks or manual efforts, security is concern, and cost is key in product development, thus device manufacturers (ODM/OEMs) are exploring opportunities to break the typical boundary of developing system firmware for their products in a closed environment. In this book, we ensure the fundamental concepts remain clear, so you can be market ready with such a migration in technology.

We wrote this book as a text for readers like you who want to explore the future of system firmware. The range of target audience could vary between grade school students, to recent college graduates working on developing firmware skill sets as per market needs, to embedded firmware/software engineers migrating product development from closed source firmware to open source firmware for product adaptation needs. This book will benefit engineers working on various bootloaders like open source firmware, UEFI, and Slim Bootloader development. As prerequisites, we assume that you are familiar with basic programming knowledge like assembly and C. The hardware topics required for understanding firmware/BIOS are included in Chapter 3. For code examples, we use predominantly C, with some pseudo code, but the idea here is that you can still understand the code logic without a thorough knowledge of a high-level programming language like UEFI.

The fundamental firmware design concepts covered in this book are mostly applicable for all SoC architectures (i.e., x86, ARM, RISC-V, etc.) with any platform design (i.e., personal computers, evaluation boards, servers, etc.). Our aim is to present these concepts and design principles in general without being tied to one particular architecture. We will present a majority of examples with widely used architecture and hardware references to make it a more real use case scenario. If a feature or functionality doesn't exist in all architecture and thus is specific to a SoC architecture, we will state this explicitly.

Acknowledgments

The system firmware journey from its origin to today's modern architecture and looking into the future is vast. It needs subject matter experts to contribute and share their knowledge to complete this journey. This book involved contributions from talented industry experts who we are honored to work with, and they deserve acknowledgement.

We would like to thank Maurice Ma and Ravi P. Rangarajan for sharing the Slim Bootloader (SBL) knowledge and architecture details as part of Chapter 4. A special mention goes to Karthik Ramasubramanian, Shelley Chen and Hung-Te Lin for their input on depicting the applicability of hybrid firmware architecture on all leading SoC platforms as part of Chapter 5.

Subrata thanks Vincent Zimmer, Ronald G. Minnich, and Stefan Reinauer for their expertise and for making this venture enjoyable and learnable. Above all, Subrata is thankful for his family, especially his wife, Barnali, and daughter, Samriddhi, who were patient with many nights and weekends consumed by this effort, and his parents, who influenced his technical curiosity, which translated into book development.

Vincent thanks Subrata for the great collaboration on this project and in other endeavors. Along with Subrata, he thanks collaborators across the different communities, standards groups, and his employer.

Introduction

"The only way to be truly satisfied is to do what you believe is great work."

—*Steve Jobs*

The definition of system firmware changes over time. Typically, it starts with no boot firmware for underlying hardware to modern computing systems where system firmware is the product differentiator, due to the level of optimization being put inside system firmware to allow configuring hardware and establish the trusted communication between operating system and hardware, and also at the same time provide electrifying performance.

For example, the minimum expectation for an end user is to see that the device is operational almost instantly by pressing the power button or holding the device in hand or starting the ignition of the car engine. Keeping the configurability of accessing underlying hardware, or ensuring instant boot, the other key criteria for system firmware is that it's trustworthy. With firmware being the closest entity in system design, it's easy to affect the hardware functionality and make it compromised. A compromised system firmware is an ultimate risk for the entire system, regardless of how secure the operating system may be. In the history of system firmware or the boot firmware evolution process, only a small group of people understand the background scene prior to booting to the operating system.

CPU vendors were using a closed and controlled environment to make sure that the platform bringing up the activity could be managed by those key people, rather than opening such knowledge in a wider manner.

The downside of this closed-group-enabling model is that the entire system firmware enabling and boot firmware development process became a "secret art" where, willingly or unwillingly, the device manufacturers had to reach such closed groups for their platform bring-up activity. Eventually this resulted in several key issues:

- ODM/OEMs had no control on their platform design and had to rely on a third party to bring up their platform.

- CPU or SoC vendors "only" trusted a selective third party for sharing the key knowledge to bring up their processors or chipset.

- They were unable to optimize the Bill of Material (BoM) cost, as a result of being dependent on third-party system firmware vendors, and they were unable to utilize engineering resources on the ODM/OEM side due to limited knowledge of the high-level proprietary closed source system firmware.

- They were unaware of SoC and/or platform security because of third-party involvement and they had no means to review the boot firmware code due to its closed source nature.

To find an amicable way out here, the market looked for a transition to a simpler, robust, transparency-enabling model of system firmware. It's not possible for SoC vendors to still be able to control the platform enabling model. In the present situation, there is more interest in knowing what's happening behind the curtain of booting to the operating system to define a transparent process in order to build a trustworthy system. There is interest in knowing how to optimize the boot firmware flow, reduce its boundaries, and make it more scalable for the operating system to leverage the privileged mode that the system firmware belongs to while talking to the hardware. This process might help to reduce the system boot time requirement for exclusive hardware/firmware-centric communication.

This is quite an attractive period for system firmware developers and companies who want to migrate their firmware development from a closed source solution to open source, to minimize their development costs, to bring transparency into product development process, and at the same time, to ensure time to market for their new products. Therefore, the key part here is choosing the right firmware solution as per their product needs.

This introduction explains the general challenge of system firmware migration and also describes what you can expect in the remainder of this book.

Migration to Open Source System Firmware

The term *migration* is being used in this book to refer to the transition of the existing firmware development model from closed source to open source, or to adopt the open source firmware development model for the new product development cycle.

This migration is not limited to porting the firmware alone; it's also an ecosystem change. For example, the program source code—whether implemented based on closed source firmware or open source firmware— is written with the capability of underlying hardware in mind. Therefore, it is very important to keep in mind the required hardware capability to develop the system firmware using an open source model is also expected to be available to support this migration.

The repository to maintain the source code is also important to ensure the real open source visibility, and to provide an opportunity for the open source community to review the source code rather than limiting the firmware development among few companies through peer review.

Finally, there is the build infrastructure that is being used to stitch other firmware ingredients (as applicable) with SoC architecture to qualify as an integrated firmware image (IFWI). Typically, different SoC vendors use their proprietary stitching tool for customization of IFWI ingredients as per the product requirement. But for migration to open source firmware development, it's expected to have a unified open source-friendly tool to meet such requirements.

The important part in this whole open source migration is the system firmware code development model. Over time, the platform-enabling strategy has gone through a rapid transition. Even a few years back, SoC vendors and device manufacturers were only considering a single entity for boot firmware, typically Unified Extensible Firmware Interface (UEFI). With an open source firmware development model, where more than one entity is combined together to call it as system firmware, this assumption won't hold. At a high level, open source system firmware may consist of two major components : boot firmware and payload.

There are several open source boot firmware options available to perform the CPU and chipset initialization. Based on the nature of the product and applicable market segment, device manufacturers choose the right boot firmware. It might also be possible that boot firmware itself may consist of several other associated firmware binaries that are restricted in nature and not necessarily available in open source due to SoC vendors or device manufacturer product requirements. This model is referred to as *hybrid* and there are sections to explain the work model to support such needs as well.

A boot firmware also needs to have a dedicated payload (typically, it doesn't have a payload integrated into it by default) to detect a special boot signature to boot to the kernel from possible boot media. A payload can be defined as another boot firmware, but in a generic manner, it doesn't need to perform specific CPU or chipset programming and is more architecture neutral and platform independent. The major task for a payload is to ensure booting to the operating system. Therefore, it's preferable to have a configurable option with boot firmware to choose the payload as per the target operating system need.

Motivation for This Book

The PC industry is going through a transition where the typical device manufacturers are willing to design their products in a more transparent manner. There is significant interest in understanding the secretive art behind booting to the operating system. This book highlights the underlying ecosystem changes. It also makes system integrators aware of the common challenges while migrating from a well-defined process to a new, evolving, open source-based firmware development, to maintain or improve the product quality and also to meet the time to market.

First, it's important to understand the legacy of the system firmware—its origin, architecture overview, and the reason why real-world firmware development is expecting this migration—with case studies. Additionally, this book provides an architectural overview of various popular boot firmware options. Types of firmware discussed will include both closed source and open source in nature, such as UEFI, coreboot, and Slim Bootloader as well as their applicable market segments based on product development and deployment requirements.

This book represents the journey of system firmware from its origin to now. Also, it captures the evolution of system firmware from complex and closed source to the modern firmware where it is still a hybrid between closed and open source. Finally, it attempts to predict the market transition about the future firmware model. This book tries to find the most simplistic boot firmware solution, using the open source firmware development. We deliver this information as a handbook to you so that you know how to choose the right boot firmware for your products and develop your own boot firmware using open source.

Who Is This Book For?

This book covers embedded system and firmware programming models. Readers are expected to be comfortable with low-level programming languages such as assembly and C. A few topics will require specific knowledge of UEFI.

As this book will focus on open source firmware developments, the target audience could vary between students interested in STEM topics, to recent college graduates working on developing skill sets as per market needs, to embedded firmware/software engineers migrating product development from closed source firmware to open source firmware for product adaptation needs.

Also, this book could be useful for engineers working in open source firmware development. A few sections will require specific domain knowledge like UEFI, as silicon vendors might be keen on using hybrid work models.

You will learn the following while reading this book:

- A comprehensive architecture overview of all market standard and popular boot firmware (a.k.a. the BIOS, the basic input and output system)

- How to pick the correct BIOS for the required target hardware

- How to design a hybrid workflow model for the latest chipset platform

- Understanding various popular payload architectures and offerings for embedded systems

    - Picking the right payload for the boot firmware solution to boot to the operating system

- Various case studies done on embedded systems with different CPU architectures: x86 and ARM-based solutions to optimize the system firmware boot time, demonstrating the power of hardware innovation that influences firmware design, usage of kernel features in firmware trusted computing boundaries, and understanding the product development cycle using open source firmware development

Overview

In general, this book is built with an assumption that you are reading the chapters in sequence. Each chapter builds on a knowledge block gained from earlier chapters. As the book progresses, you will apply this knowledge.

Chapters can be divided into two categories: developing concepts and applications. In concept chapters, you will learn about various aspects such as hardware knowledge required prior to any system firmware development, designing a minimal system firmware, and understanding various different system firmware architectures and payloads. In the application chapters, you'll build a few applications using what you've learned from the concepts chapters.

Starter: Chapter 1 provides the historical introduction about the boot firmware and different solutions available like closed source boot firmware and open source boot firmware. We will define the goals for you to create your own open source boot firmware for target hardware.

Knowing your hardware: Chapter 2 provides a detailed understanding of hardware interfaces that firmware needs to manage prior to booting to an operating system. This is a very basic understanding section for system boot firmware without which you really can't make progress on your system firmware journey.

Understanding the BIOS and its minimalistic design: Chapter 3 provides details about the BIOS. It explains the basic characteristics that a firmware has to have to call it a BIOS, as well as the minimum requirement to design a boot firmware.

System firmware architecture: Chapter 4 provides architectural details about popular or market leading system firmware along with applicable market segments because of their characteristics. The idea here is to understand the pros and cons of each offering.

Hybrid firmware architecture: Chapter 5 explains the ecosystem balance with open source firmware development using minimum closed source blobs. Open source boot firmware development has an enormous dependency on SoC vendors for providing the documentation and reference code for CPU, memory, and chipset initialization. This chapter defines the hybrid firmware architecture, which is useful to build open source firmware solutions when working with closed or restricted SoC hardware platforms.

Payload: Chapter 6 explains the necessity of the payload for the boot firmware. It provides architecture details of all popular payloads and current offerings to help users to choose the correct payload for their product.

Case studies: Chapter 7 covers a case study done on real hardware. This real-life example will help you think through innovation while designing your own open source boot firmware.

The **Appendices** include source code data types based on Chapter 7 and system firmware postcodes details. The **Glossary** and **Index** connect back to the main topics.

CHAPTER 1

Starter

"The beginning is always today."

—Mary Wollstonecraft Shelley

A journey in life teaches us that the most important aspect of a journey itself is not just reaching the destination, but rather ascribing importance to the experience gathered during the journey. This book is written to take readers through the amazing journey of firmware from its origin to today, demonstrating its firmness even on modern electronic devices and finally utilizing this opportunity to develop a specialized knowledge about different types of firmware. In the history of computer architecture and its evolution, the most underrated subject is firmware. The existence of firmware is not known to end users. If any end user ever saw the firmware screen, it was probably an awful day. Something might have been wrong on the hardware side, so the end user started exploring the way to fix it and "Here I come," said the tiny firmware, which resides deep in the hardware.

The standard academic curriculum for the next set of engineers silently ignores the importance of firmware. This creates an imbalance in the embedded device ecosystem where recent college graduates are well equipped with hardware knowledge (like transistors, microcontrollers, and even microprocessors) and software knowledge (like a deep understanding of application software, kernel operating model, artificial intelligence, and machine learning) but are ignorant of an important piece in the jigsaw

---

The original version of this chapter was revised. A correction to this chapter is available at https://doi.org/10.1007/978-1-4842-7939-7_8

© Subrata Banik and Vincent Zimmer 2022, corrected publication 2023
S. Banik and V. Zimmer, *System Firmware*,
https://doi.org/10.1007/978-1-4842-7939-7_1

puzzle: *firmware*. It's a layer that stays closer to the hardware and brings it to life. It provides an easy interface to apply patches without any additional cost of replacing or rebuilding the hardware. It's also empowered enough to orchestrate the entire platform to the operating system in a more abstract manner to maintain the generic nature of operating systems. In the last two decades, significant technological advancements in the embedded device market have impacted our regular lifestyle, socio-economic status, and more. These changes include the following examples: mobile phones are no longer a luxury device (once limited to people who could afford them 20 years ago) and have rather become a necessity today as the definition of entertainment has changed from limited shows airing on television to unlimited content over global digital platforms readily available for consumption via smart devices; popular video games are now equipped with virtual reality to track the user's motion and enable a real-world gaming experience; personal computers are now within most everyone's affordability with reduced storage (memory and disk) and lower cost; the pandemic added another dimension by necessitating digital education for kids and demanding more powerful computing devices for work-from-home experiences; and due to affordable and speedy internet services, new internet users are growing rapidly. A recent study suggests that the global embedded device market has seen a rapid revenue growth of ~$100 billion in just the last six years. Applying Moore's Law into it with the predictive advancement of semiconductors, this eventually results in higher demand for embedded systems and can easily predict the growth.

The alarming thing for the industry is that even though the demand for embedded devices is increasing, the number of firmware engineers has not. Over time, this might result in an imbalance where the embedded firmware world won't see fresh, incoming, talented engineers striving to be part of this industry. Today, most computer system college graduates are not even aware of the existence of the firmware world unless someone explicitly mentions it. In the study of computer science and engineering, the knowledge about firmware can be metaphorically presented as the famous *Platform 9¾* in J.K. Rowling's novels. The whole world of embedded firmware remains cloaked between the hardware and the operating system and is secretly maintained by a privileged group hidden from normal users' eyes. Due to the rapid growth of the Internet of Things in the last decade, there is a rise in the number of devices that need firmware to become operational and to fulfill end users' needs, such as voice assistance, smart locks, and more. With the more complicated silicon and sophisticated hardware designs, the underlying firmware that is responsible to bring the platform to life is getting more complex over time. Modern firmware development expects efficient system programming knowledge to implement solutions, even considering the space and time constraints. The non-volatile storage for keeping the firmware is limited, so an optimal implementation is required to ensure platform enabling in a time-efficient manner where the pressing of the power button starts the device immediately or opening the laptop lid is enough to see the user login without any forced delay in response.

Without any actionable improvement plan in place, there is no way the current situation can be improved with time. The current embedded industry needs to challenge the present education system and demand more focused and practical education that will help to improve the quality and also produce more ready engineers, those who are able to understand the different firmware architecture, choose the right solution from the lists of current offerings, or innovate one while designing and developing firmware for embedded systems. This chapter presents some insights into why traditional education of computer systems might have out-scoped the importance of firmware study.

Lack of Open System Design

Since the origin of the computer, the separation between hardware and software was not well known. Initially, the PC companies focused on providing the complete solution, so the hardware and software layers were very tightly coupled. Over time, this model started to become a bottleneck for innovation in the hardware space (Refer to the "Origin of the Firmware" section of this chapter). The open system design concept introduced later in the computer evolution defines the layer approach in embedded systems. Having a dedicated layer decoupled from the operating system that touches the hardware eventually led to designing the operating system more generically and in a hardware-neutral fashion. In this model, the layer that touches the bare metal hardware stays close to the hardware itself and allows for the opportunity to grow over time to support all future hardware needs.

Due to the lack of open system design concepts, any study of embedded devices today by default assumes a tightly coupled system design, where a bunch of low-level device drivers are capable of providing for the system programming. Unfortunately, that is not the case for most embedded devices available today.

Misinterpretation of Firmware Definition

The most popular definition of firmware is found in IEEE 610.12-1990 and it says "the combination of hardware device and computer instructions and data that reside as read-only software on that device." This definition is largely correct for the early generations of electronic devices where the users of the devices were limited (which translate into limited use-case enablement), with minimum hardware components attached to the motherboard, a simplistic microprocessor design, limited memory designed to have fixed operations, when security was not a prevailing concern, and when firmware updates and resilience requirements were not even known to the industry at that time.

The scope of firmware in modern embedded devices is very broad. The fundamental platform of stability and security relies heavily on the trustworthiness of the firmware layer. The *tiny* and *read-only* terms are often misleading when defining the actual scope of firmware in an embedded system today.

A better definition of firmware that depicts its relevance in the embedded system is as follows:

"**Firmware**: *An essential piece of code that is responsible for performing the underlying hardware initialization prior to handing over to the operating system.*"

A study of the embedded system and computer architecture wouldn't have ignored the value of an entity that is categorized as *essential* or *specialized* knowledge in the academic world.

Facts   NIST (National Institute of Standards and Technology) takes a special interest in the platform (the collection of hardware and firmware components of a computer system) firmware and publishes resiliency guidelines that help organizations to better prepare against potentially destructive security attacks, detect authorized changes, and ensure secure recovery from attacks.

Additionally, this chapter will show possible path findings and share an actionable improvement plan to support the growing embedded system market needed to bring more quality to embedded firmware.

Attract the Talent

The best way to prevent firmware being *a lost art* in the future is by attracting talented engineers who have a passion for contributing to this embedded space. The best class of engineers are always looking for specialization and advancement that not only helps to build their resumes but also satisfies a craving for knowledge. Interest in cutting-edge technologies related to the fields of artificial intelligence (AI), machine learning (ML), and data science are well expected. It's also important to highlight that the value of studying embedded systems and firmware is still relevant in modern times. The embedded system programming skill is considered a top-10 high-paying job in the field of computers.

It is interesting to learn the history of how firmware has maintained being value neutral to the end user over the last several decades since its origin. It's important for firmware engineers to keep it that way, as it can become value *negative* when firmware is difficult to use, has security issues, or isn't performant. The inability to patch firmware on a system with bug fixes or try to optimize the code, where the direct end user or intermediate platform builder, fosters the potential for the space of closed firmware to become 'value negative.' It can become value *positive* when users are very concerned about firmware and often rely on the firmware solutions. Over-dependency on firmware is also not a good indicator. Thus, it's an art to maintain the value of firmware in a platform that is close to *zero*. To achieve this trend consistently in millions of devices year over year definitely requires smart, focused, and talented engineers to get motivated enough to accept and excel in the embedded firmware world.

The Importance of Programming Knowledge

The simplest way to represent the firmware is as a code block that is responsible for setting or resetting a bunch of hardware registers. Over time, this demand has evolved with additional requirements of being optimized and efficient in operation. For example, a good firmware programmer pays attention to not only setting or resetting a register bit but also how optimally this operation can be done.

Table 1-1 describes a simple problem statement to help understand why programming knowledge is important in embedded firmware.

Table 1-1. *Problem Statement: Determine the Size Difference Between Code Way (6-Bits in Width) and Data Way (1-Bit in Width) in the x86 Platform*

Solution: Let's see the algorithm used in "a good programming practice" and "an optimized/efficient programming practice" to determine the size difference.

Code Way = Bit 0-5 -> 0x3f represents the code way
Data Way = Bit 0   -> 0x1 represents the data way

A good programming practice	An efficient programming practice
Algo:	**Algo:**
`((1 << Code Way) - 1) -` `((1 << Data Way) - 1)`	`((1 << (Code Way - Data Way)) - 1) << Data Way`
Code:	**Code:**
`mov  $0x3f, %ecx`	`mov  $0x3f, %eax`
`mov  $0x01, %eax`	`mov  $0x01, %ebx`
`shl  %cl, %eax`	`sub  %ebx, %eax`
`subl $0x01, %eax`	`mov  $0x01, %cl`
`mov  $0x01, %ecx`	`shl  %cl, %eax`
`mov  $0x01, %ebx`	`sub  %ebx, %eax`
`shl  %cl, %ebx`	`shl  %bl, %eax`
`subl $0x01, %eax`	
`sub  %ebx, %eax`	
Summary: Total 4 mov instructions, 2 shl instructions, and 3 sub instructions are used	**Summary:** Total 3 mov instructions, 2 shl instructions, and 2 sub instructions are used

Analysis: Each mov instruction requires 7 T-States and a sub instruction requires 4 T-States, hence, the total savings in the optimized solution is 11 T-States for a simple operation.

This approach highlights the need for embedded firmware engineers to have a deep knowledge of system programming. As per the current industry trends, the firmware engineers are typically coming from an electrical major background. A knowledge of electrical engineering would help to understand the hardware components better, but the downside of this background might be a lack in programming proficiency compared to a computer science/engineering major candidate. Hence, it's important for a firmware engineer to have a good understanding of the hardware along with being a prolific programmer. Unfortunately, the present academic curriculum is not attuned for the embedded firmware industry and requires special attention from the job-seeker to accomplish the goal. Chapter 2 provides the essential cross architecture, processor-internal knowledge that can streamline your understanding about hardware, regardless of your backgrounds and it's a prerequisite for understanding the rest of the chapters.

Specialized Education

Many different fields of computer systems provide specialized training and certification courses to support technical education for college grads, allowing professionals to upgrade their domain knowledge and provide an opportunity to learn about the new technology. For example, CCNA (Cisco Certified Network Associate) certification certifies the skills and knowledge in computer network fundamentals. OCA (Oracle Certified Associate) and OCP (Oracle Certified Professional) certifications demonstrate high-level skills in Java development.

Unfortunately, there are no specialized courses and opportunities available to gain proficiency in embedded firmware. One of the biggest reasons for such a shortcoming is due to lack of openness in the embedded system development approach. Since the origin of firmware, the majority of the firmware development and architectural innovation is limited to a few companies. The firmware knowledge is confined to engineers working for those companies and parties fortunate enough to receive that precious training about hardware components, knowledge of system programming, and getting used to the embedded system and firmware development process. The downside is that it leads to engineers who only have focused learning about a specific firmware architecture and who are thus unable to explore or learn from the other offerings. At the same time, there is a high chance that focus learning on a particular technology may become a bottleneck towards being open enough to explore more opportunities and unable to appreciate or leverage a potentially better design model than the current approach.

This book is written with the intention of breaking that prohibition about learning firmware. Our goal is to keep talented engineers in mind and motivate them to learn essential knowledge about computer systems and embedded devices to be able to thrive in the growing embedded market. The learning of firmware architecture and development aspects might help you to pick the correct system firmware from the lists that are being presented as part of this book, when designing and building your own firmware solutions for the targeted embedded system.

This chapter will further provide background information about the origin of firmware and its evolution. Additionally, we will explain a possible fork of the parallel firmware development approach in the last several decades and show the current status. We want you to be aware of the *original necessity* that inspired the invention of firmware and initiated this journey.

The remaining section of this chapter is to set your expectations for this book and also to refer to another book by us named *Firmware Development: A Guide to Specialized Systemic Knowledge.* This book provides the prerequisite knowledge to start with embedded firmware learning, plus all necessary information about different types of firmware, including underlying architectures, design assumptions, and applicable user market. At the end of this book, you will have key information for your firmware journey. The second book offers specialized firmware development knowledge like understanding the other types of firmware like non-host firmware, device firmware, and its architecture; the firmware development concepts and applications using modern high-level system programming languages; understanding the build and debug infrastructure; creating a firmware security paradigm; and a deep dive into the improvement opportunities for future firmware.

The Origin of Firmware

The Intel 8080 (eighty-eighty, shown in Figure 1-1) is the revolutionary microprocessor that changed the traditional way of designing the computer system in early 1974. Prior to the 8080, in a computer system, the separation between the hardware (processor, terminals, etc.) and software (compiler and operating system) was not known to the world. Typically, a manufacturer would build the complete computer starting from the processor to the operating system. The 8080 is the second 8-bit microprocessor design and manufactured by Intel. The 8080 was designed with a vision of being a general purpose microprocessor to meet the needs of most advanced applications (for building computer terminals, microcomputers, etc.) of that era.

Figure 1-1. *Intel 8080 processor*

Facts   In 1987, an asteroid of *Caussols'* main belt was named 8080 Intel to honor the revolutionary invention that changed the computer industry.

In 1976, Zilog (a company founded by two ex-Intel engineers) introduced the Z80 (Figure 1-2), the most popular microprocessor in the 1980s for different types of computer applications. The Z80 is an 8-bit microprocessor that was an extension and enhancement of the Intel 8080. It was used in different computer systems like desktops, home computers, portable computers, embedded systems, military applications, and musical equipment. The computer industry was evidencing a domination by the Z80 processor and the first disk operating system called CP/M (Control Program for Microcomputers). The introduction of CP/M boosted the demand of computer systems with its easy interface for installing software applications without much computer programming. The inventor of CP/M, Gary Kildall, was initially part of developing a compiler for the Intel 8080 platform (working as a consultant for Intel) to replace the system programming in assembly language. The PL/M (Programming Language for Microcomputers) is a high-level language developed by Gary in 1973 and later used while developing the CP/M operating system. The initial computer system architectures lacked modularity, resulting in additional work in the operating system to add support for new hardware interfaces. The majority of computer systems in 1973 used paper or punched tape for storage devices, which was limited in size and suffered a slow data rate. To overcome this limitation, the industry was looking for better solutions and bringing in newer hardware controllers. In 1976, IMSAI Manufacturing Corporation shipped a few workstation systems with a hard disk drive and was looking for an operating system that could support them. Gary was reluctant to add another hardware controller support into the CP/M. Rather, he separated the hardware dependent portion of

11

the CP/M and thus the notion of a basic I/O system (BIOS) evolved. In 8080- and Z80-based computer system with the CP/M operating system, the machine-dependent code (a.k.a. the BIOS) is referred as a simple bootloader that resides in the ROM (read-only memory) and manages to perform the direct communication with the hardware and an additional low-level hardware-specific file (often referred to as the hardware abstraction layer in the modern operating system) part of the operating system that interfaced with the system BIOS represented the philosophy of *firmware*.

Figure 1-2. *Zilog Z80 processor*

Since its origin, the firmware on the embedded system has made a long journey and has evolved several times in this process. The section about firmware evolution will depict the journey of system firmware to help you understand its applicability to modern devices.

Facts   In 1983, Model 100 was the first notebook-style computer that supported both the QWERTY keyboard and an LCD display. The Model 100 was based on the Intel 8085 microprocessor and supported ROM firmware-based platform booting. This was the last Microsoft product that Bill Gates developed personally, and in one of his interviews, he mentioned the nostalgia he has for the Model 100 project where he contributed significantly to the code development.

Figure 1-3 presents the relationship between the firmware and the rest of the platform components. Firmware belongs to the lowest layer in the platform stack and remains closest to the hardware. In the modern operating system, communication from the kernel layer is routed to the hardware via the firmware interface.

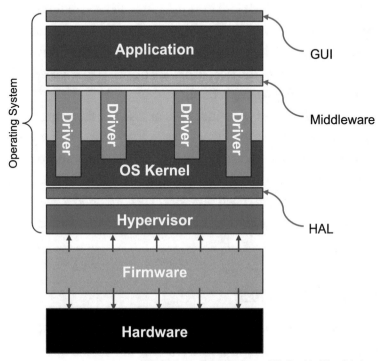

HAL: Hardware Abstraction Layer GUI: Graphical User Interface

Figure 1-3. *Firmware in the platform stack*

Although the fundamental principle of firmware remained the same, in order to support the different business requirements, the target market segment eventually created different firmware architectures. The evolution of the system programming language is one of the catalysts behind the origin of different firmware technologies. The origin of the BIOS in the CP/M platform was written in PL/M. Typically, the firmware running on the early embedded devices are known as legacy BIOSes and were written mostly in assembly. Modern firmware such as UEFI Platform Initialization-based firmware like EDKII, Das U-Boot, and coreboot are predominantly written in C with a small amount of assembly language code. This does not imply that firmware is limited to the C programming language. In fact, IEEE 1275 is written in Forth and the emergent firmware solution oreboot (coreboot without C) is written in the Rust programming language. What is important, though, is the functionality embodied in the firmware, the flow, and the interfaces of the host firmware exposed to successive layers of execution during the platform boot.

On the early platforms with Intel 8080 or Z80, the firmware was a tiny code block that stored into the PROM (programmable read-only memory) and performed the basic bootstrap operation. In later computer systems with more complex processors and platforms, the ROM chip for storing the firmware was replaced with flash memory. This provided easier ways to get fixes or allow feature upgrades on the modern computer systems, even on in-field devices.

Firmware Evolution

It's been close to 50 years since the term *basic I/O system* was first introduced by Gary Kildall and used in the CP/M based operating system platform. In the last several decades, system firmware has evolved to keep its interface still relevant with the innovation in hardware space and to accommodate the different operating systems using a unified layer of firmware. Figure 1-4 represents the growth in embedded devices over decades and how it resonated into the firmware to satisfy the demand from the next million units of devices. This section compares the evolution of firmware to the human life cycle to illustrate the maturity that came with the progression. A journey that started with a tiny read-only piece of code has evolved into a proper hardware interface for performing the hardware initialization and providing runtime services and has finally reached a phase where the firmware needs to support advanced product features (like security, resilience, etc.) to meet the modern electronic device needs.

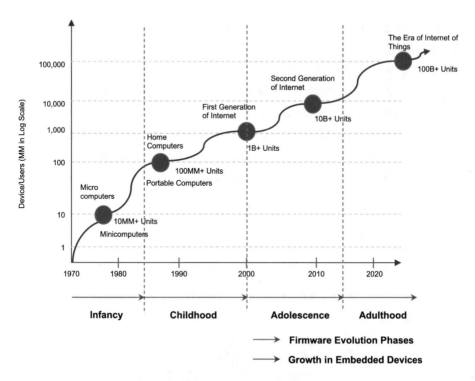

Figure 1-4. *Four phases of firmware evolution*

Infancy (Early 1970 to Mid-1980s)

The evolution of the modern computer system started with the Intel 8080 processor and the introduction of the CP/M operating system. CP/M first described the concept of decoupling the hardware programming from the operating system and keeping a dedicated layer responsible for directly communicating with the hardware. CP/M provided the simple but useful functionality required to manage the different disk controllers (floppy disks, hard disks, etc.), run the programs, receive the input from the console, display it at the video terminal, and so on.

Due to the wide application of computer systems with the CP/M operating system, continuous customization was demanded from the operating system. For example, initial hardware released with CP/M had

15

support for floppy disks and later with IMSAI 8080 for hard disk support. To support extensive serial ports usage (printers, modems, consoles, etc.) as per device manufacturer needs, CP/M was expected to have implementations for different types of serial chips. Different hardware interfaces were expected to have memory-mapped I/O or I/O-based communication for initialization. Some computer systems were designed with only a terminal while others had a video display system.

The CP/M operating system can be divided into three components:

- Basic input/output system (BIOS)

- Basic disk operating system (BDOS)

- Console command processor (CCP)

The BIOS is the machine-dependent part of CP/M and is responsible for managing the hardware controller. See Figure 1-5.

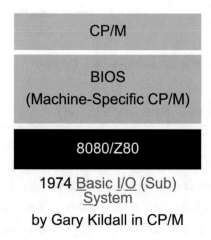

Figure 1-5. *CP/M platform layout*

For example, BIOS functions implemented in CP/M are for specific operations like communication with the console to check the status, read from (CONIN) or write to the console (CONOUT), control the disk drive read (READ) and write operations (WRITE), and more.

The BDOS implements the filesystem for CP/M and provides I/O abstraction on top of the BIOS using a specific file (almost similar to IO.SYS usage in the MS-DOS operating system) part of the operating system that performs hardware-specific operations. The CCP provides a command processing interface that takes user input from the keyboard and produces results to the terminal (serial or video). CP/M comes with a set of in-built commands to ease the operation for the user.

With the introduction of MS-DOS (the Microsoft Disk Operating System) for the 16-bit microprocessor-based computer system, the industry shifted gear from CP/M to MS-DOS. The operational model of MS-DOS was similar to CP/M and it maintained the same multi-layer architecture that separated the direct hardware communication from the rest. This helped MS-DOS to get adapted for different hardware platforms. MS-DOS introduced a concept called DOS BIOS. In DOS BIOS (also known as IO.SYS), a system file resides in the operating system and loads a self program into the memory to perform system initialization using device drivers, display splash screen, and more.

Childhood (Mid-1980s to Late 1990s)

Although the BIOS name originated in the early 70s, from a functionality standpoint, the BIOS in modern PCs originated in the mid-1980s. The pioneering company for this effort was IBM. In 1984, IBM released PC/AT (Personal Computer/AT) hardware while Microsoft built the operating system, MS-DOS, demanding a clean separation between the firmware and the operating system.

The evolution in firmware with the IBM platform is known as the PC/AT BIOS. The IBM PC/AT BIOS on the Intel 8088 microprocessor with ~40 kilobytes in size resides in a ROM chip on the computer motherboard. The original PC/AT BIOS also demonstrated the phased nature of platform firmware, and was given new phases, namely Power-On-Self-Test (POST) versus runtime. See Figure 1-6.

Figure 1-6. IBM PC/AT platform layout

A more detailed understanding of the IBM PC/AT platform and firmware, which is the backbone for even the modern system firmware can be found in Chapter 2, including interrupt handling, memory layout, CPU internal operations, and the system bus architecture.

The POST (Power-On Self-Test)

The Power-On Self-Test is used to define a series of operations performed by the BIOS after the processor becomes operational and the code block is running from the ROM. After the limited hardware component gets initialized, the BIOS loads the bootstrap loader (BSL) into the RAM (random access memory) and executes it. The bootstrap loader uses the bootstrap code to complete the boot from the disk drive. If it fails to boot to the OS, at the end of the POST, it loads the ROM BASIC module for basic I/O operations. After the platform power-on reset, the responsibility of the POST operation ends by handing over to the bootstrap loader.

Starting with the Intel 8088 CPU platform, the responsibilities of POST are

- After the CPU comes out from the reset, it jumps into the fixed memory mapped address 0xFFFF0 (20-bit addressing), also known as reset-vector on x86-based platforms. It contains a jmp instruction to start execution of the Power-On Self-Test code.

- Although the POST operation is highly platform dependent, at the high level, it involves initialization of the hardware components including the CPU and physical memory (RAM), plus additional controllers like the 8259 interrupt controller, 8237 DMA controller, 8253 timer, display controller, 8042 keyboard controller, serial and parallel interface, and disk drives (floppy and hard disk).

- The POST operation is also responsible for creating memory layout for applications to run as part of the OS layer. Hence, the BIOS prepares the memory layout table for keeping its essential data and code block for internal usage and leaves a maximum of 640 kilobytes of usable DRAM for the OS and its applications. This simple memory reporting mechanism by the BIOS is known as the BIOS data area (BDA).

Chapter 3 explains what a user should expect from the POST operation. The minimalist nature of the POST operative is different between architectures, so Chapter 3 outlines the differences in brief.

User Interface

The IBM PC/AT BIOS had first surmised the need for end users to know the failure in the hardware initialization operation. The hardware was sophisticated and it's important to identify the failure or potential bad hardware as part of the POST operation. One part of the initial user interface implemented on the PC/AT was POST codes (2-bytes data, also known as error codes), which appear either on the primary I/O port 80 or video/serial console that represented the error status and the correctable actions (if available). Error code 0x0003 signified CMOS Battery Low with the corrective action being to continue booting or abort the boot to fix the problem. Later, beep codes were a more meaningful way to draw the user's attention to a failure or to indicate the success If the computer failed the POST, the computer generated different beep notations (between a short beep or a long beep with a periodic interval) to inform the user about the source of the problem. One short beep denoted the DRAM refresh failure. Later, every BIOS vendor designed their own product-specific POST and error codes for easy detecting of failures during POST. Appendix A list common post codes and usages in computer systems.

In the mid-1990s, an advanced video/graphics user interface known as the BIOS Setup Utility was developed; it was launched or controlled using a specific key sequence. See Figure 1-7.

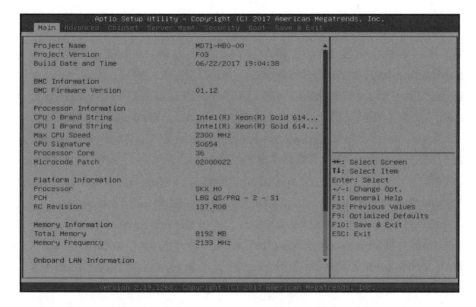

Figure 1-7. *Aptio BIOS setup utility implemented by AMI*

A user interface to allow configuration and remember user preference wasn't possible without having a place to store that information. IBM PC/AT first introduced the idea of storing those configurations into the non-volatile memory, later known as CMOS storage.

Chapter 2 of *Firmware Development: A Guide to Specialized Systemic Knowledge* explains the need for configuration tools in the firmware development approach and lists the different options available.

BIOS Services

The BIOS was responsible for performing the hardware initialization for all controllers attached to the motherboard as part of the POST. The BIOS implemented specific routines to perform the hardware components' initialization, such as input and output devices, storage devices, and serial ports. The PC/AT BIOS separated the platform initialization from the runtime services. This section covers the additional services of the BIOS leveraged by the OS and the platform.

BIOS Interrupt Call

The IBM platform leveraged BIOS interrupt calls to invoke the platform hardware from the MS-DOS layer. Traditionally, the BIOS routines were accessed by triggering the software interrupt. These BIOS interrupt calls were used by the DOS internal operations and some application layers. Such a mode of operation required high privilege. When software triggered the BIOS interrupt, the CPU redirected the interrupt to the IVT (Interrupt Vector Table) with the corresponding interrupt vector and a special routine against that interrupt vector was executed to perform the requested task. The INT instruction was used to trigger the software interrupt. This included Int13h for disk access, Int10h for video access, and Int16h for keyboard access. These Int-calls provided a service layer for both the OS boot and OS runtime.

Plug and Play BIOS (PnP BIOS)

The Plug and Play BIOS Specification defined new functionality for the system BIOS to be able to meet the computer system design goal with a Plug and Play card. A PnP system BIOS played a vital role in helping to manage the resources allocation for those card devices and ensured a successful launch of the operating system. The PnP BIOS was responsible for configuring Plug and Play cards during the POST. After the POST process was complete, control of the Plug and Play device configuration passed from the system BIOS to the OS. In order to make the Plug and Play Card initialization process independent at the system firmware side, each Plug and Play card was equipped with Option ROM, a newer standard for the Plug and Play BIOS. The system firmware called into the Option ROM to perform device initialization.

Bootstrap Loader

A bootstrap loader (BSL) is a special program that is responsible for loading the operating system. At the end of the POST operation, BIOS identifies an IPL (initial program load) device (floppy drives, hard drives, CD-ROM drives, PnP cards, etc.) and is able to load and execute an OS. BSL can identify all IPL devices in the system, prioritize them in the order the user selects, and then sequentially go through each device and attempt to boot.

Chapter 7 defines the purpose of having a separate bootstrap loader in the system firmware architecture.

With the introduction of real and protected addressing mode for the later CPU generations, the BIOS operations are also divided into two categories: CBIOS (Compatibility BIOS) to maintain backward compatibility with MS-DOS-like operating system, where all operations are running in real mode, and ABIOS (Advanced BIOS), which provides a new protected mode interface. This results in a significant change in the operational model for the OS, which limits the direct BIOS interrupt calls from the protected mode. In the 1990s, the BIOS provided more protected mode interfaces to the operating systems, such as Advanced Power Management (APM), e820, and MultiProcessor Specification (MPS).

The PC/AT BIOS became a de facto standard for computer systems for a very long time. And given the lack of a redistributable open source variant of the BIOS, various companies had to clean-room their own instances. This led to the formation of independent BIOS vendors like AMI, Award, System Soft, and Phoenix. Some of the large OEMs elected to create their own clean-room BIOSes; one of the notable first examples was Compaq.

This lack of openness and reuse led to incompatibilities over time, resulting in bug wars between Houston and Austin regarding which of the notable OEMs in those cities had the least bugs in their proprietary BIOS.

The PC/AT BIOS standard provided platform initialization and runtime interface for operating system. The latter faced structural challenges in the late 90s as the platform evolved beyond x86-CPU vendors (Intel and AMD). Specifically, the Apple Macintosh and Sun used Motorola 68k and Sparc CPUs, respectively. They could not use the x86 interrupt-calls as their abstraction for booting.

Adolescence (2000 to 2015)

The most impactful era of the embedded industry started with the revolution of the Internet in 2000. The PC industry has followed an interesting arc with more numbers of users exploring the new side of computing, resulting in improving the overall device-per-user ratio and bringing new use case and platform requirements, so processors matured to manage users' advancements. Prevailing usage of firmware runtime services by the operating system was another key motivation for further evolution in the firmware space to define more rich solutions.

Open Firmware

With the introduction of open-system design in the 1970s and the origin of firmware, the job of loading the operating system greatly involved programming I/O components present in the motherboard. The prerequisite of the platform booting to the OS is the advanced knowledge of possible I/O devices from which the operating system may be loaded. In different computer system applications like desktop computers, a new bootable device may be added later to the system and the user would expect its functionality. With rapid innovation in the hardware space in the 1990s and more devices and users, it was impractical to roll out different sets of system firmware to support new devices. Thus, to assist the growth in the hardware/systems and maintain the generics of the operating system, the firmware was rearchitected to allow abstracting the hardware characteristics while presenting to the operating system.

Originally, the Open Firmware (OF) was intended to solve those problem by creating a processor-independent firmware architecture. Probably the OF provided the first concept of hardware programming using interface specifications, where the user of the interface isn't required to know the machine-level details. An earlier section explained the concept of the PnP BIOS that was necessary to use a new device without changing the system firmware. With OF, the PnP driver was implemented in a byte-coded, machine-independent, interpreted language called FCode. Since FCode was machine independent, the same device and driver could be used on computer systems with different CPU instruction sets. The Open Firmware specification brought the requirement of modularity in firmware development and let the computer integrator choose the feature sets that were mandatory to meet the system design goal. The OF specification viewed the hardware components based on industry-standard bus specifications, so the development and debug process became more scalable. Similarly, it's easy to represent the devices attached to the system using a data structure described in OF as the device tree. See Figure 1-8.

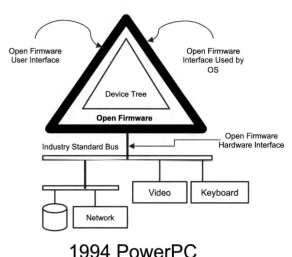

Figure 1-8. *Open Firmware architecture*

Companies like IBM, Sun, and Apple used Open Firmware for shipping platforms. In the early days of Windows NT, Microsoft engineers wrote the ARC (Advanced RISC Computing) boot firmware for non-x86-based systems.

With the introduction of the 64-bit Itanium architecture from Intel, the next generation of processor architecture needed a unified firmware solution. There were nearly two possibilities between ARC or Open Firmware. Initially, Open Firmware was considered as a solution for "how to boot Itanium," due to the fact the PowerPC booted Windows NT via OF. Later, Intel introduced Extensible Firmware Interface (EFI) in 2000, which was an outcome of the Intel Boot Initiative (IBI) program that began in 1998.

EFI ended up looking more like ARC, with a similarity between the ARC Firmware Function Vector and UEFI System Table, and both supported booting from a FAT-formatted portion of the disk. OF does have some advantages, especially for security. On the other hand, ARC muddied platform definition details in the specification and it was also not clear if ARC could be opened and extended. One interesting transition that was introduced with the ARC firmware and also seen with EFI. See Figure 1-9.

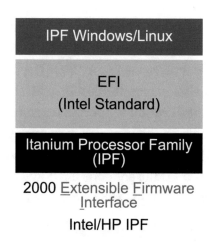

Figure 1-9. Itanium platform layout

firmware is porting of the kernel drivers into the firmware for addressing the advanced use case, For example, Windows NT NDIS miniport drivers were embedded into the firmware to support pre-OS networking. This trend continues with the block device, display, and console services in the pre-OS and also requires the runtime interface.

In 2005, Intel updated the specification and a new Unified EFI (UEFI) forum was formed to promote and manage the industry-wide adaptation of the EFI Specification for firmware development. The UEFI Forum is led by core committee representatives from different companies: Intel, AMD, Insyde, IBM, HP, Apple, Microsoft, Lenovo, Dell, Phoenix Technology, and AMI. Since then, UEFI has become the de facto standard for firmware development for computer systems.

UEFI

Unified Extensible Firmware Interface (pronounced as u-e-f-i) defines the interface between the underlying firmware and the operating system. The interface consists of data tables that contain platform-related information and separate service calls between boot and runtime; the boot service calls are used to complete the POST operation and the operating system uses the runtime service to access firmware routines.

UEFI is intended to replace the PC/AT BIOS (typically referred as the legacy BIOS) INT-calls-based communication with sophisticated C callable interfaces. The UEFI specification supports a machine-independent architecture where processor bindings assist in setting up the machine state on various CPU instruction set architectures (ISAs), commencing with Itanium and IA-32 and subsequently including 32-bit ARM and 64-bit ARM or Aarch64, along with 64-bit x86 or x64. See Figure 1-10.

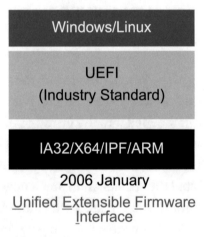

Figure 1-10. *UEFI platform layout*

Underneath the UEFI interface there are many potential implementations. One type of implementation is UEFI PI, or platform initialization. The PI specification and code lives relative to the UEFI interfaces and is divided into platform drivers and silicon component modules. These modules contain executables for the early phase of execution, or the Pre-EFI initialization (PEI), and the later Driver Execution Environment (DXE) after memory has been initialized. The DXE phase is responsible for both late platform initialization and the DXE core driver provides the basic UEFI services. See Figure 1-11.

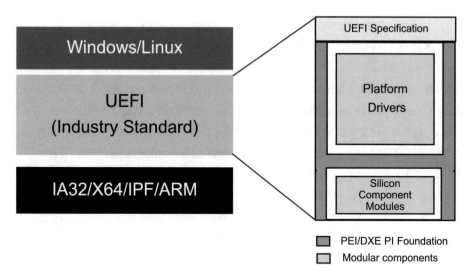

Figure 1-11. *UEFI PI model*

A detailed architectural overview of UEFI and its intrinsic operations is covered in Chapter 4.

The UEFI firmware standard provides many enhancements over the legacy BIOS implementation as a unified bootloader that can boot into multiple operating systems, implement an enriched pre-boot phase with high-level driver architecture (separate device, bus, and host-driver that introduces the modularity), and introduce security to prevent attacks on the firmware.

Between 2000 and 2015, the UEFI specification was in charge of firmware development for computer systems. All major MNCs were shipping cross architecture platforms using UEFI, such as Microsoft UEFI x64 support in Server 2008, Vista, and Win7; RedHat and SuSE OS support; and a Windows 8 client. With time, ARM 32- and 64-bit support was added into the open source Tianocore (the community supporting an open source implementation of the UEFI).

One potential downside of this evolution, though, is fragmentation. The original EFI sample from 1999 evolved into the EFI Developer Kit (EDK) to include the firmware development framework and early PI specifications, and has culminated in the EFI Developer Kit II (EDKII). The EDKII code provides many of the class drivers and generic infrastructure code with a permissive BSD style license, but the Tianocore project which hosts EDKII does not have the full silicon initialization elements of the PI code. In addition, given the permissive nature of the generic EDKII code, many vendors take a downstream fork and add their own fixes and modifications, which are rarely shared back with the community. This raise the proprietary implementation of UEFI-based system firmware, such as Aptio by American Megatrends (AMI) and InsydeH2O for server, desktop, mobile, and embedded devices. Most implementations below generic high-level code are still closed source.

The complexity of firmware increased as time progressed, as the code base and standards needed to consider more modules and interfaces for emergent I/O and memory buses (PCIe and USB standards evolved to support improved speed in data transfer). This led to a lot of fragmentation in the market where the products shipped were based upon this forest of different branches from the silicon vendors, and the code went through various hands, including independent bios vendors, OEMs, and ODMs. Figure 1-12 shows the system firmware development model using UEFI. Firmware vendors often do not rebase the firmware in the field against the latest code or fixes, especially if the products are based upon older branches. And many products do not release updates after the initial product release. This lack of updates is not observable to end users since the provenance of these various forks is not readily discernible. Thus, a system may have out-of-date capabilities or known security vulnerabilities. The traditional devices might have ignored such security vulnerabilities but, knowing the attack surfaces on modern devices are shifted from the OS and users to the firmware, emphasize the need for security in the firmware.

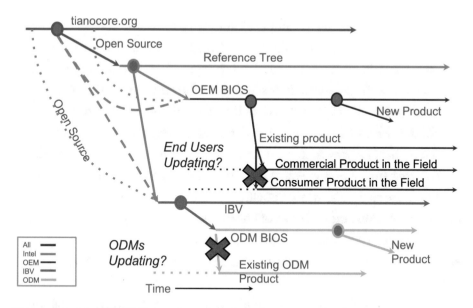

Figure 1-12. *UEFI firmware development supply chain*

The modern firmware development model has adopted an efficient version control mechanism to collaborate better across organizations, and even cross-company. Chapter 3 of the *Firmware Development* book provides the best practices being used in firmware development.

Security

The initial embedded devices with fixed ROM didn't provide an option for end users to allow updating the firmware for bug fixes on shipped devices. With the introduction of EEPROM and flash memory chips, it became easy to perform firmware updates on the production devices to allow bug fixes and feature improvement. However, this advantage brought a risk of making the entire device vulnerable to a security attack if it wasn't protected properly. Over time, attackers analyzed the dreadfulness of a low-level firmware attack, which is as good as making the entire platform paralyzed.

UEFI introduced Secure Boot to establish trust in the system firmware by creating Trusted Computing Base (TCB). The idea was to implement the smaller TCBs to verify the system firmware. Technology like Intel Boot Guard uses keying material in fuses verifies the entire system firmware. For example, on UEFI-based system firmware platforms, the Initial Boot Block (IBB) block will only execute if it is the one from the manufacturer (based on the fuse key matched). In addition, technology like a hardware root of trust such as Boot Guard may be necessary but not sufficient for the firmware to defend itself. Specifically, firmware may be composed of hundreds of thousands of lines of codes. And given industry metrics such as 1 defect per 1000 lines of code on average, the ability to potentially exploit a vulnerability and get privilege escalation into the firmware is non-zero.

Chapter 4 of *Firmware Development: A Guide to Specialized Systemic Knowledge* describes the importance of system firmware being more security compliant. Antivirus software is not enough to detect the presence of rootkit or malware in the firmware.

ACPI

The Advanced Configuration and Power Interface (ACPI) specification was developed to define a common industry standard for cross-architecture platforms to manage the motherboard device configuration and power management of the device and entire system. The ACPI specification provides interfaces that support platform-agnostic, OS-directed device configuration and power management. The key element in the ACPI specification (evolved from its predecessor) is the OS-directed configuration and power management (OSPM). The concept of ACPI is suitable for all types of computer systems like desktops, services, and mobile and embedded systems. The idea was to conserve energy by transitioning unused devices and the overall system into a low-power state when even possible.

The predecessor of ACPI was firmware-based System Power Management, known as Advanced Power Management (APM). The design philosophy for APM was to provide CPU and device power management in an OS-agnostic way. The BIOS routines for CPU power management were getting called when idle and device activity timeout were used to determine when to transition the device into low-power states. The entire power management being handled inside firmware provided flexibility for platform manufacturers to implement a wide variety of solutions without unification, thus resulting in no uniform user experience even with the same operating system but with different system firmware from another vendor.

The ACPI interface describes the hardware interface (hardware registers for implementing the chipset silicon) and firmware interface (ACPI data structures to represent the motherboard-attached devices and a control method to perform runtime operations for device configuration) and finally allow OSPM to configure the system and device power states.

In 2013, the ACPI specification came under the leadership of the UEFI forum. You'll read more about the ACPI interface and required implementation in the system firmware in Chapter 3.

Alternative Ecosystem Approach

At the same time that EFI was evolving as a response to the Itanium boot problem and engaging the existing OEM (original equipment manufacturer) and PC ecosystem with a technology evolution, the world had a desire for more openness. The LinuxBoot project commenced in 1999 as a response to supporting clusters of machines in supercomputers where the paradigm of a PC-style BIOS needing human interaction was insufficient. In fact, the boot of thousands of nodes at scale argued for having more of an OS-like capability to launch the final OS.

This is where LinuxBIOS emerged as a solution to have a more streamlined, C-based bootstrap for early platform initialization and defer richer I/O services, akin to what UEFI provides in its single-threaded programming model, to a payload. The payload could be any executive software, but given the namesake of LinuxBIOS, this payload was Linux. The rich set of capabilities of the Linux kernel were used in this supercomputer use case, specifically the threaded network stack to boot these machines at scale. See Figure 1-13.

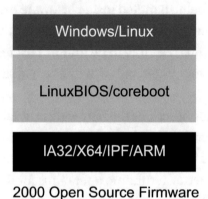

Figure 1-13. *LinuxBIOS platform layout*

The other salient aspect of LinuxBIOS, which became the coreboot project, was the community driver and a goal of maximal openness from the beginning. Unlike the evolution of the UEFI ecosystem, which introduced new technology to an existing supply chain of closed source OEM and independent BIOS vendor copyrighted solutions, coreboot fostered an environment of having the platform initialization, which is broken into bootblock, romstage, and ramstage (vs. UEFI PI SEC, PEI, and DXE) provided in GPLv2 open source. This copyleft license requires that changes to code be provided back to the community.

One coreboot engineer responded to the question of why GPL for firmware vs. the UEFI PI-based BSD license, with the following question: *"Why would someone want to hoard a bug fix, say for your hardware initialization?"* This shows in stark contrast the lack of end user value of bug wars when, in fact, host firmware is largely value-neutral to end users.

And LinuxBIOS/coreboot were not alone. Although this community and its infrastructure started on the richer x86 PC-like devices, it has expanded to IBM Open Power and ARM. One hallmark of coreboot is having a rich infrastructure for platform initialization, including x86 system management mode (SMM) and ACPI.

U-Boot from 2000 was another C-based host firmware initialization technology. It has a much simpler software model that allows it to span several hundred embedded class CPUs. It typically supports simpler devices, whereas UEFI was built for a rich supply chain and shrink-wrap OS interoperability working in tandem with ACPI. U-boot has a flattened device tree and also has a tighter coupling with the OS, often necessitating Linux kernel modifications to align with the specific U-boot instance.

In a larger sense, one can argue coreboot takes the PI aspect of UEFI style firmware and opens it up. coreboot can comprehend UEFI today as a payload, too.

A detailed architectural overview of coreboot and other bootloaders is covered in Chapter 4. Additionally, Chapter 1 in *Firmware Development* explains the extension of the firmware in a more advanced form in the future.

Adulthood (the Modern Era of Firmware Since 2015)

From the beginning of the open system design aspect in the 1970s, the one thing that has remained constant even with the evolution of the firmware is the closed-source nature. Over time, an increasing number of embedded devices are exposed to the Internet and vulnerabilities are being detected on end user devices, raising questions about the fundamental rights of the users. The security paradigm built at the operating system and application level are not enough to ensure the trustworthiness of the platform where the more privileged layer than the OS is still running unaudited code as part of the firmware. Previous generations of firmware attempted to become more comparable with the OS rather than being the essential unit in this whole platform initialization.

Openness

Modern firmware is looking for more simplistic, essential, and bare minimal hardware initialization prior to transferring control to the OS loader or the OS itself. The firmware running on the embedded devices is expected to be more mature to demonstrate the openness to witness more transparency in the platform enabling. Asus's Chromebook with Rockchip RK3399 is a classic example of achieving the openness that the industry is expecting from the matured firmware ecosystem. The typical bottleneck for the firmware not being completely developed in open-source is the first-party hardware restriction and third-party code running on the restricted hardware. The next generation hardware design (including processor and motherboard) is expected to be supportive enough to ensure open sourcing and meeting business goals in parallel.

The computer industry is looking for more openness due to two major reasons. The first is end user interest in knowing if the code block running on the underlying hardware is really trustworthy, meaning users want to know about configuration changes, bug fixes, and feature improvements when accepting the firmware update. Secondly, the developer community want freedom to fixing their own hardware without being beholden to the original device vendor. The Open Source Firmware (OSF) initiative group formed to support such a developer group and over time, it has been able to connect with the business goal. For example, the platform adhering to the Open Compute Project (OCP) is running various open-source firmware code, including coreboot, the popular open system firmware. Figure 1-14 shows the growth in coreboot firmware development in year over year (YoY) time. The coreboot project receives an average 150 commits per day in 2021.

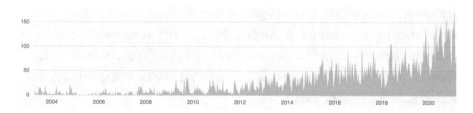

Figure 1-14. *coreboot project commits trends in YoY*

Security

The definition of security has evolved from the previous generation's embedded systems, where the manufacturer firmware implementation was assumed to be trusted running on the target hardware. Modern devices are more likely to rely on the hardware chip solution, which has proven better compared to firmware-based security. With the introduction of the OpenTitan project, the industry's first open source silicon root of trust (RoT), the future platform can envision an implementation that is more transparent, trustworthy, and secure. The entire development model of OpenTitan has actually neutralized the old claim of platform security, which is *"the less see the code, the better!",* to the current development approach where it welcomes more eyes to inspect the code, evaluate it, and contribute to the development.

Hybrid Firmware Architecture

Open Source Firmware development for product systems is not fully mainstream even in this modern era of firmware development. The restricted nature of design and development adopted by the processor vendors is one major barrier of modern embedded devices for using OSF solutions, although there is interest from different silicon vendors to support the business goal of openness in platform development even while working on a restricted silicon platform. The advancement of the separate platform initialization code from the generic code block in the previous generation provides that flexibility for silicon companies to design alternative solutions.

The introduction of a hybrid firmware architecture is the computer industry's attempt towards openness for platform enabling. The hybrid firmware architecture is meant to demystify the early platform engineering with a restricted SoC/Hardware platform to meet the TTM (time to market). See Figure 1-15.

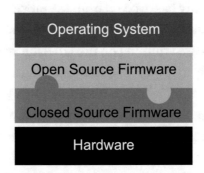

2020 Hybrid Firmware Architecture

Figure 1-15.   *Platform layout in hybrid firmware architecture*

This form of firmware development relies on two pillars: closed source firmware and open source firmware. Silicon vendors are adopting the binary-based platform initialization model to consistently maintain the closed source nature of silicon initialization. Typically, binary-based PI initialization is implemented using API/ABI, which can easily integrate with any standard boot firmware to complete the PI. Examples of closed source firmware used in hybrid firmware architecture are AMD AGESA (AMD Generic Encapsulated Software Architecture) and Intel FSP (Firmware Support Package), and closed source binaries are used in ARM Trusted Firmware Bootloader Stages (i.e., BL1 and BL3x).

The introduction of the binary PI model is a blessing in disguise for the embedded market, where an alternative approach for firmware development using open source firmware initiative boot firmware is now a reality. Chapter 5 explains the intrinsic of platform initialization while adapting this model in system firmware development.

Modern System Programming Language

As stated in the earlier section, the one of key catalysts of the firmware technology evolution is the progression of programming languages. A complicated programming language demands special knowledge and lack of inclusion for the wider community to adapt. The evolution of programming languages has been used in firmware development, starting with assembly language to exploring different high-level language offerings to finally settling with the C programming language. The majority of firmware development in the modern era is based on either C or an equivalent programming language.

The future of system programming language is in exploring more *safe* programming languages while building firmware where security and reliability are major concerns. According to one study, 70 percent of security bugs are due to memory safety issues with the programming language, which can't be prevented even by adopting any silicon RoT solution unless replaced.

The Appendix in *Firmware Development: A Guide to Specialized Systemic Knowledge* covers the evolution of system programming languages used in firmware development and calls for an action. Additionally, Chapter 1 from the same book demonstrates the platform enabled using oreboot (coreboot without C) firmware, written in the Rust programming language. See Figure 1-16.

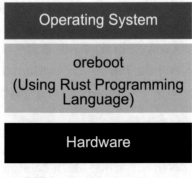

Figure 1-16. *Next generation firmware*

Distinction Between Firmware and Software

Although firmware is typically written in a higher-level language like C, it often has special requirements. These requirements begin with the environment. Specifically, firmware has a size constraint that is driven by the small ROM size and small RAM size in microcontrollers, which only have SRAM or cache that can be used before the DRAM is ready, a special processor management mode size leveraging stolen system memory, and limited stack and heap sizes.

Additional limitations include the Execution-In-Place (XIP) for the early code block. Namely, some code executes in the ROM. One aspect of this is the ROM code wherein some code has no writable global variable in the DATA section. And for this early code, such as the UEFI Platform Initialization PI, Slim Bootloader Stage1, and coreboot romstage, there is no memory management, including no virtual memory, although page tables may be used.

Beyond memory management, there are challenges with execution isolation in early code flows. For example, ring separation might or might not be available. As such, some firmware implementations just run all code in supervisor mode. And although the hardware may contain multiple CPU cores, multi-processing (MP) may or may not be enabled. In fact, most implementations of host firmware execute services on a single processor (known as bootstrap processor or BSP). Alongside MP, other common capabilities like interrupts may be enabled, but only for usages much simpler than that of operating systems. And unlike the operating system, the firmware usually interacts directly with the hardware. Finally, the firmware has its own executive infrastructure, such as a kernel and loader, distinct from those found in high-level operating systems (HLOS) like Windows or Linux or hypervisors.

Chapter 1 of *Firmware Development: A Guide to Specialized Systemic Knowledge* provides the complete spectrum of firmware development on embedded systems, which is majorly but not only limited to the system firmware development alone. A study performed on the latest laptop devices shows the presence of more than 16 different firmwares embedded on the system.

Introduction of Non-Host Firmware

The host firmware, such as EDKII or coreboot, is not the only firmware entity on the platform. A platform might have several other firmwares, which are typically under the control of the platform manufacturer including the baseboard management controller (BMC) on servers and embedded controllers (EC) on client platforms. These devices typically interact with the host firmware during the early phases of execution and may, in fact, run prior to the host firmware since they can provide a RoT for the host firmware or sequence the power capabilities of the platform.

These non-host firmware elements should be recorded by the host firmware RoT for measurement, if possible, and these non-host elements may have their RoT for updates and verifications proxied through the host. In either case, these elements are part of the platform manufacturer's TCB typically and should not be exposed to arbitrary third-party updates.

Traditionally, these firmwares are also closed-source like the system firmware over several decades, but the open-source initiative also applies to these firmwares. The Open BMC project, Chrome EC project, and Open Source Embedded Controller firmware development using Zephyr OS are examples of open source non-host platforms available on the market. Given the inclusion in the manufacturer's TCB, following the security practices for firmware development is key for having a robust product. Chapter 1 in the *Firmware Development* book describes the firmware development for BMC and embedded controllers using open source firmware initiatives.

Introduction to Device Firmware

Beyond the manufacturer's host firmware (sometimes known as the BIOS) and non-host platforms (EC, BMC, etc.), the PCI card, USB devices, and other components such as a complex programmable logic device (CPLD), field-programmable gate array (FPGA), or digital signal processors (DSP) on the system board may have their own firmware. In fact, a review of a modern client platform noted 16 different firmware elements, and a server example quoted a multiple of that figure.

There are some examples of device firmware, such as Open Sound Firmware for programmable audio devices, but in general the device firmware is opaque to and independent of the host firmware. As such, there are protocols to query these devices for their state and add them to security policy so that the host firmware can provide a holistic view of the platform state to the HLOS.

And given that the device firmware reads in on the platform security posture, construction of this firmware, just like the other non-host firmware devices, is imperative for having a robust platform experience.

Open Source vs. Closed Source

Table 1-2 represents the growth in the system firmware footprint since its origin to the latest SoC platform. The rapid growth in system firmware to make it comparable against the operating system raises questions about the ultimate vision of the future firmware: will it be open source or remain closed for another several decades? In the beginning, it was easy to ignore what resides in the 4KB boot ROM code, but in modern devices with 32MB of firmware flash, it's catching lots of eyes and many are urging it to be transparent.

Table 1-2. *Evolution of System Firmware Footprint*

Machine Type	BIOS ROM	Processor	OS
CP/M (1974)	< 4KB	8080	CP/M
IBM PC (1981)	40KB	8088	MS-DOS
PC (1999)	512KB	Pentium III	Win98
PC (2012)	4MB	Ivy Bridge	Win8
PC (2016)	8MB	Apollo Lake	Chrome OS
PC (2021)	32MB	Alder Lake	Chrome OS

In the days of CP/M, the listings of the ROM code were typically provided in the manual for a system given the small amount of source required to build these 4 Kilobyte or 8 Kilobyte images. With the advent of the PC, the original PC/AT BIOS listings were released by IBM (look at the Reference section for Chapter 1), but these sources were intended to support maintenance of the BIOS and were not for sharing or redistribution given the IBM copyright.

Today many of the UEFI implementations have a feature-reduced open source core based upon EDKII and some set of binary modules. For example, the EDKII-based open source implementation for Intel-based designs that reduce functionality at the platform layer is the Min Platform Architecture (MPA) and the silicon modules are largely abstracted through the Intel Firmware Support Package (FSP). ARM platforms have various versions of open and closed with the ARM Trusted Firmware (TF-A), and AMD has its source plus binary solution through the evolution of its AGESA design.

Each of these designs has various merits that will get discussed in several chapters of the book and challenges for the whole supply chain, from the silicon supplier to the system board manufacturer to the integrator to the enterprise or hyperscale, and finally its implication for the end users.

Summary

This chapter described the various aspects of host firmware, including its role in the platform. It provided a brief history of host firmware and its contribution towards the evolution of different standards to overcome the limitations of its previous generation, the distinction between host and device firmware, the challenges of a diffuse supply chain, and finally the need for open standards/solutions. This chapter is intended to provide context and link between the subsequent chapters of the book and also link to the other book about firmware development aspects. Hopefully, the knowledge you got from this chapter and the rest of the chapters in this book will motivate you to starting the journey with firmware and being able to design your own firmware for target hardware.

CHAPTER 2

Knowing Your Hardware

"Software comes from heaven when you have good hardware."

—Ken Olsen

This book is about designing your own system firmware for target embedded devices. The system firmware is a piece of code that runs from platform storage and is intended to perform the hardware initialization to boot to an operating system or an embedded application. If you look into your daily-used computing devices (laptop, desktop, and smartphone), infotainment devices, and/or personal assistant devices, one thing that makes these devices different from each other is their unique hardware design. If you take a deeper look into these different devices, you will find that the basic principles of operation are fundamentally the same across all of them: upon the user pressing the power button, the device starts its operation and within a short time it reaches the runtime/final system software environment (OS or applications) so that the user can make use of it. System firmware resides in the target hardware and starts while the device is being powered on and remains operational until it transfers control to the OS. The role of the system firmware is to abstract the underlying hardware from regular users. But from a developer standpoint,

© Subrata Banik and Vincent Zimmer 2022
S. Banik and V. Zimmer, *System Firmware*,
https://doi.org/10.1007/978-1-4842-7939-7_2

without having a detailed understanding of the underlying hardware architecture, you can't gather requirements for creating your own firmware solution.

This chapter highlights the value of understanding the hardware architecture prior to starting a system firmware journey. The hardware architecture that we'll look into in this chapter is generic in nature. In other words, this material will be applicable to computing devices and other embedded systems because their underlying architecture is fundamentally the same. The primary difference between these devices are the high-level system software or the application that it runs upon the system firmware completing its operation. In general, these embedded devices are a collection of controllers, microcontrollers, and I/O peripherals. Figure 2-1 shows the hardware view of a modern computing device.

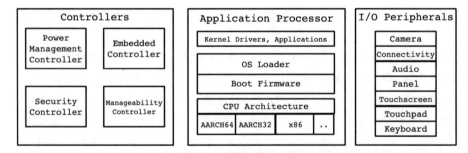

Figure 2-1. *Modern computing device hardware view*

Computer architecture is the organization of the hardware components that make up a computer system. An understanding of a computer system is nothing less than an understanding the interconnectivity of these hardware components as well as the mode of data transfer to exhibit the processing capabilities. This chapter will provide the computer architecture from a programmer's view so that you, the developer, are able to relate to the lowest-level system firmware responsibilities in an embedded system.

Computer Architecture

Computer architecture is the most widely researched area in computing since the very first time it was documented by *Charles Babbage* in 1837 as an *Analytical Engine*. The Analytical Engine provided the first general purpose computer design that combined the arithmetic-logic unit (ALU), control flow and integrated memory. In 1941, *Konrad Zuse,* a German civil engineer, built the first programmable computer. Between 1945 and 1951, the modern computer's basic model was designed by Hungarian mathematician *John von Neumann,* thus it is known as von Neumann architecture. He divided computer hardware into memory, a central processing unit (CPU) that combines the ALU and control unit, and input/output devices. All these parts are connected by a system bus. Memory and I/O devices are controlled by the CPU. Figure 2-2 shows the block diagram of *von Neumann architecture.*

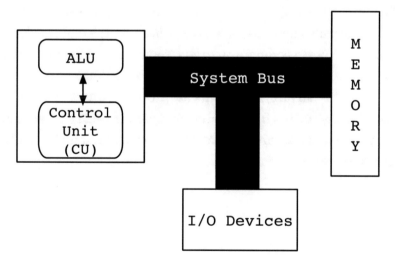

Figure 2-2. *von Neumann computer system block diagram*

Microprocessor is a term that is used widely in computer architecture; it's also known as a CPU. It combines processing logic and control logic on a single integrated circuit. A microcontroller contains one or more microprocessors along with in-built memory and programmable I/O devices that are interconnected with bus architecture. On modern computing devices, the system-on-chip (SoC) is a derivative of microcontrollers that are attached with external memory devices. The advantage of the von Neumann architecture is it's the simplest design of a control unit (CU) that gets data and instructions in the same way from a memory location. Once a memory location is assigned to a processor and if the value at that address is a number that the processor can execute, then it's an instruction, and if it is to be manipulated, then it's the data. Due to its simplistic design foundation, the von Neumann architecture is more applicable for almost all modern computers with minor modifications, such as desktop, laptops, and workstations. In contrast to von Neumann architecture, in 1947, yet another computer architecture evolved at Harvard University known as *Harvard architecture*. The main deviation in this architecture in comparison to von Neumann architecture is, *the memory for data is separate from the memory for instruction*. This means that by using the Harvard architecture the processor can simultaneously perform read instruction from memory and perform data read from and write to the memory. Figure 2-3 shows the computer system block diagram with the Harvard architecture.

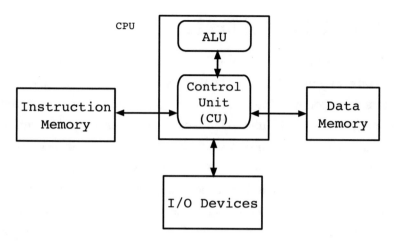

Figure 2-3. *Harvard architecture computer system block diagram*

Since the CPU concurrently accesses two memory buses, this approach allows parallel computing. The control unit for two buses makes it more complicated and more expensive, hence it is more suitable for small, embedded devices and digital signal processors.

This chapter will focus on discussing the embedded systems based on von Neumann computer architecture. There are three main subcategories of this computer architecture:

- Instruction set architecture (ISA)

- Microarchitecture

- System architecture

Instruction Set Architecture

The previous section provided the basic building blocks of computer architecture. The most important part of computer architecture is the processor. It's often referred to as the central processing unit. Everything is built around the CPU. The CPU is capable of performing read and write communication with the memory and I/O devices using the system bus.

Different CPU architectures have developed by configuring the operational speed in which data is fetched, processed, and executed in order to ensure better power or higher performance. Some processors are optimized for higher performance, while others focus on improving the system power consumption for longer battery life. Over time, based on these principles many different CPU architectures have evolved, such as ARM, x86, RISC-V, Power PC, MIPS, and SPARC.

The first step to understanding any CPU architecture is to learn its language. Unlike a verbal language, in CPU architecture any meaningful word that represents an operation is called an *instruction*. A complete range of computer instructions forms an *instruction set*. These instructions are different between different CPU architectures as instructions specify the operations to perform and the operands to use. The operands can be memory addresses, registers, or instructions. Although the instructions are written in *assembly language*, which is still human readable, the computer hardware can only understand the binaries (0s and 1s) known as *machine language*. Take a scenario of an ADD instruction using two 32-bit register operands. The first operand (destination operand), the second operand (source operand), and store the result in the destination operand (register). Figure 2-4 shows the encoding of this operation from assembly language instructions to the machine code-readable format for the processor.

Assembly Language Instruction that performs ADD ECX, EAX

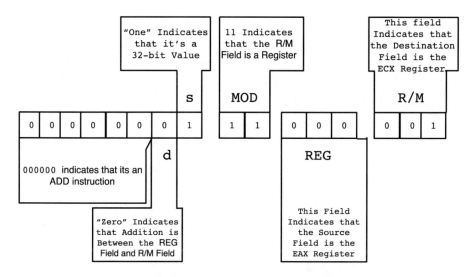

Figure 2-4. *Encoding of ADD assembly instruction into machine code*

After encoding, the machine language of instruction add ecx, eax is *01h C1h* in hexadecimal bytes as it appears in the memory in the same order.

Although the instruction set of each CPU architecture is different, it's built upon the same basic principle of computer architecture, so almost all architectures define the basic instruction sets such as memory, arithmetic, and logical and control flow operations that operate on memory or registers (I/O on x86 family processors has a separate space for accessing the I/O devices).

Here is an example of common instruction sets in cross-architecture:

Data movement instructions

Operation	x86	ARM

Set a register to a 32-bit fixed constant value	`mov r32, imm32`
	`imm32 = Immediate`
	`DWORD Value`
		`mov32 Rd, #constant`
		`Rd= Destination Reg`
		`#constant= Constant`
		`32-bit Value`

Copy data from a register to a register	`mov r32, r/m32`
	`r32= DWORD GPP`
	`register`
		`mov Rd, Rn`
		`Rn= Source Reg`

ALU operations instructions

Operation	x86	ARM

Add the values of two registers	`add r32, r/m32`
	`r/m32= A 32-bit`
	`register or memory`
	`operand`
		`add Rd, Rn, Operand2`
		`Operand2= Second`
		`operand`

Bitwise AND operations	`and r32, r/m32`	`and Rd, Rn, Operand2`

Control flow instructions

Operation	x86	ARM
Conditional branch	`cmp r32, r/m32`	`cmp Rn, Operand2`

Call a subroutine	`call r/m32`	`bl destination`
		`destination =`
		`Relative expression`

Return from a subroutine	`Ret`	`bx lr` `lr= Link Register`

Privileged/system instructions

Operation	x86	ARM
Software interrupt	int	swi

CISC and RISC

Instruction Set Architecture (ISA) vocabulary can be divided into two major categories:

- Complex Instruction Set Computer (CISC)

    - Rich vocabulary

    - A single instruction performs more work.

- Reduced Instruction Set Computer (RISC)

    - Small and reduced vocabulary

    - A single instruction performs less work.

The CISC processor architecture holds a smaller number of general purpose registers but significantly larger instruction sets. The idea behind the CISC processor is to do more operations via hardware and the software does less work, which results in a single instruction in the CISC processor being capable of performing 1,000 operations at once. This was an advantage when developers used to write their program in assembly language and external memory was costly and limited. So it made sense to create a smaller program that took less space in memory and let each instruction do more. This fundamental requirement of the CISC processor makes the processor design complicated since it needed to support a large and diverse instruction set. When external memory got cheaper and faster, the advantages of CISC weren't as great.

This thought gave birth to an alternative design named the RISC processor architecture where the idea is to make the silicon design simple and offload the complex instructions from silicon to the software programming language. This allows RISC to have large numbers of register sets, which eventually saves processors time when fetching data from the slow-speed memory. With reduced-complexity instructions, decode units also become smaller and simpler, which helps reduce the power consumption of the processing unit. A simple integer multiplication takes three cycles on a CISC processor whereas it might take only one (or two based on memory operation) cycles on an RISC processor. Also, the RISC processor uses a load-store model for memory access, which means only load and store instructions can access memory. On CISC, most instructions are allowed to directly operate on data in memory, but on RISC processors, most of the instructions work on registers only, which helps most of the instructions to complete in a single cycle. On an RISC processor, any data must be moved from memory into registers before being operated upon. With high-level programming language compilers, developers no longer need to worry about writing more code and compilers can make use of a more general purpose register set to optimize the processor's performance.

Take an example of *performing the multiplication of two numbers from a memory location and storing the results in another memory location* using CISC and RISC instructions. A single multiplication instruction can be used on CISC to load two numbers from a memory location and perform the actual multiplication operation and store the result into the destination memory location. On a RISC processor, in the absence of complex instructions, it divides the entire operations into three separate commands:

- **LOAD**: Move these two data points from the memory location into registers.

- **MULTIPLICATION**: Perform the actual operation and keep the result in the register.

- **STORE**: Move the result from the register into the memory location.

When you compare the underlying compiler generated code, you will realize that the RISC processor needs more instructions to perform the same operations. Also, the code size is bigger in RISC, but due to the fact that each instruction takes only one cycle to complete, the entire operation using either architecture takes the same number of cycles. So which ISA is better, CISC or RISC ? The answer is mixed, as both offer benefits and nowadays, there is a lot of mix-and-match between RISC and CISC-like features in cross-architectures. The classic examples of CISC processors are x86 architectures and Motorola 68xxx. RISC architecture examples include the ARM, RISC-V, and PowerPC.

Microarchitecture

Microarchitecture is the term used in computing to explain how the ISA is implemented in a particular processor. Instruction sets are like vocabulary for a computing programming language, and microarchitecture ensures how different components inside the processor are interconnected to implement those instructions. The specific components like registers, memories, ALU, EU, and others are arranged to form a processor called the microarchitecture. The overall operation performed by the CPU can be divided into three iterative loops:

- **Fetch** an instruction from the memory (or I/O).

- **Decode** the instruction.

  - Find the associated data that the instruction needs.

- **Execute** the instruction.

  - Store the results

This entire process is known as *instruction cycling* and it continuously operates on processors when powered on. Figure 2-5 highlights the various components that are part of this instruction cycling.

1. A block that is meant to fetch the data and instruction from the memory

2. Fill up the instruction queue.

3. An execution block to decode the instructions

4. Based on the nature of the instruction, perform arithmetic and/or logical operations.

5. Make use of registers and/or memory operands to store the final results.

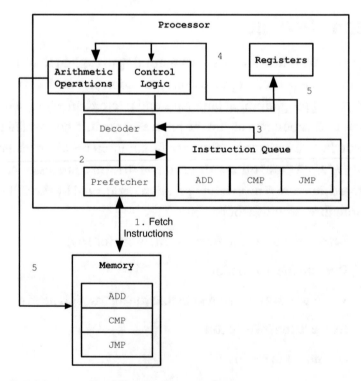

Figure 2-5. *Internals of instruction cycling*

The internals of instruction cycling provide the requirement of several hardware blocks that are essential for defining the microarchitecture of any CPU architecture. Let's take an example of basic x86 microarchitecture to understand these hardware blocks in detail.

8086 Microarchitecture

8086 and 8088 microprocessors are part of the first 8086 microarchitecture. The 8086 is a 16-bit processor, which means it can read/write data from/ to memory and I/O either in word or byte format at a time. The internal architecture of 8086 processors is divided into two units: the bus interface unit (BIU) and the execution unit (EU). They are interdependent of each other and they need additional hardware blocks as well. The following sections provide more detailed descriptions of these units.

Bus Interface Unit

The BIU provides the interface to access the external memory and I/O devices via the system bus. It is meant to perform the required data and address transfer between the memory and I/O from the outside world and fill up the instruction queue required for the execution unit. At a high level, the BIU performs operations that include

- **Address generation circuit**: Sends out physical addresses for memory access

    - The BIU has an address generation circuit.

    - It generates the 20-bit physical address using a segment and offset address as per the following formula:

Physical 20 bit address = Segment Address * 10h + Offset Address

- It fetches instructions from the memory and transfers the data to and from the memory and I/O.

    - **Bus Control Logic**: The BCL as part of the BIU generates all bus control signals like READ, WRITE for memory and I/O accesses.

    - The BIU has four *segment register*s to hold the addresses of instructions and data in memory. This is used by the processor to address the memory location. The *instruction pointer register* holds the address of the next instruction that will get executed by the EU.

- **Prefetch instruction queue**: The BIU has an instruction queue. The size of the instruction queue in 8086 is up to 6 bytes. The BIU fetches the instructions and keep up to six instructions in the queue. In order to increase the operational speed and avoid a delay while the EU is executing those executions, the BIU gets the next 6 bytes of the instruction and stores them in the instruction queue. When the EU is done with the previous instruction, it reads the next instruction readily available in the queue, thus this process is known as a prefetch instruction queue. Fetching the next instruction while the current instruction is getting executed by the EU is called *pipelining* and this results in increased execution speed. This queue gets flushed upon executing a branch instruction.

Execution Unit

The EU receives the instructions and data from the BIU, executes them, and stores the results either in the general purpose registers or stores the data in a memory location or I/O devices by passing the data back to the BIU. The EU doesn't have any way to communicate with system buses. At a high level, EU performs the following operations:

- **Instruction register**: The EU fetches an opcode from the instruction queue into the instruction registers.

    - 8086 has four 16-bit general purpose registers to store immediate values during executions and four special purpose registers (two pointer registers and two index registers) and one flag/status register.

- **Instruction decoder**: The decoder in the EU translates fetched instructions into a series of operations and sends the information to the control circuit for the execution.

- **EU control system**: The EU control system is a set of gates that control the timings, passing of the data, and other control inputs within the execution unit.

- **Arithmetic-logic unit (ALU)**: A control circuit inside the EU unit is called the arithmetic-logic unit. Figure 2-6 shows the control block diagram of the ALU. The instructions that are executed by the processor control the data flow between the registers and the ALU using the ALU data bus. The ALU is responsible for performing the arithmetic manipulation of the data in the processor via the ALU's control inputs.

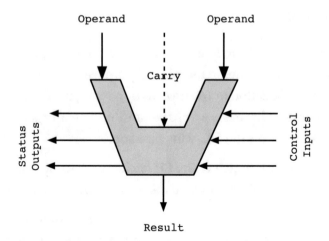

Figure 2-6. *ALU block diagram*

The ALU in the EU performs both arithmetic and logical operations such as addition, subtraction, AND, OR, and more on one or more values. These values are known as *operands.* The *results* from the operation are placed in the register or memory based on the type of destination operand.

Additionally, status outputs are special attributes known as *flags* and are based on the output result; for example, the zero flag is set if result is zero.

Figure 2-7 shows the 8086 microarchitecture elements such as the ALU and general purpose registers as part of the EU, and segment registers, address generators, instruction queue are part of the BIU. The communication between the EU and the BIU is via internal buses and the BIU provides an interface to external memory and I/O devices.

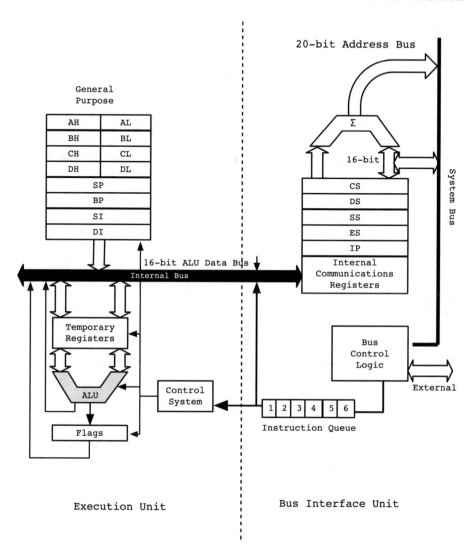

Figure 2-7. *8086 microarchitecture*

Often, there are many microarchitectures for a single architecture. Figure 2-8 shows the evolution of x86 microarchitecture by keeping the base CISC architecture but increasing the number of registers or higher max clock frequency or more pipeline stages.

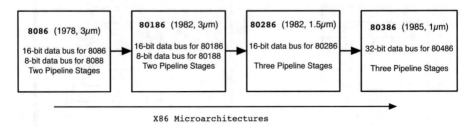

Figure 2-8. *x86 microarchitecture evolution*

System Architecture

System architecture includes all other hardware components in the computing system, apart from the processor. Although the processor is considered the heart of a computing system, other hardware blocks are also required, without which the processor alone can't perform any operation. Figure 2-9 describes the typical computer system architecture. This section provides a high-level overview of other hardware blocks that are part of computer architecture, such as:

- Memory unit

- I/O devices

- Buses

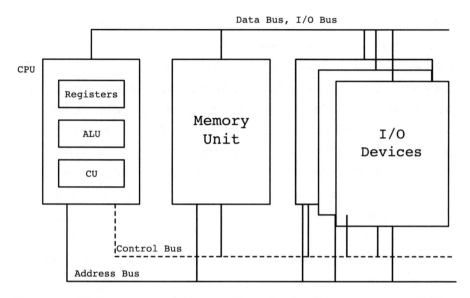

Figure 2-9. *Computer system architecture (with memory and I/O)*

Memory Unit

Typically, in a computing system, the memory is used to hold both code and data for the processor to process or manipulate. In any computer system, there are many layers that represent the different types of memory. These types can be categorized as temporary memory like memory with volatile contents, which will get lost upon device power-off, and permanent memory, mostly referred as storage memory, which is persistent across boot. Depending on the CPU architecture, upon CPU power-on, the available volatile memory can be defined as one of the following:

CPU registers: A handful of registers provide very limited memory space depending upon the CPU architecture. It's typically used by the early firmware code prior to any available memory type upon reset. It's probably the fastest memory access.

Cache: Depending on the CPU architecture, there may be different levels of CPU cache available, which provides bigger memory space compared to registers and might be sufficient to perform the early hardware initialization using limited firmware code blocks. For example, L1 cache holds cache lines retrieved from L2 cache, L2 cache holds cache lines retrieved from LLC cache, and LLC cache holds cache lines retrieved from the system memory. This provides comparatively faster access.

SRAM/DRAM: Different hardware designs are intended to overcome the limitation of limited memory available post CPU reset using the SRAM, pre-initialized memory available for firmware usage. DRAM, or the main memory, provides the much bigger volatile storage for higher-level applications. The memory access speed is lesser than cache but it's much cheaper.

The possible non-volatile memory types in the computer systems are the following:

Local disks: The permanent storage part of the computer system, possibly belonging to the I/O controller hub. It's meant to provide the higher memory space for keeping large software like the OS, system applications, and others. It's access time is much higher compared to the main memory.

Remote storage: Typically referred to as cloud storage, storage space is very high but provides the slowest memory access.

The order in which these memories are listed here is their actual initialization order by system firmware first and later by the OS. The memory units (the volatile memory outside the CPU) are connected with the processor using three different buses: the address bus, data bus, and control bus.

Facts   Another widely used memory in computer systems is CMOS, which is a low-power memory chip powered by a small battery when the system is powered off to ensure that the stored data is always preserved. It used to store boot configuration information such as drive details, keyboard type, PCI bus slots configuration, and passwords to restrict access to the system configuration window.

I/O Devices

A processor's address space can contain devices other than the memory. These devices are referred to as input/output devices (I/O). These devices can be further categories into two types.

Legacy devices: The processor has access to these devices using dedicated I/O mapped ports. Even processors can perform separate instructions to read and write into these device spaces using an I/O bus. Examples: Serial ports, parallel ports, PS2 keyboards

Modern devices: Today, a majority of I/O devices are attached to the standard PCI bus (on x86) or the AMBA peripheral bus (APB on ARM). The I/O functions are implemented in modern systems using memory-mapped addressable peripheral registers. These devices can be accessed using their memory-mapped registers. In a memory-mapped system, each register appears as a memory location at a particular address. Examples: USB, SATA, UART controllers

There are three different ways that data can be exchanged between the processor and external I/O devices:

- **Programmed I/O**: The data transfer is initiated based on the execution of an I/O instruction. In this mode of transfer, the CPU remains at an idle loop until the I/O device is ready for the data transfer. This process wastes lots of valuable CPU cycles.

- **Interrupt-initiated I/O**: The external device triggers an interrupt when it needs the dedicated service of the processor for performing any data transfer. In this mode, upon receiving the interrupt from an external device, the processor will suspend its current task and start executing the interrupt service routine (ISR).

- **Direct memory access (DMA)**: DMA allows the data to be transferred between I/O devices and memory units without the continuous involvement of the processor. DMA is intended while performing a high-speed transfer. This mode is known as direct memory access because I/O devices can directly communicate with each other using the memory buses without having any dependencies of the CPU. Here the DMA controller requests the processor to lease the system bus and the processor informs the DMA controller that the buses are available so that the DMA can take control of the buses.

Buses

Buses are the electrical signals that transfer the data from one part of the computer system to another. A typical computer system usually contains three bus types: address bus, data bus, and control bus. Additionally, the CPU architecture that allows transferring the data between the CPU and the I/O devices using programmed I/O has another bus called the I/O bus. Figure 2-10 shows the connection between the memory unit and the processor.

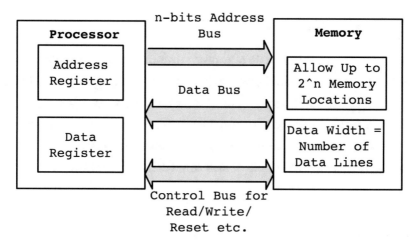

Figure 2-10. *Bus connections between memory and processor*

- **Address bus**: Unidirectional bus that carries the
  location information or address of the memory.
  Depending on the n-bit address, the processor can
  access up to 2^n memory locations.

- **Data bus**: This bus carries the data information that
  needs to be read from or written to the memory.
  Depending on the number of data lines, it limits the
  maximum size of the data variable. For example, if
  a data bus is 16 bits, then the maximum width of a
  data variable is 16 bits. The direction of this bus is
  dependent on the control bus.

- **Control bus**: The bus that provides all the control
  signals such as read or write operations to memory.
  The control bus can also pass status information after
  execution of the read/write operations like address
  errors. The control bus is also bidirectional where
  output signals are used for read, write, valid address,
  and such and the input control lines are for reset, one
  or more interrupt lines, and clock input.

CPU Internals

Earlier sections provided basic computer architecture information and the required hardware blocks for designing a computing system. Different CPU architectures have implemented their own registers, ISAs, ALUs, and control units for processing any instructions and communicating with external memory units and/or I/O devices using a specific bus. This section highlights the internals of different CPU architectures such as x86 and ARM.

Internals of x86 Processors

8086 is the first 16-bit microprocessor designed by Intel in 1978, which gave rise to the x86 processor family. The x86 processor family is generally classified as a von Neumann architecture machine. The 8086 has a 20-bit address line (A0-A19), which means it can map up to $2^{20} = 10,48,576 = 1MB$ of memory. Out of this 20-bit address line, A0-A15 are coupled with the data bus and A16-A19 are uniformly separated. As 8086 is a 16-bit processor, it has a 16-bit (D0-D15) bidirectional data bus. 8086 microprocessors perform fast operations compared to 8085 because of two separate engines, called the BIU (bus interface unit) and the EU (execution unit). The BIU is responsible for fetching the data from memory and I/O from the outside world and filling up the 6-byte-long instruction queue. The EU fetches instructions from the queue, decodes them, and executes operations.

Registers

The primary and internal data storage of the processor is known as a register. Registers are used to hold the operands and data while running an instruction. The size of a register is measured by the number of bits it can hold. In an 8086 processor, the register width is 16 bits. The first 32-bit registers were introduced with the 80386 microprocessor. Figure 2-11 shows the complete register list for x86 architecture.

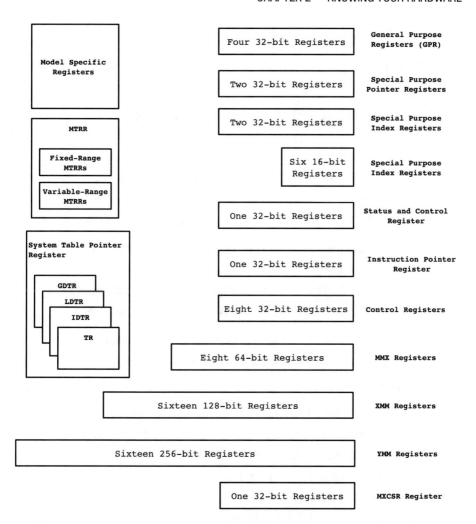

Figure 2-11. *Different registers in x86 architecture*

The x86 architecture has four general purpose registers, four special purpose registers (two pointer registers and two index registers), six segment registers, one status and control register, one instruction pointer, and architecture-specific registers as eight control registers, multimedia extension (MMX) registers, XMM, and YMM registers. Apart from these, there are other processor capability registers such as model-specific registers (MSR) and memory type range registers (MTRRs).

General Purpose Registers (GPR)

The 32-bit general purpose registers are intended to provide the following items:

- Operands for arithmetic and logical operations

- Operands to hold the memory address

- **EAX register**: This register is also known as an *accumulator register*. It works to hold the operands and results for various arithmetic and logical operations.

- **EBX register**: This register is used to hold the address of the memory location. It's also known as the base register. Wide usage of this register is in segment mode with a data segment register to hold the offset address.

- **ECX register**: This register is referred to as *a counter register* that holds the loop count during loop instruction.

- **EDX register**: This register is used to hold the upper 32-bit values along with EAX during arithmetic operations and point to the I/O port address for I/O operations. It's also known as a data register.

Special Purpose Registers (SPR)

Four special purpose registers are divided into two subcategories as pointer registers (ESP, EBP) and index registers (ESI, EDI). The 32-bit special purpose registers are intended to provide the following items:

- Operands for address calculations

- Special operands used for string instructions

- Memory pointers

- Stack pointers

- **ESP register**: This register is used to point to the stack top, also known as a stack pointer register (in the stack segment register). It's used during instructions like push, pop, call, and ret.

- **EBP register**: Base pointer registers contain the offset address in the stack segment. This is used during base addressing mode.

- **ESI register**: This register is also known as a source index register. It holds pointers to data in the segment pointed by the data segment register, such as a source pointer for string operations.

- **EDI register**: Destination index register. It holds a pointer to data (destination) in the segment pointed by the extra segment register, such as a destination pointer for string operations.

Figure 2-12 shows the alternate names and usage of both general purpose and special purpose registers.

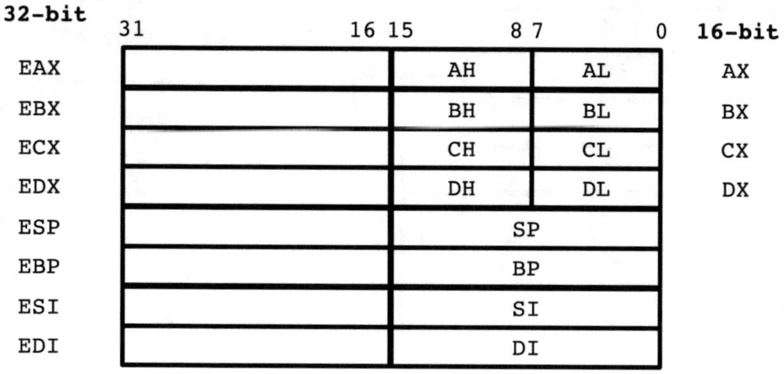

32-bit	31	16 15	8 7	0	16-bit
EAX			AH	AL	AX
EBX			BH	BL	BX
ECX			CH	CL	CX
EDX			DH	DL	DX
ESP			SP		
EBP			BP		
ESI			SI		
EDI			DI		

Figure 2-12. *Alternative register names and usage*

As shown in the figure, the 16-bit representation of these registers used in the x86 architecture between 8086 and 80286 as AX, BX, CX, DX, SP, BP, SI, and DI. Each of the lower two bytes of the 32-bit registers can be referred to by the names of AH, BH, CH, and DH (the higher-order byte between bits 15-8) and AL, BL, CL, and DL (for the lower-order byte between bits 7-0).

In 64-bit mode, registers between EAX-EDI are referred to as RAX-EDI; additionally, R8-R15 represents the eight new general purpose registers.

Segment Registers

The segment register is a special pointer that points to the segment selectors. In order to access a particular segment in memory, the segment selector for the segment must be present in that segment register. In x86 architecture, there are six 16-bit segment registers, which point to one of three types of segments: code, data, and stack. Each segment register can access 64KB of segments in memory. Figure 2-13 shows the use of different segment registers.

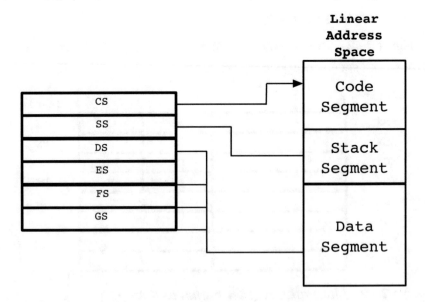

Figure 2-13. *Use of segment registers*

- **Code segment register**: The CS register holds the base address for the code segment where the current instructions being executed are stored. The processor fetches the instruction from the logical address, where the segment is pointed by the CS register and the offset is pointed by the EIP register. The CS register cannot be loaded explicitly, so it needs to be updated implicitly by some internal processor operation like a procedure call or interrupt handling.

- **Data segment register**: The DS, ES, FS, and GS registers are all points to data segments. It consists of data used by the program and is accessed in the data segment by an offset address. With the 80386 architecture, two new segment registers were added (FS, F-segment, and GS, G-segment) for general purpose programs. ES stands as an extra segment and is used by the string to hold the extra destination data.

- **Stack segment register**: The SS register points to the stack during execution of the application program. All stack operations use the SS registers to find the stack segment.

In 64-bit mode, all segment registers are treated as disabled.

Status and Control Register

The 32-bit register contains a group of status flags and control flags. This register is also known as a EFLAG register (where the lower word is known as a FLAGS register), which is used to reflect the status of an instruction of use to control the operations of the processor. Figure 2-14 shows the status and control register flag.

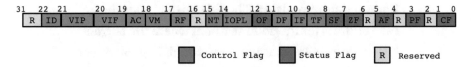

Figure 2-14. *Status and control flag (EFLAGS)*

Status flag: Indicates the results of arithmetic and logical instructions

Bit definitions	Descriptions
CF (bit 0)	**Carry flag:** Set if an arithmetic operation generates a carry or a borrow out of the most significant bit of the result. This flag indicates an overflow condition for arithmetic operations.
PF (bit 2)	**Parity flag:** Set if the least significant byte of the result contains an even number of 1 bit.
AF (bit 4)	**Auxiliary carry flag:** Set if an arithmetic operation generates a carry or a borrow out from lower nibble (D0-D3) to upper nibble (D4-D7). This flag is used in binary-coded decimal (BCD) arithmetic.
ZF (bit 6)	**Zero flag:** Set to 1 when the result of arithmetic or logical operation is zero; otherwise, it is set to 0.
SF (bit 7)	**Sign flag:** This flag holds the sign of the result. 0 indicates a positive value and 1 indicates a negative value.
OF (bit 11)	**Overflow flag:** Set if the integer result is too large a positive number or too small a negative number (excluding the sign-bit) to fit in the destination operand.

Control flag: Controls the operations of the execution unit

Bit definitions	Descriptions
TF (bit 8)	**Trap flag:** Set to enable single-step mode for debugging (user to execute one instruction at a time)
IF (bit 9)	**Interrupt Flag:** Controls the response of the processor to maskable interrupt requests. Set to 1 for interrupt enabled condition and set to 0 for interrupt disabled condition
DF (bit 10)	**Direction Flag:** Controls string instructions (MOVS, CMPS, LODS, and STOS). Setting the DF flag causes the string instructions to auto-decrement (to process strings from high addresses to low addresses). Clearing the DF flag causes the string instructions to auto-increment (process strings from low addresses to high addresses).

In 64-bit mode, this register is known as RFLAGS but bits 32-63 are reserved to 0.

Instruction Pointer Registers (IP)

EIP is the instruction pointer register that contains the offset in the current code segment for the next instruction to get executed. This register is advanced by one instruction while getting executed in linear order or it can move back and forth by the number of instructions while executing branch instructions, calling procedures, and such.

Control Registers (CR)

The control register is a set of 32-bit registers (CR0-CR7) used to change or control the general behavior of a processor. The typical usage of these registers is during processor addressing mode switch, page control, and interrupt control. Each control register has several control flags that can be set or reset based on software programming needs; for example, the CR0 bit 0 is PE (protected mode enable) and is set if the system is in protected mode; otherwise the system remains in real mode.

In 64-bit mode, this register is 64 bits long and there are few more control registers available. Additional general purpose registers include 32-bit extensions to EAX called RAX, with similar extensions RBX, RCX, and eight more 64-bit only registers R8 through R15.

Vector Registers

Vector registers hold data for vector processing done by SIMD (single instruction, multiple data).

- **MMX registers:** MMX is the first set of SIMD instructions that defines eight 64-bit registers named MM0-MM7. MMX registers can be used in different ways (in eight 8-bit modes, four 16-bit modes, two 32-bit modes, or one 64-bit mode) as operands for MMX instructions. Programmers can also use these registers as general purpose registers as per need.

- **XMM registers:** XMM registers are introduced as part of SSE (streaming SIMD extension) to overcome the problem with MMX (where FPU and MMX are unable to work at the same time). These are eight 128-bit registers named XMM0-XMM7. Later with 64-bit mode, a further eight registers XMM8-XMM15 were added. Programming can either use these registers for 128-bit arithmetic or floating-pointer operations or allow parallel operations using

  - Two 64-bit integers or

  - Four 32-bit integers or

- Eight 16-bit integers or

- Sixteen 8-bit integers or

- Two 64-bit floating-point numbers or

- Four 32-bit floating-point numbers

- **YMM registers:** A processor supporting the advanced vector extensions (AVX) uses sixteen 256-bits YMM registers (YMM0-YMM15) to perform SIMD operations. Programmers can also perform parallel operations as

  - Four 64-bit floating-point numbers or

  - Eight 32-bit floating-point numbers

The YMM registers are aliased over the order 128-bit XMM registers use for SSE, hence lower 128-bits of YMM registers are treated as XMM registers, as shown in Figure 2-15.

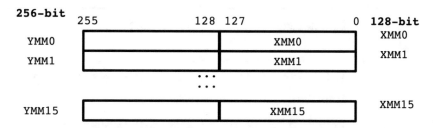

Figure 2-15. *XMM registers overlay the YMM registers*

- **MXCSR registers:** The MXCSR register is a 32-bit register containing flags for control and status information regarding SSE instructions. Bits 0-5 represent invalid operations, denormal, divide by zero, overflow, underflow, and precision, respectively. Bits 7-12 mask individual exceptions when set and initially are set by a power-up or reset.

Model-Specific Registers (MSR)

A model-specific register is a processor-specific control register used in x86-architecture for processor-monitoring events, runtime machine checks, to enable/disable certain CPU features, and for selecting memory types for physical memory. The model-specific registers were introduced with the Pentium processor (Pentium 4, Xeon P6 family), along with CPUID instructions to determine which features are present on a particular model. All MSRs can be accessed using RDMSR for reading and writing with the WRMSR instructions. As MSRs and its bit-fields have support for a finite range of processor families and models, it's recommended for programmers to make use of CPUID instruction with leaf function 01h to query and determine model-specific availability of MSRs. Many MSRs have existed between different processor generations and even architectures hence known as architectural MSRs. These "architectural MSRs" were given the prefix *IA32_*. For example:

Register address	MSR name	Description
10h	IA32_TIME_STAMP_ COUNTER	Returns the current timestamp count value
8Bh	IA32_BIOS_SIGN_ID	BIOS update signature (RO). Returns the microcode update signature following the execution of CPUID.01H.

Memory Type Range Registers (MTRRs)

Memory type range registers are a set of processor capability control registers used to optimize the memory operations for different memory types such as ROM, RAM, frame buffer memory, and memory-mapped I/O. MTRRs were introduced into the IA-32 architecture with the Pentium

Pro Processor. MTRRs are a type of MSRs that allow programmers to specify the type of caching (no caching) in the system memory for selected physical address ranges. The MTRR mechanism allows up to 96 memory ranges to be defined in physical memory using a set of MSRs that helps to specify the type of memory for each memory range. Here are the details of different memory types:

Memory type: Uncacheable (UC)

Encoding in MTRR: 00h

Description: Specifying a system memory range with this type makes the memory locations as non-cacheable. All reads and writes that appear on the system bus are executed in program order without reordering. This type of cache control is useful for memory-mapped I/O devices. When applied on the physical memory, it greatly reduces processor performance.

Memory type: Write combining (WC)

Encoding in MTRR: 01h

Description: Specifying a system memory location with this type makes the memory location as non-cacheable (same as the UC type). Writes may be delayed and combined in the write combining buffer (WC buffer) to reduce memory accesses. If the WC buffer is partially filled, the writes may be delayed until the next occurrence of a serializing event, such as an SFENCE or MFENCE instruction, CPUID execution, a read or write to uncached memory, an interrupt occurrence, or a LOCK instruction execution. This type of cache control is applicable for video frame buffers, where regardless of the write order, it is important to update memory so the written character is seen on the graphics display.

Memory type: Write-through (WT)

Encoding in MTRR: 04h

Description: Specifying a memory range with this type ensures that writes and reads to and from system memory are cached. Reads come from cache lines on cache hits; read misses cause cache fills. All writes are written to a cache line (when possible) and through to system memory.

When writing through to memory, invalid cache lines are never filled, and valid cache lines are either filled or invalidated.

Memory type: Write-protected (WP)

Encoding in MTRR: 05h

Description: Marking a system memory location with this type ensures writes are propagated to the system bus and cause corresponding cache lines on all processors on the bus to be invalidated. Reads come from cache lines when possible, and read misses cause cache fills.

Memory type: Write-back (WB)

Encoding in MTRR: 06h

Description: All types of system memory accesses like writes and reads to and from system memory are cached. Reads come from cache lines on cache hits. Write misses cause cache line fills, and writes are performed entirely in the cache, when possible. The write-back memory type reduces bus traffic by eliminating many unnecessary writes to system memory. Writes to a cache line are not immediately forwarded to system memory; instead, they are accumulated in the cache. The modified cache lines are written to system memory later, when a write-back operation is performed. Write-back operations are triggered when cache lines need to be deallocated, such as when new cache lines are being allocated in a cache that is already full.

The memory ranges and the types of memory in each range are set by groups of registers: the fixed range MTRRs and the variable range MTRRs. These registers can be read and written using RDMSR and WRMSR instructions.

- **Fixed range MTRRs**

There are a total 11 fixed range registers of 64-bits each to map fixed system memory ranges. Each fixed range register is divided into 8-bit fields to specify the memory type for each of the subranges that the register controls. Here is the list of fixed range registers:

MSR register address	Name	Description
0x250	MTRRfix64K_00000	To map the 512-KByte address range from system memory 0H to 7FFFFH. This range is divided into eight 64-KByte subranges.
0x258	MTRRfix16K_80000	To map the two 128-KByte addresses
0x259	MTRRfix16K_A0000	ranges from 80000H to BFFFFH. This range is divided into sixteen 16-KByte subranges, eight ranges per register.
0x268	MTRRfix4K_C0000	To map eight 32-KByte addresses
0x269	MTRRfix4K_C8000	ranges from C0000H to FFFFFH. This
0x26A	MTRRfix4K_D0000	range is divided into 64 4-KByte
0x26B	MTRRfix4K_D8000	subranges, eight ranges per
0x26C	MTRRfix4K_E0000	register.
0x26D	MTRRfix4K_E8000	
0x26E	MTRRfix4K_F0000	
0x26F	MTRRfix4K_F8000	

- **Variable range MTRRs**

The variable range registers are used to define memory ranges from the available system memory and set the caching policies for these ranges. Examples: Graphics memory and different memory ranges used by PCI devices. To specify these ranges, processors permit "m" variable size address ranges, using a pair of MTRRs for each range. The number "m" is provided by the MTRRCap register Bit 8:0 VCNT offset, indicating the number of variable ranges implemented by the processor.

It's recommended that system firmware read this register before creating system memory using variable range registers.

It needs two register pairs to specify a memory range. The first register is to define the base address and memory type for the range and the second register contains the mask used to determine the address range.

MSR register address	Name	Description
0x200	MTRRPhyBase0	Bit 7:0 specifies the memory type for the range. Specifies the base address of the address range. This 24-bit value, in the case max physical address is 36 bits, is extended by 12 bits at the low end to form the base address.
0x201	MTRRPhyMask0	Specifies a mask. The mask determines the range of the region being mapped. Bit 11 specifies the valid bit to enable this register pair when set.

The last register pair to specify the variable memory range is MTRRPhyBase$n$ and MTRRPhyMask$n$ where n=m-1. Here is an example of setting up the MTRR for a system with following assumptions (total system memory is 4GB and variable MTTRs are 10).

- 64MB of system memory is mapped as write-back memory (WB) for the highest system performance.

- 768MB of system memory is mapped as write-back memory for the PCI memory range and other reserved ranges.

- 8MB of system memory is mapped as write-back memory for system management mode base addresses.

- 256MB of the graphics card is mapped to write-combining memory (WC) beginning at address A0000000H.

The following table settings for the MTRRs to have the proper mapping of the system memory for this above configuration:

Registers	Base	Type
MTRRPhyBase0	0x0000000000000000	WB
MTRRPhyMask0	0x0000007fc0000000	
MTRRPhyBase1	0x0000000040000000	WB
MTRRPhyMask1	0x0000007fe0000000	
MTRRPhyBase2	0x0000000060000000	WB
MTRRPhyMask2	0x0000007ff0000000	
MTRRPhyBase3	0x0000000070000000	WB
MTRRPhyMask3	0x0000007fff800000	
MTRRPhyBase4	0x0000000070000000	WB
MTRRPhyMask4	0x0000007fff800000	
MTRRPhyBase5	0x00000000a0000000	WC
MTRRPhyMask5	0x0000007ff0000000	
MTRRPhyBase6	0x00000000b0000000	UC
MTRRPhyMask6	0x0000007ff0000000	
MTRRPhyBase7	0x00000000c0000000	UC
MTRRPhyMask7	0x0000007fc0000000	

Processor Modes

Upon reset, the x86 processor supports primarily three modes of operations: real mode, protected mode, and system management mode. There is one more special submode of protected mode known as virtual 8086 mode. Here are operational details of each mode.

Real Mode

All x86 processors come up in real mode after they are reset. This model allows for executing the basic instruction set of the 8086 processor (backward compatibility) in addition to a number of new features, such as the ability to switch into other modes. It's a 16-bit mode with 20-bit address space offering no memory protection. That's the reason this mode is also known as *real addressing mode*. In real mode, only the first 1MB (2^{20}) of memory can be addressed with the typical *segment:offset* logical address. Each segment (segment registers are CS, DS, ES, SS, etc.) is 64K bytes long (16-bit offset).

As an example, in real mode, if DS = 0x0008, then the data segment begins at address (20-bit address) = DS * 0x10 = 0x0080 and its length is 64K bytes.

In real mode, the interrupt handling is through the interrupt vector table (IVT).

Facts   A 32-bit processor has a 36-bit address bus, which means it can support up to 2^{36} = 64GB of total memory, which can't be addressed in real mode but can be addressed in protected mode.

Interrupt Vector Table

In real mode, the maximum number of interrupts is 256, so the number of vectors that can be stored in the interrupt vector table is 256. Each interrupt vector entry in the IVT takes 4 bytes because each interrupt is a 4-byte real mode pointer (in the form of segment:offset, which represents the address of a routine to be called, known as an interrupt service routine or ISR, when the processor receives an interrupt, the first two bytes represent the offset and next 2 bytes a segment). Hence, the bottom 1KB (256 * 4 bytes = 1024 bytes) of system memory is devoted to the storage of interrupt vectors. The IVT resides at a fixed location in conventional memory (below 640KB) between addresses 0x0000:0x03FF. Figure 2-16 is an example of interrupt handling using IVT with the below assumptions: the Interrupt number is 0x10, a video BIOS interrupt used for display related services

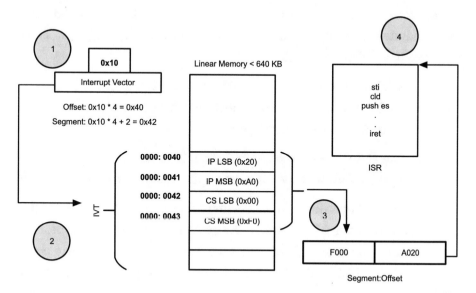

Figure 2-16. *Demonstration of Int 10h interrupt handling*

Protected Mode

Protected mode is the native state of the processor and it allows access to all instructions and features. In protected mode, memory greater than 1MB can be accessed by the software. This mode provides a separate memory area named *segments*; this segment size can be of variable length (below or above 64KB). The processor prevents software programs referencing memory outside its assigned segments. The segment registers and offset address combined create the logical memory address in protected mode, which is different compared to the real mode, although the offset usage part of the logical memory calculation remains the same. A 32-bit offset allows segments of up to 2^{32} = 4GB in length. However, the segment register contains a *selector* that selects a *descriptor* from a descriptor table. The descriptor *describes* the memory segment's location, limits, and access rights.

Selectors: A segment selector is a 16-bit identifier that is used to select a segment descriptor from a descriptor table that defines a segment. There are two types of descriptor tables:

- **Global descriptor table (GDT)**: Contains segment definitions that are applicable for all programs, also known as system descriptors

- **Local descriptor table (LDT)**: Specific to an application, also known as an application descriptor

Figure 2-17 shows the segment sector that holds a 13-bit index to select a descriptor from one of 2^{13} = 8192 descriptors available in a descriptor table. The table indicator (TI) specifies the one of descriptor table to use between GDT or LDT and requested privilege (RPL) specifies the privilege level of selector.

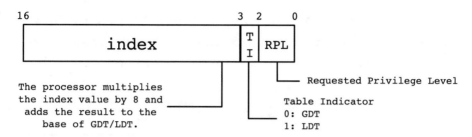

Figure 2-17. *Segment selector*

Descriptors: A segment descriptor is a data structure as part of a descriptor table (GDT or LDT) that provides the processor with the base and limit of a segment, as well as access control and status information. Each descriptor is 8 bytes long, so a descriptor table with an 8192 descriptor entry needs 8 * 8192 = 64KB of memory. It's the responsibility of the software program to create the descriptor table. Figure 2-18 illustrates the general descriptor format for all types of segment descriptors.

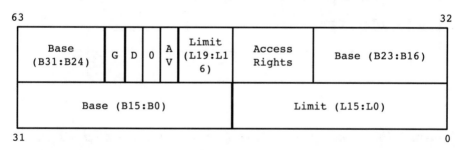

Figure 2-18. *Segment descriptors*

The two important pieces of information are that the inside descriptor is base (B31: B0) and indicates the starting location of the memory segment and limit (L19:L0) contains the last offset address (between 1 and 1MB) inside the segment. The granularity (G) bit, if set, means the limit value is multiplied by 4KB (the segment size is mapped anywhere between 4KB to 4GB).

For example, in protected mode, if the segment selector is 0x0010 = 0000 0000 0001 **0**000 that selects the descriptor 2 in the descriptor table. Figure 2-19 describes how it is mapped to system memory.

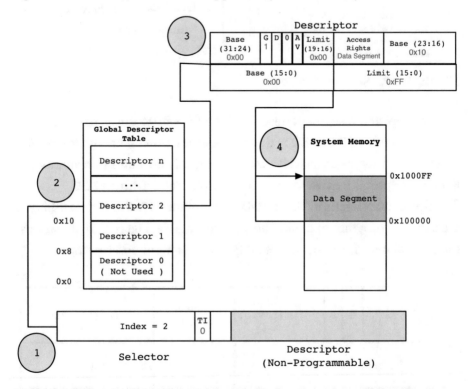

Figure 2-19. *Memory map using segment selection and descriptor*

Facts   In protected mode, control register CR4 bit 4 needs to be enabled and 4M paging is needed to access the area between 4GB and 64GB.

To control memory management, the processor provides four memory-management registers as GDTR, LDTR, IDTR, and TR.

Global Descriptor Table Register (GDTR)

The GDTR register contains the base address (32-bit or 64-bit based on the mode) and its limit (16-bit table limit for the GDT). System firmware must have one GDT defined, which is used for the entire firmware and OS programs. The first descriptor in the GDT is a "null descriptor" and is not used by the processor. The LGDT and SGDT instructions are used to load and store the GDTR register by system firmware on every power up. Refer to Figure 2-20 for details.

Local Descriptor Table Register (LDTR)

The LDTR register contains a 16-bit segment selector, base address (32-bit or 64-bit based on the mode), limit (16-bit table limit for the LDT), and descriptor attributes for the LDT. A system may have one or more LDTs. A segment descriptor of a LDT segment is present inside the global descriptor table and can be located as a LDT type. The LLDT and SLDT instructions are used to load and store the segment selector part of the LDTR register. Refer to Figure 2-20 for details.

Interrupt Descriptor Table Register (IDTR)

The IDTR register holds the base address (32-bit or 64-bit based on the mode) and its limit (16-bit table limit for the IDT). The interrupt descriptor table (IDT) represents each interrupt and exceptions with a gate descriptor for managing the interrupt or exception while a task or procedure is getting serviced. The IDT is an 8-byte descriptor array like the GDT or LDT, but unlike the GDT, the first entry of the IDT may contain a valid descriptor. There are only 256 interrupt or exception vectors, so the IDT holds only 256 descriptors (empty descriptor set to 0). The LIDT and SIDT instructions are used to load and store the contents of the IDTR register. Refer to Figure 2-20 for details.

Task Register (TR)

The TR register contains a 16-bit segment selector, base address (32-bit or 64-bit based on the mode), limit (16-bit table limit), and descriptor attributes for the TSS (task state segment). The segment selector as part of TR points to a TSS descriptor in the GDT. The information is copied from the TSS descriptor in the GDT for the current task using the base address and segment limit. The LTR and STR instructions load and read the task register. Refer to Figure 2-20 for details.

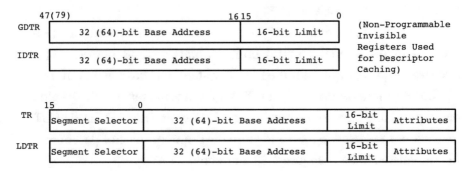

Figure 2-20. *Memory management registers*

System Management Mode (SMM)

SMM is a processor architecture feature introduced with 80386 microarchitecture. This mode provides the operating system or other high-level software a transparent mechanism for implementing power management and other OEM-specific features. Processors are allowed to enter into the SMM mode through an activation of system management interrupt (SMI). In SMM, the processor switches to a separate address space known as SMRAM (system management RAM) to save the context of the current executing program.

Virtual 8086 Mode

This mode is a sub operating mode of protected mode. In this mode, processors are allowed to execute 8086 software in a protected and multi-tasking environment.

Interrupt

An interrupt is defined as an unexpected flow of control that affects the current flow of execution and transfers the control to somewhere else that depends upon the ISR. The routine that gets called up when the interrupt is triggered is called the interrupt service routine (ISR). An interrupt is an event that triggers the processor to jump from its current program counter to a specific point in the code. This involves the processor saving its state of execution and beginning execution of an interrupt handler. Hence, an interrupt can also be referred to as a new program control that executes and transfers control to the main program after complete execution of the interrupt.

Interrupts are basically one of the foundational principles of computer architecture. There are two types:

- **Software interrupts**: Used as instructions as per ISA, which causes a context switch to an interrupt handler. Example: Used in BIOS routines.

- **Hardware interrupts**: Implement a way to avoid a processor's idle cycles in a polling loop, waiting for I/O devices to generate an event.

Earlier sections provided details about IVT and its calculation mechanism based on the processor operating mode (real mode and protected mode). Mainly interrupts can be classified into two categories :

- **NMI (non-maskable interrupt)**: Its priority is first and it can't be delayed.

- **INTR (interrupt request)**: A maskable interrupt that can be delayed. The processor provides a control mechanism to manage the interrupt servicing by the processor core. The interrupt enable (IF) flag in the EFLAGS register only affects the hardware interrupts. Clearing the IF flag will not prevent the execution of a trap or exception. The *clear interrupt enable flag instruction (cli)* instruction clears the IF flag and maskable hardware interrupts will not be handled. To reenable the interrupts within a hardware interrupt service routine, the *set interrupt enable flag instruction (sti)* instruction explicitly turns them back on. *int* is an assembly language instruction for x86 processors for generating a software interrupt. It takes the interrupt vector number formatted as a byte value as it supports a maximum of 256 interrupt and exception vectors.

In general, interrupt events get generated by timer chips, keyboards, serial ports, parallel ports, disk drives, the CMOS real-time clock, mice, sound cards, and other peripheral devices to the processor through either programmable interrupt controller (PIC) or 8259, local advanced programmable interrupt controller (LAPIC), input/output advanced programmable interrupt controller (I/OAPIC), or message signaled interrupt (MSI).

Programmable Interrupt Controller

The legacy interrupt controller has two cascaded 8259s with 15 available IRQs (interrupt request) (IRQ2 is not available to connect the 8259s), an interrupt request output line named INTR, an interrupt acknowledgement line named INTA, and data lines for communicating the vector number. The legacy interrupt control delivers the interrupt request and interrupt vector to the CPU using its output INTR PIN, which is connected to CPU INTR signal. Figure 2-21 describes an interrupt handling mechanism using PIC.

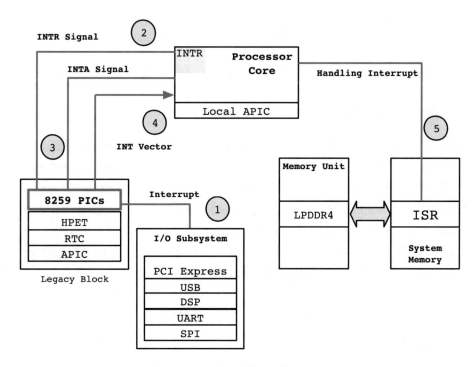

Figure 2-21. *Legacy interrupt handling flow*

Steps to handle an interrupt request from the I/O subsystem using the PIC

---

1. The I/O device has triggered an IRQ to the CPU. The IRQ signal is received by the PIC. Example: A user pressing a key triggers an IRQ.

2. The PIC sends the interrupt request to the CPU using its INTR PIN.

3. Upon receiving the interrupt request, the CPU sends an interrupt acknowledgement (INTA) to the PIC.

4. The PIC further sends the 8-bit interrupt vector to the CPU. Example: INT 9 is a keyboard interrupt.

5. The CPU preserves its current state into the stack and fetches the corresponding ISR from the interrupt vector table.

Advanced Programmable Interrupt Controller

The APIC is a more advanced interrupt controller than the legacy PIC. The APIC is used for IRQ routing and sending interrupts between processors in the multiprocessor systems. At the system level, APIC splits into two parts: one residing in the CPU (called the local APIC or LAPIC) and the other residing in the I/O subsystems (called the IOxAPIC). The LAPIC and IOxAPIC communicate over system buses. This reduces the interrupt latency over the standard interrupt controller.

Local Advanced Programmable Interrupt Controller

There is one LAPIC in each processor in the system. The LAPIC is capable of receiving the interrupt from processor interrupt pins as internal sources and from an external I/O APIC. Each LAPIC has a set of APIC registers in it that control the delivery of the interrupts to the processor core. The local APIC performs two primary functions for the processor:

- Provides local pending of interrupts, nesting and masking of interrupts, and handles all interactions with its local processor.

- Provides inter-processor interrupts and a timer to its local processor.

Figure 2-22 describes the interrupt handling mechanism using LAPIC.

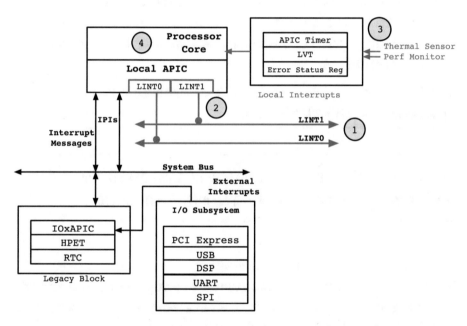

Figure 2-22. *Internal interrupt handling flow using the LAPIC*

Steps to handle interrupt request from internal sources using the LAPIC

---

1. The processor's internal interrupt pins like LINT0/1, the APIC timer, the performance-monitor counters, and the thermal sensors can trigger local interrupts. Example: The LINT1 pin is going to be used as an NMI interrupt.

2. Upon receiving a signal from a local interrupt source, the LAPIC receives it.

3. The LAPIC creates the local vector table (LVT), a group of 32-bit APIC registers that allow the software to specify the manner in which the local interrupts are delivered to the processor core. Example: To implement a LVT LINT1 register for an interrupt at LINT1 pin.

4. The LAPIC delivers the interrupt to the processor core using an interrupt delivery protocol (e.g., the INTR/INTA/EOI protocol).

Facts   The LAPIC can also receive an IRQ from the I/O APIC and route it to the processor core using an interrupt message.

I/O Advanced Programmable Interrupt Controller

The IOxAPIC is used to receive the external interrupt from the associated I/O devices and redirect them to the CPU in a more advanced manner than the legacy PIC. In systems with multiple I/O subsystems, each subsystem can have its own set of interrupts. Each interrupt pin is individually programmable as either edge or level triggered. The interrupt vector and interrupt steering information can be specified per interrupt. The IOAPIC unit consists of a set of interrupt input signals, a 24-entry by 64-bit interrupt redirection table, programmable registers, and a message unit for sending and receiving interrupt messages over the system bus. Figure 2-23 describes the interrupt handling mechanism using the IOxAPIC.

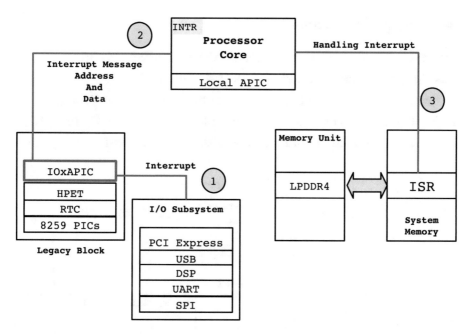

Figure 2-23.   *IOxAPIC interrupt handling flow*

Steps to handle interrupt request from internal sources using the IOxAPIC

---

1. The I/O device triggers an interrupt to the IOxAPIC.

2. The IOxAPIC delivers the interrupt to the processor in the form of a 32-bit memory write cycle with a known format for address and data as defined in the interrupt message address and interrupt message data.

3. After this 32-bit memory write cycle is received by the processor, the CPU preserves its current state into the stack and fetches a corresponding ISR from the interrupt vector table.

Message Signaled Interrupt

The MSI is an alternative to traditional interrupts which rely on dedicated pins to trigger an interrupt. PCIe devices that use MSIs trigger an interrupt by writing a value to a particular memory address. Typically, the bootloader does not use the MSI for interrupt handling. Figure 2-24 describes the interrupt handling mechanism using the MSI.

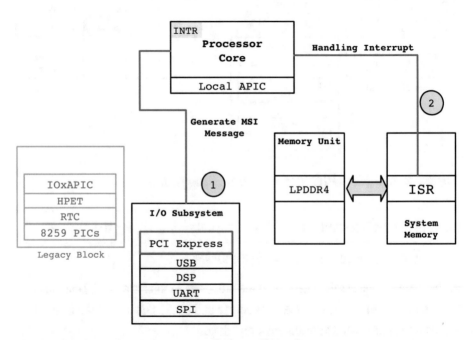

Figure 2-24. *PCIe-MSI interrupt handling flow*

Steps to handle interrupt request from internal sources using the MSI

---

1. PCIe devices generate MSI messages and write to the CPU.

2. The CPU preserves its current state into the stack and fetches the corresponding ISR from the interrupt vector table.

Timers

In computer architecture, a timer is a device that is used for measuring and signaling the end of time intervals. It's also used for recording or indicating the time. In software programming, a timer can be used to control the sequence of an event or process. Computer systems usually have at least one timer. Typically, the computer architecture provides two types of hardware devices to help with time keeping: a real-time clock and a system timer.

Real-Time Clock

On the computer architecture, the real-time clock (RTC) provides a nonvolatile device (CMOS) for storing the system time. The RTC continues to keep track of time even when the system is off using a small battery typically included on the system board. The RTC also has a timer that gets used by system firmware.

System Timer

In computer programming, a system timer is an essential component. The main idea behind a system timer in an architecture-agnostic manner is to be able to trigger interrupts at a periodic rate. A system timer is often configurable and used as a digital counter capable of incrementing or decrementing and operating at fixed frequency. When the counter reaches zero, it triggers an interrupt. On x86, the primary system timer is 8254, a programmable interval timer (PIT).

The 8254 is a general purpose, multi-timing element that can be treated as an array of I/O ports (0x40-0x43) in the system software. It's also used for accurate delay generation under software control.

The newer hardware also includes a HPET (high precision event timer), which is an evolution of the PIT concept and is likely to be used by operating systems, not by the bootloader. Other x86 time sources are the local APIC timer and the processor's time stamp counter (TSC).

Internals of ARM Processors

An ARM processor is one of the family members of a reduced instruction set computer (RISC) architecture-based CPU developed by Advanced RISC Machines (ARM). The first ARM design with a 32-bit processor was the ARMv3 (the ARMv1 used a 32-bit internal structure but the address space was limited to 26-bit, $2^{26} = 64$ MB of main memory).

Instruction Sets

Due to the RISC-architecture design the ARM processor follows a simple ISA where the majority of instructions are executed in a single cycle so that they can operate at higher speed. All instructions are 32 bits long. The ARM instruction sets follow a load-store architecture:

- Data processing instructions only act on registers.

- All data processing instructions have the same instruction format.

- Combined ALU and shifter for high-speed bit manipulation

- First operand always register - Rn

- Second operand is sent to the ALU via a barrel shifter. The ARM doesn't have support for shift instructions hence it uses barrel shifter, a mechanism to perform shift operations as part of other instructions.
  For example, a left shift uses lsl #4 and multiplies by power of two.

- Limited direct memory access instruction with auto-indexing addressing modes

In order to improve the speed of the instruction flow to the processor, the ARM uses a pipeline. It allows several operations to execute concurrently using a three-stage pipeline:

- **Fetch**: Instructions fetched from memory. The program counter (PC) points here.

- **Decode**: Decoding of registers used in instructions.

- **Execute**: Registers are read from the register bank, perform ALU and shift operations, and finally write back to the register bank.

The ARM processor also has a 16-bit instruction set called Thumb (in ARMv8-M baseline, the Thumb instruction set is replaced with a subset of the Thumb-2 32-bit instruction set).

Processor Modes

The ARM supports different processor modes, depending upon the architecture version. Typically, it has six operating modes.

Mode number	Processor mode	Description
0x10	User (usr)	Unprivileged mode, which allows it to run most application programs
0x11	FIQ (fiq)	Fast interrupt request: The processor is entered when a high priority (fast) interrupt is raised.
0x12	IRQ (irq)	Interrupt request: This mode is used for general-purpose interrupt handling. The processor enters when a low priority (normal) interrupt is raised.

(continued)

Mode number	Processor mode	Description
0x13	Supervisor (svc)	The processor enters on reset and when a software interrupt instruction is executed.
0x17	Abort (abt)	This mode is used to handle memory access violations.
0x1B	Undefined (und)	The processor enters into this mode when an undefined instruction is executed.

Apart from these, there is an additional mode since ARMv4 has System (sys), a privileged user mode.

Exception Levels

The processor supports different exception levels to ensure the firmware and/ or the software running on the application processor doesn't have the same level of access rights to be compliant with product security requirements. For example, since the application processor powers on until reaching to the user interface, it runs different types for firmware, middleware, software, and finally applications, where each entity should be configured with its privilege to access system resources. At the high level, this is the purpose of defining the exception level so that an entity running at non-trusted privilege level doesn't have the capability to configure the system.

On the ARM architecture, the exception levels are referred to as ELx, with x as a number between 0 and 3. The lowest level of privilege is referred to as EL0 (or unprivileged level of execution) and EL3 is considered as the highest privileged execution level. In a typical scenario, the application code runs at EL0, a rich operating system runs at EL1, EL2 is used by a hypervisor, and EL3 is reserved for the low-level firmware execution. Refer to the "Trusted Firmware" section in Chapter 3 for a more detailed overview of ARM exception levels and communication between nonsecure and secure worlds.

Registers

ARM has a total of 37 32-bit registers, which includes 30 general purpose registers between r0-r15 and few others that are governed by the processor mode, one dedicated program counter, one current program status register (cpsr), and five saved program status registers (spsr) for privileged mode. Figure 2-25 shows the ARM register organization.

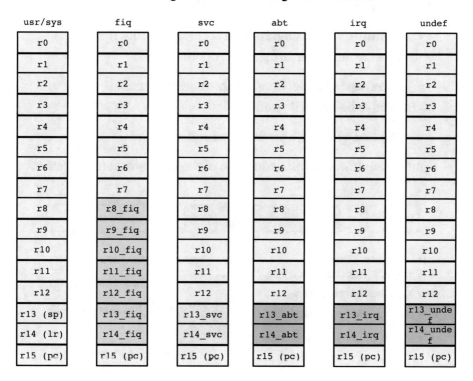

General Register and Program Counter

usr/sys	fiq	svc	abt	irq	undef
r0	r0	r0	r0	r0	r0
r1	r1	r1	r1	r1	r1
r2	r2	r2	r2	r2	r2
r3	r3	r3	r3	r3	r3
r4	r4	r4	r4	r4	r4
r5	r5	r5	r5	r5	r5
r6	r6	r6	r6	r6	r6
r7	r7	r7	r7	r7	r7
r8	r8_fiq	r8	r8	r8	r8
r9	r9_fiq	r9	r9	r9	r9
r10	r10_fiq	r10	r10	r10	r10
r11	r11_fiq	r11	r11	r11	r11
r12	r12_fiq	r12	r12	r12	r12
r13 (sp)	r13_fiq	r13_svc	r13_abt	r13_irq	r13_undef
r14 (lr)	r14_fiq	r14_svc	r14_abt	r14_irq	r14_undef
r15 (pc)	r15 (pc)	r15 (pc)	r15 (pc)	r15 (pc)	r15 (pc)

Program Status Registers

cpsr	cpsr	cpsr	cpsr	cpsr	cpsr
	spsr_fiq	spsr_svc	spsr_abt	spsr_irq	spsr_undef

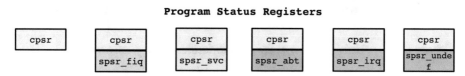

Figure 2-25. *ARM register organization based on processor mode*

Each mode can access a particular set of registers (r0-r12) and r15, r13-r15 are special registers, where r13 is the stack pointer, r14 is the link register, and r15 is the program counter. Special instructions are required to access CPSR and SPSR program status registers.

Program Status Registers

The processor has one CPSR and five SPSRs for exception handlers to use. The program status registers contain the following:

- **Condition code flag**: Holds information about the most recently performed ALU operation

- **Interrupt disable**: Controls the interrupt enable/disable between irq and fiq

- **Mode**: Defines the processor mode

Figure 2-26 shows the bit definitions of the program status registers.

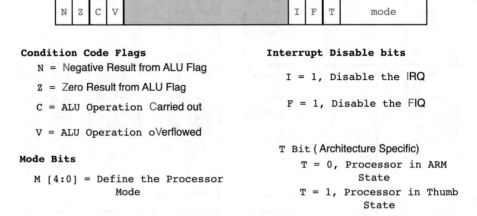

Figure 2-26. *ARM program status registers bit definitions*

During an exception in an ARM state, the contents of the CPSR are copied into the spsr_mode register. The appropriate exception mode is set in the CPSR register along with the processor state. It stores the return address into the link register and sets the program counter to the vector address. This transfers control to the exception handler. Upon return, the exception handler restores the CPSR from the spsr_mode register and restores the program counter with the return address (previously saved into the link register).

Program Counter Registers

The program counter is accessed as r15. It is incremented by the size of the instruction executed. In ARM states, all instructions are 32 bits in length. Software programs can explicitly load the PC directly using data processing instructions, such as `mov pc, r0`. While executing, the PC doesn't hold the address of the current executing instruction like other architectures. The address of the current instruction is typically held using PC-8 during ARM state.

Facts   ARM recommends using the BX instruction to jump to an address or to return from a function, rather than writing to the PC directly.

Processor Architecture

Figure 2-27 illustrates the processor core design, which is a combination of CPU registers and ALU units.

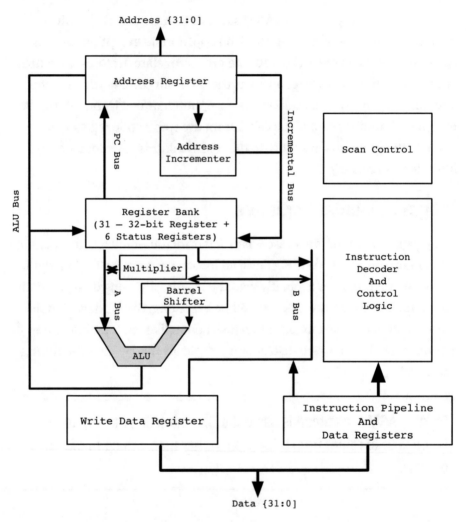

Figure 2-27. *Typical ARM core diagram*

ARM has a 32-bit address bus A[31:0] and 32-bit bidirectional data bus as D[31:0] along with control bus signals like read/write enable, reset, and others. Communication between processors and other I/O devices happens at address and data lines. The CPU core consists of a processor core and other function blocks like cache and memory management blocks. Figure 2-28 shows the ARM CPU core hardware block diagram.

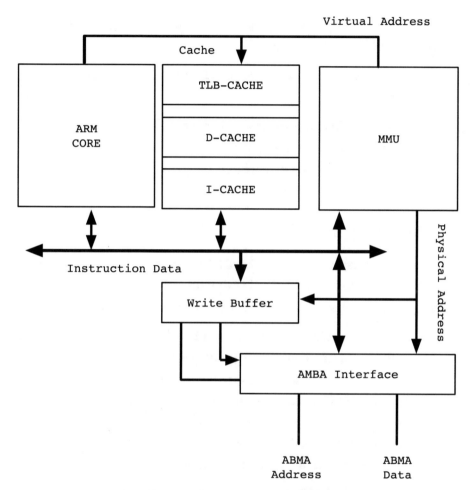

Figure 2-28. *ARM CPU core hardware block diagram*

Caches

A cache is a small, fast memory that holds the recently used memory values. It's part of the same chip as the processor and works based on the property of *locality*, which means that the program tends to execute the same instruction many times on the same data. Access to an item that is present in the cache is called a *hit* and unavailability of that item in the cache is known as a *miss*. An ARM processor can have one of the following two organizations for the cache:

- **A unified cache**: A single cache for both instructions and data

- **Separate instruction and data cache**: This is a modified Harvard architecture, which allows a dedicated instruction cache (ICache) and data cache (DCache) and a write buffer.

Memory Management Unit

The memory management unit or MMU is responsible for translating all CPU virtual addresses into physical addresses. Additionally, it controls the memory accesses. A MMU hardware unit has the following functions:

- **Translation look-aside buffer (TLB)**: The TLB contains a translated entry for the virtual address and the access control logic to determine access if permitted. If access is permitted, then MMU provides an output physical address corresponding to the virtual address; otherwise, MMU signals abort. The TLB-cache holds 64 translated entities for the virtual address.

- **Control logic**: This controls whether a program has no-access, read-only, or read-write access to the memory area. The level of access is also affected by the processor operating mode (mode[4:0]).

The MMU hardware block is connected to the ARM memory bus architecture (AMBA) interface, which provides a 32-bit address bus and data bus to connect peripheral devices. Refer to the "Bus Architecture" section for more details about the ARM memory bus architecture (AMBA).

System Memory Map

The processor core needs to interface with either internal or external memory units to make sure that higher-level system programs can run freely. The prime responsibility of the system firmware is to create the system memory map based on the total system memory minus the memory reserved for various devices to calculate the total available memory. The total available memory is what is being advertised for operating system and application usage. This section demonstrates how the memory space is partitioned and the use of the separate memory regions on the x86 processor supporting 39-bit addressing, meaning $2^{39} =$ 512GB of addressable memory space.

The entire system memory range is divided into four ranges:

- Legacy address range (between 0 - 1MB)

- Main memory address range (between 1MB - TOLUD)

- PCI memory address range (between TOLUD - 4GB)

- Main memory upper address range (between 4GB - TOUUD)

Legacy Address Range

The legacy address range is mapped at the base of the system memory. It is the first 1MB (1 * 1024 * 1024 bytes) of the memory. This area is divided into the following address regions:

- Memory range between 0 - 640KB

- Memory range between 640KB - 1MB

Conventional Memory Range

System memory below 640KB is known as conventional memory, also called base memory. It's the first 640KB (640 * 1024 bytes) of the memory. This memory region is segregated into the following parts:

Alignment type	Range	Size
Interrupt vector table	0x000 – 0x2FF	768 bytes
BIOS stack area	0x300 – 0x3FF	256 bytes
BIOS data area	0x400 – 0x4FF	256 bytes
Application memory area	0x500 – 0x9FFF	~638 kilobytes

Upper Memory Range

In legacy memory maps, the upper memory range refers to memory between 640KB and 1024KB (0xA0000 - 0xFFFFF). The upper memory region is divided into the following parts:

Alignment type	Range	Size
Legacy video area	0xA0000 – 0xBFFFF	128 kilobytes
VBIOS area	0xC0000 – 0xC7FFF	32 kilobytes
Expansion area	0xC8000 – 0xDFFFF	96 kilobytes
Extended system BIOS	0xE0000 – 0xEFFFF	64 kilobytes
BIOS/firmware	0xF0000 – 0xFFFFF	64 kilobytes

- **Legacy video area**: The legacy 128KB VGA memory range/frame buffer range is mapped between 0xA0000 to 0xBFFFF. This range can be further mapped into video memory when used in graphics mode between

0xA0000 to 0xAFFFF. Memory range 0xB0000 - 0xB7FFF is used to hold all text currently displayed on the screen when video is in monochrome text mode; in color text mode, memory range 0xB8000 - 0xBFFFF is used.

- **Programmable attribute map**: The compatibility memory range from 0xC0000 to 0xFFFFF is named the programmable attribute map (PAM) memory area. Each section has read enable and write enable attributes. CPU registers between PAM0 to PAM6 are used to map this configuration space.

- **VBIOS area**: A dedicated address space for legacy video option ROM, used to initialize the display and provide display-related legacy services using int 10h.

- Extended system BIOS area (0xE0000 - 0xEFFFF) and system BIOS area (0xF0000 - 0xFFFFF) are usually 128KB long and are used to address the ROM. In some cases, 0xE0000 address range can also be used for option ROM execution.

Facts   An option ROM is firmware usually residing on a plug-in card (may also be present on the system board). It's intended to isolate a hardware device by providing an abstract interface that implements device-specific functions. The optional ROM header holds the signature 0x55,0xAA, followed by length of the initialization code and a 4-byte option ROM initialization vector address.

Main Memory Address Range

The memory address range is extended from 1MB to the top of the lower usable DRAM (TOLUD) that is permitted to be accessible by the processor as per the TOLUD register. All memory access to this range by the processor routes to the DRAM range unless specified by other memory ranges (such as TSEG or video memory). Figure 2-29 shows the separation of the main memory address range.

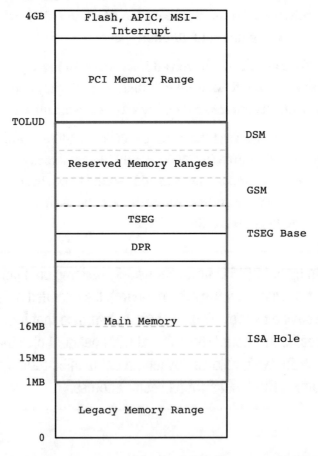

Figure 2-29. *Main memory address range (between 1MB to TOLUD)*

- **Main memory**: This memory range is available for system programs to use. It's also referred to as OS visible memory, without any additional memory access logic. This memory range is typically calculated between 1MB to TSEG - DPR.

  ISA hole: An optional memory range between 15MB to 16MB region, it's reserved using the host bridge device register le gacy access control (lac). All memory transactions targeting this region will route the request to the DMI if a hole is being created.

- **TSEG** (top of main memory segment): This region is used to specify the amount of memory space required while operating in system management mode (SMM). The start of this memory range is configured by the system firmware using the TSEG base register in the host bridge device. A software programming running in other modes (than SMM) won't have access to this range. Hence, this range would be treated as a memory hole for the OS.

- **DPR** (DMA protected range): This range only applies to DMA access and GMADR transactions. It serves the purpose of providing a memory range that is only accessible to processor streams. This range is configured using the DPR register in the host bridge device. The system will set up a memory range between 0 to (TSEG base - DPR size - 1) for DMA and (TSEG base - DPR size) as no DMA.

- **Reserved memory ranges**: This memory range is between (TSEG Base + TSEG limit) to TOLUD. It combines various other device-specific reserved ranges as the following:

  - **Data of stolen memory (DSM)**: This range is used to specify the base address of graphics data stolen DRAM memory. This range is only available if the internal graphics device is enabled. It acts as graphics memory when an internal graphics device is enabled. The BIOS determines the DSM base by subtracting the graphics data stolen memory size (the host bridge device register) from TOLUD.

  - **GTT stolen memory (GSM)**: This range contains the base address of stolen memory for the graphics translation table (GTT) entries. This range is only available if the internal graphics device is enabled. The BIOS determines the GSM base by subtracting the GTT graphics stolen memory size (the host bridge device register) from the DSM base.

PCI Memory Address Range

This address range, from the top of low usable DRAM (TOLUD) to 4GB is mapped to the DMI interface. There are a few exceptions for assigning the resource to host the bridge device (i.e., PXPEPBAR, MCHBAR, and DMIBAR and integrated graphics configurations like GMADR, GTTMMADR, etc.). Some of the MMIO BARs may be mapped to the upper PCI memory address range (above TOUUD). System firmware allocates MMIO and/or IO resources to PCI devices belonging to this address range.

There are subranges within the PCI memory address range, mapped between 4GB - 20MB for the APIC configuration space, the MSI interrupt space, and the BIOS address range. System firmware to ensure PCI device resources must not overlap with these ranges. Figure 2-30 describes the PCI memory address range.

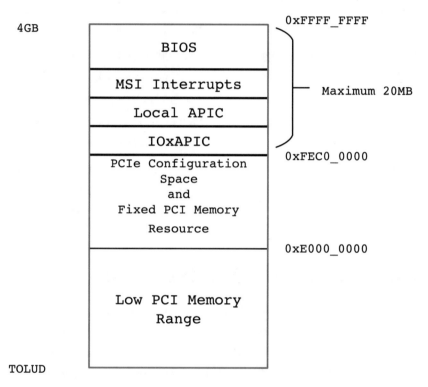

Figure 2-30. *PCI memory address range (between TOLUD - 4GB)*

MMIO address	Target	Description
TOLUD - 0xFEBFFFFF	PCI devices, PCIe root ports, and devices	The system BIOS performs the PCI enumeration to probe the PCI and PCIe devices on the bus and allocate resources either fixed or dynamic.
0xFEC00000 - 0xFEC7FFFF	IOxAPIC	IOxAPIC spaces are used to communicate with IOxAPIC interrupt controllers.

(*continued*)

MMIO address	Target	Description
0xFEC80000 - 0xFED00000	Local APIC	The local APIC registers are memory mapped to this address. Note: The mapped address is not fixed.
0xFEE00000 - 0xFEF00000	MSI interrupts	Any PCIe device or DMI device may issue a memory write to 0FEEx_xxxxh. This memory writes along with the data to the processor as an interrupt message transaction.
0xFF000000 - 0xFFFFFFFF	BIOS area	The processor begins execution from the BIOS area after reset. This region is positively decoded to DMI.

Main Memory Upper Address Range

Since the processor supports a 39-bit address, the main memory size can be greater than 4GB. The main memory upper address range is used to map system memory beyond 4GB to the top of upper usable DRAM (TOUUD). To configure that TOM, the TOUUD and REMAPBASE/REMAPLIMIT registers become relevant.

Top of Upper Usable DRAM

For physical memory greater than 4GB, the TOUUD register helps to identify the address range in between the 4GB boundary and the total amount of addressable DRAM. TOUUD reflects the top of the memory minus the higher PCI memory range (and any other reserved range) when remap is disable. If remap is enabled, then TOUUD points to the REMAPLIMIT.

Memory Remapping

The memory remapping window base and limit is programmable using the REMAPBASE and REMAPLIMIT registers. The bottom of the remap window is defined by the value in the REMAPBASE register. The top of the remap window is defined by the value in the REMAPLIMIT register. An address that falls within this window is remapped to the physical memory starting at the address defined by the TOLUD register.

The following is the algorithm used to calculate the DRAM address used for an incoming address above the top of physical memory made available using reclaiming:

```
IF (ADDRESS_IN[38:20]  >= REMAPBASE[35:20]) AND
(ADDRESS_IN[38:20] <= REMAPLIMIT[35:20]) THEN
ADDRESS_OUT[38:20] = (ADDRESS_IN[38:20] - REMAPBASE[35:20]) +
0000000b & TOLUD[31:20]
ADDRESS_OUT[19:0] = ADDRESS_IN[19:0]
```

Top of Memory

The TOM register reflects the total amount of populated physical memory. The BIOS determines the memory size reported to the OS using this register.

Upper PCI Memory Address Range

The range is between the top of memory and TOUUD. The value of the TOUUD register in the host bridge device is used to point to the start of this memory range. The PMLIMIT register in the host bridge device determines the end of this memory range. Access to this range is forwarded to either the high-speed PCIe controller attached to the northbridge or to the southbridge via the DMI. Figure 2-31 illustrates the different address ranges that are part of this region.

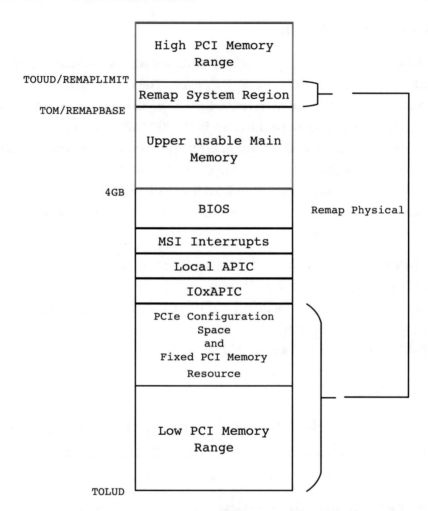

Figure 2-31. *Main memory upper address range*

Bus Architecture

The motherboard (also called the mainboard) is the vital printed circuit board in a computer system that allows communication between the CPU, memory unit, and peripherals. These motherboard components are connected to each other by a bus, an internal connection used to send signals (control and data) between the processor and other motherboard components. These buses are capable of transmitting data either using parallel or serial communication. Figure 2-32 shows a typical computer system with different buses.

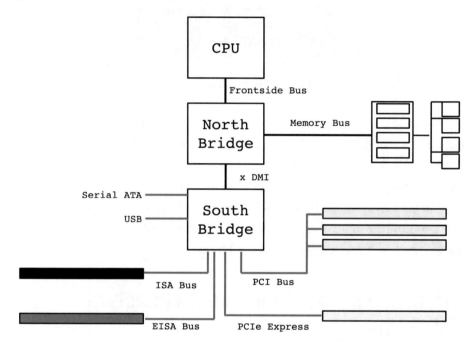

Figure 2-32. *Different peripheral buses on the motherboard*

This section discusses the peripheral buses used to connect the I/O devices. Based on the operating speed and the power efficiency, these buses are standardized. Among many other computer buses, this section focuses on the ISA, EISA, PCI and PCIe, USB, and SATA buses.

Industry Standard Architecture (ISA) Bus

The ISA bus is designed to connect peripheral cards to the motherboard. ISA was developed by a team led by IBM as part of the IBM PC project in 1981. It originated as an 8-bit bus and later extended to 16-bit standard in 1984. See Figure 2-33.

Figure 2-33. *ISA slots on a motherboard*

IBM used the original 8-bit version as a buffered interface to the external bus of the Intel 8088 processor used in the original IBM PC. With the introduction of Intel 80286 CPU, a 16-bit version of ISA was used on IBM AT computers. The operating bus speed was 4.77MHz (with an 8-bit bus) or 6/8MHz (with a 16-bit bus). The ISA bus on the motherboard was eventually replaced due to the performance bottleneck and was augmented with additional high-speed buses.

Extended Industry Standard Architecture (EISA) Bus

The EISA bus architecture was introduced in 1988. It extended the ISA bus from 16 bits to 32 bits. The EISA extended the advanced technology (AT) bus architecture that allowed more than one CPI to share the bus. It also extended the bus mastering support to access 4GB of memory. The EISA bus operated at a speed of 8.33MHz and transferred data at a rate of 32MBps. See Figure 2-34.

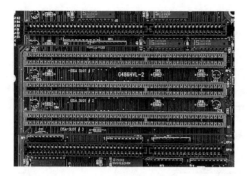

Figure 2-34. *EISA slots on a motherboard*

Due to underlying cost factors these buses were not widely used in client devices; rather, they were used in server space for bandwidth-intensive tasks like disk access and networking hence. The majority of EISA cards were either SCSI or network cards.

Peripheral Component Interconnect (PCI) Bus

The PCI bus architecture was introduced by Intel in 1992. It provides a connecting bridge between the CPU and other system devices such as memory, display controller, and I/O peripherals. The PCI bus supports both 32-bits (at a bus speed of 33MHz) and 64-bits (at a bus speed of 66MHz) and operations data rates of 133MBps (in 32-bit width) or 1GBps (in 64-bit width). It provides flexibility to support the older standard (ISA, EISA) expansion cards as well. Figure 2-35 illustrates a typical computer system where every device on the motherboard is a PCI device. Each device over a PCI bus has a unique identity using a bus and device number. PCI devices are either a single function or multifunction devices.

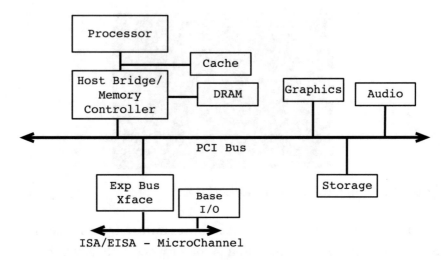

Figure 2-35. *PCI system block diagram*

A PCI device defines three different physical address spaces: configuration address space, memory address space, and I/O address space.

Memory address space: Typically, this space is used to access the device registers and function; it's the general-purpose address space. The PCI spec recommends that a device use memory space even if it is a peripheral. An agent can request between 16 bytes and 2GB of memory space. The PCI spec recommends that an agent use at least 4kB of memory space to reduce the width of the agent's address decoder.

I/O address space: This space is where basic I/O devices are mapped, such as serial ports and legacy keyboards. The PCI spec allows an agent to request 4 bytes to 2GB of I/O space.

Configuration address space: The configuration address space is 256 bytes in size and can be accessed with the read/write configuration cycle to configure the PCI hardware. Every PCI device must implement the configuration address space. The 256 bytes of configuration space is divided into two parts:

- Generic PCI header, the first 64 bytes (between 0x00 - 0x3F)

- Device-dependent region, the next 192 bytes (between 0x40 - 0xFF)

Figure 2-36 describes the PCI configuration space. The generic PCI header region fields are used to uniquely identify the devices over the PCI bus.

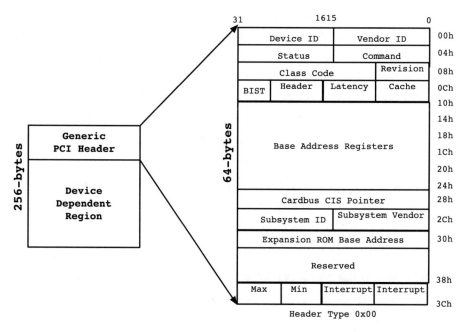

Figure 2-36. *PCI configuration space*

Vendor ID (read-only): This field identifies the device manufacturer. For example, 0x1002 is the vendor id for an AMD/ATI vendor.

Device ID (read-only): This vendor-specified field is used to identify the specific device over the PCI bus. For example, 0x6861 is the AMD graphics card device id.

Header type (read-only): This byte identifies the layout of the next part of the generic header (beginning at byte 0x10 in the configuration space) and also indicates if the device is a multi-function device. Value 0x00 between bits (6:0) specifies a generic device, value 0x01 specifies a PCI-PCI bridge, and value 0x02 specifies a CareBus bridge. If bit 7 is 1, then the device has multiple functions; otherwise, it's a single function device.

In PCI bus topology, a function is a representation of a logical device. If a package contains one function, it's referred to as a single-function PCI device, such as an integrated graphics device at bus 0, device 2, and function 0. A package that contains two or more functions is referred to as a multi-function PCI device, such as when several PCI devices like eSPI (function 0), audio (function 3), Smbus (function 4), and SPI (function 5) are attached to PCI bus 0, device 31. Each function has its own addressable configuration space. The system firmware needs to ensure that system resources (MMIO or I/O) assigned to one function do not conflict with the resource assigned to the other devices.

Class code (read-only): This field is used to specify the generic function of the device. In an integrated graphics device, the class code indicates it is a display controller device.

Facts   When reading a configuration space for a PCI device, if it returns 0xFFFF for the Vendor Id and Device Id, it's a non-existent device.

There are other configurable (read-write) fields inside the PCI configuration space that are used to access end-point devices and configure those devices to communicate with the CPU using an interrupt.

Base address registers (read-write): The PCI device needs to implement this register(s) to allow access to internal device registers of the function either using memory or I/O accesses. The lowest bit field offset is used to specify the type of access required. See Figure 2-37.

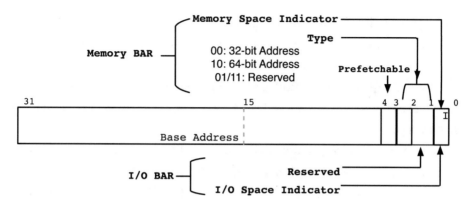

Figure 2-37. *Base address register (memory and I/O)*

The system firmware uses the BAR to determine the device-required address space and then assigns those ranges as part of the PCI enumeration process.

The system software needs to perform a decoding in order to determine the device-required address space from the base address register. Decoding of a register is disabled using the command register before determining the size of the base address register. System software saves the original value read from the register (BAR) and then writes all 1s to the 32-bit register (0xFFFFFFFF) and reads it back. The device-required size calculation can be done by first cleaning the encoding information bits (bit 0 for I/O and bits 3:0 for memory) and then inverting all 32-bits and incrementing by 1. The final result value is the memory or I/O device range size. In an I/O type base address register, ignore the upper 16 bits (bits 31:16). The original preserved value of the base address register is restored prior to enabling the decode range in the command register of the device. For a 64-bit BAR address, the decoding mechanism remains the same, except it needs an additional 32-bit register write and then it reads them back and combines the result into a 64-bit value.

Interrupt line (read-write): It is used to communicate interrupt line routing information. System firmware writes the routing information into this register as it initializes and configures the system. The value in this register indicates to which input of the system interrupt controller the device's interrupt pin is connected.

Interrupt pin (read-write): This field specifies which interrupt pin the device uses between INTA# - INTD#. 0x00 means the device doesn't use an interrupt pin.

There are other configuration fields in the PCI configuration space, but they are outside the scope of this chapter. The system software uses two DWORD I/O locations as CONFIG_ADDRESS (0xcf8) and CONFIG_DATA (0xcfc) to read and write the PCI configuration space. It needs bus, device, function, and register to access the configuration space as the following:

- **Bus:** An encoded value used to select buses between 1 - 256 in a system

- **Device:** This field is used to select one of 32 devices on a given bus.

- **Function:** To select one of eight possible functions (between function 0 - 7) on a multi-function device

- **Register:** An encoded value (a byte width) is used to select a DWORD in the configuration space of the target.

Facts   System software can use MMIO-based access as well to read/write the PCI configuration space using the following formula (for PCIe):

```
> PCIEXBAR + bus << 16 | device << 11 | function <<
8 | register
```

Enable the bit 31 configuration space prior to writing this DWORD address to CONFIG_WRITE and read/write from the CONFIG_READ I/O port.

Since the PCI bus provides the multi-bus topology, it needs to define a mechanism that allows the host bridge or PCI-PCI bridge to decide whether to decode that cycle or pass it to the next available interface. Figure 2-38 provides the different PCI configuration cycles.

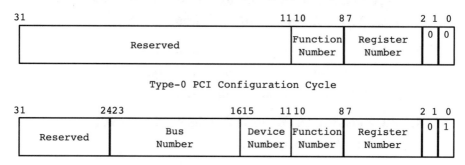

Figure 2-38. *Types of PCI configuration cycles*

Type 0 PCI configuration cycle: A Type 0 configuration cycle is used to select a device on the bus where the transaction is being run, so specifying the bus number is not required. The register number and function number are used to specify the target and the target is selected during the configuration access when its IDSEL signal is asserted.

Type 1 PCI configuration cycle: A Type 1 configuration cycle is used to pass a configuration request from the primary bus to the secondary bus segment unless the secondary bus interface is matched with the bus number given as part of the Type 1 configuration cycle. Refer to the sections below for details about the PCI configuration cycle translation between Type 1 to Type 0 in single host-bridge and multi-bridge scenarios.

1.   Bridges (both host and PCI-to-PCI) that need to generate a Type 0 configuration transaction use

the device number to select which IDSEL to assert.
The function number is provided on bits (10:8) and
the register number is provided on bits (7:2). The
software must ensure bits (1:0) are "00" for a Type 0
configuration transaction.

2. A Type 0 configuration transaction is not propagated
   beyond the local PCI bus and must be claimed by a
   local device or terminated with master-abort.

3. If the target of a configuration transaction resides
   on another bus (not the local bus), a Type 1
   configuration transaction must be used.

4. All targets except PCI-to-PCI bridges ignore Type 1
   configuration transactions.

5. PCI-to-PCI bridges decode the bus number field to
   determine if the destination bus of the configuration
   transaction resides behind the bridge.

   a. If the bus number is not for a bus behind the bridge, the
      transaction is ignored.

6. The bridge claims the transaction if the transaction
   is to a bus behind the bridge.

7. If the bus number is not to the secondary bus of the
   bridge, the transaction is simply passed through
   unchanged.

8. If the bus number matches the secondary bus
   number, the bridge converts the transaction into a
   Type 0 configuration transaction.

9. The bridge changes bits (1:0) to "00" and passes bits
   (10:2) through unchanged.

10. The device number is decoded to select one of 32 devices on the local bus.

11. The bridge asserts the correct IDSEL and initiates a Type 0 configuration transaction.

Peripheral Component Interconnect Express (PCIe) Bus

The PCIe bus replaces the legacy, shared, parallel buses with a high-speed, point-to-point, serial computer expansion bus standard. This specification was approved in 2002. The introduction of serial technology provides the performance, and this bus consumes less power than PCI. See Figure 2-39.

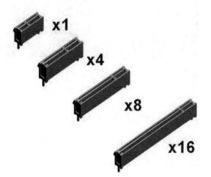

Figure 2-39. *Different PCIe slots*

The PCIe bus supports hot plug, meaning it supports runtime device insertion and removal without any additional power cycle.

The data transmitted over the PCIe bus is a serial transmission that works in full-duplex mode. The data transmission uses this bus through two pairs of wires called *lanes*. Each lane is capable of transferring data at a rate of 250MB/s in each direction and each slot is configurable from 1 to 32 lanes. For example, a PCIe device with 8 lanes (x8) can support a bandwidth up to 2GB/s.

Serial AT attachment (SATA) Bus

SATA is a computer bus that is used to connect mass storage devices such as hard disk drives, solid state devices (SSDs), and optical devices to the motherboard. The first SATA specification was released in 2001 as a replacement of the legacy parallel ATA (PATA) interface. A device attached to this bus can operate at a speed of 6GBps. See Figure 2-40.

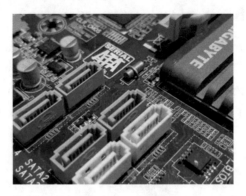

Figure 2-40. *Direct SATA slot*

The system firmware needs to configure the SATA operational mode from the available modes as IDE (integrated drive electronics), AHCI (advanced host controller interface), and RAID (redundant array of independent disks). The IDE mode supports compatibility and is mostly not recommended for modern hardware. Modern systems recommend a SATA controller to use in AHCI mode due to its better performance (with the native command queuing (NCQ) feature, which optimizes multiple read/write commands). In RAID mode, it copies data to multiple drives and ensures no data loss even during disk failure.

Universal Serial Bus (USB)

USB is an industry-wide standard for a plug-and-play interface that allows a device to communicate in both slave mode (where a USB device is attached with computer motherboard and used as a data transfer operation) or even in master mode (where the host system is used to debug the target system using the USB debug interface). Also, USB connectors are used for charging other portable devices. The first USB specification was introduced in 1996. Since then, the USB specification has evolved to the latest USB4 specification. Here are the high-level specification details:

USB specification	Device types	Details
USB 1.x	Type-A, Type-B	The port specification allows data transfer at the rate of 1.5MBps for low speed and 12MBps for full speed devices.
USB 2.0	Type-A/B, Mini-A/B, Micro-USB cables and connectors, On-The-Go (OTG)	This specification introduces a transfer rate of maximum 480MBps, thus the name of high speed USB. Additionally, this specification makes it possible for two USB devices to communicate with each other without any additional USB host. A USB cable charging specification is also introduced in this revision.
USB 3.x	Type-A/B, Type-C	The USB 3.x specification provides improves power management and transfer rate efficiency. USB 3.0 is known as SuperSpeed USB, and it supports up to 5.0GBps transfer rate. The USB 3.1 specification is known as SuperSpeed+ and it allows data transfer at a rate of 10GBps using Gen 2 revision. The USB 3.2 specification introduces transfer modes over a USB-C connector with a data rate of 10 and 20GBps.
USB 4	Type-C	This specification is based on the Thunderbolt 3 protocol specification that supports up to 40GBps throughput. It supports backward compatibility of USB specifications along with DisplayPort and the PCI Express specification.

During system boot, when a peripheral device is attached via USB, the system firmware needs to implement logic to detect the type of device and automatically binds with an appropriate device driver to support data transfer between the host system and device. The data transfer can occur in any of four types.

Control transfer*: This type of transfer is used to obtain the device information and configure the device or control the device. Any transfer that targets the default endpoint is called a control transfer.

Interrupt transfer: Devices that need a guaranteed response use this type of transfer. Peripheral devices such as keyboard and mice use this type of data transfer.

Isochronous transfer: This is for devices that operate at a fixed data rate but might cause data loss without any interruption in transfer. For example, audio and video data uses isochronous transfers.

Bulk transfer: Use this transfer mode for large amounts of data, such as transferring files to a USB mass drive or from a printer or a scanner. Except for low-speed endpoint USB devices, all other endpoint devices support bulk transfer.

ARM Advanced Microcontroller Bus Architecture (AMBA)

The AMBA defines a multilevel busing system with a high-speed system bus and lower-level peripheral bus. These two buses are linked via a bridge that serves as the master to the peripheral bus-attached slave devices.

AMBA High-Speed Bus (AHB)

The AHB is used to connect high-speed peripherals and memory devices. The AHB provides wider data bus configuration like 64/128/256/512/1024 bits. This bus provides separate read (HRDATA) and write (HWDATA) buses.

AMBA Peripheral Bus (APB)

The APB is used to support low-speed peripherals like UARTs, I2C, and SPI. The APB consists of a single bus master called the APB bridge, which acts as a slave on the AHB. The bridge divides the operating clock and makes it able to be used for lower-speed devices. All devices on the APB are slaves to the master. This bus uses a single clock, pclk.

Figure 2-41 shows the AMBA buses including AHB and APB.

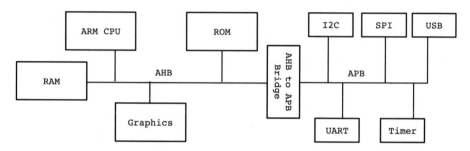

Figure 2-41. *ARM buses including AHB and APB*

Platform Runtime Power Management

The earlier sections provided information that can be used while performing the initialization of the motherboard components as part of the system firmware execution, starting with the processor initialization, then enabling the memory unit, and finally configuring the peripherals. The system firmware is not only responsible for perform the motherboard-associated device initialization and handing over to the OS, but it also needs to ensure runtime device configuration and power management. The Advanced Configuration and Power Interface (ACPI) specification provides the interface for enabling OS-directed motherboard device configuration and power management (typically, known as OSPM) for all platform devices and even entire systems. The ACPI specification evolved from its predecessor, Advanced Power Management (APM), which was a BIOS-based system power management implementation. The ACPI interface and OSPM are intended to apply to all modern computing systems with a concept of energy conservation by keeping the unused devices into lower-power states and putting the entire system in a low-power state when all device prerequisites are met. ACPI is neither a software specification nor a hardware specification, but still it touches both the platform hardware and software while handling the configuration and power management. This section provides a high-level overview of the ACPI as an interface specification comprising both hardware and software elements. Figure 2-42 illustrates the platform hardware and software components that interface with the ACPI.

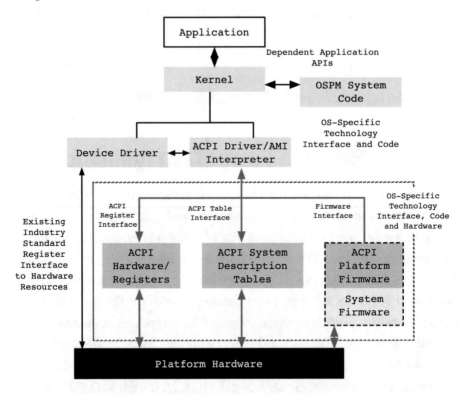

Figure 2-42. *ACPI system overview with runtime components*

There are three main components of the ACPI:

- ACPI hardware/registers

- ACPI system description tables

- ACPI platform firmware

ACPI Hardware/Registers

ACPI hardware/register components provide an interface that allows an ACPI-compliant OS to access the ACPI-compliant hardware platform. In this context, hardware is treated as a programming model that allows read/write into dedicated chipset registers (memory or I/O mapped), program sleep, or wake capabilities. ACPI classifies the hardware into two categories: fixed and generic. Fixed hardware/registers need to follow the ACPI specification while generic categories have flexibility in their implementation.

Fixed Hardware/Register

ACPI defines a register-based interface for fixed hardware, for example power management control and status register, timer register, and general-purpose event registers to reduce operational latency. It allows the OSPM to communicate with these registers directly without being dependent on specific device drivers. This helps the OSPM to handle the wake process without loading the entire OS. This table lists the fixed hardware register blocks residing inside the ACPI system descriptor tables (the FADT has specific pointers to the different fixed hardware register blocks used by OSPM).

Registers	Register blocks	Register grouping
PM1a_STS	PM1a_EVT_BLK	PM1 Event Registers
PM1a_EN		
PM1b_STS	PM1b_EVT_BLK	
PM1b_EN		
PM1a_CNT	PM1a_CNT_BLK	PM1 control registers
PM1b_CNT	PM1b_CNT_BLK	
PM2_CNT	PM2_CNT_LEN	PM2 control register
PM_TMR	PM_TMR_BLK	PM timer register
P_CNT	P_BLK	Processor control registers
P_LVL2		
P_LVL3		
GPE0_STS	GPE0_BLK	General purpose event registers
GPE0_EN		
GPE1_STS	GPE1_BLK	
GPE1_EN		

Each register block has one status and one control/enable register. Each bit in these registers defines an event. Typically, system firmware needs to configure the control/enable status and the status register is hardware signaled. An event will trigger only when the equivalent control and status bits are enabled. For example, the PM1Enable register bit 8 represents the enablement of the power button, so when the user presses the power button, the PM1Status register bit 8 will set to 1 and will eventually trigger the power button event.

Generic Hardware/Register

The generic hardware model allows the registers to reside in one of the following five address spaces. These registers can be accessed/ programmed using the ASL control method.

- System IO

- System memory

- PCI address space

- SMBUS

- EC

A device's generic hardware programming model is described through an associated object in the ACPI namespace. Here is an example of accessing the legacy IO port 80 as part of the ACPI control methods (encoded in AML):

```
OperationRegion (DEB0, SystemIO, 0x80, 1) // Port 80
Field (DEB0, ByteAcc,NoLock,Preserve)
        { DBG8, 8,}                        // 8-bit register space
```

ACPI System Description Tables

ACPI tables describe the interface to the hardware, some constraints to the hardware, specifics for the fixed blocks of registers, and the address of the register block. Many ACPI tables contain the definition blocks implemented using a pseudo-code type of language, the interpretation

of which is performed by the OS. The pseudo-code language is known
as ACPI Machine Language (AML), generated from the ACPI Source
Language (ASL) part of the system firmware.

An ACPI table is initiated with a root system description pointer
(RSDP). During OS initialization, the OSPM must have an RSDP pointer
structure from the platform. The system firmware should look for a
RSDP pointer entry in the system memory. This approach is bootloader
implementation specific.

Facts   With coreboot as the bootloader, the OSPM finds the RSDP
structure between memory space 0xE0000-0xFFFFF with the "RSD
PTR " signature. On the UEFI-enabled system, the OSPM locates the
RSDP structure by locating the EFI Configuration Table within the EFI
System Table. The EFI Configuration Table consists of the ACPI x.x
specification GUID.

These ACPI tables must have ACPI definition blocks that include the
Differentiated System Description Table (DSDT) and the Secondary System
Description Table (SSDT) describing motherboard devices in a hierarchical
format known as the ACPI namespace. Each ACPI namespace has control
methods used by the OS while enumerating the device or by OSPM for
configuration and power management. The most common ACPI tables are

- Root System Description Table (RSDT)

- Extended System Description Table (XSDT)

- Fixed ACPI Description Table (FADT)

- Firmware ACPI Control Structure (FACS)

- Differentiated System Description Table (DSDT)

- Secondary System Description Table (SSDT)

ACPI Platform Firmware

Portions of the firmware that are compatible with the ACPI specifications are known as ACPI platform firmware or ACPI BIOS. The ACPI BIOS can be divided into two parts:

Pre-OS boot: Cook all ACPI tables, set up ACPI HW registers, and initialize global non-volatile ACPI variables. Consider to be C coding. Pre-Boot ACPI BIOS are general ACPI tables like FADT, CSRT, FPDT, and MADT.

Post-OS boot: Prepare and populate the runtime code for OS drivers and services to communicate with hardware. Establish an interface between the OS and underlying hardware. Implemented using the ACPI Source Language "ASL" coding (compiled version known as AML and interpreted by the OSPM during boot). Post-boot ACPI BIOS is part of DSDT and SSDT tables.

DSDT provides resources for the OS to enumerate platform devices and also implement interfaces for sleep, wake, and some restart operations. Let's take an example of how the ACPI platform firmware handles sleep state transition (between S0 to Sx, where x=3, as S3 or 5, as S5):

ACPI BIOS implementation of S0->Sx transition

The OSPM decides to place the system into a sleep state. Program SLP_TYPx and SLP_EN.

The OSPM invokes the _TTS control methods to indicate the possible sleep state that the system would like to transit to (1 - S1/ 2 - S2/ 3 - S3/ 4 - S4). (Optional)

The OSPM analyzes all devices capable of waking up the system and from which sleep state. The _PRW named object under each device is examined, as well as the power resource object it points to.

(continued)

ACPI BIOS implementation of S0->Sx transition

The OSPM places all devices into their respected Dx states using native drivers. If the device is not wake-capable, then it is put into the D3 state.

The OSPM executes the _PTS control method, passing an argument that indicates the targeted sleep state.

The OSPM saves any processor contexts other than the local processor into memory.

The OSPM writes the OS waking vectors into the FACS tables in memory.

The OSPM executes the _GTS control method, passing an argument that indicates sleep state entered. (Optional)

The OSPM clears the WAK_STS register in the PM1a_STS/PM1b_STS FADT Table register.

The OSPM saves the local processor context into memory.

The OSPM sets GPE enabled-registers to ensure that all appropriate wake capabilities are properly programmed.

The OSPM writes SLP_TYPb with the SLP_EN bit into the PM1b_CNT register.

The OSPM loops on the WAK_STS register in PM1a_STS/PM1b_STS FADT table on a periodic basis.

The system enters into the low-power state as specified.

ACPI Source Language Overview

The ACPI source language is intended to provide information and mechanisms in form of definition blocks with operating system to perform operations like

- Resource allocation for devices
- Power management control

- Generic event description and control

- Device configuration

- I/O, PCI and memory region access

The system firmware needs to write the ASL and the compiler compiles it to AML and then the generated AML embeds into the system firmware-created ACPI system description tables. The OS bootstrap reads those description tables and interprets and executes the control methods or interprets and stores them for later execution.

System Power States

ACPI enforces the OSPM-directed device and system power transitions, employing user preferences and device usage knowledge by the applications, prior putting the devices in or out of low-power states. Combining the device and processor operating states, OSPM decides to put the entire system into a low-power state. The OS uses the ACPI control methods to support these hardware power state transitions. These power states describe the state of a system at a point in time. There are four-types:

- Define global system states between G0 - G3

- Define device power states between D0 - D3

- Define CPU power state between C0 - Cn (n = least CPU state, depending on the processor type)

- Define sleep states between S0 - S5

Facts   Modern Standby is the newest active idle state in the client device segment and it provides an instant on/off user experience, similar to smartphones.

Figure 2-43 shows the relationship between different platform component power states and their impacts over the entire system power states.

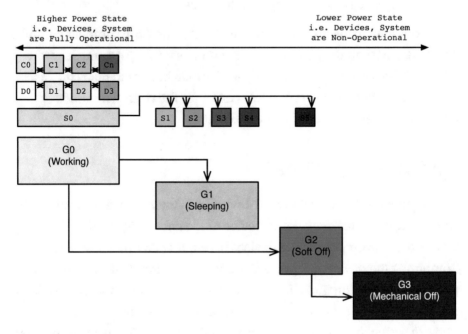

Figure 2-43. *System power states*

Summary

This chapter started with computer architecture and provided an overview of the basic computer design along with its subcategories as in instruction set architecture (ISA), microarchitecture, and system architecture. While discussing the ISA in detail, it also provided the different types of instruction set architectures (i.e., CISC and RISC) and CPU internals based on those two architectures and applications in x86 and ARM CPUs, which includes registers, processor modes, interrupts, and processor architecture. There were also detailed sections about the memory unit and various peripherals communicating with the CPU using the different bus architectures and their comparative benefits. Additionally, it provided the required knowledge that a system firmware should have while transferring control to high-level system software like the OS, as in a system memory map based on the motherboard components, providing a runtime interface to manage the device configuration, and power management at runtime.

The layout for this chapter was carefully designed to ensure that you really do understand these basic hardware concepts well because several components introduced here are going to be used repetitively in the rest of the chapters in this book.

This chapter provided in-depth knowledge about the system hardware and its internal components that you should possess prior to starting the journey of system firmware. You may have started working on system firmware or low-level device drivers for computing systems without having much detailed knowledge about the domain, and it might take several months or years of work exposure to understand the underlying hardware and its native interfaces. Hence, this chapter has written with immense care based on the real-work experiences of the authors to make sure that, while reading this chapter, you will be able to understand it well, connect several topics being discussed as part of this chapter, and use this knowledge in next chapters, which cover the operation relationship between system hardware and firmware.

CHAPTER 3

Understanding the BIOS and Minimalistic Design

"Simplicity is the ultimate sophistication."

—Leonardo da Vinci

In the modern computing era, we are surrounded by many consumer electronics devices. These devices have extended their boundary from being computing "only" devices to "companion" devices, namely devices that are used for daily needs including smart home aids, smart appliances, and smart gadgets. From an end user's standpoint, the device is operational only after it is booted to its GUI and/or connected with the network to operate in faceless mode (example: soft robotic devices) using a remote or applications. The entire device bring-up process, starting with the user pressing the device's power button to the device getting booted to the UI, remains unnoticed by its user. This process is responsible for bringing the device to life after executing a series of complex CPU initialization sequences, performing the physical memory (also known as RAM) initialization to let applications use the main memory for improved

© Subrata Banik and Vincent Zimmer 2022
S. Banik and V. Zimmer, *System Firmware*,
https://doi.org/10.1007/978-1-4842-7939-7_3

efficiency, increasing the capabilities, and finally performing the chipset initialization to boot the OS (Windows, Linux or one of its flavors, or macOS) from the boot media.

The tiny piece of programming sequence that is responsible for such operations is known as the BIOS. The BIOS resides in the target hardware itself and is fetched by the processor upon coming out from the reset as part of a power-on sequence.

There are many different types of firmware that exist based on the underlying hardware requirements like system boot firmware, device firmware, platform security firmware, and manageability firmware. Each firmware has its minimum requirements to complete its assigned task to initialize the underlying hardware and/or abstract the hardware to higher level applications. This chapter will focus on the system boot firmware and provide details about what a BIOS is, what basic characteristics the firmware has to perform to qualify as a BIOS, and the minimum requirements to design a BIOS.

This information will be helpful for you when you go to create your own system firmware for a target embedded system. It won't be possible to do unless you understand the basic expectation from the BIOS. The upcoming chapters will guide you in choosing the appropriate boot firmware for the target hardware.

What Is the BIOS?

The BIOS, as the acronym suggests, is responsible for the basic input/output system. The term *BIOS* is relevant with the word "boot." Typically, in computer terminology, the boot is referred to as bootstrapping, which is the startup process that takes place automatically after a computer power-on without any manual input. Thus, a BIOS is known as a boot program or boot sequence specially designed for such usage, where it starts its execution by performing a bunch of instructions at the early boot phase in the absence of physical memory and later performs a series of operations to initialize the main memory where it can load dynamic libraries, install several services for efficient boot usages, and finally initialize the boot media (example: eMMC, SATA, SSD, NVMe, UFS, or USB) or boot from a network (example: PXE boot or netboot) to load the OS and associated drivers and applications.

The term *bootloader* can be used in many ways in computer programming; in many cases, the bootloader is also referred to as a special operating system software block (e.g., boot.efi as the EFI bootloader to boot an EFI-aware OS; ARM Core Bootloader is typically used by smartphone OSes) that is responsible for loading the operating system from the block device into system memory. This chapter and Chapter 4 will use bootloader as semantics of *booting,* as in booting up an embedded system. Hence in the context of this book, bootloader is used as a synonym for the BIOS when it comes to initializing the CPU and hardware and still relying on the OS loader to load and run the OS.

Working Principle of BIOS

As mentioned, the BIOS is the first executable piece of code run by the processor after the user presses the power button. Thus, the boot firmware needs to adhere to certain characteristics to qualify as a BIOS:

- **Self-supporting**: A bootloader is a boot program for bringing up the device without any user input, hence the design principle needs to be self-supportive. *Self-supportive* means that the bootloader is capable of starting its execution from its residence. Typically, it's the reset vector (refer to later sections for details) which is an address, where upon a reset, the processor goes to find the first executable instruction. This address is dependent on the target hardware architecture, and the bootloader needs to get patched into this address. The entire bootloader boot sequence is designed such that it doesn't depend on any user interaction to perform the basic hardware initialization. All the boot phases are part of the bootloader hardware initialization process, which is written in such a way that it's aware of the prerequisites prior to starting execution of the next phase. For an example, if the boot program is dependent on the main memory, then the stage prior to that will first ensure that the main memory is being initialized and readily available.

- **Simple**: The whole purpose of the bootloader is to perform initialization of the underlying hardware. It collects the most diverse hardware data and prepares the device list while booting to higher-level software like the OS. Post booting to the OS, the drivers and applications can make use of the hardware without knowing the exact programming details to initialize the hardware interfaces. The expectation from the boot program is a simple interface without any high-level programming language due to the fact that the bootloader starts its execution from a state where RAM is not even available, and it needs a simple robust mechanism during the boot phase to access the hardware registers directly.

- **Boot**: When the hardware initialization process is complete, the bootloader will have a boot device list prepared. Depending on the type of bootloader, it can either decide to transfer the call to another firmware called a payload or continue the same to find the special boot signature (or boot record) from the available boot devices to boot to the kernel. If it fails to find the boot signature, an unsuccessful attempt to boot to the OS would result in a recovery boot where the device is dependent on booting from a removable recovery media. If the bootloader and payload are independent firmware binaries, it needs a standard communication method to pass the hardware and platform information to know the possible boot devices.

The BIOS design aspect that this chapter is going to highlight is with an assumption that the bootloader is only responsible for performing the hardware initialization, preparing the boot device lists, and passing that information to the payload. The payload is in charge of booting to an operating system or equivalent to make use of the embedded system.

Where Does the BIOS Reside?

Based on the platform reset architecture, the BIOS can reside in two different places:

1. The BIOS is stored in the flash memory (SPI NOR) on the target motherboard hardware. This is the widely used platform design where the SPI NOR is used as firmware boot media. SPI NOR designates the serial peripheral interconnect (SPI) bus upon which the NOR flash is attached. NOR flash is distinct from NAND in that it is memory mapped, byte-addressable, bit and byte writable but only bulk erasable, with the erase operation spanning either an 8KiB or 64KiB section of the device. Typically, on x86 platforms, the default reset architecture supports the boot from SPI NOR. Figure 3-1 shows the high-level block diagram of an IA-based platform to highlight where the BIOS is located in the hardware.

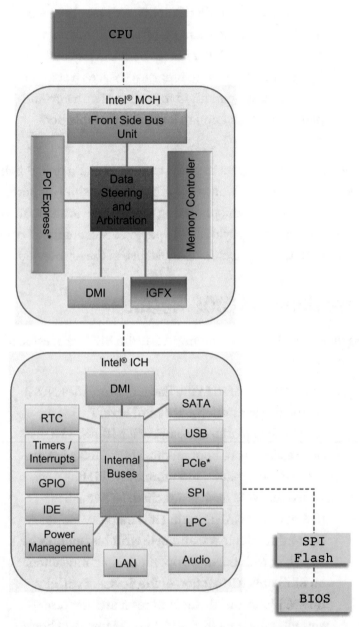

* PCI Express can be Located At Both MCH (as Slot x1/4/8 etc.) and PCH (as M.2 Slot)

Figure 3-1. *Hardware block diagram to locate the BIOS*

2. Alternatively, on smaller computing devices the BIOS is located as part of the block device. This is a cost-effective approach where the BIOS is part of the block device boot partition (BP) and the OS is located in the general purpose partition (GPP). Most handheld devices follow this reset mechanism.

All discussions in this chapter are based on the assumption that the BIOS resides in the SPI flash (as shown in Figure 3-1), which is a slave device attached to the SPI controller.

BIOS Work Model

The BIOS works as an intermediate layer between the underlying hardware and the target operating system, as shown in Figure 3-2. As soon as the CPU comes out from the reset, the bootloader needs to get the boot process going. The first major task that the BIOS supports is the initialization of the main memory to load the operations into the main memory, which is essential for the next set of tasks.

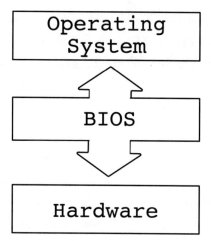

Figure 3-2. *High-level function of a bootloader*

In the second step, the BIOS performs the chipset and CPU initialization and loads the kernel or the high-level system software that controls the devices through drivers. Apart from this, there is still some work that the bootloader performs that remains unnoticed in the boot process. Figure 3-3 provides the system simplified boot flow so you can understand the bootloader work model. This boot flow includes

- **Pre-CPU reset**: By definition, a bootloader is designed to be self-supporting. Hence the firmware layout as part of the SPI flash has to be explicit to point to the required binaries (ROM patch) for associated microcontrollers that take part in the prior CPU reset activities. The final BIOS binary generation (described in more detail as part of the "Stitching Tools" section in Chapter 2 of *Firmware Development: A Guide to Specialized Systemic Knowledge*) process needs to ensure that upon the CPU release from reset it is able to jump into an address where the bootloader is located.

Note   In the most simplistic platform design, where no other microcontrollers are involved prior to the CPU reset process, you certainly can ignore the pre-CPU reset sections from the BIOS work model.

- **POST (Power-on self-test):** The boot program responsible for performing the required hardware initialization. Due to the size restriction where only a limited portion of the SPI flash is memory mapped and physical memory is not available, the bootloader tasks can be divided into two major phases as Stage 1 (a.k.a. pre-memory phase) and Stage 2 (a.k.a. post-memory phase).

- **Stage 1:** Typically, this is executed as a part of the SPI mapped memory or part of the temporary memory in the absence of the real main memory. All modules that are part of Stage 1 are mapped as eXecute-in-Place (XIP) where modules are executed in a host address space where the SPI flash is being mapped.

- **Stage 2:** Main memory is initialized as part of Stage 1, and it loads Stage 2 into the memory. Stage 2 is executed from main memory. It is responsible for performing the hardware initialization, creating the device lists, and passing the platform-centric information to the OS loader/payload stage.

- **OS loader/payload:** Depending on the type of bootloader, the OS loader may or may not be part of the bootloader program. Regardless of where the payload is located, the bootloader passes a set of information that is required for the OS loader to initialize an input, an output device (optional to display some informative text or take some special key sequence), and most importantly the boot devices list to boot to the OS. Chapter 6 describes the payload in more detail.

- **After Life (AL):** Typically, in normal eyes the bootloader is only responsible for performing the most essential hardware initialization to boot to the OS and its job ends once the OS loader hands over the control to the boot manager. But that's not the case anymore with modern operating systems. As highlighted before in the "BIOS Work Model" section, that bootloader works as a mediator between hardware and OS. Hence, certain pieces of code stay in the system memory even after the bootloader has transited. These types of services are referred to as bootloader's AL in this book.

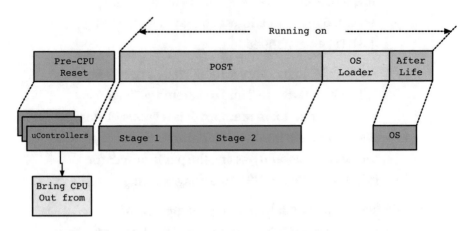

Figure 3-3. *Bootloader simplified boot flow*

Types of BIOS

The BIOS in modern consumer electronics devices is responsible for initializing and testing the system hardware components and loading an operating system from a mass memory device. Although *BIOS* is a generic terminology used to initialize the underlying hardware as mentioned in the "BIOS Work Model" section (performing POST operations), other features like the OS loader and AL characteristics make it a product differentiator for each platform. The platform owner goes with their own specification of BIOS firmware that suits the target hardware and operating system needs the most. For an example, coreboot is the official boot firmware solution used on the Chrome OS platform, whereas other Windows-based platforms rely on UEFI to provide the required boot and AL (runtime) services.

Based on the wide usage model across client, servers, IoT, and automotive platforms, there are different types of bootloaders:

- **coreboot**: An extended firmware for embedded platforms that is designed with the principle of being open, secure, simple, and offering an instant boot experience for its users. coreboot is an Open Source Firmware (OSF) project that aims to provide lightweight and lightning fast performance with only the bare minimum hardware initialization to load and run operating systems. In fact, coreboot doesn't by default come with any OS loader so it's just meant to perform the hardware initialization. It needs a dedicated payload to load and run the target operating system.

- **UEFI (Unified Extensible Firmware Interface)**: An interface created to communicate between the OS and platform firmware. It is a specification that is used to write the firmware program that performs basic hardware initialization (most similar to what's done by the traditional BIOS) to hand over the platform to its operating system. There are other specifications as part of UEFI that provide details on internal interfaces used to communicate between different parts of the platform firmware. UEFI has the OS visible interfaces in the main UEFI specification and the underlying interfaces in the platform initialization (PI) specification. There are several reference implementations of UEFI and PI, including the EFI Developer Kit II hosted on tianocore. Tiano was the codename of the initiative that created the precursor to PI, namely the Intel Platform Innovation Framework for the Extensible Firmware

Interface, or "Framework" specifications, and the original implementation known as the EFI Developer Kit (EDK), which was the precursor to EDKII.

- **SBL (Slim Bootloader)**: An open-source boot firmware build with the principle of being small, fast, secure, extensible, and configurable running on Intel x86 architecture. SBL is designed with the modular approach by providing hardware initialization and then launching a payload to boot to the OS. SBL leverages the build system and library infrastructure of EDKII.

- **U-Boot (Universal Boot Loader)**: U-Boot is an open source bootloader consisting of a first stage (where U-Boot is responsible for configuring the memory controller and performing the hardware configuration) and a second stage (where it performs the required operations to load an OS from the available device lists) of a bootloader. Typically, it is used as a bare-bone bootloader for embedded systems or evaluation hardware. It is available almost for all possible CPU architectures (ARM, RISC-V, x86, etc.). U-boot also has an implementation layer supporting UEFI that is independent of the PI specification and EDKII reference code.

- **Trusted Firmware**: Provides an open source reference implementation of secure world software for ARM architecture. This specification allows SoC developers and OEMs to implement their required bootloader code by complying with the implementation specification. The purpose of Trusted Firmware is to create a foundation for trusted execution environments

(TEEs) on CPUs or secure processing environments
(SPEs) on microcontrollers where it reduces duplicate
efforts by adhering to standardizing on a single
implementation framework.

Chapter 4 will provide the detailed architecture overview of each boot firmware type.

Some of these boot firmwares don't have an OS loader integrated by default so they need a dedicated payload to meet the OS loading characteristics of a BIOS firmware. A few popular ones include

- **Tianocore**: An open source implementation of the UEFI payload that was developed using the EDKII and PI specifications. coreboot only performs the hardware initialization and then relies on the payload to handle the boot logic. The Tianocore payload can be integrated into the coreboot boot image; residing in the SPI flash would load the UEFI-aware operating system. Figure 3-4 shows the different usage models of Tianocore as a payload.

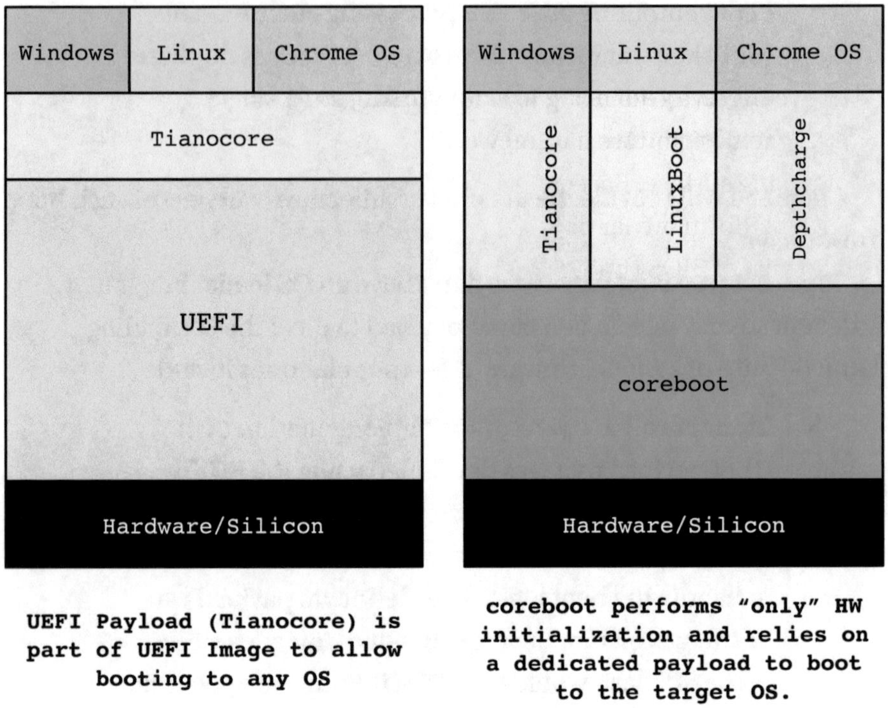

Windows	Linux	Chrome OS
Tianocore		
UEFI		
Hardware/Silicon		

UEFI Payload (Tianocore) is part of UEFI Image to allow booting to any OS

Windows	Linux	Chrome OS
Tianocore	LinuxBoot	Depthcharge
coreboot		
Hardware/Silicon		

coreboot performs "only" HW initialization and relies on a dedicated payload to boot to the target OS.

Figure 3-4. *Different usages of the Tianocore payload*

- **Depthcharge**: The bootloader for the Chrome OS platform. The main goal of Depthcharge is to provide a small, simple, secure (using vboot), and efficient payload, integrated with coreboot to boot to the Chrome OS.

- **LinuxBoot**: An open source firmware initiative to replace any proprietary firmware modules meant to boot Linux or an equivalent OS with a Linux kernel. The Linux kernel works here as a payload located in the SPI flash as part of the BIOS binary. LinuxBoot is intended to remove unnecessary code from the boot firmware (UEFI DXE phase, coreboot ramstage, SBL stage 1B, U-Boot SPL) and relies on the Linux kernel and runtime services to perform the boot logic to boot to the OS.

In modern computing devices, usage of the legacy BIOS has faded at a rapid speed. The legacy BIOS had its own complexity in programming the native hardware using assembly language or relying too much on device-specific firmware like Option ROM (OpROM), which could increase the attacking surface. Based on functionality, adaptability, and operating speed, a platform owner decides which firmware to choose from the available list of BIOS (boot firmware and OS loader) options to replace the legacy BIOS concept like OpROM with a modular and driver-based approach while initializing the hardware and booting to the OS.

Designing a Minimalistic Bootloader

It's almost difficult for end users to differentiate the presence of the BIOS from higher-level system software like operating systems, drivers, and applications on a production system. It's expected that end users and the platform owners of the device only bother knowing about the details about the system hardware and the capabilities of the operating system running on the device. But it's also important to understand the underlying bootloader design as well for several reasons:

- The underlying boot firmware (i.e., the BIOS) provides consistent behavior across different architectures (e.g., ARM, x86, RISC V, etc.).

- Firmware, being closest to the hardware, is meant to provide better control of the platform.

- It abstracts the underlying hardware by providing a flexible interface to the OS.

- **Dealing with bugs**: Working on a real hardware platform increases the chances of working around hardware or SoC defects. Firmware is close to hardware and provides the lowest turnaround time to get the bug fixed without altering the hardware or updating the OS. Updating the BIOS is thus comparatively easier.

The above reasons should be enough to motivate you to understand the underlying bootloader. Also, this book is committed to helping you create your own system firmware and be able to boot the target embedded systems. Prior to that, it's important to understand the bootloader's minimum requirements and design schema.

The different types of BIOSes provide several different frameworks or interfaces to ease the OS-to-hardware communication. But the underlying working model is almost the same across different bootloaders. Hence this section provides the minimalistic bootloader design with the required sequence in which a typical BIOS performs all recommended hardware initialization even on a cross-architecture platform.

Minimalistic Bootloader Design on x86 Platform

With growing customer demand for creating more performance-oriented systems with a limited power envelope, it forces the SoC vendors to bring more efficient microcontrollers into the SoC design along with the native CPU. This makes the reset architecture even more complicated to ensure that firmware running in these microcontrollers also gets periodic updates, since they aren't exempt from defects either. Hence the firmware image as part of the SPI flash doesn't just hold the BIOS region alone; rather it needs to have ROM patch binaries for all possible microcontrollers that take part into the SoC reset flow. Due to the fact that the bootloader design expects it to be self-supporting, here is the list of items that you need to consider when designing a minimalistic bootloader on x86 platform.

SPI Flash Layout

All boot-critical firmware components are stitched together, and the integrated firmware image is called the IFWI (integrated firmware image). The IFWI is stored in the SPI flash. The integration process for firmware ingredients is important on the x86 platform to ensure that all microcontrollers prior to the CPU reset are able to apply the ROM patch and let the CPU come out from reset. It's important to ensure that upon reset the CPU is able to fetch code from the BIOS region without any manual intervention.

Figure 3-5 depicts the firmware integration on a typical x86 platform.

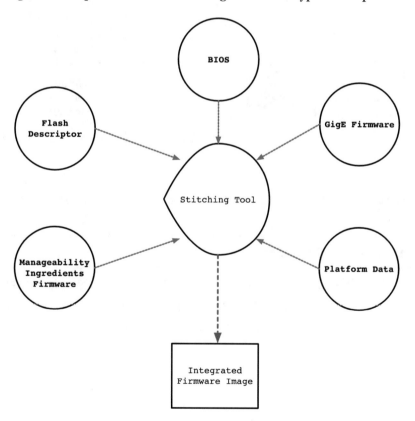

Figure 3-5. *Firmware integration process*

Refer to Figure 3-6 for the detailed flash layout.

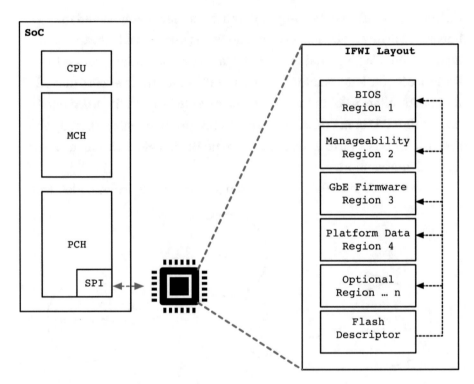

Figure 3-6. *IFWI flash regions are mapped from flash descriptors*

Region	Name	Description
0	Descriptor	In the SPI controller, a size of 4KB flash descriptor, located at the base of the SPI flash, splits the flash layout into regions and provides access control to each region.

Here are the flash descriptor region register details:

Flash Region 0 (flash descriptor) register

Bit range	Default	Access	Description
30:16	0h	RO/V	**Region limit (RL)** This specifies address bits 26:12 for the Region 0 limit. The value in this register is loaded from the contents in the flash Descriptor.FLREG0 region limit.
14:0	0h	RO/V	**Region base (RB)** This specifies address bits 26:12 for the Region 0 base. The value in this register is loaded from the contents in the flash Descriptor.FLREG0 region base

Similarly, there are other flash region registers to describe the base and limit for other flash regions as part of the IFWI image as below. The flash controller must have a default region base of 0x7FFF and region limit to 0x0 within the flash controller in case the number of regions specified are not in use.

Region	Name	Register	Calculate base and limit
1	BIOS	Flash Region 1 (BIOS) register	Region base (RB) = Flash (Descriptor.FLREG**x** & 0x00000FFF) << 12
2	Manageability ingredients	Flash Region 2 (IFWI) register	Region limit (RL) = Flash (Descriptor.FLREG**x** & 0x0FFF0000)
3	GigE firmware	Flash Region 3 (GbE) register	>> 4	0xFFF
4	Platform data	Flash Region 4 (platform data) register	**x** = Flash region index

Here are details about the other flash region sections as part of the IFWI:

Region	Name	Description
1	BIOS	The BIOS region is at the top of the SPI flash so that this region can be mapped into system memory. By default, all x86 platforms map a maximum of 16MB of SPI flash at the top of 4G in the host address space.

This map is controlled by the BIOS Decode Enable register either as part of LPC or SPI based on where SPI flash is attached.

This register allows PCH to simply decode these ranges as memory access when enabled for the SPI flash.

Bit range	Default value	Description
Bit 0	1h	Enables decoding of 1MB of the following BIOS range: 0xFF00_0000 : 0xFF0F_FFFF
...	....	....
Bit 15	1h	Enables decoding of 1MB of the following BIOS range: 0xFFF8_0000 : 0xFFFF_FFFF

Region	Name	Description
2	Manageability ingredients	This region is divided into two parts: initialization section (code) and data region. The initialization section starts from the offset 4KB, covering the ROM patch. If the ROM patch doesn't exist, then the region size is 0. The data region is followed by the code region.

(continued)

Region	Name	Description
3	GbE firmware	The GbE region and any optional flash regions will be added as required into the SPI flash layout after the manageability region and prior to BIOS region.
4	Platform data	

The above sections provided detailed descriptions so you can understand how to create a SPI flash layout and map the BIOS region and several other boot-critical regions while creating an IFWI image, as applicable based on the platform reset architecture. On x86 platforms, the CPU reset is not guaranteed and the bootloader won't be able to perform its operation if you haven't followed the proper recommendations when creating the SPI flash layout. If you want to create your own system firmware for x86-based embedded systems, the proper understanding of these sections is important.

Take a look at the sample SPI flash layout (64MB) from a Xeon processor-based server platform under the Cedar Island codename. The BIOS region is placed at the top of the SPI flash as shown here:

```
FLASH@0xfc000000 64M {
 SI_ALL@0x0 0x2fe8000 {
     SI_DESC@0x0 0x1000
     SI_GBE@0x1000 0x2000
     SI_ME@0x3000 0x2fd5000
     SI_PT@0x2fd8000 0x10000
 }
     FMAP@0x03000000 0x800
     RW_MRC_CACHE@0x3000800   0x10000
     COREBOOT(CBFS)@0x3010800
}
```

BIOS Region (~16MB)	03FF_FFFFh
NVS Data Region	0301_0800h
	0300_0800h
OEM Data	0300_0000h
Unused	
	02FE_8000h
Platform Data Region	02FD_8000h
CSE Region (~46MB)	
	0000_3000h
GbE Region	0000_1000h
Flash Descriptor Region	0000_0000h

Pre-Reset Flow

When the user presses the power button, the expectation is that the CPU will immediately come out from reset and start fetching code from the SPI flash. But in reality, there are more underlying steps involved prior to the CPU being ready to execute the first instruction. The duration between the user pressing the power button to the CPU fetching the first BIOS code is called the pre-reset phase. The boot flow in this phase typically involves hardware sequencing, so the hardware waits for the power supply to get settled to its nominal state and the microcontrollers that are part of SoC boot architecture come out from reset and start running from their ROM. This pre-reset flow is complex and highly dependent on the SoC architecture, so the flow is not generic enough to apply on all possible x86 platforms. The pre-reset flow that we will discuss here is based on the IA-architecture.

Prior to that, let's understand the associated controllers and microcontrollers that are part of this reset flow:

CSE (Converged Security Engine):

- Intel Quark x86-based 32-bit CPU, 384KB SRAM, ROM present.

- First microcontroller active after power-on reset

- Responsible for retrieving all firmware from the SPI flash and verifying it prior to allowing other microcontrollers to load their firmware.

- CSE firmware has four different firmwares in it.

  - **ROM**: First piece of firmware code that runs after reset, allows fetching and validating other CSE bring up firmware from SPI flash.

  - **RBE** (ROM boot extension)

  - **BUP (bring-up process)**: Responsible for configuring the shared SRAM and loading the other boot firmware into SRAM

  - **Runtime**: Micro kernel and runtime applications

PMC (Power Management Controller):

- 32-bit ARC controller, 64KB local instruction memory, 16KB local data memory, ROM present.

- Responsible for platform-wide power management during active and idle device states

- PMC is also responsible for enhanced low power states like S0ix

PUNIT:

- 8051 based microcontroller

- Performs similar functionality as the PMC for the North Complex IP block.

- Determines the package C-states based on the system idleness and latency tolerance reporting by the various IP blocks on the North Complex

- Communicates periodically with PMC to apply comprehensive platform power management policies.

SPI Flash (BIOS region)

- The BIOS on IA-based platforms is divided into three blocks:

  - **IBBL (Initial Boot Block Loader)**: This stage runs from the shared static RAM (SRAM), which is shared by the host CPU and the security controller (i.e., CSE) and is mapped to the top of the 4GB memory region. For example, in coreboot, the bootblock acts as IBBL. For UEFI, it's the SEC phase.

  - **IBB (Initial Boot Block)**: This stage is executed from temporary memory known as cache as RAM (CAR). For example, in coreboot, the romstage acts as IBB. For UEFI, it's the PEI phase.

  - **OBB (OEM Boot Block)**: This stage is executed from system DRAM. For example, in coreboot, the ramstage and rest phases act as OBB. For UEFI, it's the DXE and rest phases.

Here is the pre-reset boot flow that involves these controllers, the microcontrollers described above, and of course the host CPU:

1. Upon pressing the power button, the CSE comes out from reset and the ROM starts its execution.

2. The CSE ROM sets up the CSE SRAM.

3. The CSE ROM authenticates and loads the RBE to the SRAM.

4. The CSE RBE loads the PMC firmware to the SRAM and the PMC consumes it.

5. The CSE RBE authenticates and loads the BUP to the SRAM.

6. The CSE BUP configures the shared SRAM and maps portions of the SRAM into the host CPU address space.

7. The CSE BUP loads the uCode (microcode) patch to shared SRAM.

[If Boot Guard is enabled, then the CSE can perform additional steps to load the Key Manifest (KM) and Boot Policy Manifest (BPM) into the SRAM as well. In this flow, we shall ignore this step.]

8. The CSE BUP creates the FIT (firmware interface table) with

    a. A pointer to uCode

    b. A pointer to IBBL hash

9. The CSE BUP verifies and loads the IBBL.

10. It notifies the PMC and PUNIT to power up the North Complex and CPU.

11. The CPU/PUNIT applies the uCode patch from the shared SRAM according to the FIT, where the uCode is loaded into the CPU and the pCode is loaded by the PUNIT.

12. The CPU starts executing the IBBL from the reset vector.

Figure 3-7 provides the pictorial representation of the entire pre-reset boot flow where the CPU is out from reset and ready to run the BIOS region.

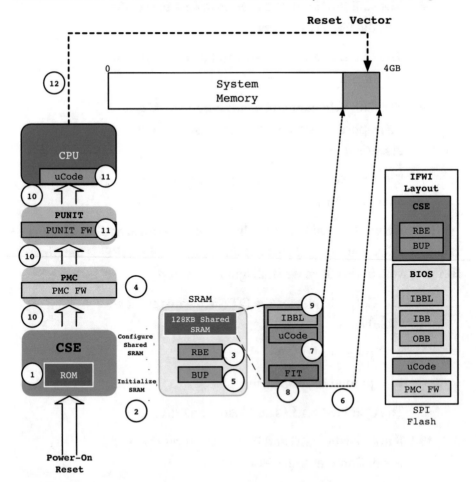

Figure 3-7. *IA-based platform pre-reset boot flow*

Minimal Bootloader Flow (Post Reset)

The prior sections provided details of the prerequisites that allow the CPU to start running the boot program upon coming out from the reset. This section provides the minimum bootloader design to allow an IA-based platform to boot an OS. A few steps that are part of this minimalistic bootloader design are subject to change (addition, deletion, or refactoring) based on the target hardware and/or specific OS requirements.

Host CPU at Reset Vector

After the bootstrap processor (BSP) comes out from reset, the location where the processor will go and find the first instruction to execute is known as the reset vector. The reset vector typically contains branch instruction that point to the start of the boot firmware. Hence a reset vector can also be defined as a pointer where the processor should always start its execution. The reset vector address is specific to the CPU architecture. For example,

- On the x86-based platform, the reset vector is patched at address 0xFFFF_FFF0.

- For the ARM family of processors, the reset vector is at the 0x0000_0000 address. This is the case for Motorola 68000 and PIC18 processors.

As we are discussing the x86-based bootloader design, let's understand how this reset vector is mapped. The whole chip is mapped to the system memory (as mentioned above using the BIOS decode range) but due to protection of the flash device, not all ranges are readable. The shared SRAM is mapped into the top of the CPU address space (Step 6 in the pre-reset flow). This access is located at the top of the SPI flash - 16 bytes (i.e., the top of 4G (0xFFFF_FFFF) - 0x10 (16 bytes) = 0xFFFF_FFF0). The IBBL is part of a shared SRAM executed from the reset vector. The code is written in assembly as at this point no stack or cache as RAM is being set. Figure 3-8 shows the typical IA system memory map at power-on.

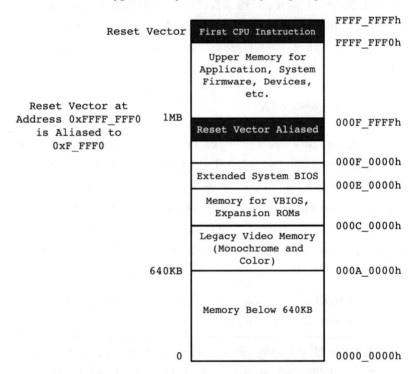

Figure 3-8. *Typical IA-based platform power-on memory map*

Processor Operational Modes and Mode Switching

On the x86 processor, from the boot firmware and general purpose operations standpoint, let's discuss two widely used operating modes:

- **Real mode**: Also known as real address mode. Upon the CPU coming out from reset or with any hardware reset, the processor starts operating in real mode. This mode provides a 16-bit code execution mode and a 20-bit segmented memory address space that can help to access a total of 1MB of addressable memory.

In real mode, interrupts are handled using the interrupt vector table (IVT).

- Protected mode: Since the i386 processor, x86 architecture has added 32-bit native operating mode support for processors to overcome the limitation of maximum accessible memory up to 1MB in real mode. This mode provides flexibility for system firmware to access higher address memory and still maintain backward compatibility based on the operations needed.

  In protected mode, the interrupt descriptor table (IDT) is used to handle the interrupt and the global descriptor table (GDT) is used to determine the segment-based addressing.

After power-on, the BSP always starts in real mode. All processor resources are reset. The memory management unit (MMU) and cache are not yet available. The top 12-bit address line being asserted as high allows access to the bootloader code directly from the SPI flash mapped into below 1MB of memory (20-bit address as 0xFFFxx or physical address 0xFFFx_xxxx) in real mode. The BIOS will continue in this mode unless it executes the first long jump; at that time, the processor will enter into protected mode by following the recommended programming.

Switching to protected mode

1. Disable the maskable hardware interrupt using the `cli` instruction.

2. [Optional] Load an IDT with a NULL limit to prevent the 16-bit IDT being used in the protected mode before a 32-bit IDT is set.

3. Construct two temporary GDTs.
   - GDT[0]: NULL
   - GDT[1]: Typically, one data and one code GDT entry with a base = 0 and size = 4GB. (Refer to Figure 3-9 for the GDT entry.)

4. Execute the LGDT instruction to load the GDTR to point to the temporary GDT.

5. Load a MOV CR0 instruction that clears the PG, AM, WP, NE, TS, EM, and MP flags and sets the CD, NW, and PE flags.

6. Immediately after that, perform a far JMP or far CALL that clear the real mode instruction queue and also reset the code segment (CS) register. Reload segment registers DS and ES with a GDT[1] descriptor, so both point to the entire physical memory space.

7. After entering into protected mode, the original CS base address of 0xFFFF_0000 is retained (used as a macro to restore the CS register) and execution continues from the current offset in the EIP register.

8. Execute the STI to enable the maskable hardware interrupt and continue the necessary hardware operation.

Figure 3-9 shows an example of GDT in gcc syntax that contains the NULL descriptor, a 32-bit code selector (0x8), and a 32-bit data selector (0x10). This is required because in protected mode all memory mappings are 1:1, meaning all logical addresses are equivalent to a physical address.

```
gdt:
        /* selgdt 0, unused */
        .word   0x0000, 0x0000              /* dummy */
        .byte   0x00, 0x00, 0x00, 0x00

        /* selgdt 0x08, flat code segment */
        .word   0xffff, 0x0000
        .byte   0x00, 0x9b, 0xcf, 0x00 /* G=1 and 0x0f, So we get 4Gbytes
                                          for limit */

        /* selgdt 0x10,flat data segment */
        .word   0xffff, 0x0000
        .byte   0x00, 0x93, 0xcf, 0x00
```

Figure 3-9. *GDT for protected mode in coreboot (source: src/arch/x86/gdt_init.S)*

The bootloader may need to switch to real mode from protected mode based on certain use cases like executing legacy Option ROM, using a legacy OS loader, resuming from S3, and so on.

Pre-Memory Initialization

The IBBL runs from the shared SRAM in the absence of physical memory, so the following code is responsible for setting up the cache as RAM (CAR). Figure 3-10 describes the cache hierarchy on x86 platforms, where L3 cache is shared between all the cores. It is called before accessing memory and is usually referred to as the last level cache (LLC).

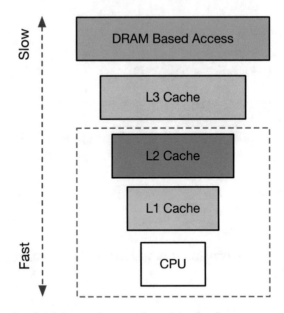

Figure 3-10. *Cache hierarchy on the x86 platform*

NEM (Non-Evict Mode)

The boot code requires temporary memory in the absence of main
memory for setting up the stack that is required for a C program execution.
The BIOS implements a temporary memory by configuring the BSP cache
in non-evict mode. For many generations, NEM mode has run from the
LLC. Memory doesn't exist, so all read/writes must be confined to the
cache; otherwise they're lost. NEM has a strict requirement of maintaining
a 0.5MB buffer between the code and data sections. This makes the
bootloader's job difficult where IBB doesn't fit in the available LLC size.
To overcome this limitation, many bootloader designs use Cache
Allocation Technology (CAT), which provides a mechanism that ensures
data is always in the cache (minimum one way locked for data) while
code lines are replaced. This mechanism is also known as enhanced NEM
(eNEM), which allows bigger code blocks to run from the LLC.

Early Chipset Initialization

A few controllers are required to program during the early boot phases like UART for enabling the serial console. This process requires programming the PCI configuration space's base address registers (BARs), enabling the I/O and MMIO space. Depending on the chipset, there are prefetchers that can be enabled at this point to speed up the data transfer from the flashed mapped device. There may be other controllers that can be accessed either over the PCI bus or memory mapped devices prior to memory initialization.

Memory Initialization

Initialization of the memory controller is the key responsibility of the boot firmware. This initialization process depends on the DRAM technology and the capabilities of the memory controller. The memory controller integrated inside the SoC provides an opportunity for the SoC vendors to supply the memory reference code (MRC) and required documentation to know the configurations allowed on a platform. At a high level, MRC is developed based on the DRAM technology by following the JEDEC initialization sequence. This involves running several training algorithms in 32-bit protected mode by considering a few board configuration parameters. PC-based memory configurations are based on dual inline memory modules (DIMM). There is a very wide range of DIMM configurations on embedded systems based on the module configuration as soldered down/memory-down solutions or socketed memory solutions. These configurations vary between the number of ranks, memory controllers, runtime control of resistive compression (RCOMP), and delay locked loop (DLL) capabilities. (Refer to Chapter 7's "Adopting Hybrid Firmware Development Model" section for details) These capabilities allow the memory controller to change components such as the drive strength to ensure flawless operation with temperature variations and with aged hardware.

The majority of embedded systems are populated with soldered down DIMMs on the motherboard so the BIOS doesn't need to perform the dynamic configuration; rather, the BIOS is specifically built for the target configuration using the vendor-supplied serial presence detect (SPD) data hard-coded as part of the BIOS. If the platform supports a socketed memory module, then the DIMM configurations are read through a special, tiny serial EEPROM chip. These chips contain specification-defined information about the capabilities of the DRAM configuration such as SPD data, which is readable through a SMBUS or an I2C interface. It is also possible to provide hard-coded SPD data for EPROM-less devices in case of socketed DIMM.

All this configuration data needs to be gathered as part of the memory initialization process to feed into the MRC code in order to make main memory available.

Post Memory Initialization

Today the firmware boundary is prolonged due to the fact that lots of IP initializations and application processors initializations are dependent on the main memory being initialized. For example, the basic foundation block for security enforcement has to wait until the DRAM is available. Once the main memory has been initialized, here is the minimum list of operations being performed.

Memory Test

The idea here is to ensure the integrity of the main memory by writing and reading back the test patterns (the most common ones are Zero-One and Walking 1/0). This operation is done as part of MRC prior to transferring the call into DRAM-based resources. For systems with fast boot requirements, it doesn't make sense to run this operation at all boot paths (cold or warm boot).

Shadowing

In the absence of physical memory, the BIOS modules (IBBL and IBB) are expected to run as part of XIP. This makes the boot process slower. Once main memory is available, the BIOS performs a shadowing operation of further modules from the SPI flash into DRAM-based memory. This process requires the bootloader stages being built with relocation enabled so that the program starts to execute from RAM.

Tear Down the CAR

While the BIOS is operating using the CAR as temporary memory, the data and code stacks are part of the BSP cache. Now with main memory being initialized, the need for the CAR is over, hence the need to tear down the CAR. The stack must be set up before jumping into the main memory. The stack top needs to get identified based on the main memory availability after reserving the required memory range (refer to Figure 3-11). The stack counts down, so the top of the stack must be placed with enough memory to be allocated for the maximum stack.

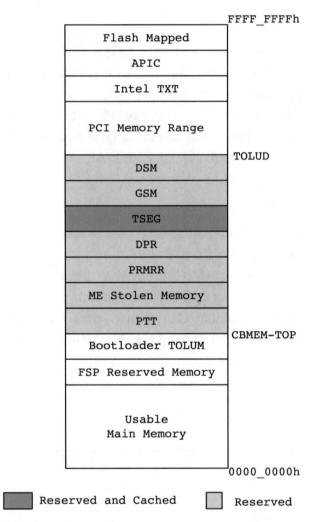

Figure 3-11. *System memory map on an IA-based platform*

Since the processor cache using temporary memory is already being torn down, now the need is to enable caching ranges based on DRAM resources. The bootloader makes use of the variable memory MTRRs to specify the different caching ranges. The first entry in each pair is MTRR_PHYSBASEn and it defines the base address and memory type for the ranges. The second entry, MTRR_PHYSMASKn, contains a mask to specify the range limit. The n indicates variable MTTR pairs between 0 to 7.

MP (Multi-Processor) Initialization

In a typical CPU architecture, there is more than one logical processor in it. As a result, the CPU initialization process is not only limited to the BSP. The other logical processors available in a CPU architecture in case of a multi-CPU core environment are known as application processors (APs). It's the responsibility of the BSP to bring the APs from the dormant state and perform the initialization with identical features enabled for the BSP. Before going to the AP initialization process, let's understand the underlying command used in this initialization process.

Startup Inter-Processor Interrupt (SIPI)

To wake up the other logical processors apart from the BSP, the BSP sends a SIPI to each application processor, indicating the physical address from which the APs should start executing. All APs start in real mode so this address where APs will jump after reset must be below 1MB of memory and be aligned on a 4-KB boundary.

The MP initialization can be divided into two major phases:

- BSP initialization sequence, to let the APs out from the reset

- AP initialization sequence, to let the APs perform the feature programming

BSP Initialization Sequence

The boot-strap code typically performs the following operations:

1. Initializes memory

2. Loads the microcode update into the processor

3. Initializes the MTRRs

4. Enables the caches

5. Loads start-up code for the AP to execute into a 4-KByte page in the lower 1MB of memory

6. Switches to protected mode and ensures that the APIC address space is mapped to the strong uncacheable (UC) memory type. Determines the BSP's APIC ID from the local APIC ID register (default is 0).

7. Save the BSP used MSRs and MTRRs.

8. Performs the following operation to set up the BSP to detect the presence of APs in the system and the number of processors (within a finite duration, minimally 10 milliseconds):

   • Sets the value of the COUNT variable to 1

   • In the AP BIOS initialization code, the AP increments the COUNT variable to indicate its presence. The finite duration while waiting for the COUNT to be updated can be accomplished with a timer. When the timer expires, the BSP checks the value of the COUNT variable. If the timer expires and the COUNT variable has not been incremented, no APs are present or some error has occurred.

9. Broadcasts an INIT-SIPI-SIPI sequence to the APs to wake them up (newer AMD and Intel CPUs don't even need second SIPI and a delay between INIT and the first SIPI) and initialize them. If the software knows how many logical processors it expects to wake up, it may choose to poll the COUNT variable.

If the expected processors show up before the 10 millisecond timer expires, the timer can be canceled and skip to step 10.

10. Reads and evaluates the COUNT variable and establishes a processor counts

11. If necessary, reconfigures the APIC and continues with the remaining system diagnostics as appropriate

AP Initialization Sequence

When an AP receives the INIT SIPI, it begins executing the BIOS AP initialization code at the vector encoded in the SIPI.

The AP initialization code typically performs the following operations:

1. Waits on the BIOS initialization lock semaphore. When control of the semaphore is attained, initialization continues.

2. Loads the microcode update into the processor

3. Syncs the BSP MSRs and MTRRs

4. Enables the cache

5. Determines the AP's APIC ID from the local APIC ID register and adds it to the MP and ACPI tables and optionally to the system configuration space in RAM

6. Initializes and configures the local APIC. Configures the AP's SMI execution environment. (Each AP and the BSP must have a different SMBASE address.)

7. Increments the COUNT variable by 1

8. Releases the semaphore

9. Executes one of the following:

- The CLI and HLT instructions (if MONITOR/MWAIT is not supported), or

- The CLI, MONITOR and MWAIT sequence to enter a deep C-state

10. Waits for an INIT SIPI

Figure 3-12 provides a snapshot of the MP CPU feature programming as part of IA-based platform using coreboot bootloader.

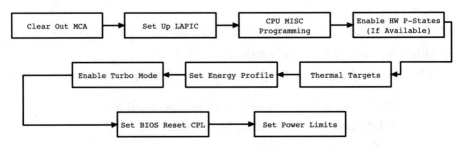

Figure 3-12. *MP feature-enabling sequence (using coreboot on an IA-based platform)*

Late Chipset Initialization

The early chipset initialization is already being done in the pre-memory phase. This stage performs the initialization of the remaining chipset devices that take part in the payload or early kernel initialization process. This list may widely vary between the underlying hardware and target OS features. At a high level, the minimal operations in this phase are

- General purpose I/O (GPIO) programming

- Interrupt configuration

- PCI enumeration

- Graphics initialization

- Boot media initialization (USB, SATA)

GPIO Programming

The GPIO controller is an elemental part of the SoC PCH. The GPIO controller part of SoC may have one or more GPIO communities. Each community consists of one or more GPIO groups, which consist of a number of GPIO PINs. Several functionalities of each IP/device inside SoC can be multiplexed to a particular I/O PIN. The configuration of the PINs must be set prior to the use of the IP/device. This PIN can either be configured to be a special function (typically known as a native function) or a general purpose I/O PIN. If a PIN is configured as GPIO, then it's direction can be configured as input or output with respect to the SoC IP/device. For an example, UART Rx and Tx PINs are programmed as native functions. The GPIO state may be configured for PINs that are configured as outputs. It's recommended that developers refer to the board schematics to know the exact GPIO configuration based on the target hardware.

Interrupt Configuration

Interrupts are like events and are used by endpoint devices to communicate something to the CPU. For example, for user input on the HID, in absence of an interrupt, the CPU would have had to poll all the platform devices, resulting in wasting CPU time.

There are three types of interrupts:

- **Hardware interrupts**: Interrupts coming from hardware devices like a keyboard or timer

- **Software interrupts**: Generated by the software `int` instruction

- **Exceptions**: Triggered by the CPU itself in response to some erroneous conditions like "divide by zero" and such

On the x86 platform, a combination of the following is used to handle interrupts:

- **PIC (programmable interrupt controller)**: The simplest way to handle interrupts on x86 platforms where PIC receives interrupt requests from the endpoint device and sends them to the CPU. The PIC contains two cascaded 8259s with 15 IRQs (IRQ2 is not available since it is used to connect the 8259s). The BIOS programs the IRQs as per the board configuration. Figure 3-13 shows a reference block diagram of the BIOS configuring the IRQ.

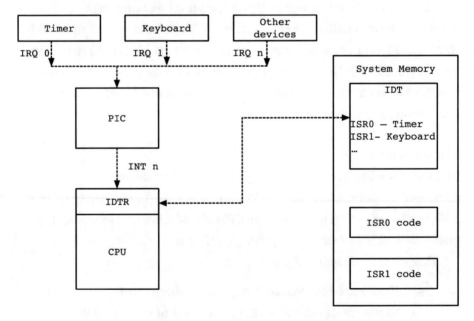

Figure 3-13. *BIOS configuring the interrupt in PIC mode*

- **LAPIC (local advanced programmable interrupt controller)**: APIC is a more advanced interrupt controller than PIC. The APIC design is split into two components: local components (LAPIC) integrated into the processor and I/O APIC on a system bus. There is one LAPIC in each processor in the system. LAPICs may support up to 224 usable interrupt vectors. Vector numbers 0 to 31, out of 0 to 255, are reserved for exception handling by x86 processors.

- **IOxAPIC (input/output advanced programmable interrupt controller)**: The IOxAPIC is present inside the Integrated Controller HUB (ICH) or Platform Controller Hub (PCH). The IOxAPIC has support for 24 interrupt lines. Each IRQ has an associated redirection table entry that can be enabled/disabled and selects the vector for the associated IRQ. Typically, the BIOS is expected to program interrupts in IOxAPIC mode as it provides the improved latency.

Refer to Figure 3-14 for the interrupt handling mechanism on x86-based platforms. There are eight PIRQ pins named PIRQ[A#: H#] that routed individual IRQs to the PIC and the PIC forwards the single interrupt to the CPU based on the BIOS programming (GPIO IRQ Select; the valid value is 14 or 15). Alternatively, ICH/PCH also connects those PIRQs to eight individual IOxAPIC input pins.

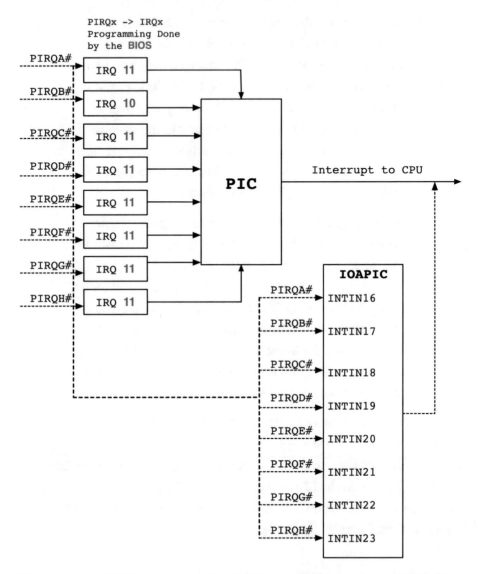

Figure 3-14 *BIOS programming PIRQx# to IRQx in PIC or IOAPIC*

PCI Enumeration

The Peripheral Connect Interface is a standard bus used in an x86-based SoC design to connect various controllers to it. The bootloader is responsible for enumerating the PCI buses to detect the PCI devices present and create the complete PCI device list. Later, it allocates the DRAM-based resources to those PCI devices. The PCI enumeration is a generic process that might take several milliseconds based on the number of devices attached to the PCI bus and the speed at which the CPU is operating. Most embedded systems have SoC internal devices attached to Bus 0, hence a static PCI device list (similar to `src/mainboard/google/zork/variants/baseboard/devicetree_dalboz.cb`) where the device location (i.e., the bus) and function are known. Of course, there are external devices sitting behind PCIe root ports which need an additional child device enumeration. After discovering the entire PCI device list, the BIOS needs to allocate and enable the resources, which includes

- MMIO space

- IRQ assignments as described in an earlier section

- Locating the Option ROM (also known as expansion ROM) and executing if available based on platform need

A few of the PCI devices that are typically used in embedded systems are the on-board graphics controller, USB controller, Serial ATA (SATA), and SPI. The BIOS must ensure that these devices have resource allocations for future use.

Graphics Initialization

Graphics initialization is considered as the sign of life for embedded devices with displays attached. The BIOS detects the on-board graphics controller or the off-board discrete graphics card on the PCIe root port. Let's limit this discussion up to the internal graphics controller. On legacy platforms, the BIOS locates the expansion ROM inside the graphics controller, also known as video BIOS (vBIOS) and executes it for display initialization. Modern systems with UEFI rely on Graphics Output Protocol (GOP), and open source firmware uses libgfxinit for graphics initialization on embedded systems.

Boot Media Initialization

Typically boot device initialization is the responsibility of a payload program. Boot firmware is responsible for detecting the boot devices over the standard PCI bus and performing the resource allocation. The payload has several device drivers for the required boot device: USB or SATA. With USB, the payload needs to have the standard XHCI controller drivers and USB bus drivers, followed by the USB device drivers. As USB is a generic specification, the payload needs to have a mass storage driver to support booting from the USB media.

Similarly, the boot firmware is expected to perform the SATA controller mode setup prior to payload. Also, it implements the Port Mapping register and Port X Enable (PxE) bit(s) of the Port Control and Status register to enable the unused SATA ports based on runtime device detection. Typically, on client segments, SATA controllers are expected to program in AHCI (Advanced Host Controller Interface) mode while server platforms configure the SATA controller in RAID mode.

Booting to the OS

The OS loader is responsible for managing the required communication while booting to an OS. The boot firmware might need to provide different sets of information based on the target OS (between a UEFI-aware OS and a legacy OS). This section will limit the discussion to booting to a legacy OS. While booting to a legacy OS, the OS bootloader is loaded into a memory location below 1MB , so it switches into processor real mode and jumps to the location. The following section specifies the expectation from the boot firmware while booting to a legacy OS.

OS Handoff Lists

Here are the minimum requirements from a boot firmware while booting to the OS and boot firmware to create several tables that the OS needs as part of the post memory initialization process:

- E820 table

- Programmable interrupt routing (PIRQ) table

- Multi-processor specification (MP) table

- System management BIOS (SMBIOS) tables

- Advanced configuration and power interface (ACPI) tables

e820 Table

As discussed (Figure 3-11 as part of the post memory initialization), the BIOS is responsible for defining the cacheable range and creating system memory maps. It is also responsible for providing that system memory map to the OS so that the OS is aware of what regions are actually available to use and what all ranges are reserved. The ACPI specification describes the entries in this table.

There are different ways to provide this information to the OS. For example, an UEFI-aware OS relies on the EfiMemoryMap call from the kernel to a real UEFI memory map. In a legacy OS, the most widely used mechanism is to use real mode interrupt service 0x15, function 0xe8, sub-function 0x20 (hence its INT15, 0xe820), which the BIOS must implement. The e820 table defines the following address range types:

e820 Type	Name	Description
1	RAM	This range is the available RAM usable by the operating system.
2	Reserved	This range of addresses is in use or reserved by the system and is not to be included in the allocatable memory pool of the operating system's memory manager.

(continued)

191

e820 Type	Name	Description
3	ACPI	ACPI reclaim memory. This range is available RAM usable by the OS after it reads the ACPI tables.
4	NVS	ACPI NVS memory. This range of addresses is in use or reserved by the system and must not be used by the operating system. This range is required to be saved and restored across an NVS sleep.
5	Unusable	This range of addresses contains memory in which errors have been detected. This range must not be used by OSPM.
7	Persistent memory	OSPM must comprehend this memory as having non-volatile attributes and handling distinct from conventional volatile memory.

With some bootloaders like coreboot, the e820 table has an entry of type 16, which is unknown to the Linux kernel. coreboot marks the entire cbmem as type 16 rather than attempting to mark the RAM as reserved. Here is sample example of the e820 table from an x86-based platform:

```
BIOS-e820: [mem 0x0000000000000000-0x000000000009ffff] usable
BIOS-e820: [mem 0x00000000000a0000-0x00000000000fffff] reserved
BIOS-e820: [mem 0x0000000000100000-0x000000005bffffff] usable
BIOS-e820: [mem 0x000000005c000000-0x00000000707fffff] reserved
BIOS-e820: [mem 0x00000000c0000000-0x00000000cfffffff] reserved
BIOS-e820: [mem 0x00000000fc000000-0x00000000fc000fff] reserved
BIOS-e820: [mem 0x00000000fd000000-0x00000000fe00ffff] reserved
BIOS-e820: [mem 0x00000000fed10000-0x00000000fed17fff] reserved
BIOS-e820: [mem 0x00000000fed80000-0x00000000fed83fff] reserved
BIOS-e820: [mem 0x00000000feda0000-0x00000000feda1fff] reserved
BIOS-e820: [mem 0x0000000100000000-0x000000048f7fffff] usable
```

Programmable Interrupt Routing Table

The first PCI interrupt routing table provided by the x86 BIOS is the $PIR table. This table describes how the PCI interrupt signals are connected to input pins on a PIC. In addition, these details can be used by the operating system to program the interrupt router directly.

Multiprocessor Specification Table

The multiprocessor specification table is required if a system has more than one processor present. The signature of this table is _MP_. More details can be found in the multiprocessor specification (MP Spec).

System Management BIOS Table

On booting the system, the BIOS will create the SMBIOS table with the signature _SM_ and put it into the system memory. This table provides information about the underlying system hardware and firmware and is used by some OS-based applications. A popular consumer of SMBIOS tables is the dmidecode command, which provides hardware-related information such as processors, DIMM, BIOS, memory, and serial number.

Creation of ACPI Tables

ACPI defines an interface between the ACPI-compliant OS and platform HW via the system BIOS to control core power and system management.

To provide HW vendor flexibility in choosing the implementation, ACPI uses the concept of tables like system info, features, and other control methods.

- Describe the interfaces to the hardware

- The ACPI table is initiated with the root system description pointer (RSDP). During the OS initialization, the OSPM must have an RSDP pointer structure from the platform.

- The platform BIOS should look for the RSDP pointer entry in the system memory. This approach differs between a legacy BIOS and a UEFI implementation.

- The platform design should specify what ACPI table system the BIOS should populate.

- Figure 3-15 shows the sample ACPI table structure, where all ACPI tables have standard header format (signature/length) apart from table-specific information or a pointer to another table structure.

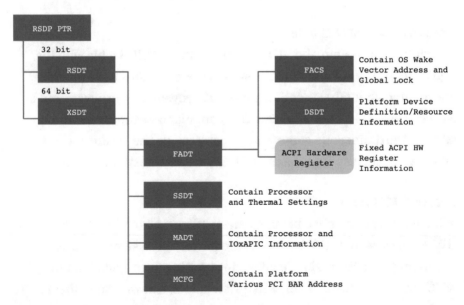

Figure 3-15. *Sample ACPI table structure*

BIOS Runtime Services

Apart from the boot services, many bootloaders also provide runtime capabilities that coexist with the main operating system, also known as runtime (RT) services. Typically, it's expected that a BIOS job is done once the system is able to find the boot media and load the kernel but there is certain access where the OS relies on the system BIOS. A widely used application of a RT service is BIOS ASL (ACPI Source Language) code, which is used by kernel devices and ACPI drivers. Apart from that, there may be other services as part of the bootloader runtime service table, such as get/set time, get/set wakeup time, access to the non-volatile memory like SPI flash using a get/set variable, resetting the system, and more.

Another hidden but available AL service is usage of SMM triggered by the System Management Interrupt (SMI). This allows accessing the SMI handlers part of SMM memory written by the bootloader from the OS layer with the highest privilege level.

BIOS AL Services

In the event that the main operating system crashes or issues a shut-down, there is a final set of capabilities known as After Life (AL) services. Typically, it's expected that the OS will shut down gracefully. In the event of an OS panic or failure, a hardware watchdog timer (WDT) may reinvoke the firmware, say the TCO SMI source. In this case, the firmware can quiesce the hardware and create a firmware error log prior to issuing a hard reset, such as an 0xCF9 write. Figure 3-16 shows a x86-based embedded system boot flow with a minimalistic bootloader design approach.

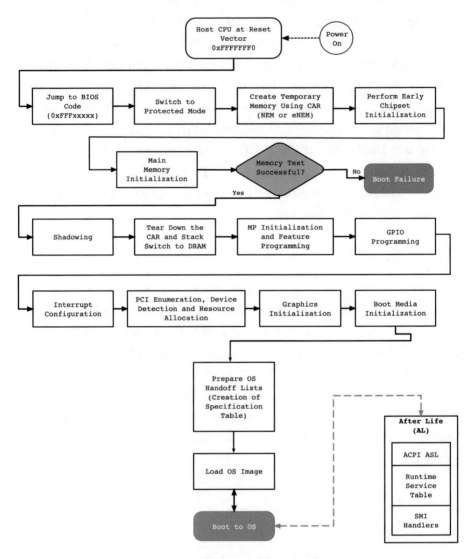

Figure 3-16. *System boot flow with a minimalistic BIOS design*

Minimalistic Bootloader Design on the ARM Platform

A bootloader design on the ARM platform is way different than what we have discussed so far on the x86 platform. On the ARM platform, the minimalist bootloader design needs to implement the Trusted Board Boot (TBB) feature. The TBB feature allows the platform to be protected from malicious firmware attack by implementing a chain of trust (CoT) at each firmware level up to the normal world bootloader. Trusted Firmware (TF) implements a subset of the TBB requirements for ARM reference platforms. This section describes the minimalistic design of TF on the ARM platform.

Trusted Firmware

The TBB sequence starts when the user presses the power button until it transfers the control to firmware running as part of a normal world bootloader in DRAM. The TF is a reference implementation of secure world software for processors implementing both the A-Profile and M-Profile of the ARM architecture. The TF for A-Profile ARM processors is known as TF-A, and Trusted Firmware-M (TF-M) provides a reference implementation of the platform requirements for ARM Cortex-M processors. The scope of this section is limited to TF-A, an open source implementation focusing on trusted boot including Exception Level 3 (EL3) code.

The ARM architecture defines four exception levels (EL0, EL1, EL2, and EL3). These exception levels are associated with software execution privileges.

- EL0: The lowest privileged execution level, also referred to as the unprivileged level of execution

- EL3: The highest privileged execution level, which is used to control access to the secured world. Switching between a non-secure state to a secure state or vice-versa can be done only when the software executes at the EL3 privilege level.

This table shows the partitioning of software based on the processor exception level:

Exception level	Description and usage
Non-secure world EL0	Unprivileged applications downloaded and running from the app stores
Non-secure world EL1	Operating system kernels run at EL1 exception level
Non-secure world EL2	Bootloader running from DRAM. Virtualization applications from vendors run at this exception level.
Secure EL0	Trusted OS applications
Secure EL1	Trusted OS kernels from trusted OS vendors. Starting with AArch64 architecture, it allows firmware to run at Secure EL1.
Secure EL3	Secure firmware from SoC vendors, secure monitor, trusted ROM firmware runs at this exception level.

Trusted Firmware utilizes the processor exception levels and associate this with Trusted Execution Environment (TEE), so that the trusted firmware running part of Secure World and other firmware running in DRAM are from Non-Secure World. Figure 3-17 shows the software layers of TF on an ARM system.

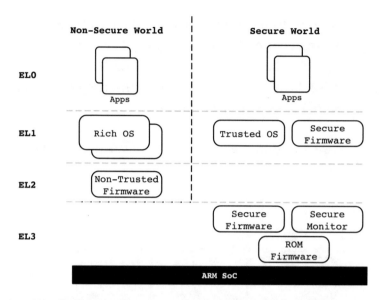

Figure 3-17. *Software/firmware layers of TF on an ARM system*

In order to create a more scalable kernel image that can work on all platforms, the ARM platform firmware is looking for a standard that allows interaction with the hardware platform based on certain firmware interfaces. Trusted Firmware has created some of these standards to make this possible:

- PSCI (Power State Coordination Interface)

- SMC (Secure Monitor Call) Calling Convention

Power State Coordination Interface

This creates an API that can be used to perform device power management by OS vendors for supervisory software working at different privilege levels. The idea here is that when supervisory software running as part of the non-secure world requests to manage the device power (i.e., power off the system), the request context is transferred to the secure world platform firmware, which might need to communicate with the trusted OS. This interface is designed to provide a generic implementation that

allows rich OS, non-trusted firmware, trusted OSes, and secure firmware
to interoperate when power is being managed. This interface also allows
it to work along with other firmware tables (examples: ACPI and FDT
(Flattened Device Tree)). Figure 3-18 provides an example of a platform
shutdown request being managed with PSCI.

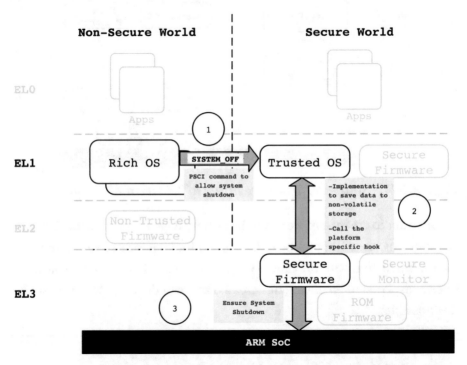

Figure 3-18. *SYSTEM_OFF PSCI command from non-secure world*

SMC Calling Convention

This defines a standard calling mechanism for the Secure Monitor Call
(SMC) instruction in the ARM architecture. In the ARM architecture,
synchronous control is transferred between the non-secure world to the
secure world through SMS exceptions. These calls may then be passed
on to a trusted OS in Secure EL1. It eases out the integration of several
software layers, such as a rich OS, virtualization application, trusted OS,
secure monitor, and system firmware.

TF Architecture

Based on the underlying ARM architecture (between 32-bit ARM processor AArch32 and 64-bit ARM processor AArch64), the Trusted Firmware is divided into five stages (in the order of execution):

Stage name	Firmware name	Applicable for AArch32	Applicable for AArch64
Boot Loader Stage 1 (BL1)	Processor Trusted ROM	Yes	Yes
Boot Loader Stage 2 (BL2)	Trusted Boot Firmware	Yes	Yes
Boot Loader Stage 3-1 (BL31)	EL3 Runtime Firmware	No	Yes
Boot Loader Stage 3-2 (BL32)	EL3 Runtime Firmware (for AArch32) Secure EL1 Payload (for AArch64)	Yes	Optional
Boot Loader Stage 3-3 (BL33)	Non-Trusted Firmware	Yes	Yes

As part of the initialization process, these boot firmwares use different memory regions for loading, verifying, and execution:

- Regions are only accessible by the secure world elements like ROM and trusted SRAM. There may be some implementations that also use a region in the DRAM as trusted DRAM only for secure operations.

- Regions are accessible by both the non-secure and secure world, such as non-trusted SRAM and DRAM.

Firmware Configuration

The Firmware Configuration Framework (FCONF) provides the flexibility at each bootloader stage to allow for configuring the platform dynamically. The bootloader stage can specify a firmware configuration file and/ or hardware configuration file that was previously hardcoded into the firmware code. This framework uses the Flattened Device Tree (FDT) format that is passed to the firmware during the bootloader load process. These configuration files are

- FW_CONFIG: The firmware configuration file that holds platform configuration data shared across all boot loader (BLx) images. The FW_CONFIG expects a dtb_registry node with the information field like the physical loading address of the configuration, maximum size, and image id.

- HW_CONFIG: The hardware configuration file that can be shared by all bootloader stages and also by the unsecured world rich OS

- TB_FW_CONFIG: The Trusted Boot firmware configuration file shared between BL1 and BL2 stages

- SOC_FW_CONFIG: The SoC firmware configuration file used by BL31

- TOS_FW_CONFIG: The trusted OS firmware configuration file used by the trusted OS (BL32)

- NT_FW_CONFIG: The non-trusted firmware configuration file used by the non-trusted firmware (BL33)

Each bootloader stage can pass up to four arguments via registers to the next stage. When dynamic configuration files are available, the firmware configuration file is passed as the first argument and the generic hardware configuration is passed as the next available argument for the next bootloader stage. For example, FW_CONFIG is loaded by the BL1 and then its address is passed in arg0 to BL2.

Firmware Image Package (FIP)

The FIP allows packing all possible bootloader images along with configuration files and certificates for boot stage authentication into a single archive that can be loaded by the TF from the non-volatile platform storage (for FVP, it's the SPI flash). This package also consists of a dedicated driver (`drivers/io/io_fip.c`) to read data from a file in the package. The FIP creation tool (`tools/fiptool`) can be used to pack specified images into a binary package that can be loaded by the TF from platform storage.

Firmware Authentication

Trusted Firmware has an authentication framework as part of the TCB requirement that allows verification of all bootloader images. TF does this by establishing a CoT using public-key cryptography standards (PKCS).

A CoT on the ARM platform relies on trusted components such as

- A SHA-256 hash of the root of trusted public key (ROTPK), stored inside the trusted root-key storage register

- The BL1 image running as part of the trusted ROM

The CoT certificates are categories as Key and Content. Key certificates are used to verify public keys that have been used to sign content certificates. Content certificates are used to store the hash of a bootloader image. An image can be authenticated by calculating its hash (using SHA-256 function) and matching it with the hash extracted from the content certificate.

Boot Loader Stages

Figure 3-19 shows a simple TF boot flow on the ARM FVP platform. Trusted ROM and trusted SRAM are used for trusted firmware binaries and non-secured DRAM is used for non-trusted bootloaders. BL1 originally sits in the trusted ROM at address 0x0 (RO block). Its RW data is relocated at the base of the trusted SRAM at runtime. BL1 loads the BL2 image into the top of trusted SRAM to run at the EL3 exception level.

BL2 loads BL31 images between BL1 and B2 in the trusted SRAM. BL31 then loads the first non-secure bootloader BL33 into the non-secure memory running as an EL2 exception level. BL33 then performs the remaining platform initialization and boots to the rich OS.

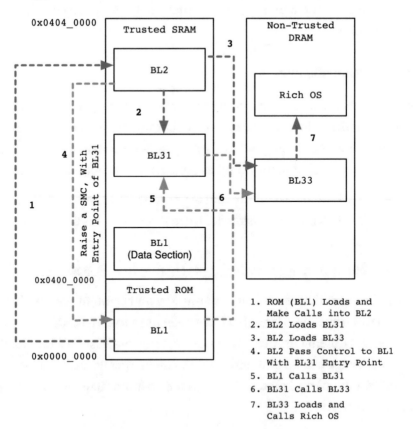

Figure 3-19. Minimalistic bootloader operations in an ARM TF

Here is the detailed description of each bootloader stage and its minimal architecture:

Bootloader stage 1: The first stage of TF is designed to execute upon a platform hitting the reset vector from the trusted ROM at EL3. The BL1 code starts at 0x0000_0000 in the FVP memory map. The Data section of BL1 is placed inside a trusted SRAM base at address 0x0400_0000. The operations performed by this stage are as follows:

- **Identify the boot path**: Upon the CPU release from reset, BL1 needs to perform a unique identification to detect the boot path between the warm and cold boot. This is a platform-specific implementation. For example, the ARM FVP relies on a power controller to distinguish between a cold and warm boot.

- **Set up exception vectors**: BL1 sets up simple exception vectors for both synchronous and asynchronous exceptions.

- **MMU setup**: BL1 sets up an EL3 memory translation by creating page tables to cover the physical address space.

- **Control register setup**: BL1 performs enabling of several control registers, which helps other bootloaders running at different exception levels (for example, instruction cache, intra-cluster coherency, use of the HVC instruction from EL1, FIQ exceptions are configured to be taken in EL3, etc.).

- **Platform initialization**: BL1 performs the following initialization:

  - Initialize the UART controller.

- Determine the amount of trusted SRAM required to load the next bootloader image (BL2).

- Configure the platform storage to load the BL2 binary at a platform-specific base address.

- Pass control to the BL2 image at Secure E1, starting from its load address.

- If the dynamic configuration file is available (TB_FW_CONFIG), BL1 loads it to the platform-defined address and makes it available for BL2 via arg0.

Bootloader stage 2: BL2 performs the next level of Trusted Firmware initialization that loads both secure and non-secure bootloader stages. BL2 runs from the Secure EL1. The operations performed by this stage are as follows:

- **MMU setup**: BL2 sets up a Secure EL1 memory transition by creating page tables to cover the physical address space in a similar way as BL1.

- **Platform initialization**: BL2 performs the following initialization:

  - BL2 calculates the limits of DRAM (main memory) to determine whether there is enough space to load the BL33 image.

  - BL2 uses a platform-defined base address to load the BL31 image into trusted SRAM.

  - If the ARM architecture supports a BL32 image, then BL2 is also responsible for loading BL32 into trusted SRAM.

  - BL2 also initializes the UART controller.

- Platform security is initialized to allow access to controlled components. BL2 loads and verifies the trusted key and other bootloader (BL3x) key certificate.

- BL2 loads the non-secured bootloader from non-volatile storage into non-secured memory (DRAM). The entry point address of the BL33 image is passed to BL31 as BL2 relies on BL31 to pass control to BL33.

- BL2 raises an SMC to pass control back to BL1 with a BL31 entry point. The exception is handled by the SMC exception handler as part of BL1.

Bootloader stage 3-1: This image is loaded by BL2 and BL1 passes control to BL31 at EL3. BL31 executes from trusted SRAM. The functionality perform by BL31 is as follows:

- BL31 perform the similar architectural initialization being done by BL1 as BL1 code was running from the ROM, so BL31 allows an override of any previous initialization done by BL1.

- BL31 creates page tables to address the physical address space and initializes the MMU.

- BL31 overrides the exception vectors earlier populated by BL1 with its own exception vector table.

- **Platform initialization**: BL31 performs the following initialization:

  - BL31 ensures that the required platform initialization is done to help the non-secure world bootloader and software run correctly.

- BL31 is also responsible for executing the non-secure world bootloader BL33 based on the platform memory address populated by BL2.

- BL31 also initializes the UART controller.

- It initialize the generic interrupt controller.

- It initialize the power controller device.

- It initialize the runtime services of the software and firmware running in the non-secure and secure world at an exception level lower than EL3 will request runtime services using the SMC instruction. The EL3 runtime services framework enables different service providers to easily integrate their services into the final product firmware. For an example, for power management of the ARM system, PSCI is the interface used by non-secure or secure world software.

Bootloader stage 3-3: BL2 loads the BL33 image into the non-secure memory. BL33 is the first bootloader call outside the secure world, so platform owners can decide to use any BIOS solution as BL33. BL33 images can be any boot firmware like UEFI, coreboot, or U-Boot. BL31 initializes the EL2 or EL1 processor context for a non-secure world cold boot, ensuring that no secure state information finds its way into the non-secure execution state. BL31 uses the entry point information provided by BL2 to jump to the non-trusted firmware image (BL33) at the highest available exception level (mostly EL2; if not available, then EL1). The functionality perform by BL33 is as follows:

- **Platform initialization**: BL33 performs the following initialization:

- As memory is available and initialized, it performs the required set up for stack for running the C programming code.

- Initializes the UART controller for the serial console

- Has a non-volatile driver to access the system firmware

- Sets up MMU for caching if BL33 is running from non-secure SRAM.

- Performs GPIO programming and moving bootloader code from SRAM to DRAM (if not done already)

- Creates firmware code based on standard specifications like ACPI and SMBIOS.

- Performs boot device initialization and transfers control to the OS bootloader as part of the non-secure world

Figure 3-20 shows the Trusted Firmware boot flow which summarizes all these different bootloaders' minimalistic operational designs to perform SoC and platform initialization in a secure manner and finally boot to an OS.

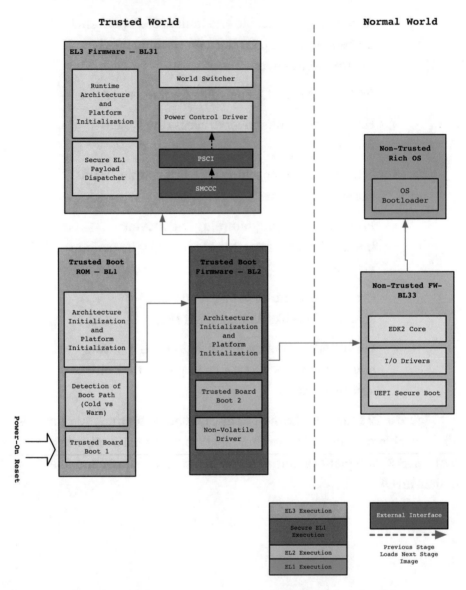

Figure 3-20. *Trusted Firmware minimalistic bootloader flow*

Summary

This chapter captured the roles and responsibilities that a system firmware needs to perform in order to be called a BIOS. We discussed in detail the types of BIOSes and their working principles. Additionally, this chapter revealed the minimalistic bootloader design across different CPU architectures. The chapter also resolved the mystery of the system initialization process prior to CPU reset (i.e., the pre-reset phase) and its prerequisites, and provided a detailed understanding of reset and various other boot and runtime operations made by the bootloader to ensure all required hardware and platform components are initialized as part of the bootloader execution. Having a minimal understanding of BIOS design in cross-architecture will help you create your own system firmware based on the target embedded system.

CHAPTER 4

System Firmware Architecture

"God is in the details."

—*Mies van der Rohe*

Architecture is a process that is used for developing a product. This process includes planning, designing, and constructing. Similarly, the firmware architecture represents the skeleton structure that a firmware implementation will build upon. The primary idea behind system firmware architecture is to design a minimalistic, robust, scalable, and fast solution that can be applied across different computer systems and embedded devices. Architecture demands a deeper knowledge of the applied domain.

Hence, Chapter 2 provided adequate details about the motherboard components (starting with processors and associated units like memory and peripheral devices) and its interfaces (communication between these motherboard components using various buses) while Chapter 3 covered the minimalistic system firmware design proposal based on platform hardware knowledge. When creating system firmware for the target embedded system, the developer needs to choose the right firmware

© Subrata Banik and Vincent Zimmer 2022
S. Banik and V. Zimmer, *System Firmware*,
https://doi.org/10.1007/978-1-4842-7939-7_4

solution from the diverse lists of available bootloaders. Without knowing the architecture of these bootloaders, it's difficult for developers to choose the correct system firmware for targeted hardware. This chapter will provide details on system firmware architecture from a programming environment perspective that involves understanding the boot phases, the interface to the platform hardware, and passing information to the operating systems.

Since this book is about open source firmware development, this chapter will emphasize popular open source bootloader architecture.

Unified Extensible Firmware Interface (UEFI): UEFI is a specification for developing system firmware on modern hardware. It's an interface between the firmware and the operating system. The primary principle of UEFI architecture is to create a modular and scalable interface that can be used as a unified framework (with minimal changes) for different hardware platforms. This chapter will analyze UEFI architecture in detail and its benefits over other bootloaders to guide you when to use UEFI as a boot solution.

coreboot: coreboot is an alternative approach for designing boot firmware solution with minimalistic, fast, and bare minimum hardware programming to make the system usable and pass the control to the suitable OS loader program (called the payload) for further booting to the OS. Due to the fact that it performs minimal programming, it doesn't impose any high-level specification while implementing firmware, so it's more applicable for embedded systems where direct access to the hardware is the minimum requirement. In this chapter, we will discuss the coreboot programming model and the architectural changes being done to make the firmware development process more modular and scalable across different SoC platforms with higher testing integrity.

Slim Bootloader (SBL): An open-source boot firmware designed for specific market segments like Internet of Things (IoT) devices where the requirement is for a lightweight, instant boot and flexible bootloader. Similar to coreboot, SBL separates the hardware initialization from the boot logic so that it can serve for the wider market requirement where the product choice of operating system could be from popular OSes like Windows and Linux to embedded OSes or RTOSes with minimal hardware initializations. Slim Bootloader's code base is optimized for fast boot using EDKII libraries.

UEFI Architecture

This section provides a brief overview of the UEFI architecture, previously known as the Extensible Firmware Interface (EFI), which defines an interface between the operating system and platform firmware. This interface provides several data tables that contain platform-related information, various services (boot and runtime), drivers and a path for platform devices to the OS loader for booting an OS or an OS-neutral value add application. It also needs to perform several hardware-specific initializations in order to collect platform-related information that can be used while preparing data for the service tables. Figure 4-1 shows the UEFI architecture overview.

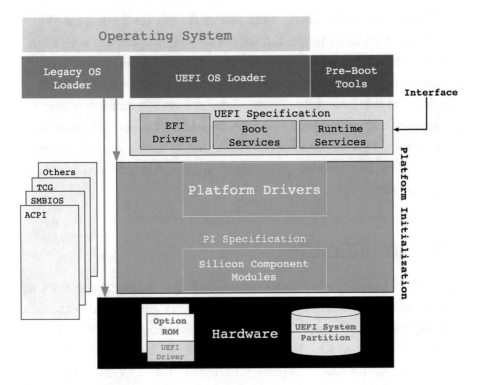

Figure 4-1. *UEFI architecture overview*

At a high level, the UEFI architecture is divided into two parts.

UEFI: It's a pure interface specification that is focused on booting or passing information and control to the next layer, typically referred to as an operating system loader. It's also capable of providing OS runtime services. All expectations from UEFI are part of the UEFI specification.

PI (Platform Initialization): Platform initialization focuses on initializing the hardware components since the platform reset. It defines the boot control being transferred from one phase to another phase and interoperability between the firmware modules as part of platform initialization. In fact, PI also implements the tables and services provided by the UEFI specification. The PI specification is the evolution of Intel Framework specifications, with additional capabilities.

UEFI and PI are interdependent interfaces required to create the system firmware using the UEFI architecture. UDK (the second generation of the EFI Development Kit (EDK) is EDKII), the UEFI Development Kit, is an open source project that provides the implementation of these specifications. Hence, any system firmware developed using open source EDKII should specify the underlying UEFI and PI specifications as well. For example, the latest development (as of May 2021) can be referred to as UEFI spec 2.9 and PI version 1.7.

UEFI Specification

Typically, a motherboard component includes a processor, a memory unit and various I/O devices and system firmware that is responsible for perform the required initialization prior to transferring the control to the OS loader. But as per the UEFI specification, it provides a programmatic interface between the OS, add-in drivers, and system firmware. These interfaces and services belonging to the UEFI specification are accessible by the operating systems, high-level software, and pre-OS applications. This section provide the architectural aspects of the interface. As per UEFI specification 2.9, here are few key concepts of UEFI that you need to understand:

- Objects
- UEFI images
- EFI services
- EFI system table
- Protocols
- Handling databases
- Events
- UEFI driver model

- Driver connection process

- Device paths

- EFI byte code (EBC)

Objects

Objects are the number of instances that UEFI-based firmware can manage through various services. Figure 4-2 shows the various object types of UEFI. The widely used objects are the following:

- EFI system table

- Handles

- Protocols

- Events

- Memory

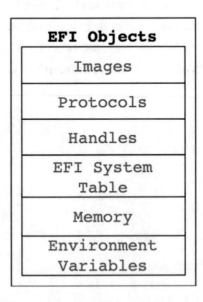

Figure 4-2. *Objects managed by UEFI-based system firmware*

Here is an example of the UEFI firmware managing several objects.

The UEFI specification introduces the concept of object-oriented thinking in system firmware programming, where each structure (handles, protocol, events, etc.) is represented as an object in the central object repository.

```
Status = gBS->InstallProtocolInterface (
        &gImageHandle,                 // Handle Object
        &gEfiShellProtocolGuid,
        EFI_NATIVE_INTERFACE,
        (VOID*)(&mShellProtocol)    // Protocol Object
        );
```

In the above example, the UEFI driver is installing a shell protocol object, which is part of the handle database. The handle database is composed of objects called handles and protocols; it's also the central repository for the objects maintained by the UEFI-based firmware. There are some UEFI drivers that may access the environment variable (depending on implementation, accessing stderr, stdin or stdout, etc.). Also, some UEFI drivers may use the platform timers and counters.

UEFI Images

This section describes the types of UEFI images, a set of files defined by UEFI that contain executable code. All UEFI images contain a PE/COFF image header, which follows the format defined by the Microsoft Portable Executable and Common Object File Format Specification. The image header contains information about the image type and processor type. The executable code can be for IA32, IA64, x64, ARM, RISC-V, or generic EBC, indicated by the machine code type field of the image. An UEFI image can be from the following three image types:

Image type	PE32+ subsystem type	Value
Application	EFI_IMAGE_SUBSYSTEM_EFI_APPLICATION	10
Boot services drivers	EFI_IMAGE_SUBSYSTEM_EFI_BOOT_SERVICE_DRIVER	11
Runtime drivers	EFI_IMAGE_SUBSYSTEM_EFI_RUNTIME_DRIVER	12

UEFI images can be located in different supported platform hardware, such as UEFI-aware Option ROMs on a PCI card device, UEFI-based system firmware in system ROM, UEFI-OS loader in block devices, and/ or LAN servers. All UEFI images are loaded into memory through the EFI_BOOT_SERVICES.LoadImage() Boot Service. UEFI images are not compiled and linked into a specific address; rather the PE32+ loader allows the entire PE32+ image to be completely loaded into the memory. After that, it performs all required relocation fix-ups. This allows the image to be position-independent and placed anywhere in the system memory. Once the UEFI image is loaded, it can be started with a boot service call to StartImage(). The header of the UEFI image contains the AddressOfEntryPoint that is called by EFI_BOOT_SERVICES.StartImage(). The entry point of a UEFI module always receives two parameters:

- ImageHandle: The firmware allocated handle for the EFI image. This allows UEFI modules to install events, protocols, and other services using the same image handle.

- SystemTable: A pointer to the EFI System Table. It allow access to all UEFI services that are available in the platform.

Apart from that, the operation performed by the UEFI image at the entry point varies depending on the type of the UEFI image and the purpose for that module. For example, the SimpleTextInOutSerial driver installs the EFI simple text input and output protocol at its entry point, SimpleTextInOutEntryPoint.

This table describes the types of UEFI images:

Application

An UEFI image of type application can be loaded either from system memory or non-volatile storage into the system memory by the boot manager or other UEFI application. Upon loading into the system memory, the application will start its execution at its entry point and automatically be unloaded from the memory when the image returns from the entry point or calls the exit() boot service function. The common examples of UEFI applications are the EFI Shell, the Flash updater utility running from the EFI shell, and diagnostic utilities. It's expected that none of the application instances will be part of system memory upon its exit.

There is one special type of UEFI application called an OS loader. It calls EFI_BOOT_SERVICES.ExitBootServices() to transfer the control to the operating system after it ensures that all of the required OS infrastructure is ready. At this stage, all boot time services will be eliminated, and the platform will have only runtime services.

(continued)

Drivers

An UEFI image of type driver can be loaded by the boot manager, UEFI core firmware, or by other UEFI applications. The UEFI drivers behave differently from UEFI applications after being loaded into the memory. Instances of UEFI drivers remain in the system memory unless it returns an error. After the driver is returned or exited from its entry point with success, it remains in memory and provides services to the other drivers, applications, or the OS. At a high level, the services provided by the drivers can be divided into two types: boot service drivers and runtime drivers.

Boot service drivers: The boot time drivers are loaded into memory by allocating the code and data as a type of `EfiBootServiceCode` and `EfiBootServiceData`. Hence, UEFI boot service drivers are terminated when `ExitBootServices()` is called, and all memory resources consumed by the UEFI boot service drivers are released.

Runtime drivers: The runtime drivers are loaded into memory by allocating the code and data as a type of `EfiRuntimeServiceCode` and `EfiRuntimeServiceData`. Hence, these types of memory are available even after the OS loader has taken control of the platform when the boot service `ExitBootServices()` is called. These services can be used by the runtime drivers while the operating system is running. For example, all of the UEFI variable services are required for managing multiple boot devices and security variables on the target systems.

Apart from these types, there are different types of drivers defined by the UEFI specification as service drivers, initializing drivers, root bridge drivers, bus drivers, device drivers, and hybrid drivers. The UEFI specification provides a special type of driver model as UEFI driver model; the bus, device, and hybrid drivers belong to this category.

UEFI driver model: Drivers that follow the UEFI driver model described in the UEFI specification aren't allowed to touch the hardware or start the device-related services at the entry point. Rather, at the entry point of a driver, it registers a set of services that allow the driver to be started and stopped based on the platform initialization demand.

(continued)

UEFI Services

The purpose of the UEFI interface is to provide a common abstraction layer while running the UEFI-based system firmware image that includes UEFI drivers, UEFI applications, and UEFI OS loaders. The EDKII provides a number of library functions that simplify the use of UEFI services and make the UEFI-based system firmware development process more modular and robust by increasing the readability while reducing the maintainability and code size, because UEFI modules can communicate between each other utilizing these services without duplicating code. This section provides an overview of the services defined by UEFI. The UEFI boot services and the UEFI runtime services are two categories of UEFI services as per the specification.

UEFI boot services

This section describes the UEFI boot services. During boot, the system resources are owned by the firmware and are controlled using the boot services interface functions. These functions can be either defined as *global* functions, meaning they are accessible for all system firmware modules, or *handle-based* functions, which are accessible for a specific device. Figure 4-3 provides a high-level list of boot services categories. Until the system control is present inside the firmware, the boot services function can be accessed, even from the UEFI application (including UEFI OS loaders). ExitBootServices is the function call that terminates all instances of boot services.

(continued)

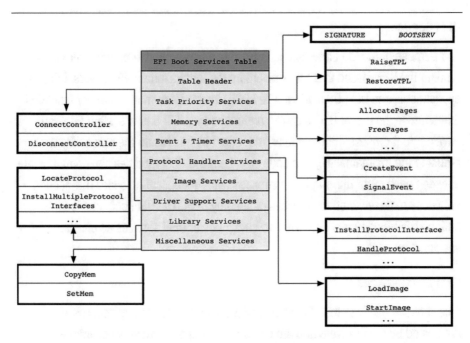

Figure 4-3. *EFI boot services table with functions*

By design, the ExitBootServices() call is intended for the operating system to indicate that its loader is ready to assume control of the platform and other resource management. Hence, the boot services are available up to the point where the OS loader is preparing to boot to the operating system. Once the UEFI OS loader takes control of the system and completes the operating system boot process, the only available services that remain are runtime services. The following code snippet shows an example of UEFI boot services. CopyMem() is part of the UEFI boot service used to copy a number of bytes from the source buffer of the memory copy to the destination buffer.

(*continued*)

```
#include <Uefi.h>
#include <Library/UefiBootServicesTableLib.h>
VOID *
EFIAPI
InternalMemCopyMem (
  OUT      VOID                        *Destination,
  IN           CONST VOID         *Source,
  IN           UINTN                     Length
  )
{
  gBS->CopyMem (Destination, (VOID*)Source, Length);
  return Destination;
}
```

UEFI Runtime Services

This section describes the UEFI runtime service function. The purpose of the runtime services is to abstract the platform hardware implementation from the OS. The runtime service functions are available both at the boot process and at runtime while the OS is running. While the OS loader and the OS use the runtime services, they need to call the SetVirtualAddressMap() service to switch into flat physical addressing mode to make the runtime call. Figure 4-4 describes the UEFI runtime service table and its functions.

(continued)

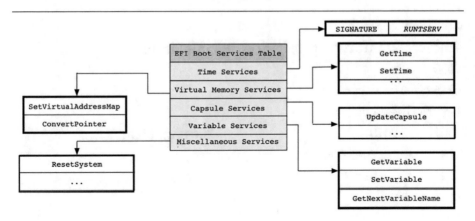

Figure 4-4. *EFI runtime services table with functions*

All the memory used by the runtime services must be reserved to ensure that those memory ranges are not being used by the OS. UEFI is responsible for defining the hardware resources used by the runtime services, so the OS can synchronize with those resources to make sure the OS never uses those resources while runtime service calls are being made. The following code snippet shows an example of the UEFI runtime services. ResetSystem() is part of the UEFI runtime service that allows a platform cold reset.

```
#include <Uefi.h>
#include <Library/UefiRuntimeServicesTableLib.h>
//
// Perform platform Cold Reset
//
VOID
EFIAPI
ResetCold (
 VOID
 )
{
 gRT->ResetSystem (EfiResetCold, EFI_SUCCESS, 0, NULL);
}
```

EFI System Table

UEFI uses the EFI system table, a very important data structure in UEFI, which contains pointers to the runtime and boot services table, configuration table, basic input and output console, and other miscellaneous pointers. Figure 4-5 shows the definition of the EFI system table. Prior to calling the EFI_BOOT_SERVICES.ExitBootServices() function, all of the EFI system table fields remained valid. After an operating system has taken control of the platform and with a call to ExitBootServices(), only the Hdr, version information (FirmwareVendor, FirmwareRevision), RuntimeServices, NumberOfTableEntries, and ConfigurationTable fields remain valid.

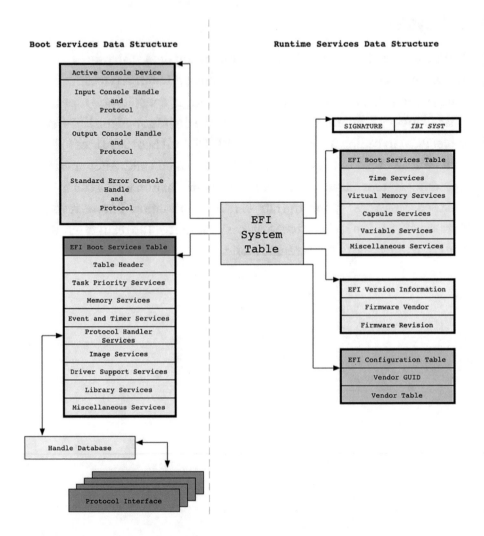

Figure 4-5. *EFI system table with data structures*

This section provides details about the EFI system table and its associated table entries. Earlier sections provided details about UEFI boot services and runtime services, so this section will only focus on the remaining table and other fields.

EFI configuration table: The ConfigurationTable field in the EFI system table is a pointer to the system configuration tables. Each entry of the table is described by the EFI_CONFIGURATION_TABLE structure. This structure contains a set of GUID and table pointer pairs. A platform might have more than one configuration table, so the NumberOfTableEntries field holds the number of system configuration tables in the ConfigurationTable buffer.

During the firmware boot, the UEFI firmware defines a number of custom and industry standard configuration tables into the EFI system table's configuration table including the following:

- EFI DXE services table: A table that holds the header for the DXE service table and services used by the DXE core like dispatcher and global coherency domain services.

- EFI_MEMORY_TYPE_INFORMATION: Provides the EFI memory types as per the specification.

- Industry standards define tables accessed as UEFI configuration tables on UEFI-based systems including

  - EFI_ACPI_TABLE_GUID

  - SAL_SYSTEM_TABLE_GUID

  - SMBIOS_TABLE_GUID

Apart from that, the EFI system table holds the handle and protocol for the active console input, output, and standard error console device.

Here is the sample code snippet to initialize the contents of the EFI system table using the template:

```
EFI_SYSTEM_TABLE        *gDxeCoreST = NULL;
//
// Allocate the EFI System Table
```

```
// Use the templates to initialize the contents of the EFI
System Table
//
gDxeCoreST = AllocateRuntimeCopyPool (sizeof (EFI_SYSTEM_
TABLE), &mEfiSystemTableTemplate);
ASSERT (gDxeCoreST != NULL);
```

Protocols

The extensible and modular nature of UEFI has been built around the protocols. The protocol is an agreement between UEFI drivers in order to exchange information. It follows the producer and consumer model, where one UEFI driver installs a variety of protocols using handles and any consumer UEFI driver that want to use that information needs to pass the unique identifier to retrieve the protocol interface structure. Each protocol has a specification that includes the following:

- A unique ID (GUID) that can help to identify the protocol in the handle database

- The protocol interface structure

- The protocol services

The UEFI protocol is typically a combination of several function pointers and data structures. Each protocol is associated with a unique GUID, which can be also referred to as the protocol's real name and used to find the protocol in the handle database. Figure 4-6 shows the construction of a protocol. The UEFI driver implements several protocol-specific functions and creates a structure that holds the pointers to those protocol specific-functions and private, device-specific data. The UEFI driver registers them with the boot service EFI_BOOT_SERVICES. InstallProtocolInterface() using a handle.

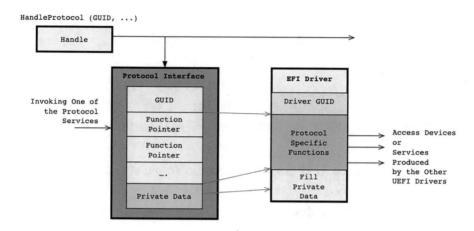

Figure 4-6. *Construction of a protocol*

The table below shows the actual implementation of a protocol where the firmware determine if the handle supports any given protocol specified by protocol's GUID passed to EFI_BOOT_SERVICES.HandleProtocol() or EFI_BOOT_SERVICES.OpenProtocol(). If the device supports the requested protocol, a pointer to the defined protocol interface structure is returned. The protocol interface structure can be used to call the protocol-specific services.

```
extern EFI_GUID gEfiSimpleTextInProtocolGuid;
typedef struct _EFI_SIMPLE_TEXT_INPUT_PROTOCOL  EFI_SIMPLE_
TEXT_INPUT_PROTOCOL;
//
// The EFI_SIMPLE_TEXT_INPUT_PROTOCOL is used on the
ConsoleIn device.
//
struct _EFI_SIMPLE_TEXT_INPUT_PROTOCOL {
  EFI_INPUT_RESET      Reset;
  EFI_INPUT_READ_KEY   ReadKeyStroke;
  //
  // Event to use with WaitForEvent() to wait for a key to be
    available
```

```
  //
  EFI_EVENT              WaitForKey;
};
EFI_STATUS                        Status;
EFI_HANDLE                        Handle;
EFI_SIMPLE_TEXT_INPUT_PROTOCOL    *SimpleTextInput;
//
// Open the Simple Text Input Protocol BY_DRIVER.
//
Status = gBS->OpenProtocol (
                 Handle,
                 &gEfiSimpleTextInProtocolGuid,
                 (VOID **) &SimpleTextInput,
                 This->DriverBindingHandle,
                 Handle,
                 EFI_OPEN_PROTOCOL_BY_DRIVER
                 );
ASSERT ((Status == EFI_SUCCESS) || (Status == EFI_ALREADY_STARTED));
```

Here is a list of some widely used UEFI protocols defined by the specification:

Protocol	Description
EFI_LOADED_IMAGE_PROTOCOL	Provides information on the image
EFI_DEVICE_PATH_PROTOCOL	Provide the location information of the device
EFI_SIMPLE_TEXT_INPUT_ PROTOCOL	Protocol interface for devices that support simple console text input
EFI_BLOCK_IO_PROTOCOL	Protocol interface for device that support block I/O accesses
EFI_PCI_IO_PROTOCOL	Protocol to abstract memory, I/O, PCI configuration, and DMA accesses to a PCI root bridge controller

Globally Unique Identifier (GUIDs)

A unique identifier used in UEFI-based firmware is specified by a GUID, a unique 128-bit number defined by the Wired for Management (WfM) 2.0 specification. Protocols are named using a GUID. The code snippet is a GUID definition. Developers need to generate a GUID when creating an image, protocol, or device as defined in UEFI.

```
//
// 128 bit buffer containing a unique identifier value.
//
typedef struct {
  UINT32  Data1;
  UINT16  Data2;
  UINT16  Data3;
  UINT8   Data4[8];
} EFI_GUID;

//
// The global ID for the Simple Text Input Protocol.
//
#define EFI_SIMPLE_TEXT_INPUT_PROTOCOL_GUID \
  { \
    0x387477c1, 0x69c7, 0x11d2, {0x8e, 0x39, 0x0, 0xa0, 0xc9,
    0x69, 0x72, 0x3b } \
  }
```

Facts   The GUIDGEN utility is used on Windows machines (or the uuidgen command under Linux) to generate GUIDs. Other GUID generation utilities may be found on the Internet.

Handle Database

The *handle database* contains objects called *Handles* and *Protocols*.
Handles are a collection of one or more protocols, and protocols are data
structures that consist of function pointers and data fields. During platform
initialization, the system firmware, UEFI modules, and UEFI applications
will create handles to register protocols to those handles. The handle
database can be accessed globally, meaning any UEFI module can install
a protocol on a handle, pass a handle identifier to check if it supports a
given protocol, and check if the device supports the device path protocol.
The handle database is built dynamically by calling the boot service
`InstallProtocolInterface()` function. It's like the central repository for
the objects that are managed by the UEFI-based firmware. Each handle
is identified by a unique handle number, a *key* to an entry in the handle
database. Figure 4-7 shows the representation of the handle database.

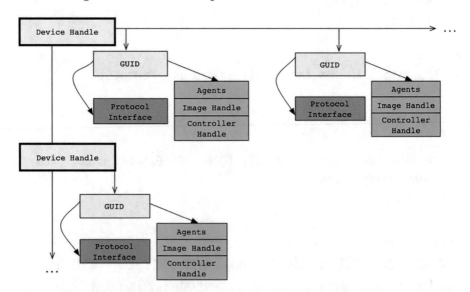

Figure 4-7. *Handle database*

Apart from handles and protocols, each protocol interface includes a list of *agents* that are consuming the protocol interface. This information is critical to ensure that UEFI drivers can safely start or stop any services on a given handler. An agent can consist of an *image handle,* used to identify the driver or application that is consuming the protocol interface, or a *controller handle,* which identifies the controller that is consuming the protocol interface.

Events

As UEFI doesn't support interrupts, it needs to provide an option for developers who may want to use an interrupt driven driver model. Events are the solution for that kind of usage. They're objects that provide a synchronous and asynchronous call back upon a particular occurrence. The UEFI specification defined a bunch of boot services for managing event, timer, and task priority at the preboot. A UEFI image allows operations like create, close, signal, and wait for events; setting timers; and raising and restoring task priority levels. The following three elements are associated with every event:

- The Task Priority Level (TPL) of an event

- A notification function

- A notification context

The notification function will execute based on its associated event change in state (for a wait event, the function will notify whenever the event is checked or waited upon) or being signaled (from the waiting state to the signaled state). The notification context is passed into the notification function each time the notification function gets executed. The TPL is to define the priority in which the notification function is executed. There are four TPL levels that are defined by these specifications:

Task priority level	Values	Description
TPL_APPLICATION	4	The lowest priority level in which UEFI images are executed
TPL_CALLBACK	8	Defined for most notified functions
TPL_NOTIFY	16	An intermediate priority level at which most I/O operations are performed
TPL_HIGH_LEVEL	31	The highest priority level for any event to operate

TPLs are used for the following purposes:

- To define the priority between more than one event in the signaled state at the same time. In these cases, the notification function associated with higher priority will be executed first.

- To create locks to avoid multiple functions (one in normal execution and one triggered by the event) accessing the shared data structure at the same time while getting executed. A lock can be created by temporarily raising the task priority level to TPL_HIGH_LEVEL.

UEFI Driver Model

Drivers that follow the UEFI driver model share the same characteristics of EFI drivers and applications. However, the UEFI driver model allows more control by the driver by separating the driver loading into memory from its being operated on the host controller, bus, or endpoint device. UEFI drivers that follow this model are registered with EFI_DRIVER_BINDING_ PROTOCOL on the driver's image handle. These drivers are not allowed to touch the controller at the entrypoint, so they install the driver binding protocol after loading the driver and exit successfully. Figure 4-8 shows the driver initialization using the UEFI driver model.

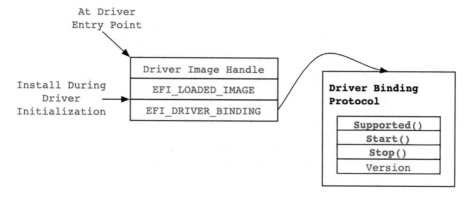

Figure 4-8. *Device initialization using the UEFI driver model*

Later boot stages (discussed in the "Platform Initialization" section) will make use of these handles to identify the best drivers for a controller. The UEFI Driver Model defines the following two basic types of UEFI boot time drivers: device drivers and bus drivers. A driver that has characteristics of both a device driver and a bus driver is known as a hybrid driver. Device drivers and bus drivers have distinguished operations to perform at the Start() and Stop() services of the EFI_DRIVER_BINDING_ PROTOCOL.

EFI Driver Binding Protocol

This section provides a high-level overview of the EFI_DRIVER_BINDING_ PROTOCOL. All UEFI drivers that follow the UEFI Driver Model must install at least one instance of this protocol at its entry point. This protocol controls the behavior of the driver on the controller. It provides three services to operate on a controller based on the given image handle:

- **Supported**: A service to test if a driver supports a given controller. This service is called by the EFI boot service ConnectController.

- **Start**: If a controller is supported, then the driver will start using the controller. Based on the type of driver, it performs additional operations besides initializing the controller and publishing the required protocols for other drivers or applications to use. For example, bus drivers create child handles for devices that are visible on the bus, so a PCI bus driver may discover and enumerate all PCI devices on the bus and create handles for all child controllers in its first call to Start().

- **Stop**: Stops a controller using this driver. This service is called by the EFI boot service DisconnectController.

Driver Connection Process

UEFI allows the extension of the platform firmware by loading the UEFI drivers and UEFI applications. The driver connection process is performed by the system firmware to make all the hardware controllers, buses, and devices available for the boot manager for further booting to the OS loader or the UEFI application. The EFI boot service EFI_BOOT_SERVICES. ConnectController() is called with a given ControllerHandle to identify the best driver for the controller.

```
EFI_STATUS   Status;
UINTN        HandleCount;
EFI_HANDLE   *HandleBuffer;
UINTN        Index;
```

```
Status = gBS->LocateHandleBuffer (
                AllHandles,
                NULL,
                NULL,
                &HandleCount,
                &HandleBuffer
                );
if (EFI_ERROR (Status)) {
  return Status;
}

for (Index = 0; Index < HandleCount; Index++) {
  Status = gBS->ConnectController (HandleBuffer[Index], NULL,
  NULL, TRUE);
}

if (HandleBuffer != NULL) {
  FreePool (HandleBuffer);
}
```

The ConnectController() function is called at BDS phase to connect
all current system handles (using AllHandles) recursively. If the handle
is a bus type handler, all children also will be connected recursively.
This will make sure that application and OS loader will have access to all
UEFI-defined services as required to boot an operating system from a boot
medium. See Figure 4-9.

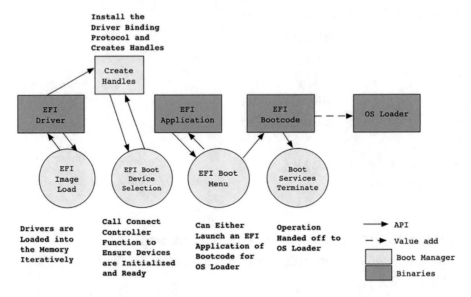

Figure 4-9. *UEFI-based system firmware connecting drivers*

Device Paths

A device path is used to define the programmatic path to a device. It allows us to determine the physical location of the device that the interfaces are abstracting. EFI defines a protocol EFI_DEVICE_PATH_PROTOCOL that is attached with a device handle, located in the handle database to help system firmware include drivers, applications, and operating system loaders to identify the hardware that the device handle represents. The device path protocol provides a unique name for each physical device, called a namespace. A device path is a data structure that is a collection of one or more device path nodes, as shown in example below. The next table shows an example of partition #1 of an IDE hard disk holding a boot target attached to a PCI IDE controller attached to PCI root bridge #0.

PCI Root Bridge #0 using a standard ACPI device path

```
Acpi (PNP0A03, 0)
```

A PCI IDE controller (Bus 0: Device 0x17: Function 0) is attached to the PCI Root Bridge #0

```
Acpi (PNP0A03, 0)/Pci(17|0)
```

Device path for the IDE hard disk attached to the PCI IDE controller

```
Acpi (PNP0A03, 0)/Pci(17|0)/Ata (Primary, Master)
```

Initializing partition #1 of an ATA drive

```
Acpi (PNP0A03, 0)/Pci(17|0)/Ata (Primary, Master)/HD(Part1,
Sig00000000)
```

EFI OS loader located in partition #1 of an ATA drive

```
Acpi (PNP0A03, 0)/Pci(17|0)/Ata (Primary, Master)/HD(Part1,
Sig00000000)/"\EFI\Boot"/"OSLoader.efi"
```

A device path structure doesn't contain any pointer hence its position is independent. The UEFI specification defines six types of device path nodes to describe device paths, shown below, and is terminated by a special device path node called an *end device path node*.

Type of device path node	Description
Hardware	Describe the device that appears on industry-standard buses that are directly accessible through processor memory or I/O cycles. Example: devices on the buses like PCI
ACPI	Devices that are specified using HID, CID, and UID, meaning they can't be defined using standard bus terminologies. Example: PCI root bridges
Messaging	Devices that belong to industry standard buses but can't be accessed using processor memory or I/O cycles. Example: USB and ATA need dedicated bus protocol for communication
Media	Hard disk, CD-ROM, and file paths that support multiple directory levels
BBS (BIOS boot specification)	These device path nodes are used only in a platform that supports BIOS INT services.
End of hardware	To mark the end of a device path

EFI Byte Code

This section defines EBC, a pseudo or virtual machine that can interpret a predefined instruction set. EBC virtual machines can provide platform- and processor-independent mechanism binaries. EBC Option ROM images are architecture-independent and they are not limited to a predetermined, fixed maximum size. EBC interpreters can be implemented for any processor architecture. The advantages of EBC are abstract and extensible design, processor independence, and OS independence. EBC also facilitates the removal of legacy infrastructure and provides exclusive use of EFI services such as Option ROM.

The VM supports an EBC instruction set that performs data movement, data manipulation, branching, and other miscellaneous operations typical of a simple processor. The EBC virtual machine utilizes a simple register set. There are two categories of VM registers: general purpose registers and dedicated registers. All registers are 64-bits wide. There are eight general-purpose registers (R0-R7), which are used by most EBC instructions to manipulate or fetch data. Dedicated registers are the instruction pointer (IP) and the flags (Flags) register. All EBC images are in the PE32+ format. A given EBC image must be executable on different platforms, independent of whether it is a 32- or 64-bit processor.

UEFI defines the EFI_EBC_PROTOCOL protocol that allows execution of EBC images. The code below shows the services provided by EFI_EBC_PROTOCOL, which are typically loaded into Option ROMs. The image loader will load the EBC image, perform standard relocations, and invoke the CreateThunk() service to create a thunk for the EBC image's entry point. The entry point of an EBC image holds the EBC instructions, so it is not directly executable by the native processor. Therefore, when an EBC image is loaded, the loader must call the EbcCreateThunk service to get a pointer to native code (thunk) that can be executed, which will invoke the interpreter to begin execution at the original EBC entry point.

```
#define EFI_EBC_INTERPRETER_PROTOCOL_GUID \
  { \
    0x13AC6DD1, 0x73D0, 0x11D4, {0xB0, 0x6B, 0x00, 0xAA, 0x00, \
    0xBD, 0x6D, 0xE7 } \
  }

struct _EFI_EBC_PROTOCOL {
  EFI_EBC_CREATE_THUNK          CreateThunk;
  EFI_EBC_UNLOAD_IMAGE          UnloadImage;
  EFI_EBC_REGISTER_ICACHE_FLUSH RegisterICacheFlush;
  EFI_EBC_GET_VERSION           GetVersion;
};
```

Platform Initialization Specification

The PI Specification is another part of the specification published
by the Platform Initialization Working Group (PIWG) that describes
interoperability between firmware components from different providers.
This specification works in conjunction with the UEFI specification. The
contains of this specification can be divided into the following:

- Core code and services required by the pre-EFI
  initialization (PEI) phase

- Core code and services required by the Driver
  Execution Environment (DXE)

- Basic PI firmware storage concepts include firmware
  volumes, firmware file systems, PEI PEIM-to-
  PEIM interfaces (PPIs) and DXE protocols, and
  implementation of hand-off blocks (HOBs).

- Management mode core interface

- Standards

Figure 4-10 shows the architectural and operational overview of the PI
specification.

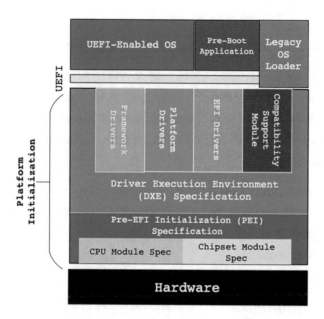

Figure 4-10. *Architectural and operational overview of PI*

PI describes the phases of boot control from the platform reset to the booting until the operating system, including the internal interfaces between these different firmwares.

This chapter explains the boot phases and the internal interfaces used during the boot. The UEFI-based system firmware divides the boot phases into the following:

- **Security (SEC) phase:** This phase inspections the very first opcode that the system will execute after coming from reset on to ensure that the system firmware image is trustworthy.

- **Pre-EFI initialization phase:** An intermediate stage that is responsible for discovering memory and preparing a resource map for the next phase (DXE).

The early information gathered in this stage transits to the DXE phase using the PEI-to-DXE handoff.

- **Driver execution environment (DXE) phase:** This phase is responsible for creating foundation code that publishes a set of services and creates a dispatcher to find and load the appropriate EFI drivers for the set of devices.

- **Boot device selection (BDS) phase:** The primary task of this stage is to find and load the boot manager. This component is responsible for determining the target OS to boot.

- **Transient system load (TSL) phase:** This phase allows service interfaces to be available to OS loaders before the platform is taken over completely by the OS kernel.

- **Run time (RT) phase:** This phase provides a set of drivers that remains operational even after OS has taken the platform control.

- **After life (AL) phase:** This phase is designed to allow platform firmware to execute after the OS in the case of voluntary or involuntary termination of the OS like hardware failure or OS crashes.

Figure 4-11 shows the PI boot phases.

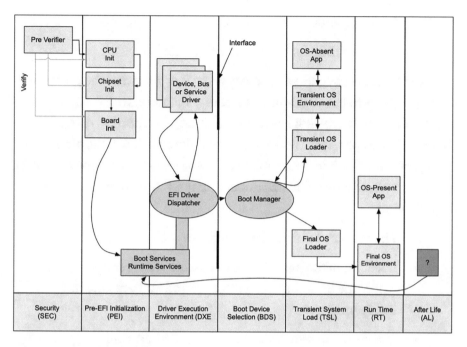

Figure 4-11. *PI boot phases*

Security Phase

The SEC phase is the first phase in the PI architecture representing the root of trust in a platform that has core root-of-trust maintenance from the reset vector. The responsibilities of the SEC phase are as follows:

- Contains the RESET vector for handling a platform reset event

- Initializes the temporary memory

Facts   On the x86 platform, the SEC phase is responsible for making use of processor cache as RAM (CAR) in the absence of real physical memory and performing any specific early processor-related operations like protected mode switches.

- Passing handoff information to the PEI foundation

- Serves as the root of trust in the system

The SEC phase begins with power-on so it expects that the processor has capabilities to produce some temporary memory, which might be processor cache, system static RAM (SRAM), or a portion of the DRAM mapped physical memory, and prior knowledge of the platform configuration like where this temporary memory can be mapped. The SEC phase is required to provide information to the PEI foundation including the following:

- The results of the processor built-in self-test (BIST)

- Location of the boot firmware volume (BFV), from where the SEC phase will discover and authenticate the PEI foundation

- Location and size of the temporary memory and the stack

In addition to that, the SEC phase can provide a set of services like the Security PPI and a Trusted Computing Group (TCG) PPI. These services allow the Core Root-of-Trust Module (CRTM) to have the necessary services to authenticate the PEI foundation, and the PEI foundation can also reuse these services using PPI without reimplementation.

Pre-EFI Initialization Phase

The PEI phase of the PI architecture is invoked right after the SEC phase in the boot flow. The PEI phase uses the temporary memory as a call stack to dispatch the Pre-EFI Initialization Modules (PEIMs) and populate the PEI services. The responsibilities of the PEI phase are the following:

- Provides a standardized method of loading and invoking specific initial configuration routines for the processor, chipset, and motherboard

- Initializes the permanent memory

- Initializes enough of the system, passes information in form of HOBs, and allow instantiation of the DXE phase

- Determines the system boot path in any machine reset and recovers from corruption of the firmware storage space

Typically, the PEI phase is intended to do the minimalist tasks listed above to provide a stable base for follow-on phases. The PEI phase provides a common framework that allows independent implementation of initialization modules. Figure 4-13 shows the operational diagram of the PEI phase. This framework consists of the following parts.

PEI Foundation

The processor architecture independent portable executable binary responsible for performing these operations:

- Dispatching the PEIMs using PEI Dispatcher

- Determining the boot mode for ensuring fast resume with minimal platform initialization through firmware code

- Initializing the permanent memory

- Invoking the DXE loader

- Providing a set of common core services used by PEIMs, called PEI Services

- Assisting PEIMs in communicating with each other

PEI Services

A system table named the PEI Service Table (EFI_PEI_SERVICES) is created by the PEI Foundation as part of PeiMain.c, which is a collection of functions manifested by the PEI Foundation when the services' initialization requirements are met. These services can be divided into these classes:

Type of services	Function	Description
PPI	InstallPpi, ReInstallPpi, LocatePpi, NotifyPpi	Allows intermodule calls between PEIMs and tracks using a database maintained in temporary RAM
Boot mode	GetBootMode, SetBootMode	To identify the platform reset scenarios like S3, S5, normal mode
HOB	GetHobList, CreateHob	Creates data structures called HOBs to pass information between the PEI and DXE phases
Firmware volume	FfsFindNextVolume, FfsFindNextFile, etc.	Finds PEIMs and other firmware files in the firmware volumes.
PEI memory	InstallPeiMemory, AllocatePages, Copy/SetMem, etc.	Provides memory management services for both temporary and permanent memory
Status code	ReportStatusCode	Provides system firmware progress and error codes (part of Appendix A)
Reset	ResetSystem	Allows resetting the system. Example: warm, cold reset of the system

In absence of physical memory, a pointer to the PEI Service Table is passed as an argument of the PEIM's entry point and also to part of each PPI.

PEI Dispatcher

The PEI Dispatcher is a state machine implemented by the PEI Foundation. Its job is to hand control the PEIMs in an orderly manner. The PEI Dispatcher consists of a single phase. During the execution of this phase, the PEI Foundation examines each file in the firmware volumes that contain files of type PEIM. A dependency expression (*TRUE* or *FALSE*) is code associated with each driver that describes the dependencies that must be satisfied for that driver to run. It examines the dependency expression (depex) within each firmware file to decide if a PEIM can run. Once the dependency expression is evaluated to TRUE, the PEI Foundation passes control to the PEIM with a true dependency expression. The PEI dispatcher will exit after it has evaluated all of the PEIMs that are part of the exposed firmware volume.

Pre-EFI Initialization Modules

PEIMs are specialized drivers that encapsulate processor, chipset, device, or other platform-specific functionality. Due to the fact that PEI phase is executed while minimal hardware resources are available, the PEI phase provides mechanisms for PEIMs to locate and invoke interfaces to communicate between other PEIMs or the PEI Foundation. These PEIMs reside in ROM in either a compressed or uncompressed format depending on the memory that it will operate on.

PEIM-to-PEIM Interfaces (PPIs)

PEIMs communicate with each other using a structure called PEIM-to-PEIM Interface. Each PPI is named using GUIDs to allow the independent development and register a unique interface into the identifier database without any naming collision. The PPIs are defined as structures that contain functions and data. The PEIM must register a PPI into the PPI database using InstallPpi() or ReInstallPpi() PEI services. A consumer PEIM uses the LocatePpi() PEI service to access the interface. Based on operations, PPIs can be divided into two types:

- **PPI services**: A PEIM provides a function and/or data for another PEIM to use using PPI services.

- **PPI notifications**: A PEIM to register for a callback when another PPI is registered with the PEI Foundation

Firmware Volumes (FVs)

PEIMs reside in Firmware Volumes. The Boot Firmware Volume (BFV) contains the PEI Foundation and PEIMs. The PEI phase supports the ability to have multiple firmware volumes.

Hand-Off Blocks (HOBs)

UEFI-based system firmware performs platform initialization as part of PEI phase prior transferring the control to the DXE Foundation. The platform information required to pass from the PEI phase to the DXE phase uses a mechanism called a HOB. It's a processor microarchitecture independent data structure with a header and data section. The header definition is common for all HOBs and allows any code using this definition to know two items:

- The format of the data section

- The total size of the HOB

The sequential list of HOBs available in permanent memory is referred to as the HOB list. The HOB list must contain at least one HOB named the Phase Handoff Information Table (PHIT) HOB, the first HOB in the HOB list that describes the information as physical memory used by the PEI phase and the boot mode discovered during the PEI phase, and one or more resource descriptor HOBs as per firmware need. Only PEI components are allowed to make additions or changes to HOBs. Once the HOB list is passed into DXE, it will be treated as read-only for DXE components. Figure 4-12 describes the PEI-to-DXE handoff.

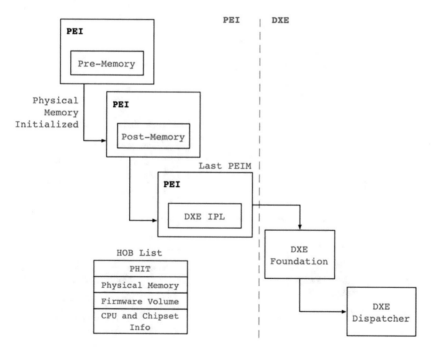

Figure 4-12. *PEI-to-DXE handoff*

Dispatch of the DXE Foundation

After dispatching all PEIMs from the firmware volumes, the PEI dispatcher job is complete and it invokes a special architectural PPI named DXE Initial Program Load PPI (EFI_DXE_IPL_PPI) to discover and dispatch the DXE Foundation and components that are needed to run the DXE Foundation. The DXE IPL PPI passes the HOB list from PEI to the DXE Foundation while it invokes the DXE Foundation. See Figure 4-13.

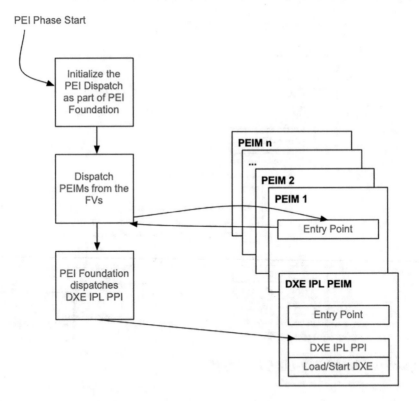

Figure 4-13. *Operational diagram of the PEI phase*

Driver Execution Environment Phase

The DXE phase defined by UEFI-based system firmware is where the majority of the platform initialization is performed. The PEI phase prior to the DXE phase is responsible for initializing the permanent memory in the platform so, regardless of the DXE phase being in the system ROM, it gets loaded and executed from the physical memory. At the end of the PEI phase, the system state information is passed to the DXE phase through HOBs. The responsibilities of the DXE phase are as follows:

- Initializes the processor, chipset, and platform components and provides interfaces (as Boot Services, Runtime Services and DXE Services) to the OS or UEFI applications

- The DXE and Boot Device Selection (BDS) phases work together to establish consoles and attempt the booting of the OS.

As per the DXE specification, the components in the DXE phase include

- **DXE Foundation**: The DXE Foundation produces a set of UEFI Services.

- **DXE Dispatcher**: The DXE Dispatcher is responsible for discovering and executing DXE drivers as per the order in the Firmware Volume.

- **A set of DXE drivers**: The DXE drivers are responsible for platform initialization and providing software abstractions for console and boot devices.

These components work together to initialize the platform and provide the services required to boot an OS.

DXE Foundation

The DXE Foundation is a boot service image that produces the EFI system table and the associated set of UEFI services: UEFI boot services, UEFI runtime services, and DXE services. The DXE Dispatcher is also part of DXE Foundation and is responsible for discovering and dispatching the DXE drivers after resolving their dependency expression as they appear in the Firmware Volumes. The DXE Foundation consumes the HOB list and architectural protocols to provide the UEFI services.

The DXE Foundation only has dependency on the HOB list from its previous operational state, hence instances of the prior phases can be unloaded once the HOB list is passed to the DXE Foundation. The DXE Foundation is a microarchitecture-neutral implementation that is abstracted from the platform hardware through a set of architectural protocol interfaces. The DXE Foundation is also responsible for maintaining the Handle Database.

DXE Dispatcher

The DXE Dispatcher is one component of the DXE Foundation. The firmware control is handed to the DXE Dispatcher after the DXE Foundation is initialized. The DXE Dispatcher is responsible for loading and invoking DXE drivers found in Firmware Volumes. The DXE Dispatcher searches for drivers in the firmware volumes described by the a priori file (optionally) and dependency expressions that are part of the drivers. After the DXE drivers whose dependency expressions evaluate to TRUE have been loaded and executed by the DXE Dispatcher, control is transferred from the DXE Dispatcher to the BDS Architectural Protocol. The BDS Architectural Protocol is responsible for establishing the console devices and attempting the boot of the OS.

DXE Drivers

We've already provided details about the DXE drivers and types. The expectation for the DXE drivers is to perform the initialization of the processor, chipset, and platform and to produce the DXE Architectural Protocol and other protocol services used to abstract the platform hardware.

DXE Architectural Protocols

The DXE Foundation is abstracted from the platform hardware through a set of DXE Architectural Protocols. DXE drivers that are loaded from firmware volumes produce the DXE Architectural Protocols, functions that are consumed by DXE Foundation to produce the EFI boot services and EFI runtime services. The early DXE drivers produce the DXE Architectural Protocols, so the DXE Foundation can produce the full complement of EFI boot services and EFI runtime services. Here are a few examples of DXE Architectural Protocols:

BDS Architectural Protocols	Provides an entry point that the DXE Foundation can call to transfer the control to the BDS phase
Variable Architectural Protocols	Provides the services to read/write volatile environment variables

Figure 4-14 shows the operational diagram of the DXE phase.

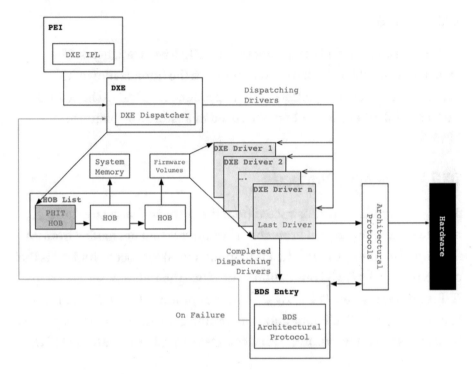

Figure 4-14. *Operational diagram of the DXE phase*

Boot Device Selection Phase

The system firmware control is transferred to the BDS phase after DXE
Dispatcher has executed all the DXE drivers. The BDS Architecture
Protocol is discovered in the DXE phase and the control is transferred into
its entry point after these two conditions are met:

- All of the DXE Architectural Protocols have been
  registered in the handle database. This condition is
  required for the DXE Foundation to produce the full
  complement of EFI boot services and EFI runtime
  services.

- The DXE Dispatcher does not have any more DXE drivers to load and execute.

The BDS phase is responsible for establishing consoles (Console IN, Console OUT, and Standard Error), enabling the boot devices required to boot an OS and implementing the platform boot policies. If there is an error in the BDS phase and it can't make forward progress, it will reinvoke the DXE Dispatcher (as shown in Figure 4-14).

Transient System Load Phase

The BDS phase is terminated when an OS loader is executed. The Transient System Load (TSL) is primarily the OS vendor-provided EFI application. The OS loader creates all required infrastructure for ensuring the successful loading of an operating system. It calls the boot service ExitBootServices() that frees up all of the boot service components and those resources are not available for use by the operating system. At this stage, the only available services are the runtime services and the firmware enters into the Runtime (RT) phase.

Runtime Phase

The RT phase can coexist with the operating system being operational and running. The system control now is with the platform OS. UEFI has a limited set of runtime services (discussed earlier) that are available for the OS to use. The most common runtime services are being used to perform reset of the platform and the usage of the real-time clock. While the OS uses the runtime services, it needs to call the SetVirtualAddressMap() service to switch into flat physical addressing mode to make the runtime call.

After Life Phase

The BDS phase (via TSL) is terminated when the OS loader is executed and the OS is successfully booted. At that stage, only a small set of UEFI is left behind to support recovery from any catastrophic scenarios due to hardware or OS failures. This is called the AL phase.

This summarizes the responsibility of the PI specification and the interoperability between the UEFI and PI specifications combined the system firmware architecture using UEFI. This section provided a brief overview of all key terminologies used in the UEFI architecture and the boot flow to understand where these concepts are applied.

coreboot Architecture

This section provides a brief overview of coreboot, an open source firmware project begun in 1999 (originally named as LinuxBIOS and later renamed to coreboot in 2008) with a goal of creating system firmware for embedded systems that can do the minimum hardware initialization required to transfer control to an OS loader (payload) and run an operating system. Figure 4-15 provides a coreboot architecture diagram to highlight that coreboot design and development philosophy, which is different from the UEFI architecture. Unlike the UEFI architecture, coreboot doesn't provide a separate specification for initializing platform components and abstracting devices access through an interface to higher-level system software. In fact, coreboot doesn't provide any specification.

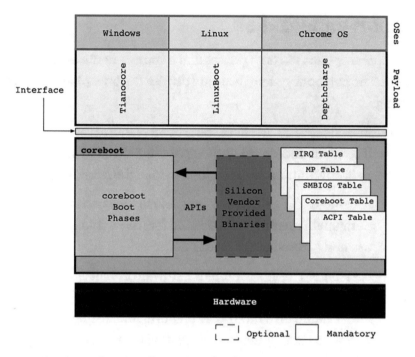

Figure 4-15. *coreboot architecture overview*

This is made possible by moving the interfaces and resident services to the payload. coreboot supports a variety of payloads that can provide user interfaces, file system drivers, applications, and boot managers to load the OS. Popular payloads in use with coreboot are Tianocore (used for launching EFI-aware Windows OS and native UEFI diagnostic tools), LinuxBoot (for Linux distributions on servers), or Depthcharge (a specific OS loader for ChromeOS platforms). coreboot uses a very minimal interface to the payload and a small piece of code is left behind in the system to provide the runtime services.

Platform Initialization

This chapter explains the boot phases and internal interfaces used during the boot. The coreboot system firmware divides the boot phases into the following:

- **bootblock**: The first boot stage upon platform reset, it contains code for early processor initialization and performs minimal initialization to load the next stage.

- **romstage**: Typically, it's responsible for performing permanent memory initialization for the next stage to use and early chipset initialization.

- **ramstage**: The most complex hardware initialization is performed by this stage, like multiprocessor initialization on a multi-core platform, initializing peripheral components, and creating the required infrastructure to transfer the control to the payload.

- **payload**: An OS loader program is separate from coreboot and retrieves platform state information using the coreboot interface. Also, it uses a static library named libpayload, part of the coreboot project to get access to SoC, platform device drivers required to boot to an operating system. Chapter 6 provides details on payload.

Apart from that, there are two further stages (one is optional and one is intermediate):

- **verstage**: An optional stage in the coreboot project, used to establish the trust in the system firmware boot process. verstage is part of Read-Only Firmware block, loaded by the bootblock to validate the Read-Write/ Updatable firmware section in the flash layout prior loading in memory.

- **postcar**: An intermediate stage used to tear down the temporary memory and load the ramstage. It's typically used in x86-based system firmware design.

Figure 4-16 shows the coreboot platform initialization boot phases.

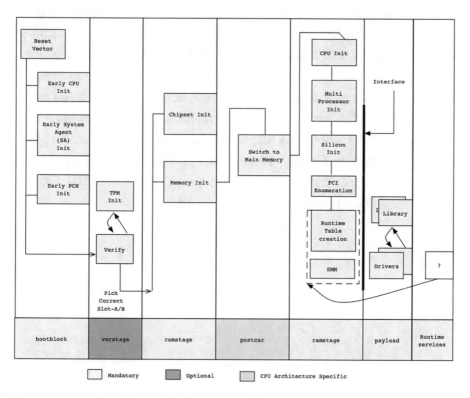

Figure 4-16. *coreboot platform initialization boot phases*

These coreboot stages are compiled as separate binaries and are inserted into the CBFS (coreboot file system). The components inside the CBFS can be placed as compressed or uncompressed based on their usage. For example, the bootblock stage is executed immediately after CPU reset (typically running from SPI mapped memory) so it is kept uncompressed while ramstage and payload are compressed with LZMA. Each stage loads the next stage at a given address (after decompressing if applicable). To improve the boot performance, some stages are relocated and loaded into permanent memory and also cached in CBMEM for faster resume.

CBFS: CBFS provides a mechanism that allows us to have the independent blobs as part of the system ROM. It's a data structure used to store essential information about the ROM that can be used by both the coreboot CBFS implementation while locating any blobs as well as utilities while creating the final ROM image. Cbfstool is a utility for managing the CBFS components during the final firmware image (.ROM) generation process. CBFS components are placed in the ROM starting at the offset data field in the cbfs_header data structure. Each CBFS component has its own header that contains a magic field to identify the CBFS, len, type, checksum and offset. Figure 4-17 shows the coreboot ROM layout of ChromeOS platform that contains three cbfs as COREBOOT (RO) cbfs, FW_MAIN_A (RW) cbfs, and FW_MAIN_B (RW) cbfs.

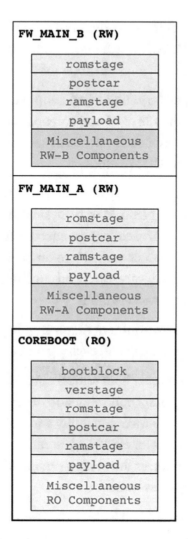

Figure 4-17. *CBFS layout*

Bootblock

The bootblock is the first stage of coreboot that is executed upon the CPU coming out from reset. In the multicore processor scenario, the bootblock code runs on the Boot Strap Processor (BSP) in a memory-constrained manner in absence of real physical memory. Based on the

CPU architecture, the bootblock code runs from either system static RAM (SRAM) or a portion of the SPI that is memory mapped. Operations performed by the bootblock phase include the following:

- Processor-specific initialization as applicable. For example, on the x86 platform, coreboot needs to perform processor mode switch or set up MMU for caching on the ARM platform.

- Setting up the temporary ram (as Cache as RAM, a.k.a. CAR) in absence of SRAM or if physical memory is not yet available (CPU architecture-specific. In ARM TF boot flow, coreboot is loaded into physical memory by Trusted Boot Firmware, BL2) and configuring memory and the interrupt access table

- Preparing the environment to run C code, like setting up the stack and heap and clearing memory for BSS

- Early initialization of boot critical devices like the power management controller and the event controller to manage device wake capability and wake source, the I/O decode range for enabling the early console, and enabling caching for the memory mapped region to speed up the access process

- Decompressing (if applicable) and loading the next stage. The bootblock loads the romstage or the verstage if the system firmware has selected the verified boot.

Figure 4-18 represents the operations performed by the bootblock stage pictorially.

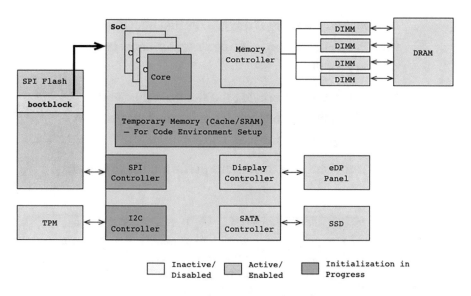

Figure 4-18. *Operational diagram of the bootblock stage*

Verstage

The verstage represents the root of trust in a platform that has core root-of-trust maintenance in the read-only (RO) CBFS, a write-protect mechanism to ensure this code block can't get updated by the in-field firmware update process. The responsibilities of the verstage are as follows:

- The verstage provides a vb2_shared_data, used to share data between vboot API calls. It holds various key information like fw_slot, recovery_reason, and vb2_ context, another data structure that is used for firmware verification.

- The verstage installs a handle that is used to verify a file before it's loaded from CBFS or accessed.

- This stage initializes the Trusted Platform Module (TPM) so that the firmware can read and/or update the key indexes for the keys used to sign the rewritable

firmware and kernels. If this is a normal boot and
the TPM initialization fails, the system reboots into
recovery mode.

- Upon successfully verifying the slot from the Read-
  Write (RW) firmware block, it loads romstage from RW
  CBFS and jumps to the romstage.

Figure 4-19 represents the operations performed by the verstage
pictorially.

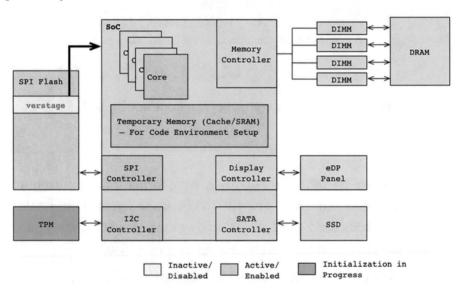

Figure 4-19. *Operational diagram of verstage*

Romstage

The romstage is the first stage invoked by the verified boot firmware from
the RW CBFS if verified boot is enabled, or this stage is invoked right after
the bootblock in the boot flow. This stage is executed from the temporary
memory and it performs DRAM initialization. The responsibilities of the
romstage are as follows:

- Performs early device initialization, such as PMIC, SMBUS, the security controller part of SoC, and more

- Initiates DRAM initialization. The DRAM initialization process involves running SoC vendor-specific routines that train the physical memory at different voltages to ensure the device can be operable at different frequencies and temperatures. Typically, either SoC vendors provide the DRAM initialization code blocks in the form of a proprietary binary to integrate with coreboot or as Trusted Firmware, part of the SoC binary that does the initialization of DRAM and loads romstage into physical memory.

Facts   On x86 platforms, SoC vendors provide the silicon initialization code as part of reference code like FSP for Intel and AGESA for AMD, although AMD has also started adopting the FSP specification. The FSP specification provides an API named FSP-M (M stands for Memory) which does memory reference code for doing the DRAM initialization. Chapter 5 provides more details on the FSP specification.

- Creates CBMEM based on a Top of RAM DRAM base minus the size of bootloader reserve range to save the CBMEM header

CBMEM

CBMEM is a generic runtime storage interface for keeping the timestamp, event log, boot console log redirected to memory, enabling stage caching for faster resume, tables for ACPI, SMBIOS, MP, and more. This memory range is accessible for the rest of the boot phases and is available to the operating system as reserved as part of the e820 table.

In-Memory Database (IMD)

IMD resides in the cbmem region for creating a dynamic cbmem infrastructure. It allows cbmem to grow dynamically as things are added. The IMD data structure has two regions: IMDR as a large region for the IMD root pointer and small regions. These regions have their static size allocation as per imd.h. It grows downwards in memory from the provided upper limit and root size, so new allocation in IMD regions will always be located below the last allocation region. Regions may be removed, but the last one added is the only that can be removed.

Relocatable Modules (rmodules)

This concept is introduced to support relocation of the boot stage, like modules that are supposed to get dispatched post memory and need more space to create infrastructure code, so they are expected to relocate them from SPI mapped memory into DRAM-based memory. For .elf files as part of coreboot project, those that are supposed to get executed post physical memory being initialized and not using SPI mapped memory, is using rmodtool to generate position independent code and data block. cbfstool is the tool used to parse and convert ELF type files to *rmodules*.

- Romstage loads the next stage, postcar (if available), into the DRAM and starts execution.

Figure 4-20 represents the operations performed by the romstage pictorially.

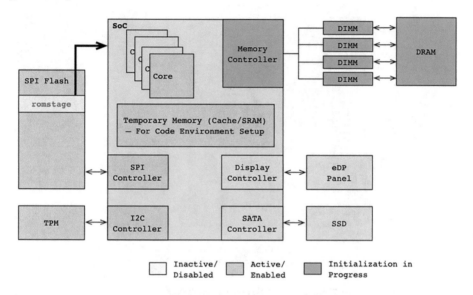

Figure 4-20. *Operational diagram of romstage*

Postcar

The postcar stage is the first stage on the x86 platform that runs from the DRAM after the physical memory is available. Compared to other boot stages, it's the smallest in size. The responsibilities of the romstage are as follows:

- Tears down the CAR setup

- Runs code from regular DRAM after the postcar tears down the CAR

- Loads the ramstage into memory

Figure 4-21 represents the operations performed by the postcar pictorially.

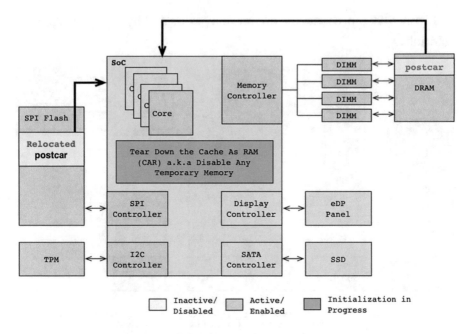

Figure 4-21. *Operational diagram of postcar*

Ramstage

The ramstage boot phase defined by coreboot is where most of the platform initialization is performed. The romstage phase, prior to the ramstage, is responsible for initializing the system physical memory and postcar loads the ramstage into memory, regardless of whether the ramstage located inside RW CBFS is part of system ROM. It gets relocated and executed from the DRAM. Entries added into the CBMEM during romstage are available in ramstage as well. The responsibilities of the ramstage are as follows:

- In ramstage, CBMEM is reinitialized where the romstage buffer is concatenated with early ramstage buffers.

- Performs multiprocessor initialization. The process brings all available application processors (APs) out from reset and allocates a dedicated stack to operate independently.

- Performs SMM relocation for each logical processor and migrates the SMM handle from the default location into the TSEG region

- Advanced chipset initialization of all SoC associated and third-party components. For example, display initialization can be done using either an on-board display controller or a discrete display card; silicon reference code handles the on-board display controller initialization whereas coreboot uses Option ROM or a display driver to perform discrete display initialization.

Facts   On x86 platforms, SoC vendors provide the reference code binary (FSP) responsible for managing SoC-specific device initialization with an API named FSP_S (S stands for Silicon). Chapter 5 provides more details on the FSP specification.

- Performs PCI enumeration, resource allocation, enables the resource, and initializes the device. All these tasks are performed using a boot state machine and motherboard (or mainboard) configuration files, called *device trees*.

Boot State Machine

At the entry point of ramstage (inside the main() function of the lib/hardwaremain.c file), static boot entries are scheduled. A boot state walker function is responsible for making a callback at state entry

(BS_ON_ENTRY), executing a state function (using run_state()) to complete the assigned task for that state, and making the final callback at state exit *(BS_ON_EXIT)*. The boot state machines are divided into the following states and developers can associate any callbacks with these state entry/exit events, similar to UEFI event handling.

Boot state	Description	Operations
BS_PRE_DEVICE	Before any device tree actions take place	
BS_DEV_INIT_CHIPS	Initializes all chips in the device tree	dev->chips_ops->init()
BS_DEV_ENUMERATE	Probes the device tree	dev->chips_ops->enable_dev() dev->ops->enable() dev->ops->scan_bus()
BS_DEV_RESOURCES	Assigns resources to devices	dev->ops->read_resources() dev->ops->set_resources()
BS_DEV_ENABLE	Device enable/disable	dev->ops->enable_resources()
BS_DEV_INIT	Initializes the device	dev->ops->init()
BS_POST_DEVICE	Performs all device operations	dev->ops->final()
BS_OS_RESUME_CHECK	Checks for OS resume to avoid creation of additional runtime tables	acpi_find_wakeup_vector()
BS_OS_RESUME	Checks for OS resume	acpi_resume()

(continued)

Boot state	Description	Operations
BS_WRITE_TABLES	Writes coreboot tables	dev->chip_ops->final()
BS_PAYLOAD_LOAD	Loads a payload into memory	payload_load()
BS_PAYLOAD_BOOT	Executes the loaded payload	payload_run()

Device tree

A device tree is a static data structure that describes the hardware layout of the system, mostly used by ramstage-related operations (but available for all boot phases) like PCI enumeration to probe the devices, dynamic ACPI table generation, and such. It's also used to configure the mainboard components.

Facts   The device tree used in coreboot is not related to the open firmware device tree or the device tree blob (DTB) used to describe platform hardware to the Linux Kernel.

The default device tree configuration for the mainboard is present inside the baseboard directory devicetree.cb, which can be overwritten using variant specific overridetree.cb. util/sconfig is the tool that is used to compile the device tree files in a coreboot project to generate the static device configuration (static.c). The firmware configuration table is also part of the mainboard devicetree.cb file; it starts with a special token as fw_config and terminates with *end*. This table provides device tree examples and override rules.

Device tree objects	devicetree.cb	overrridetree.cb	Final static configuration
Configuration data (override tree takes priority)	"PchHdaDspEnable" = "1"	"PchHdaDspEnable" = "0"	"PchHdaDspEnable" = "0"
Configure device node (override tree takes priority)	device pci 1f.2 off end	device pci 1f.2 on end	device pci 1f.2 on end
Add a child device (both child devices become siblings under same parent)	device pci 15.1 on chip drivers/i2c/generic register "hid" = ""ELAN0001"" device i2c 10 on end end end # I2C #1	device pci 15.1 on chip drivers/i2c/hid register "generic.hid" = ""GDIX0000"" device i2c 5d on end end end # I2C #1	device pci 15.1 on chip drivers/i2c/generic register "hid" = ""ELAN0001"" device i2c 10 on end end chip drivers/i2c/hid register "generic.hid" = ""GDIX0000"" device i2c 5d on end end end # I2C #1

- After it's done with platform hardware initialization, ramstage is also responsible for creating interface tables to inform the payload or operating system, including

  - Advanced Configuration and Power Interface (ACPI) tables

  - System Management BIOS (SMBIOS) tables

  - coreboot tables

  - Device Tree Table updates (applicable for ARM)

Figure 4-22 describes table creation using the coreboot ramstage boot stage machine.

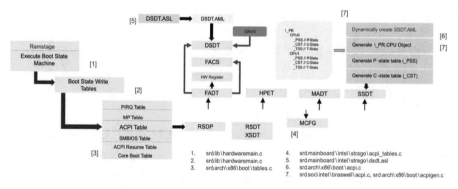

Figure 4-22. *Table creation using coreboot*

- Performs chipset lockdown and protects memory reserved ranges

- Loads payload from CBFS into memory and jumps to it

Figure 4-23 represents the operations performed by the ramstage pictorially.

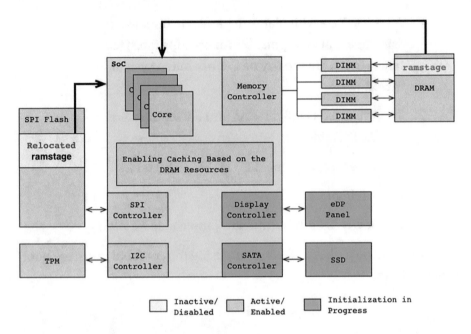

Figure 4-23. *Operational diagram of ramstage*

Payload

The payload is a separate firmware block present inside coreboot CBFS that is responsible for booting to an operating system. Libpayload is the library for common payload functions and hardware drivers that allow reading and parsing the various coreboot tables. Any information that coreboot wants to pass to the payload is in the form of a SYSINFO table.

The SYSINFO table provides the required information that the payload would like to have about the underlying hardware and platform, such as serial port number, base address of the serial port, system memory range, video framebuffer for user interaction, SPINOR layout, board details, boot media details like size, coreboot file system details like base and size and any product-related data as VPD (vital product data). Figure 4-24 represents the state of the platform hardware at the end of ramstage and when control is with the payload.

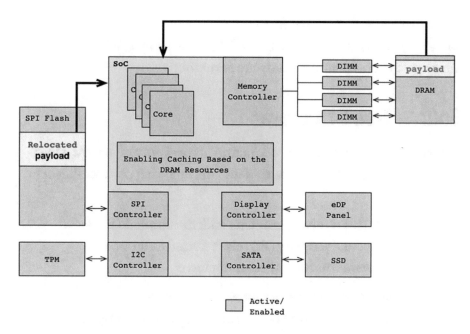

Figure 4-24. *System hardware state at payload*

Chapter 6 offers a detailed architecture overview about different types of payloads that can be integrated with coreboot to create the final ROM for the embedded system.

Runtime Services

Since coreboot is meant to provide the bare minimal hardware initialization and transfer the control to the payload, it doesn't provide detailed runtime services like UEFI. Since the operating system might still need to access some hardware registers at runtime, it's the responsibility of the boot firmware to provide a minimal interface that can be available even after coreboot has exited.

On the x86 platform, System Management Mode (SMM) is a CPU mode that is configured by ramstage and provides several SMM handlers that can be accessed by the kernel driver. For example, x86 runtime event logging relies on SMI. Apart from that, Open Source Firmware Device Tree Tables (on ARM), ACPI tables, and ACPI Source Language (ASL) objects are used to access platform hardware at runtime.

Source Tree Structure

This section describes the code structure of coreboot projects. At a high-level, the code structure can be split into the following parts as shown in Figure 4-25:

- **SoC**: This directory contains initialization code for SoC intellectual property (IP) (also referred as on-board hardware controllers) components.

- **Mainboard**: Software representation of OEM/ reference hardware design, built based on underlying SoC support

- Architecture-specific and generic device drivers to support SoC and mainboard code

- **Proprietary silicon initialization binary**: SoC vendor-provided binary blobs that abstract all silicon-related initialization using fewer APIs, called from coreboot, to work with the latest chipsets in an open source environment. On x86 platforms, SoC vendors provide the silicon initialization code as part of reference code like FSP for Intel and AGESA for AMD, although AMD has also started adopting the FSP specification. Refer to Chapter 5 to understand more about the proprietary silicon blobs' operational models and design principles.

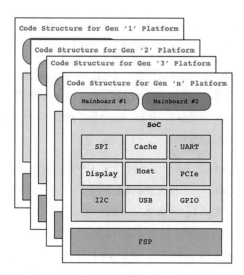

Figure 4-25. *Traditional x86-based platform coreboot code structure*

The following sections provide details on coreboot code structures and architectural changes for IA platforms.

SoC Code Structure

Typically, SoC code structures for the IA platform consists of early CPU and chipset initializations required for interfacing with FSP APIs (as per the FSP specification), which further initiates the initialization of remaining hardware controllers associated with the SoC die. The SoC code structure as part of coreboot project is responsible for performing the following operations:

- Early CPU initialization and temporary memory setup driver, typically known as the CPU or Cache code block

- Implementing device drivers to access hardware controllers to perform non-memory or I/O cycle read/write operations, such as the SPI device driver inside the SoC directory

- Setting up devices prior to FSP, like TPM over I2C, the UART controller for debugging, and such

- Apart from that, SoC device setup that is not handled by FSP like PCI enumeration, ACPI code for SoC devices, and managing the GPIO controller and associated GPIO communities

Figure 4-25 shows the number of SoC IP components that reside inside the SoC directory. This is increasing due to more complex SoC designs. Historically, the upstream coreboot code development started for a new SoC by copying the generation 'n'-1 SoC directory structure into the 'n' SoC. It increases the redundancy in the IPs initialization code for generation over generation SoC projects inside coreboot. Redundant code across various SoC directories implies higher maintenance overhead for reviewers and maintainers.

To solve this problem, latest IA-based platforms hosted in coreboot follows the *converged IP model* (even AMD has adopted this code development model for its latest SoCs) as it translates the actual hardware development model into firmware that runs on the underlying hardware. The coreboot code development using *converged IP model* is the exact snapshot of the SoC design, where the same IP component is reused over different SoCs with minor version changes, which is opaque to system firmware while initializing that IP. This model brings a new code structure into the upstream coreboot project named *common code*, a common pool of IP libraries used by various SoC products belonging to the same microarchitecture to create system firmware for the current SoC and even applicable for future SoCs as well. The new code development model makes the SoC code structure much simpler by utilizing common APIs based on the different configurations.

Common Code Architecture

Intel proposed coreboot SoC code development using the converged IP model in 2016. The first generation of common code was called common code phase 1.0. Figure 4-26 provides the common code architecture diagram.

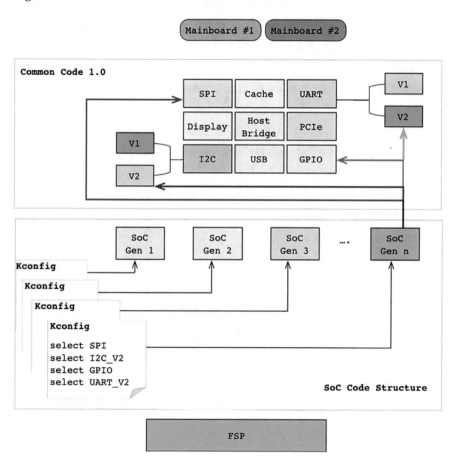

Figure 4-26. *Converged IP model-based coreboot code structure*

With the common code phase 1.0 design, the SoC directory has a dedicated Kconfig file that is used to maintain the IP versioning and SoC specific overrides for the common code. For example, the GPIO common block has all GPIO configuration logic and access mechanisms for the hardware controller but the hardware register definitions and GPIO community is different across different SoCs, so the SoC code structure to have those register layers and boot stage-specific SoC information alone required by common code block and mainboard to perform IP initialization.

When the mainboard code tries to access a SoC code structure, it can either make a direct call into a common code block or a respective SoC call redirects it into common code APIs. The problem with the common code 1.0 design is that the register layer residing in dedicated SoCs is now looking redundant even with multiple SoC reuses of the same CPU core and/or with incremental PCH. Common code 1.1 introduced a concept of a common register layer across different SoCs to further optimize the SoC code structure. See Figure 4-27.

Facts   There is one more proposal named Common Code 2.0 to create a common boot stage (i.e., bootblock, romstage, etc.) entry and exit across different SoCs, which would further optimize the SoC code structure and streamline the hardware initialization performed by different SoCs.

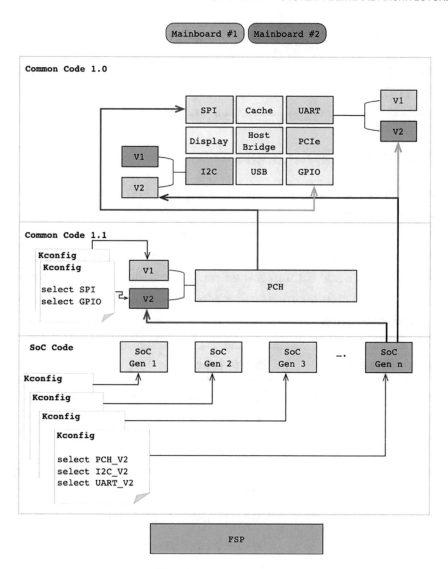

Figure 4-27. *Common Code 1.1-based coreboot code structure*

Adopting the Common Code design principle when developing new SoC for a coreboot project helps to reduce the code density by more than 50% with higher code reusability and improved code quality with maturity from different SoC generation platform development.

Facts   Prior to adopting the common code design, in 2016, the IA-SoC code density was 17.8K LOC. On the latest platform, it is around ~7K LOC.

Mainboard Code Structure

The Mainboard directory inside a coreboot project is built on SoC support and common code, as mentioned in the prior sections. Typically, the mainboard code structure is intended to provide the configuration parameters to SoC and common code blocks. Regardless of the underlying CPU architecture and without going deep into the motherboard design details, a typical mainboard directory consists of files/sub-directories that include the following:

Sample code structure	Descriptions
dsdt.asl, mainboard.asl	Static ACPI table entries for all motherboard devices
*.fmd file	Flash layout file for platform
devicetree.cb	Platform configuration file that includes port and peripherals
spd, romstage.c	On-board memory configuration
mainboard.c	Board-level callbacks
gpio.c	Mainboard GPIO configuration

In the traditional motherboard development approach, either the SoC vendor or the platform owner (assume Google in the case of the ChromeOS platform) provides the reference board hardware design that is applied while designing the firmware. Later, OEMs/ODMs come up with their own motherboard schematics based on the reference hardware design. Figure 4-28 shows the traditional hardware enabling model and its firmware representation in mainboard code structure.

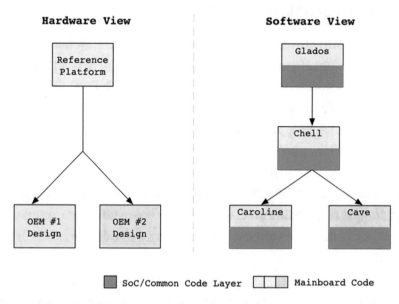

Figure 4-28. *Traditional mainboard enabling model and software view*

This model had a significant shortcoming as each mainboard directory has its own duplication of work (i.e., interfacing with SoC and common IPs, board gpio programming, on-board memory configuration, on-board device configuration, population of static ACPI on-board device entries, etc.) without actually being able to represent the hardware design level reusability. It limited the scope of scaling to all OEMs and meet faster TTM. Also, the software stack didn't provide flexibility for OEMs to reuse hardware components from other hardware designs.

To overcome this limitation, coreboot rearchitected the mainboard code structure with introduction of the following.

Dynamic Generation of the ACPI Table

SoC and platform devices are described to an operating system using the ACPI Differentiated System Description Table (DSDT), which is loaded at boot, or in Secondary System Description Tables (SSDTs), which are loaded at boot or loaded dynamically at runtime. In the traditional model, platform device entries are typically static, so the DSDT was sufficient but brought redundancy across different mainboards. Hence, SSDTs is used to improve the modularity of the platform description by creating runtime device nodes based on device tree properties. Generic driver code as part of ramstage is responsible for creating those device nodes at runtime. This table provides the code snippet to generate dynamic device nodes as part of SSDT.

device pci 15.1 on
  chip drivers/i2c/
  generic   1
    register "hid" =
    ""ELAN0001"" 2
    device i2c 10 on
    end 3
  end
end # I2C #1
	1. Generic I2C driver used for device node creation
	2. Describes the ACPI name object _*HID* as
	  Name(_HID, "ELAN0001")
	3. Provides a I2C resource description as part of
	  _CRS with a slave address as *0x10*
	  Name (_CRS, ResourceTemplate ()
	  { I2cSerialBus (0x10, ControllerIn
	  itiated, 1000000, AddressingMode7B
	  it, "_SB.PCIO.I2C1")})

Baseboard and Variant Structure

The baseboard and variant structure is introduced into the mainboard directory to be able to represent the hardware enabling model into the software stack as well.

Mainboard directory: The mainboard directory is the representation of the reference hardware design, which acts as a base hardware schematic for all OEMs design. Hence, it contains all common code shared by different boards based on reference design. This directory contains `romstage.c, mainboard.c, chromeos.fmd`, and more.

Baseboard: The baseboard represents the default hardware configuration that is common across different OEMs designs but still can be overridden by variants if required, such as the *__weak* implementation of the GPIO configuration table, devicetree.cb, and on-board memory configuration parameters like SPD.

Variants: A tiny code block that is an overlay on top of the baseboard to specify pieces that are specific to the OEM design and different from the default configuration provided by the baseboard, such as the GPIO configuration table for the variant, memory configuration parameters, and allowing the overriding default devicetree.cb using variant-specific overridetree.cb with certain rules as explained in ramstage section. Typically, the variant directory inside the coreboot mainboard is intended to be maintained by the specific OEM as per their hardware design.

Figure 4-29 describes the current mainboard code structure which optimizes the redundant code across different OEM mainboards.

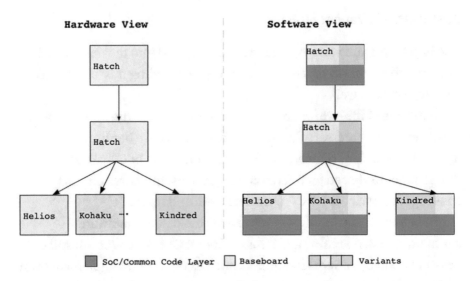

Figure 4-29. *Current mainboard enabling model and software view*

This new code structure has certain rules that make the current model more scalable with more APIs and configurable parameters:

- Variants can only access the code present within the Mainboard directory. It allows overriding the Baseboard code structure alone as applicable.

- Mainboard code either accesses the Common Code/Architecture/Generic libraries/drivers or SoC directories.

- Common Code calls SoC-specific overrides as applicable.

Proprietary Silicon Initialization Binary

Chapter 5 provides the architecture specification of SoC vendor-provided proprietary reference code binary that performs the initialization of on-die components. Typically, an x86 platform uses such a binary model for SoC initialization, called the FSP specification.

```
┌─────────────────────────────┐
│ FSP                         │
├─────────────────────────────┤
│      Temporary RAM          │
│      Initialization         │
├─────────────────────────────┤
│    Memory Initialization    │
├─────────────────────────────┤
│    Silicon Initialization   │
├─────────────────────────────┤
│      Notify Callbacks       │
└─────────────────────────────┘
```

It allows the bootloader to communicate with FSP through standard APIs and to configure SoC hardware using policies known as Updatable Product Data (UPD). The coreboot stages (bootblock, romstage, ramstage) implement wrapper code to pass required configuration data while calling the required FSP APIs.

Slim Bootloader Architecture

Slim Bootloader (SBL) is a flexible, lightweight, open source bootloader solution. It was initially designed to meet unique requirements for Intel platforms in the IoT market, such as fast boot, small footprint, secure boot, easier customization, permissive license, and more. Back in 2018, Slim Bootloader made its first public appearance during the Open Source Firmware Conference (OSFC) event and was published on GitHub with a BSD-2-Clause-Patent license. Slim Bootloader began its journey with the Intel Apollo Lake platform and QEMU virtual platform support. Since then, it's grown with addition of more IA platform support including Coffee Lake, Whiskey Lake, Tiger Lake, Elkhart Lake, and QSP Simics platforms. Now it is a generic bootloader offering on many IA platforms.

The Slim Bootloader architecture leverages many existing works done by popular system firmwares. For example, it adopted the UEFI EDKII build infrastructure to provide rich build toolchain support across different OS environments, integrated Intel FSP API infrastructure for scalable silicon initialization, and reused many existing UEFI EDKII library interfaces to minimize the development and porting effort.

Although Slim Bootloader leverages a lot from the UEFI EDKII project, the platform initialization flow is quite different from EDKII. From the execution flow perspective, Slim Bootloader is much closer to coreboot, which maintains a linear boot flow and decouples OS boot logic from the platform initialization through a separate payload module. See Figure 4-30.

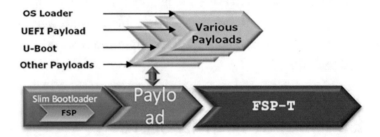

Figure 4-30. *Slim Bootloader architecture*

As shown above in Figure 4-30, Slim Bootloader conducts very basic platform initialization by utilizing the Intel FSP interfaces and then transfers control to a payload of the user's choice to complete the OS boot logic. The payload can be selected as required by the use case. For example, for a small IoT device that demands fast boot, a RTOS such as VxWorks can select a lightweight OsLoader payload to boot through the multi-boot protocol, while use cases requiring Windows can launch an UEFI payload.

Boot Stages

As stated earlier, the Slim Bootloader architecture divides the platform initialization from the boot logic, also referred to as the payload stage. The platform initialization can further be categorized into Stage 1 and Stage 2. Stage 1 is primarily responsible for bringing up the system main memory, and Stage 2 is responsible for initializing the remaining platform hardware. The payload is responsible for loading and booting the OS or the pre-boot application.

Stage 1

Slim Bootloader Stage 1 is the pre-memory stage and is responsible for early platform initialization and system main memory initialization. A lot of modern platforms provide support for some sort of auxiliary or temporary memory in the early boot phase, and Stage 1 can utilize this resource to create the proper execution environment required by the system main memory initiation.

On some platforms, the initial space that can be used for startup code execution is very limited. For example, on the Apollo Lake platform, only 32KB of CSME shared RAM can be used for initial bootstrap. In this case, it is required to further split Stage 1 into two different substages: Stage 1A and Stage 1B. Stage 1A does bare minimum platform initialization, and then loads and transfers it to Stage 1B. And Stage 1B does the memory subsystem initialization and then loads and transfers to Stage 2. Stage 1A needs to maintain a very small footprint to fit into the limited execution space, whereas Stage 1B can hold more complicated code flow because of less constraints on execution space. See Figure 4-31.

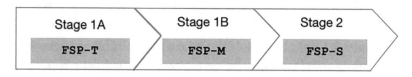

Figure 4-31. *Slim Bootloader platform initialization*

Stage 1A

When coming out of reset, the processor may be in a very raw state and may need very basic initialization before the rest of the platform can be initialized. Stage 1A sets up the initial startup environment to support the execution of the following stages. It performs the following initializations:

- Initializes the processor and switches to 32-bit flat mode or 64-bit long mode based on the desired processor execution mode. When Stage 1A code starts execution, there may not be a stack available and so assembly language code may be used to avoid stack dependency.

- Sets up temporary memory for use as a temporary stack. This is accomplished by interfacing with the Intel FSP-T TempRamInit API

- Switches to C programming

- Establishes bootloader global data in the temporary memory

- Initializes debug device to enable early debug message output

- Loads Stage 1B into the desired location and then transfers the control to Stage 1B.

Stage 1A code is assumed to be executed in place (XIP) from a read-only medium. Typically, it is flash or ROM, but it can also be shared SRAM that the host CPU has no write access to, or a CPU cache region that does not allow self-modifying. As such, any write to the data section, such as global variables, should be avoided. In some special cases, after the temporary memory is available, it might be desirable to move Stage 1A into the temporary memory for certain reasons. If such migration is required, Stage 1A will relocate itself into the new location and continue the remaining execution flow from the new location.

Stage 1A includes the FSP-T binary component. FSP-T provides an interface to help initialize the CPU cache as temporary memory.

Stage 1B

The primary purpose for Stage 1B is to bring up the system main memory so that it has more resources to execute the remaining stages. It performs the following initializations:

- Early platform-specific initialization, such as GPIO and SPI

- Determines the desired boot mode

- Detects the board ID

- Loads and verifies platform configuration data

- Initializes the main memory. This is accomplished by interfacing with the Intel FSP-M FspMemoryInit API.

- Switches the stack to system main memory and migrates the bootloader global data from the temporary memory to system main memory

- Initializes cache for optimal performance. This is accomplished by interfacing with the Intel FSP-M TempRamExit API.

- Loads Stage 2 into main memory, verifies, and then transfers the control to the Stage 2 entry point

Since the temporary memory is available, Stage 1B can be executed from either flash or temporary memory. To make the code generic for both cases, similar to Stage 1A, any writes to the Stage 1B data section should be avoided, even when Stage 1B is executed from the temporary memory.

To reduce the image footprint on flash, Stage 1B can even be compressed in flash and then decomposed into the temporary memory for execution if the temporary memory size is sufficient.

Stage 1B includes the FSP-M binary component.

Stage 2

Stage 2 is the post-memory stage and is responsible for the remaining platform initialization including processor, chipset, PCI bus, I/O devices, and ACPI. Stage 2 code is executed from system main memory and can be compressed to reduce the footprint.

It performs the following initializations:

- Completes the silicon initialization by interfacing with the Intel FSP-S FspSiliconInit API

- Saves non-volatile (NVS) data into flash

- Multi-processor (MP) initialization

- PCI enumeration and resource allocation

- ACPI and SMBIOS initialization

- Sends Intel FSP notifications by interfacing with the Intel FSP-S FspNotifyPhase API

- Prepares HOBs to pass the required platform initialization information to the payload

- Loads and jumps to the payload

Stage 2 includes the FSP-S binary component.

Payload

Slim Bootloader depends on payloads to perform OS booting logic or any purpose-driven functionalities. In general, the payload can be implemented independent of specific platform hardware through the abstracted platform interface. Slim Bootloader Stage 2 will construct the required payload interfaces and pass them into the payload entry point as a parameter.

Payload Interface

The Slim Bootloader payload interface adopts the HOB data structure defined by the PI specification to abstract platform information. Each HOB describes a piece of information associated with a specific platform function block, and a list of HOBs provides overall platform information. This HOB list is passed into the payload entry point for consumption. In this way a payload can extract the required platform information to standardize the hardware device initialization. It allows the exact same payload binary to run on multiple different platforms.

Built-in Payloads

For convenience, Slim Bootloader provides two default built-in payloads: OS Loader (OSLD) payload and Firmware Update (FWU) payload.

- **OS Loader Payload: The** OSLD payload is primarily used for customized OS boot flow. It implements Linux boot protocol, multiboot protocol and also supports loading and executing ELF and PECOFF images. It provides a simple and fast path to boot Linux-based OS, RTOS, hypervisor, or customized applications. It is capable of booting from many different boot devices including USB, NVMe, eMMC, SD, UFS, and SATA. It supports different disk partitions (MBR, GPT), different file systems (RAW, FAT, EXT2/3), as well as different boot image formats (Multi-Boot, ELF, PECOFF, FV).

Further, the OSLD payload provides a shell command line interface to assist the debug.

- **Firmware Update Payload: The** FWU payload is primarily used for power fail safe fault-tolerant system firmware updates. It can support ME/SPS firmware updates in the flash ME region and a Slim Bootloader component in the flash BIOS region, such as microcode, configuration data blob, and external payloads. The fault tolerance is provided through a redundant boot partition mechanism. All boot-critical firmware components have duplicated copies in boot partitions. If one partition cannot boot after a firmware update, it is possible to switch back to the other boot partition that has not been updated yet and perform recovery. The current firmware update state will be stored in flash devices. If the firmware update is interrupted for some reason, the next boot will resume the update flow until it fully completes.

Figure 4-32 shows the firmware update high level flow in Slim Bootloader.

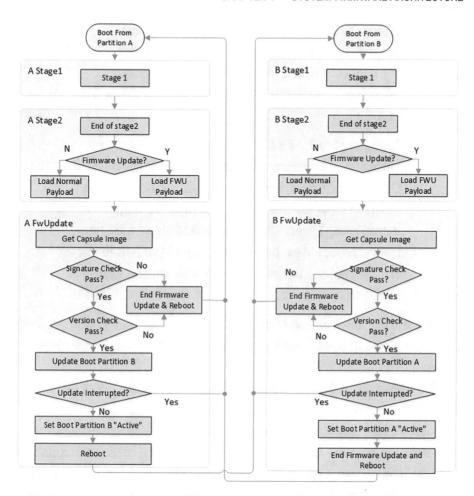

Figure 4-32. *Slim Bootloader firmware update flow*

External Payloads

There are many external payloads that can be integrated into Slim
Bootloader to provide specific functionality. The UEFI payload and Linux
payload are very popular external payloads for Slim Bootloader.

- **UEFI Payload:** The UEFI payload provides a
  UEFI specification compliant interface on top of a

bootloader. It is built from the open source EDKII project, and it extends the capability of a bootloader to support many UEFI applications (UEFI Shell, MemTest86, etc.) and UEFI-aware OSes (Windows, Linux, etc.).

- **Linux Payload:** The Linux payload uses the Linux kernel itself to perform the tasks required by a payload. Once the Linux payload is booted, it can be used as a normal OS, or further load and launch the targeted OS kernel using kexec. Slim Bootloader follows the Linux boot protocol to prepare the required boot parameter structures, load the kernel and InitRd images, and finally transfer the control to the kernel entry point.

Beyond the UEFI payload and the Linux payload, many other payloads can be used as required, such as the U-Boot payload and MicroPython payload.

Multiple extremal payloads can coexist within a Slim Bootloader image. This is done by packing multiple payload images into an Extended Payload (EPLD) container component. The platform can select a proper payload ID at runtime to determine which payload to boot for current flow. For example, on many platforms Slim Bootloader provides the capability to select the OS Loader payload or the UEFI payload using a GPIO input pin.

In summary, the Slim Bootloader payload architecture provides great flexibility to customize the bootloader targeting very specific purposes by leveraging lots of existing firmware solutions.

Boot Flow

Slim Bootloader defines several standard boot modes to control different boot paths. The primary supported boot modes are normal boot mode, S3 boot mode, S4 boot mode, and firmware update boot mode.

Normal Boot Mode

The normal boot mode is the most common boot flow observed on a platform boot. In this mode, Slim Bootloader will go through Stage 1A, Stage 1B, Stage 2, and Payload to complete the boot. The detailed flow is illustrated in Figure 4-33.

Figure 4-33. *Slim Bootloader boot wlow*

To speed up the boot flow, the FSP might provide a faster path to restore the memory controller state programmed on the full training path if the memory configuration is not changed. If supported, Slim Bootloader will save the MRC training data returned by FSP into a dedicated flash region on the very first boot after flashing. On the following boots, the saved training data will be loaded and fed back into FSP to enable fast memory initialization. Slim Bootloader will compare the saved training data with the one returned by FSP on every boot to see if the data needs to be updated. If so, the new data will be written into flash and used for the next boot.

S3 and S4 Boot Modes

Platform S3 and S4 boot flows defined by ACPI specification might need special handling in boot firmware.

For the S3 boot path in Slim Bootloader, most of the early boot flows are almost identical to the normal boot path except for the memory initialization. When the S3 boot path is detected, the FSP will initialize the memory in a special way such that the memory content can be preserved across the S3 cycle.

The other difference starts from Stage 2 where the ACPI initialization occurs. On the S3 boot path, the ACPI tables will not be constructed or loaded again. Instead, it remembers the ACPI table memory range populated on the normal boot path and reuses the same memory on the S3 boot path. The S3 boot path does not hand over to payload like normal boot path. Rather, it jumps into the waking vector provided by the ACPI FADT table. All the required FSP and board notifications will be signaled before jumping to the OS waking vector.

For S4 boot path, it is treated the same as normal boot flow on Slim Bootloader. Slim Bootloader ensures the memory map is consistent across S4 boot cycles.

Firmware Update Boot Mode

Slim Bootloader provides a special boot path for firmware update. The Firmware Update Boot Path is special in that the FWU payload is enforced to launch when FWU mode is detected. It provides a platform opportunity to recover the faulty firmware.

FWU mode can be triggered from Slim Bootloader Shell command fwupdate or from OS through the ACPI and WMI interfaces. When the FWU mode is activated, the firmware has higher privilege to access many platform resources. For example, the flash device is not write-protected yet, and many interfaces are not locked down either. As such, it is not allowed to continue the normal boot flow when the system is in FWU boot mode. A platform reboot must be issued to switch back to the normal boot path after the FWU process is fully completed.

Flash Layout

SBL contains all critical boot components with redundant copy on boot flash so that if one of them is corrupted due to a hardware defect or firmware update process, Slim Bootloader is able to recover from the second copy to boot, thus reducing the risk of bricking the board due to failures.

Flash Map

Flash map is a data structure to describe the binary component layout within a Slim Bootloader image. It contains a flash map header and a component array. The header provides overall information for the image, and each array entry describes the information for a specific component including ID, offset, size, and attributes.

Slim Bootloader embeds the flash map structure into Stage 1A at a fixed offset close to the end of the image. At the early Stage 1A, this flash map structure is copied into the Slim Bootloader global data region located in the temporary memory. Then it can be further used to locate many other components within the current boot partition.

The most seen Slim Bootloader component IDs are listed in this table:

ID	Component description
SG1A	Stage 1A
SG1B	Stage 1B
SG02	Stage 2
CNFG	External platform configuration data
UCOD	Microcode patch
MRCD	Memory training data
VARS	Variable data
KEYH	Hash store
PYLD	Default built-in payload
FWUP	Built-in firmware update payload
EPLD	Extended payload container
RSVD	Reserved
EMTY	Empty

Redundant Partitions

Slim Bootloader supports redundant flash partitions to improve the robustness of the firmware boot flow. When a redundant flash partition is used, the Slim Bootloader image can have redundant regions to hold the boot critical components. In this way, if any boot critical component in one partition is corrupted for any reason, the system can try to boot from the other partition for recovery following a reboot.

Slim Bootloader utilizes the flash top swap feature to support redundant boot partitions. However, since the top swap size supported by the silicon is very limited, the top swap region might not have sufficient space to hold all required boot critical components. To address this, Slim Bootloader introduces new extra redundant regions below the top swap regions to manage redundancy.

Facts   Top swap inverts an address on access to SPI and firmware hub, so the processor believes it is fetching the alternate boot block instead of the original boot-block. The size of the boot-block and setting of this field must be determined by the BIOS developer. If this is not set correctly, then the BIOS boot-block recovery mechanism will not work.

In the sample redundant flash layout shown in Figure 4-34, TOP_SWAP_A and TOP_SWAP_B are the top swap regions, and their size should match the size supported by the silicon. Each region contains Stage 1A component. REDUNDANT_A and REDUNDANT_B are the extended redundant regions and the size can be adjusted as needed. Each region contains Stage 1B, Stage 2, configuration data, and a firmware update payload. Together, TOP_SWAP_A and REDUNDANT_A in partition A contain all of the critical components required for the firmware update flow. TOP_SWAP_B and REDUNDANT_B in partition B contain a secondary copy of those critical components. The other components in NON_REDUNDANT region are not required on the recovery firmware update flow. And NON_VOLATILE region is used to keep tracking the firmware update states.

```
+-----------------------------------------------------------------------+
|                            FLASH   MAP                                 |
|                     (RomSize = 0x00400000)                            |
+-----------------------------------------------------------------------+
|   NAME    |    OFFSET   (BASE)      |    SIZE     |       FLAGS        |
+-----------+-------------------------+-------------+--------------------+
+-----------------------------------------------------------------------+
|                            TOP  SWAP  A                                |
+-----------------------------------------------------------------------+
|   SG1A    |  0x3f0000(0xFFFF0000)   |  0x010000   | Uncompressed, TS_A |
+-----------------------------------------------------------------------+
|                            TOP  SWAP  B                                |
+-----------------------------------------------------------------------+
|   SG1A    |  0x3e0000(0xFFFE0000)   |  0x010000   | Uncompressed, TS_B |
+-----------------------------------------------------------------------+
|                            REDUNDANT  A                                |
+-----------------------------------------------------------------------+
|   KEYH    |  0x3df000(0xFFFDF000)   |  0x001000   | Uncompressed, R_A  |
|   CNFG    |  0x3de000(0xFFFDE000)   |  0x001000   | Uncompressed, R_A  |
|   FWUP    |  0x3c6000(0xFFFC6000)   |  0x018000   | Compressed   , R_A |
|   SG1B    |  0x396000(0xFFF96000)   |  0x030000   | Compressed   , R_A |
|   SG02    |  0x37e000(0xFFF7E000)   |  0x018000   | Compressed   , R_A |
|   EMTY    |  0x360000(0xFFF60000)   |  0x01e000   | Uncompressed, R_A  |
+-----------+-------------------------+-------------+--------------------+
|                            REDUNDANT  B                                |
+-----------------------------------------------------------------------+
|   KEYH    |  0x35f000(0xFFF5F000)   |  0x001000   | Uncompressed, R_B  |
|   CNFG    |  0x35e000(0xFFF5E000)   |  0x001000   | Uncompressed, R_B  |
|   FWUP    |  0x346000(0xFFF46000)   |  0x018000   | Compressed   , R_B |
|   SG1B    |  0x316000(0xFFF16000)   |  0x030000   | Compressed   , R_B |
|   SG02    |  0x2fe000(0xFFEFE000)   |  0x018000   | Compressed   , R_B |
|   EMTY    |  0x2e0000(0xFFEE0000)   |  0x01e000   | Uncompressed, R_B  |
+-----------+-------------------------+-------------+--------------------+
|                            NON  REDUNDANT                              |
+-----------------------------------------------------------------------+
|   EPLD    |  0x0d3000(0xFFCD3000)   |  0x20d000   | Uncompressed,  NR  |
|   PYLD    |  0x0b3000(0xFFCB3000)   |  0x020000   | Compressed   ,  NR |
|   VARS    |  0x0b1000(0xFFCB1000)   |  0x002000   | Uncompressed,  NR  |
|   EMTY    |  0x001000(0xFFC01000)   |  0x0b0000   | Uncompressed,  NR  |
+-----------+-------------------------+-------------+--------------------+
|                            NON  VOLATILE                               |
+-----------------------------------------------------------------------+
|   RSVD    |  0x000000(0xFFC00000)   |  0x001000   | Uncompressed,  NV  |
+-----------+-------------------------+-------------+--------------------+
```

Figure 4-34. *Slim Bootloader flash layout with redundancy*

Board Configuration

To enable easier board customization, Slim Bootloader utilizes configuration elements to manage the board variations. Configuration elements can be further categorized into static configuration and dynamic configuration.

Static configuration is build time knobs that can be used to control if a certain option needs to be built into the final bootloader image or not. Once configured, it is not possible to change it afterwards unless a new image is built. Static configuration usually provides better image size control since unused features can be easier stripped out for the image build. On the contrary, dynamic configuration allows you to enable or disable certain configuration knobs at boot time under certain conditions. It provides better flexibility to allow the same code to dynamically adapt to the current execution environment.

Static Configuration

Static configuration in Slim Bootloader is very similar to Kconfig used in Linux kernel configuration. It provides configuration options used during the build process, such as flash layout definition, board supporting, and CPU feature set enabling.

There are many common static configuration options defined in BootLoader.py at the root of the tree. It also provides the default values for these options. A platform can override these default values in its BoarcConfig.py located under the platform package.

Dynamic Configuration

Slim Bootloader adopted the YAML file format to describe dynamic platform configurations, such as memory configuration, GPIO configuration, and boot option configuration. All configuration options are defined in a top level YAML file. And this top level YAML file can further include child YAML files to represent the full configurable options available on a platform. Each individual configuration set carries a unique configuration tag ID in the YAML file.

To support multiple boards in a single bootloader image, a DLT file is introduced to describe the board-specific configuration variation. Each board can have one DLT file associated with it, and it is identified by a unique board ID. The changes listed in a DLT file will be applied on top of the baseline YAML to create the final configuration set specific to that board ID. See Figure 4-35.

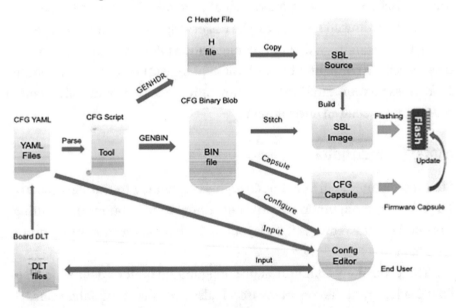

Figure 4-35. *Slim Bootloader configuration flow*

As illustrated in Figure 4-35, a tool will parse the configuration YAML and DLT files to generate configuration C header files and configuration binary blobs. They will be compiled together with the Slim Bootloader source to create the final flash image. To make it easier for the end user, a GUI Python script ConfigEditor is provided in Slim Bootloader to view and modify the platform configuration options. The changed configuration binary blob can be saved back into a DLT file for later use or used as input to create the configuration capsule image. Through the firmware capsule update process provided by FWU payload, the new configuration blob will be updated into the flash at runtime. Eventually, the new configuration will take effect from the following boot.

At the early boot stage (Stage 1B), the configuration binary blob will be retrieved from flash and then loaded into memory for verification. If it passes, this configuration data will be appended into a configuration database in memory. This database will be the central place to provide configuration information for Slim Bootloader. Platform code can use a board ID and a configuration tag ID to uniquely find a configuration option that is applicable for this board.

Source Tree Structure

The Slim Bootloader source tree structure is very similar to the open sourced UEFI EDKII source tree. It groups modules along with required libraries and definitions into packages. The tree structure alignment helps the code reuse between the EDKII source and the Slim Bootloader source.

A basic Slim Bootloader source tree contains base tools, bootloader common and core packages, payload package, and platform and silicon packages.

Base Tools

Slim Bootloader base tools are directly adopted from the UEFI EDKII project to provide an EDKII-compatible build infrastructure. As such, the Slim Bootloader build process inherits the wide build toolchain support including GCC, Microsoft Visual Studio, and Clang across multiple OS environments including Windows and Linux.

For Slim Bootloader, many unused base tools, such as VfrCompiler, BrotliCompress, EfiRom, and so on, are stripped out to reduce the number of the files required. On the other side, some new tool, such as Lz4Comporess, is added to achieve faster image decompressing performance while maintaining a very small footprint for the decompression code itself.

Bootloader Common and Core Package

Slim Bootloader core and common packages are the central location for the code that is shared across all platforms. The core package provides primary stage execution flow, core libraries, and Python scripts used for Slim Bootloader meta-file generation. The common package provides generic libraries used for various purposes such as boot device access, file system access, console input and output, crypto interfaces, and decompression interfaces. Some of the common packages such as MdePkg and IntelFsp2Pkg are located separately to maintain compatibility with the EDKII source tree.

Many of these common and core libraries are ported directly from EDKII MdePkg or MdeModulePkg with minor changes to remove the UEFI and PI dependencies.

Silicon Package

The Slim Bootloader silicon package holds the silicon-specific source code, binaries, and configurations. A typical silicon package contains Intel FSP header files and binaries; microcode binaries; silicon-specific libraries for Stage 1A, Stage 1B, and Stage 2; silicon IP-specific libraries such as GPIO control, PCH access, HECI interface; and so on.

In general, silicon packages can be reused without changes if the platform uses the same silicon. Most of the silicon initialization customization is fully abstracted by the FSP UPD settings or platform configuration data.

Platform Package

The Slim Bootloader platform package holds the platform-specific code and configuration. A typical platform package will contain board configuration Python scripts; platform ACPI tables; platform YAML configurations; board DLT files; platform-specific libraries for Stage 1A, Stage 1B, and Stage 2; platform integrated graphics VBT binaries; IFWI stitching scripts; and so on.

Most of the board customization will be done in this package. If the board hardware design is very close to an existing board that is already supported by Slim Bootloader, then in many cases the customization can be simplified by creating a new board DLT file with a new unique board ID and modifying the related configuration values to match the hardware board design. For example, if only the memory subsystem is different, memory related configuration can be added into the board DLT file for customization. On the other hand, if the board hardware design involves more changes, code customization can be done within this package to provide board specific initialization, such as Super I/O chip initialization.

Payload Package

Slim Bootloader payload package contains standard payload libraries and the built-in OsLoader payload and firmware update payload implementations. New customized payloads can be also developed on top of the payload libraries to extend the Slim Bootloader capability. A basic Slim Bootloader source tree contains base tools, bootloader common and core packages, payload package, and platform and silicon packages.

Summary

This chapter provided a detailed architecture overview of UEFI, coreboot and Slim Bootloader system firmwares. It should help you choose the correct bootloader solution for your target hardware by understanding the communication interface between high-level operating system and low-level platform hardware.

UEFI implements a robust specification to separate platform initialization (PI Specification) from passing that information across different firmware modules to an OS loader or an operating system (using the UEFI Specification) and provides runtime services for OS drivers or applications to use. Additionally, UEFI has ability to use large hard-drive or boot partitions up to 8ZB (zettabytes, $8x2^{70}$ bytes) and it provides a pre-boot environment that allows running a diagnostics utility as an EFI application.

coreboot is a minimal representation of system firmware that performs mandatory hardware initializations required to pass the control to the payload. coreboot has intentionally separated the platform initialization from the interface required to communicate with the OS to ensure a smaller footprint, instant boot, and lesser runtime service to meet security requirements. This chapter also emphasizes the flexible code architecture of coreboot that allows improvements over the time for providing better scalability, making the platform more configurable, ease while porting new SoC and/or mainboard using SoC common code model, and base-variant code structure.

Slim Bootloader is a flexible, lightweight, open source bootloader solution that is designed to meet unique requirements for the IoT market, such as fast boot, small footprint, secure boot, and easier customization. This chapter provided details to understand the SBL architecture, boot flow, and required interface to communicate between modules and payload. Additionally, you explored the code structure and board configuration so you can get involved in creating the system firmware using SBL if it meets the platform design requirement.

Figure 4-36 shows a comparison between UEFI, coreboot and SBL to help you understand that the working principle of system firmware is typically the same as they all are focused on performing hardware initialization and hand offs to the payload, but they have their own specification which you need to consider when choosing one for target embedded systems.

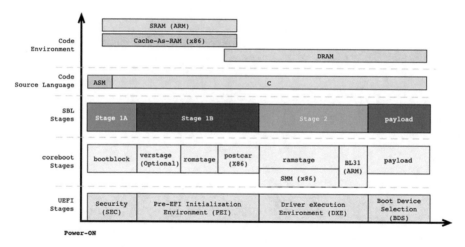

Figure 4-36. *Comparison between SBL, UEFI, and coreboot*

Chapter 2 provided platform hardware knowledge that you should possess to start you journey on system firmware, Chapter 3 outlined what is called a minimalistic system firmware requirement, and this chapter provided the required knowledge on bootloader architecture that can be used when implementing the system firmware. Chapter 7 has case studies using these bootloader solutions to address unique platform requirements.

CHAPTER 5

Hybrid Firmware Architecture

"People who are too fastidious towards the finite never reach actuality, but linger in abstraction, and their light dies away."

—Hegel

Once upon a time, a difference between hardware and the software running on the underlying hardware didn't exist. The fundamental idea was to improve the computing, ease the manual effort, and create more scalable and economical solutions for wider adaptation. The initial computing devices were meant for special usages. Users of those machines were typically programmers or researchers, possibly belonging to well-funded organizations where it was comparatively easy to maintain the device costs and the additional cost of expensive software. It became challenging when it came to the commercialization of computers where the hardware cost itself was so high that it was tricky to additionally bear the cost for expensive software. Different inventors developed the idea of making computers more affordable for general users. The most well-received idea was to slowly decouple the hardware and software to eventually bring down the entire cost. In this process, many companies started developing their own software solutions and distributing using different philosophies.

© Subrata Banik and Vincent Zimmer 2022
S. Banik and V. Zimmer, *System Firmware*,
https://doi.org/10.1007/978-1-4842-7939-7_5

Within such a chaotic situation arose the free software movement. The open source movement is one such fork from the free software movement, which started in the late 1980s with the vision of non-proprietary software. This movement emphasized the need for having free distribution of source code used in production software. The term *free software* is used not to define monetary freedom; rather, it focuses on bringing more open-source code visibility from outside the group of specific software development companies and provide the freedom in terms of modification to specify what a user needs rather than forcing the user to settle with what a software development company decides on behalf of the user.

Over time, the open source software movement has evolved and in the modern era is posing questions about fundamental rights for users:

- Open source is about empowering the users, allowing the user to know what is running on the device when accepting an automatic firmware or software update.

- Typically, open source development is inclined more towards defining the trust via transparency, whereas with proprietary software there is always a fear of being unethical or compromised due to its restricted nature.

Apart from meeting the basic fundamental rights for the users to see, alter the source code, and reapply the changes on the underlying hardware, the open source movement is also sensitive about the global geopolitical issues and committed to providing freedom from getting cornered by a supreme power to a relatively constrained nation.

Open source software has long been used by several government agencies due to not only its availability as being free of cost but its provision under a license that allows anyone to change, improve, and extend the software without bothering about political treaties or alliances. The advantage of this open source approach is to ensure continuous support and development of the software by different parties if the original developer or the parent company (rather, country) decides to stop supporting it during a crisis situation (due to consumers of the software belonging to a non-treaty nation). There are more specific reasons for government agencies to mandate the usage of open source including:

- **Trust**: An open source development approach with wider contributors across the globe naturally brings more trust for a government agency to adopt the solution rather than being developed within a particular economic or technological ground.

- **Vendor-independent support**: Typically, all forms of proprietary software have defined maintenance timelines. Post expiry of that timeline, the original company might not be responsible for supporting bug fixes, incremental feature development, and more. Additionally, there is no guarantee that a vendor's business won't get diluted over time. In such a case, who is responsible for maintenance? It's not always feasible for government agencies to migrate to a newer software infrastructure in such cases due compatibility, security issues, and funding limitations.

  Additionally, there might be some specific requirement that each government agency might like to implement (security features, etc.) which are not generic enough for the public. Also, it's not possible for technology companies to support individual drops of the same software across different users.

- **Security**: Security is the biggest concern for government agencies where proprietary software has zero code visibility. So, it's not possible to perform the security audits. In the past, several security researchers have proven the fact that proprietary software may

contain known vulnerabilities, poor security, and
fragile encryption mechanisms. Without having access
to the source code, one can't fix these and might expose
the platform to attackers.

Facts   In recent years, government agencies are seeing more cyber
attacks. One such example is the Distributed DoS (Denial of Service)
attack on the Russian Defense Ministry on July 16, 2021. The attack
knocked the ministry's website offline for around an hour before the
experts were able to rectify the issue and bring systems back online.

The open source software movement is more concerned about freedom
and ensuring trust with the known fact that software runs as part of the
System Protection Ring 0 to Ring 3. Ring 0 is considered as the most privileged
level where the kernel operates and Ring 3 is considered as the least
privileged for running applications or programs. Interestingly, underneath
the kernel layer there is the more privileged entity running in the form of
the system firmware, which is capable enough of directly accessing the bare
hardware without any abstraction. Another book from the same author,
named *Specialized Systemic Knowledge*, provides a detailed overview of the
security protection ring and components running part of it and presents the
necessity of security in the firmware layer. It is important to ensure the code
running as part of the firmware layer also has ample visibility in open source
and provides the freedom that the open source software movement envisions.
The German government is deeply supportive of engaging with open source
firmware for building custom hardware platforms.

Chapter 1 shed light on the origin of system firmware and useful background information about the firmware journey. This chapter will highlight the state of modern system firmware and what bifurcation has been done over a period of time to solve several challenges with either the open source or proprietary firmware development models. Additionally, we will introduce the hybrid firmware architecture, a way to balance the open source firmware development ecosystem even with restricted CPU or SoC architecture.

Understanding the System Firmware Development Model

Figure 5-1 illustrates the firmware evolution on the x86-based SoC platform, which is the most widely used CPU/SoC architecture platform for personal computers. Traditionally, firmware development on x86-based platforms has been considered closed source since its origin. Early days of platform enabling was considered using a legacy BIOS, which lacked modularity and also demanded special programming knowledge. These factors constrained the openness of system firmware at the origin and push the entire firmware development under the cloak for a longer period unless there was an initiative that demands the openness.

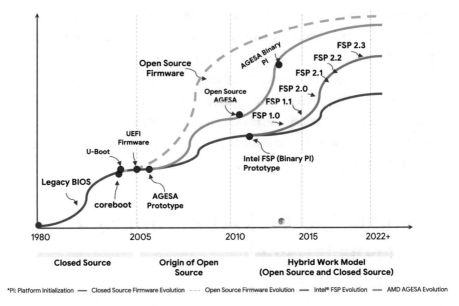

Figure 5-1. *Firmware evolution on x86-based SoC platforms*

The Open Source Initiative (OSI) talks about the same freedom to see the source code running on the restricted hardware, with the ability to modify it for improvement and fix bugs quickly without getting locked into a particular vendor dependency. Several open source firmware initiatives like coreboot started at the same time to get rid of the closed nature of platform enabling. The trickiest part of this open source firmware development approach is getting commitment from the silicon vendors. Silicon vendors are expected to ensure that silicon recommended programming materials are available for the open community without any restriction or additional licensing need. Unfortunately, this is still a wish list even today (after ~40 years of system firmware maturity) for the open-source community. The "Challenges Seen by Silicon Vendors with Open Sourcing" section tries to capture the potential bottleneck from the silicon vendors' viewpoint.

With the introduction of Unified Extensible Firmware Interface (UEFI), the entire platform enabling effort has been divided into two parts.

Generic

The core modules are responsible for providing the infrastructure for the rest of the platform initialization needs. They are guided by the standard specification and maintained by the industry-leading governing bodies. Source codes are typically available for viewing but need specific licensing for altering or extending them.

Platform Initialization (PI)

The actual source code responsible for hardware initialization is typically considered as the most privileged code in terms of execution priority or as a candidate qualified for restricted access. This further ensured that the system firmware remained closed source for the next several decades until a group of silicon firmware engineers innovated an alternative platform initialization model utilizing APIs. These API-based platform initialization designs have ensured seamless integration of silicon reference code with different boot firmware architectures, such as boot firmware adhering to the UEFI/PI specification, coreboot (earlier known as LinuxBIOS), or a legacy BIOS. AMD Generic Encapsulated Software Architecture (AGESA) is a great example; it was initially committed to deliver open source based platform initialization for AMD's Family 15h processors (known as AMD Opteron). Figure 5-2 shows the principle design guideline for platform initialization code to work seamlessly with any standard boot firmware.

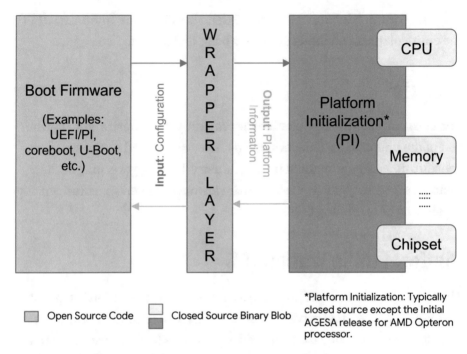

Figure 5-2. *Typical platform initialization guidelines*

Although Figure 5-2 is mostly influenced by AGESA design guidelines, it is not too different from Intel's Firmware Support Package (FSP) which is another extension of platform initialization using binary blobs. The main reason for AMD's AGESA and Intel's FSP continuing as binary-based PIs is due to stringent enabling strategies between internal development and external (open source) releases. This involves extra effort for periodic releases after removing any restricted code and eventually lacks a process that feeds those open-source changes/recommendations back into the main trunk. It's been identified as a very large and time-consuming task on the silicon vendor's side, which demands both development and legal involvement and eventually might result in delaying processor milestones and releasing new chipsets to the market. Instead adhering to the open source-based platform initialization model (as initially proposed), the x86-based silicon vendors later adapted the binary PI which claims the following benefits:

- Tested and validated by silicon vendors prior to customer and IBV (independent BIOS vendors) integration

- Intended to do heavy lifting on the silicon vendors' side with trained silicon engineers and provide a better interface for standard boot firmware integration

- Provides well encapsulated, easy to integrate, and customize binary PI blobs

- Offers a defined release process that includes documentation to understand the integration responsibilities at the boot firmware side

- Easy integration for silicon errata fixes at different product life-cycles, without deeper understanding of silicon operations

This approach of a binary-based PI is against the fundamental principle of the open source movement, which doesn't encourage getting stuck with vendors providing the bug fixes or feature implementation. Specifically, 2014 can be considered as the year for the alternative firmware development approach for the Chrome OS platform, which demands more freedom in platform enabling with open source firmware initiatives. Even today it lacks any good real alternative approach by x86-based silicon vendors that support open-source based firmware development for early SoC platforms. The closed source binary PI model is a forced choice for the Chrome OS platform to meet the business goals.

In summary, the firmware development model in last several decades can be divided into three major parts. The closed source firmware development is the case at the present with the majority of system firmware used for embedded devices. With the origin of open source, the idea is to replace the proprietary firmware code with an open source implementation, but unfortunately it lacks dedicated support from silicon vendors. Finally, the hybrid work model is an attempted to balance the open-source firmware development with a minimal, essential platform initialization binary supplied by the silicon vendors. This chapter will elaborate the design principles of various hybrid firmware architectures with a demonstration of platform enabling using the hybrid work model.

Understanding the System Firmware Supply Chain

Typically, an open-source firmware development approach makes the community more empowered and flexible enough to provide feature enhancements or bug fixes as applicable. The traditional system firmware development model is a kind of a dictatorship by the silicon vendors to follow the ecosystem built for platform enabling. A deeper look into Figure 5-2 will help you understand this ecosystem better with a proper example. It consists of three major blocks: boot firmware, a wrapper layer, and platform initialization. These blocks represent the supply chain used for platform enabling.

Platform Initialization

Typically, in the context of the system firmware development model, platform initialization is a combination of both silicon initialization and the targeted board initialization. But in this context, the platform initialization term is used to represent the code block that is responsible for silicon initialization alone and shared by silicon vendors.

In the traditional model (outside of an API-based binary model), the sample code being used for silicon initialization is shared among IBVs for their code readiness (the underlying assumption in the platform enablement model is that IBVs are responsible for the maintenance of the system firmware (a.k.a. BIOS code) for OEM/ODMs). Every IBVs has their own proprietary BIOS codebase to abstract the hardware initialization and further provide APIs for other layers for utilization. Aptio (code name for the proprietary BIOS solution developed by the American Megatrends a.k.a. AMI) expects the additional porting of silicon vendor-provided sample silicon initialization code to adhere to the Aptio infrastructure. Similarly, the InsydeH2O UEFI firmware solution focuses on the maximum utilization of a silicon vendor-provided sample package without many modifications. Later the IBV BIOS code is further shared with dedicated original equipment manufacturers (OEMs) and original design manufacturers (ODMs) to add product-specific features like enabling a pre-boot touch screen, on-screen keyboard, pre-boot connectivity, launching a hardware diagnostic utility, and more. Finally, after adding the boot firmware-specific layer, which focuses on the board configuration, the OEM customized system firmware is used for platform enabling.

This process illustrates a continuous effort that runs typically bi-weekly on the IBV/ODM/OEM side and starts with the silicon vendor releasing sample silicon initialization reference code.

Wrapper Layer

Typically, the wrapper layer is considered as an open-source layer that works as a transformation layer between the boot firmware and the platform initialization binary blob in a hybrid work model. A good example to understand the application of wrapper layer is the AGESA wrapper implemented as part of an open source coreboot vendor code implementation (`https://github.com/coreboot/coreboot/tree/master/src/vendorcode/amd/agesa`). The vendor code calls a routine in the wrapper and the wrapper code is responsible for modifying the input parameters to meet the AGESA interface requirement to transfer the call further into AMD's generic routine. Upon return, the wrapper code again modifies the return parameters to meet the vendor code's needs and return to the caller. The direct communication between the boot firmware and the PI layer is strictly prohibited. In the case of Intel's FSP design, several EDKII package modules work as wrapper layers. Specifically, IntelFsp2Pkg is the one responsible for transferring the call into and from the silicon initialization layer to and from the boot firmware layer.

Boot Firmware

In the context of a hybrid work model, the boot firmware can be considered using one of the open-source system firmware architectures. Chapter 1 in *Specialized Systemic Knowledge* provides a detailed work model using coreboot and EDKII Min-Platform as boot firmware for the IA SoC platform. Typically, the responsibility of boot firmware in the hybrid model is to provide configuration parameters as per the target hardware prior to transferring the call into silicon vendor-provided binary PI implementation and performing the specific hardware initialization (outside the scope of silicon programming, like the BoM/peripheral components initialization, like GPIO programming, etc.).

To summarize, the supply chain used on a traditional x86-based platform enablement model demands too much manual porting and this process might be erroneous due to more human involvement. The modern platform-enabling model adopted by silicon vendors relies on boot firmware-agnostic application binary interfaces (ABIs) like library implementations (AGESA) from AMD or the firmware support package (FSP) from Intel, rather relying on IBVs to prepare the codebase, distribute among ODMs/OEMs, and finally provide bug fixes at each level.

Spectrum of Open and Closed Source System Firmware

A detailed analysis of the open and closed source system firmware benefits and downsides is shown in Figure 5-3 based on the authors' years of service in firmware development and contributions to various open source firmware initiatives.

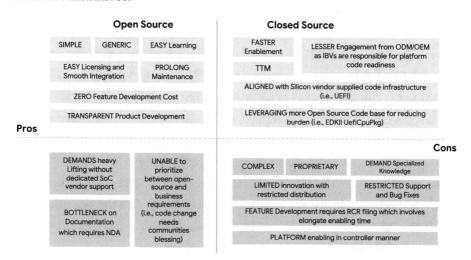

Figure 5-3. *Deep analysis of the impact of open and closed firmwares*

Figure 5-3 attempts to outline the scope for both firmware development approaches at a very high level.

On the brighter side, the open source firmware development model focuses on simplicity in every approach, like in terms of licensing requirements, coding complexity, developing based on a standard software interface without much abstraction, and not demanding intensive training to be a subject matter expert. As highlighted in earlier sections, the open source development model provides freedom from getting stuck in vendor-specific services for product maintenance, additional feature enablement, fixing bugs, and more. Although the project development cost (in terms of monetary value) is not pivotal for making the decision about picking open or closed source firmware for product development, if that is also a concern, then open source community projects are supportive of being cost effective and transparent for product development. On the other hand, the closed source firmware development model is more focused on meeting business goals like the silicon time to market (TTM) timeline. In order to meet those business goals, closed source firmware often disregards the commitment towards the open source community. The closed source model has existed over the last several decades, so from the OEM side it is a proven success path for launching the product year by year. The adaptation of a closed source model might also keep the source code implementation aligned to the silicon vendor-supplied code infrastructure. Even with the closed source-based firmware development approach in last few years, there are some positive steps of reducing the closed source burden by attempting feature development using open source implementations. For example, Intel FSP adapted the open source EDKII module UefiCpuPkg for multiprocessor initialization instead of relying on closed source implementation.

On the flip side, using open source firmware development on a restricted SoC platform demands significant heavy lifting without dedicated commitment from the SoC vendors in terms of providing the minimal documentation for silicon-recommended programming. If the required documentation is available, there is no guarantee that the documented programming steps are correct and that adhering to the same will help to reach the desired goal. Often this documentation is carried forward from the previous generation SoC platform without having the actual hardware programming sequence captured. Often, updating the document to match the actual programming recommendation is an afterthought. Having an open source first model for firmware development at times appears challenging when one needs to prioritize between aligning community feedback and meeting business requirements, as there might be cases where a code change list (CL) is mandatory for platform enabling but the community wants more documentation and clarification, which needs alignment with SoC providers and other internal stakeholders inside the silicon vendor. Closed source firmware development has major bottleneck of not having basic code visibility, a limited timeline for getting bug fixes, new feature implementation subjected to internal alignment on the silicon vendor side, and finally a single binary that serves all users requirements forces features on the user even when the user is skeptical about the specific feature.

The idea behind the hybrid firmware development model is to benefit from both (open and closed source) approaches and be flexible enough to inherit only the positive side from either proposal. The hybrid firmware approach tries to demystify firmware development on restricted SoC platforms to meet the TTM. For example, the Intel SoC platform is not supportive enough to ensure open source firmware (OSF) development to meet the TTM. Ensure platform enabling using open-source firmware with minimal/essential binary blobs in order to meet the silicon product launch timeline. For example, the Chrome OS platform with Intel SoC has adopted a hybrid work model that combines

- coreboot, an open source firmware

- And various closed source binary blobs running on the host CPU (i.e., FSP) and essential microcontrollers (i.e., CSE, PMC, etc.) to ensure the successful platform enablement

The combination of open and closed source blobs remain constant (with specific firmware binary name changes such as PSP instead CSE firmware) while ensuring platform enablement using the AMD SoC for the Chrome OS platform.

Current Industry Trends with Hybrid Firmware

As highlighted in Figure 5-1 about the firmware evolution on x86-based SoC platforms in the last several decades, the situation is indifferent even for non-x86 based SoC platforms as well. At present, all leading silicon vendors are reluctant to prioritize the silicon initialization using the open source firmware initiative. This creates challenges for the business groups (for Chrome OS devices) that are committed to the open source firmware development to accept some kind of intermediate path to continue making progress in platform initialization. Figure 5-4 exhibits the current industry trends with hybrid firmware for the Chrome OS platform.

Although the ideal business goal is to develop firmware for APs used in the Chrome OS platform using open source firmware initiatives, Figure 5-4 is the ground reality with the different SoC platforms used in Chrome OS devices. There are multiple closed source binary blobs being integrated with open source coreboot (which is the primary boot firmware for Chrome OS devices) to define the bootable recipe with those restricted SoC platforms.

The tables provide a brief overview of how different closed source binary blobs are used across AMD, Qualcomm, and MediaTek's SoC platform. Additional sections will demonstrate platform enabling using hybrid firmware on Intel SoC platforms.

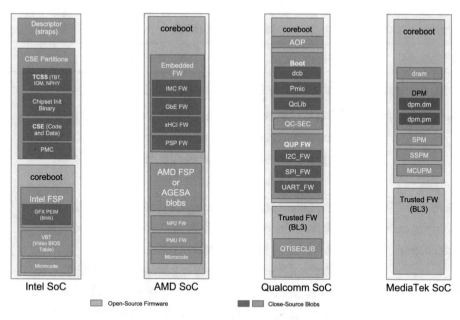

Figure 5-4. *Hybrid firmware model across leading SoC vendors*

Hybrid firmware on the generic AMD SoC platform

Firmware	Description
IMC firmware	Firmware used for the integrated microcontroller
GbE firmware	Firmware for the AMD Gigabit Ethernet LAN controller
xHCI firmware	Firmware for the xHCI controller
PSP firmware	The Platform Security Processor (PSP) is an ARM-based Isolated security co-processor on the AMD SoC platform running independently from the x86 processors.
Microcode	On x86-based platforms, microcode blobs are used to load the patch table for CPUs.

(continued)

331

Hybrid firmware on the generic AMD SoC platform

Firmware	Description
PMU firmware	Firmware for the PHY microcontroller unit
MP2 firmware	The MP2 is an ARM processor programmed as an I2C controller. Used for touchscreens and touchpads on modern laptops and uses the PCI interface for host x86-based communication.
coreboot (running on host x86 processor)	The open-source boot firmware is used on the AMD SoC platform for platform initialization. All these closed source blobs reside into the coreboot *cbfs*. coreboot is flexible enough to perform silicon initialization by using the AMD binary PI interface on older AMD platforms or using an adapted FSP specification-based API interface.
Silicon initialization (running on host x86 processor)	The restricted silicon initialization code block is abstracted and delivered as a binary blob; can be integrated with any standard boot firmware (coreboot in this example of the Chrome OS platform). Performs silicon initialization using API callbacks into the closed source silicon library. There are two possible ways the silicon initialization blobs is designed: 1. **FSP**: Fixed Entry and Exit based APIs are defined by the Intel specification and implemented by AMD. Refer to later sections for more details. 2. **AGESA**: A binary PI library with more APIs (compared to the FSP) does the silicon initialization. Refer to later sections for more details.

(*continued*)

Hybrid firmware on Qualcomm Snapdragon 7c Platform

Firmware	Description
AOP	Firmware used for the Always On Processor (AOP). The AOP is capable of managing the DDR frequency dynamically and controlling the self-refresh for the DRAM memory block for better power consumption during the idle mode of the system.
Boot	dcb.bin, Pmic.bin, and QcLib.elf are binaries that are part of this category and are responsible for performing operations such as • SoC boot • PMIC initialization • DDR initialization **dcb.bin**: The blob that contains the DDR setting and DDR training data. Host firmware running on the CPU passes a table with DDR training data to QcLib for permanent memory initialization and further stores the memory training data into non-volatile storage to avoid retraining over consecutive boots. **Pmic.bin**: Binary blob that holds Power Management IC (PMIC) settings. If coreboot is used for the host firmware, the romstage passes the table with PMIC settings data to QcLib for performing SoC clock and PMIC configuration. **QcLib.elf**: Silicon binary blob loaded by coreboot romstage for performing the DRAM and power management controller initialization. The romstage part of coreboot has a specification-defined input and output mechanism to pass and retrieve the information to and from QcLib.

(continued)

Hybrid firmware on Qualcomm Snapdragon 7c Platform

Firmware	Description
QC-SEC	A highly trusted secure image developed as part of Qualcomm Technologies (QTI's) secure boot feature to ensure loading of the trusted execution environment (TEE). Upon execution, this image will configure the access control of the system by isolating the memory used for trusted execution from the less-privileged/non-trusted execution.
QTISECLIB	Trusted Firmware-A (TF-A) implements the EL3 firmware layer for QTI, and QTISECLIB is used as a library for TF-A compilation. The APIs that are part of this library are responsible for performing operations like – PSCI initialization – Interrupt registration and managing – Providing an API wrapper for crash reporting
QUP firmware	The Qualcomm Unified Peripheral (QUP) serial engine provides a general purpose data path for connecting independent protocol-specific logic. The external interface types like Serial Peripheral Interface (SPI), I2C, and UART mini-cores can be independently used to communicate with the FIFO buffer as part of the QUP serial engine. This blob contains firmware required for I2C, UART, and SPI core initialization as per the configuration type.
coreboot (running on host x86 processor)	coreboot is the running part of TF-A as the BL33 bootloader responsible for platform- or board-specific initialization. Refer to Chapter 3's "Minimalistic Bootloader Design on the ARM Platform" section for more details.

(continued)

Hybrid firmware on the MediaTek MT8192 platform

Firmware	Description
MCUPM firmware	Firmware for the MCUSYS power management. While using coreboot as the boot firmware on the MediaTek platform, the MCUPM firmware resides in coreboot cbfs and is loaded into MCUPM SRAM by coreboot at the ramstage boot phase.
SSPM firmware	Secure System Power Manager (SSPM) is responsible for adding power-related features like CPU DVFS, thermal control, and more. SSPM firmware is loaded into SSPM SRAM as part of the ramstage initialization process.
SPM firmware	System Power Manager (SPM) is able to turn off the power such as DRAM self-refresh and the clock while the kernel triggers the suspend or Vcore DVFS features. coreboot loads `spm_firmware.bin` from cbfs into DRAM and SPM DRAM loads it from the DRAM into SPM SRAM.
DRAM	`dram.elf` is responsible for performing the full DRAM calibration and provide the training data to the boot firmware for restoring into the non-volatile memory for faster consecutive boots. coreboot calls into the dram init entry point (_start) with a configurable data structure (named dramc_param struct) to perform the DRAM initialization and the return value is stored into the flash RW region.

(continued)

Hybrid firmware on the MediaTek MT8192 platform

Firmware	Description
DPM	DRAM Power Management (DPM) firmware is used for the DPM hardware controller; it's responsible for performing the DRAM low-power operations like self-refresh and disable PLL/DLL when the DRAM is not in use. DPM firmware has two parts: • DPMD as data part (dpm.dm) • DPMP as program part (dpm.pm) DPM binaries (dpm.dm and dpm.pm) are loaded into SRAM by coreboot.
coreboot (running on host x86 processor)	coreboot is the running part of TF-A as non-trusted firmware a.k.a. the BL33 stage. coreboot is responsible for platform initialization using native coreboot drivers and additionally by loading several closed source blobs as mentioned in this table for operations like DRAM initialization and power management IC's initialization.

To summarize, the hybrid firmware development used by leading SoC vendors with various different firmwares can be divided into two major categories:

- **Firmware that is running on the coprocessor** and is essential to bring the host processor to life. AMD's PSP firmware and QC's AOP firmware are closed source firmwares from the previous tables.

- **Firmware that is running on host processor** after host processor is released out of reset can be further divided into two categories:

- Firmware responsible for performing silicon initialization and typically released as a closed source binary blob with multiple APIs for integration with other bootloaders. Examples: AMD's AGESA and QC's QTISECLIB

- The open-source firmware code running on the host CPU, being the context master and often calling into other restricted silicon blobs using given APIs. For example, coreboot on the Chrome OS platform seamlessly runs on both x86 and ARM platforms and is able to manage platform initialization using one or more closed source binaries. Chapter 4 provides more details about various open-source firmware architectures.

Later sections of this chapter provide a deep dive into the silicon vendors' supplied firmware that runs on the host processor for x86 and ARM SoC platforms.

Challenges Seen by Silicon Vendors with Open Sourcing

Since the historical past of platform enabling journeys the firmware development model always remains closed and deeply controlled by the silicon vendors. Silicon vendors typically rely on hardware partners like OEMs/ODMs for building the reference hardware platform using the silicon supplied by them and on software vendors like ISVs/IBVs to develop the software and firmware using the same hardware components and additionally provide support like bug fixes and maintenance. The current platform enabling model demands more openness in this traditional approach, which means challenges for silicon vendors to revamp the enabling model.

Based on several years of working experience in that closed-source firmware development and enabling model at IBV and on the silicon vendor side, here are some insights on the potential challenges for silicon vendors regarding the demand for openness.

To simplify this discussion, this section will focus on listing challenges seen by the silicon vendors in open-sourcing proprietary silicon initialization code.

Datasheet Dependency

System firmware programming can be defined as a simplistic process where a bunch of chipset and CPU registers are programmed as per the given guideline. Typically, the registers that get programmed by the silicon reference code are not always documented as part of externally or publicly available datasheets. Silicon engineers or the release owner may not be sufficiently empowered to bring those required registers into the public documentation first before fixing known bugs. Additionally, this may delay program milestones with a dependency on external documentation with every code change. Many of the registers programmed into the silicon reference code are considered as "restricted secrets" based on the initial attributes assigned by the silicon team. The potential reasons could be register accesses over proprietary bus interface, interfacing with the power management controller for better power savings, and more.

As per the open source programming model and reviewers' expectations, all registers that are programmed by the silicon reference code should get documented in the external datasheet with non-restricted access.

Third-Party IP Restrictions

Developing silicon reference code involves engaging with third-party IP owners as well for integrating their components. Typically, this process starts with third-party component owners sharing their reference code under a specific license which forbids silicon vendors from redistribution. For example, Memory Reference Code (MRC) shared by memory vendors is prohibited from further distribution as part of silicon reference code. Similarly, discrete GPU initialization code using third-party modules can't reside in the silicon reference code release. OEMs need to engage with specific independent hardware vendors (IHVs) to make those reference codes available.

Silicon Reference Code Development Without Compatibility

Typically, silicon reference code is developed without ensuring backward compatibility, which poses a challenge to determine the percentage of code that is actually carried forward from the previous generation. Unless a version control method for hardware registers is used in system firmware programming, it's hard to justify if all registers belonging to a newer chipset are restricted and can't have open source visibility. The fact behind AMD's aggressive open source silicon development plan with AGESA didn't last long due to a massive IP legal review on the codebase every time before external release without any traceability of running additional review only on newly added silicon code for specific CPU/SoC generation incrementally rather than brute force method. The entire process became expensive in terms of time and effort and caused problems on the business side, like delaying the product shipment. Later AMD decided to only support AGESA-based binary blobs for platform initialization.

Early Platform Enabling with Non-PRQ'ed Silicon

Product Ready Quality (PRQ) is when a silicon is ready for shipment. In the modern platform enabling model, the hardware and software vendors have been engaging with silicon vendors since the first silicon power-time, even cases for early platform bring up, partners are engaging with silicon vendors during pre-silicon readiness using emulation models. In such cases, working on non-PRQ silicon trends to have more workarounds and bug fixes due to the nature of the engagement. The silicon team finds it hard to implement workarounds for such early defects in the public domain (open-source). Additionally, there is a myth that demonstrating more silicon bugs in the public domain before the product launch might impact the business and make the shareholders concerned about the future product health. This might eventually downgrade the company valuation in the open market.

Distinguished Product Features

Firmware is always closest to the hardware and is often used for reserved engineering to get more insights into the underlying hardware. Any new hardware interface developed as part of a silicon product would definitely require firmware to initialize it. Early open-sourcing of silicon reference code that includes any of distinguished product features might reveal an advantage over the competition prior to the product launch.

Limited Customer Demand

Typically, platform enabling, customization, and support activity for silicon vendors is still managed by IBVs. They predominantly use proprietary closed source code for OEM/ODM platform development. In current platform-enabling models across different operating systems (Windows, Mac, Chrome, Android, Linux, etc.), the customer's voice that demands open-source-based silicon development is still very limited.

From the business side, Google Chrome OS platforms are very keen on having that freedom in platform development along with a very limited group of companies like System76. Facebook (Meta) also shares the vision of open source firmware for their server platforms. In general, having an ecosystem that requires more open source visibility even with silicon reference code would help silicon vendors think about possible ways out. For example, the evolution of the closed source-based firmware development model to the modern hybrid firmware model is the value addition done by the voice, which demands more freedom. Both x86-based silicon vendors adopted the same firmware support package (FSP) specification for delivering the binary-based platform initialization blobs for the open-source firmware integration.

Closed-Source Mindset

Until and unless there is a specific business reason of making things restricted or confidential, there is a thin line between what can be qualified as closed source over open source. It's a decision made by a few key business folks with *great power* and the rest just adhere to the same. An argument against this mindset could be a business decision that gets redefined over a period of time and allows opportunity for rectification is benefited the most rather than getting sucked into the history old principle.

Looking at Intel's FSP evolution on the core side of the business since 6th Generation of Core Processor, codename SkyLake till latest 12th Generation Core Processor, codename Alder Lake, one argue could be that, except the Memory Initialization blob (known as FSP-M and, deals with memory technologies), others (FSP blobs for Silicon Initialization and its associated call-backs) are good candidate for open source due to its backward compatibility over last several generation of SoCs (and its interface) and captured well as part of the external SoC programming document.

Documentation Is an Afterthought

The silicon reference code implemented by silicon vendors is not derived from a single source document. Much of the code lacks supporting documentation that justifies the flow inside the silicon reference code or calls out the interdependency between various chipset initializations. A good documentation that highlights the minimal silicon reference code design could be a good starting point for the open-sourcing discussion.

Importance of a Specific System Firmware Architecture

In an ideal scenario, a silicon vendor should just focus on developing and releasing sample silicon programming code that is easy for the ecosystem to accept and use for the product intercept. The highest priority should be given to the business value rather than being affiliates with a particular system firmware architecture for developing silicon reference code.

Take the example of Intel's FSP development. The wrapper layer, IntelFsp2Pkg, has been developed for FSP and is already available as part of the open-source EDKII project. The rest of the FSP development is tightly coupled with the UEFI PEI (pre-EFI initialization) phase. Multiple PPIs (PEIM-to-PEIM interfaces), GUIDs (globally unique identifiers), and HOBs (hand-off blocks) published by Intel's FSP are outside of the FSP specification and only get consumed by the UEFI platform code. A study done using Intel's core processor FSP codebase reveals that out of 21 PPIs being published by FSP as part of the FSP-M and FSP-S blobs, only 5 are used by the FSP module itself. So, the missing piece of the information here is whether those unattended PPIs are being installed inside the scope for silicon reference code and are mistakenly implemented inside FSP or are meant for being consumed by entities outside FSP (i.e., UEFI platform code). A UEFI platform-independent FSP development might have broadened the scope for Intel's FSP open source discussion.

These are just a few high-level thoughts against the open-sourcing discussion from the author's den, without knowing about anything that might actually prohibit the SoC vendors from getting into a more open-source friendly development model.

Challenges Faced by the Open Community with Closed Sourcing

Looking at the evolution of the platform enabling model in the last one decade, it's important for silicon vendors to stay focused on the open community feedback. It often appears that individuals who are part of open communities also belong to the developer forum. For any silicon vendor, it's key to keep the developer community happy and stay connected with them. Here is the summary of community feedback over the last several years when the silicon vendors forced more closed sourced binary blobs for platform initialization.

Security

The biggest challenge with the closed source binary model is lack of code security audit opportunities. Additionally, there is no traceability about incorporating security audit feedback into the firmware code base. The code development is a manual process, and it is expected to have coding defects. The industry average is about 10-20 defects per 1k LOC. In most of cases, the defects that remain unreported are attributed to security threats. It is possible to achieve zero defects in a product but that involves cost, so the cheapest way to ensure quality is by allowing more eyes to review the code. This is the bottleneck with the current silicon programming model.

Facts   NASA was able to achieve zero defects in their Space Shuttle Flight Software development process, but at a cost of thousands of dollars per line of code.

Platform Enabling

With the current platform enabling model, every new platform power-on requires some kind of support from the silicon vendors. Due to multiple binary blob dependencies, it's difficult to debug any issues that deal with those restricted microcontrollers' initializations. Such exclusive dependency over silicon team representatives in platform enabling might not be a very sustainable model even for silicon vendors as at times scaling projects initiated by ODMs might run longer than the available support window on the silicon side.

Motivation Is Lagging

The open source firmware community provides zero-cost consultation, debug, bug fixes, and feature implementation. The only thing that the community wants is support from silicon vendor engineering in terms of getting the right documentation and/or code visibility without any difficulty. Having limited or no commitment from silicon and hardware vendors at times causes motivational issues for the open source community.

Hard to Debug

Debugging is an inevitable part of system firmware development. The closed source approach prohibits the flexibility of source code-based debugging on the hardware platform. It's hard to detect failures if a closed source binary blob just stops booting. Chapter 4 of *Firmware Development: A Guide to Specialized Systemic Knowledge* provides more details on the debug methodology across different SoC architecture and hardware platforms.

Additionally, the hybrid firmware model often limits the debuggability due to non-uniform debug libraries between open and closed source code bases. It's the same with other report status libraries such as post code and timestamps. For example, on hybrid firmware models on Intel-based platforms using coreboot open source boot firmware, one needs to explicitly build FSP binaries in debug mode to get integrated into the coreboot image. This is because Intel FSP and coreboot don't share a debug library even though both use the same hardware debug interface like serial UART over CPU or PCH LPSS. Moreover, the open source community might not have access to FSP debug binaries for fear of leaking the silicon initialization flow.

Ungoverned Growth for Closed Source Blobs

Due to unaccountability and less governance to tap on the features that went inside these closed source blobs and eventually rises the blobs footprint, are real concerns for product integrators. Typically, developers give more importance to enabling a new feature without bothering about the implications for the platform in terms of increasing the boot media size and a longer platform boot time. Additionally, the fuzzy responsibility between the silicon vendor-provided PI binary and the open source boot firmware creates unwanted duplication of work, resulting in a larger boot media size. In a study done between Intel's 6th generation core processor and 11th generation core processor, the silicon reference binary blob size increased by 2x times.

In summary, the open-source community sees this as the opportunity for the silicon vendor not to limit the improved scope only to the process and silicon technology used for building world-class products. A revamp in the platform enabling model is required to make it much easier and scalable with time. The advocacy that this chapter is doing about defining the hybrid firmware work model is to improve the ecosystem by offering feedback from both sides (the silicon vendors and the open source community), which needs to be considered when developing system firmware for future platforms.

Hybrid Firmware Architecture

Earlier sections of this chapter emphasized the challenges that the industry is facing with a goal of more code visibility for firmware development. Unfortunately, at the same time, the business goals and the restricted nature of the platform enabling model on the hardware side is deferring that desire. The hybrid firmware architecture is an approach that demystifies firmware development on restricted SoC and/or hardware platforms. Figure 5-4 described the present industry platform enabling model across leading SoC vendors and none of these approaches are supportive enough to ensure open source firmware development to meet the business goal of TTM.

This section provides a brief overview of the hybrid work model that combines the various system firmware architectures explained as part of the earlier chapters. The remaining sections highlight work-related details to enable the platform using hybrid firmware architecture. Additionally, a case study of a restricted SoC platform using this model will help readers too. Prior to that, let's understand a few ground rules that qualify a firmware for getting into a hybrid firmware architecture.

Ground Rules

Figure 5-5 pictorially represents the hybrid firmware architecture with some ground rules that ease the platform enabling.

Rule 1: Ensure platform enabling using open source firmware being the context master and integrate minimal/essential binary blobs for platform initialization. For example, the Chrome OS platform with Intel SoC has adopted a hybrid work model that combines the following:

- coreboot, open-source firmware

- Various closed source binary blobs either running on the host CPU (i.e., Intel's FSP binaries) or on essential microcontrollers (i.e., on Intel's platform CSE Firmware, PMC firmware, etc.)

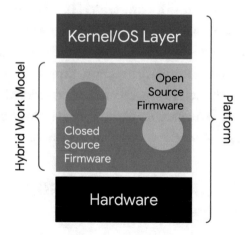

Figure 5-5. *Hybrid firmware architecture*

Rule 2: Typically, closed source and open source firmwares have their own distribution licensing and back and forth call limitations. Hence, binary blobs that are required to execute in the context of open-source firmware should implement ABIs for communication. The ABI way of implementing communication makes this approach more generic and scalable beyond a fixed system firmware architecture.

Rule 3: Prohibit direct communication between open source firmware running on a host CPU as a context master and closed source binary blobs. The communication between the two should be routed via a wrapper layer as highlighted in Figure 5-2. The wrapper layer is responsible for receiving the call from the external boot firmware (can be referred to as open-source firmware) and translating the input parameters to route the call into specific hardware blocks inside the closed source PI binary.

Rule 4: Allow redistribution of those close-source binaries without any restriction. This will ensure that the open community engages in the platform bring up with limited silicon vendor support.

Rule 5: Ensure every closed-source binary blob is equipped with a header to retrieve its version information. Additionally, integrating a closed binary into the code base requires descriptive information of the support git bisect in the future for any critical issue debugging.

Although the open source community expects to have zero closed source binary in firmware projects, knowing the limitations in the other approach, as discussed in the earlier section, firmware development using a hybrid firmware architecture is used on those restricted SoC platforms. This section defines the ownership in the hybrid firmware development model and their dependency over the platform enabling.

Firmware Development Using Hybrid Firmware Architecture

Figure 5-5 shows the three major tiers of a platform: hardware layer, firmware, and software layer.

Hardware layer: Typically remains closed source and consists of different hardware control blocks.

Firmware layer: Running code to perform the hardware initialization on the top of the hardware layer. This can either run open or closed source firmware based on the actual hardware design on the host CPU or coprocessors residing deep inside SoC.

Software/kernel layer: The highest layer is the kernel, which relies on the button layer for bringing the hardware controllers to life so the applicable device driver can get loaded. It's capable of holding the firmware and loading it into the hardware controller using device driver.

The firmware layer belonging to hybrid firmware architecture used for platform enabling can further be divided between firmwares used prior to the main processor or host CPU reset and firmwares used post host CPU reset for initialization of the platform components for ensuring booting to software/kernel layer.

Types of firmware development in the hybrid work model

Pre-CPU reset firmware development	Any firmware that is essential for bringing the host processor out from the reset belongs to this category. Typically, firmwares run as part of a microcontroller and are released as a binary blob that is considered closed source. In general, closed source blobs are released by SoC vendors either using private GitHub repositories or distributed over release portals. Examples: PSP firmware on the AMD SoC platform, CSE firmware on Intel SoC platform
	The open source firmware project coreboot has dedicated submodules to support hosting these SoC vendor-provided binaries.
Post-CPU reset firmware development	This type of firmware starts executing immediately after the host CPU comes out from reset. Depending on the nature of the platform initialization operation, it might require communication between both open and closed source binaries using ABI. In general, the communication takes place in the context of open source coreboot being the initiator.

(continued)

Types of firmware development in the hybrid work model

Let's take an example of a coreboot project with the latest AMD SoC platform. This firmware category can further split into three subcategories with defined owners for development:

Silicon PI binaries: A closed source API-based implementation is validated and released by a silicon vendor. In this example, AMD can either provide FSP binaries or an AGESA PI blob for integration with coreboot. The rest of the platform bring up code has significant dependency over this piece of binary blob.

SoC layer inside coreboot that gets implemented around silicon PI binaries and essential pieces of silicon initialization required prior to calling into those ABI blobs. In general,, silicon team engineers are also responsible for developing this code block in open source. The completion of SoC code development depends on both the SoC layer and associated silicon PI binary blobs.

The mainboard layer is developed utilizing the SoC code. Typically, the expectation from this layer is to perform the platform-specific initialization that is dependent on target hardware. This includes board specific GPIO (general purpose input/output) configuration, DRAM configuration, and configuration of peripherals attached to the motherboard. In the coreboot development model, the mainboard layer is a combination of the baseboard (the base schematics used for the mainboard design) and variants (one or more derived schematics design based on the baseboard). ODM engineers take the lead in the mainboard development.

Submodules inside coreboot/ third-party projects	Description
Blobs	Various closed-source binaries for platform initialization
amd_blobs	Proprietary blobs for AMD SoC
Fsp	Intel's released FSP binaries and header files for coreboot integration
qc_blobs	Blobs for the Qualcomm SoC platform

Conventional Closed Source Firmware in the Hybrid Work Model

This section will discuss briefly the post-CPU reset firmwares specifically developed by silicon vendors and released as PI binaries in cross-architecture platforms. The silicon vendor-provided binaries are developed with the principle of maximizing reusability among different boot firmwares to support the wider ecosystem. Additionally, all these silicon vendor-supplied binaries are released to achieve a faster platform bring up without bothering about silicon or hardware learning and paying too much attention to the BIOS development guide or datasheets for the implementation.

A brief overview about these conventional closed source firmwares will help you understand the hybrid firmware architecture better.

Overview of AMD's AGESA and Its Work Model

The AMD Generic Encapsulated Software Architecture (AGESA) is a silicon initialization procedure library designed to enable AMD hardware and software partners to seamlessly develop their features without worrying about silicon initialization. This section provides a high-level overview about the interface used in the procedure library and provides some guidelines about how to integrate this PI blob with an open-source bootloader.

The introduction of AGESA had happened mostly 15 years ago with a goal of supporting open source silicon initialization for AMD's Opteron processors. With AGESA providing the procedural library implementation, it has become easy for partners to integrate with the standard host firmware architecture as per business requirements. Figure 5-6 shows the AGESA working model where each hardware component has its own block (example: AMD Block 1, Block 2, etc.) and at the outer layer, each block is supported with a wrapper.

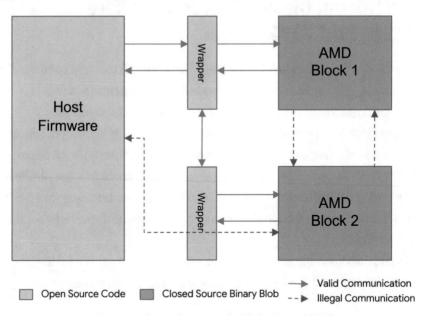

Figure 5-6. *AMD AGESA communication interface*

The wrapper layer helps to keep the AMD's hardware block generic and scalable for multiple generations. To accomplish this, the attempt is to limit the number of entry points or ABIs. Additionally, it aligns the entry points based on the boot state instead of the actual feature programming. The boot firmware (assume coreboot in this case) can call into a routine part of this wrapper. This architecture uses the concept of the initializer function, where the wrapper code receives the input parameter, allocates space for the interface data structure, assigns it based on the input parameter, and finally performs the call to AMD generic routine. After the main function has finished the execution, the wrapper code again modifies the return parameters to match the expectation from the boot firmware caller function and releases the interface data structure. Figure 5-7 describes the calling convention for setting up the code environment after the host CPU comes out from reset using the AmdInitEarly interface.

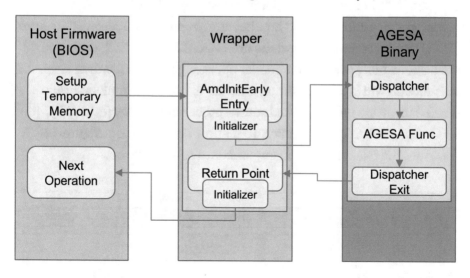

Figure 5-7. *Setting up temporary memory using the AGESA interface*

Each procedure has been designed to achieve a fixed goal, thus the number of procedures are also limited. Additionally, each entry point has a prerequisite to meet so the host firmware needs to account for that as well. All entry points to the AGESA software use a prefix, Amd for example. AmdInitEntry is used to establish the program environment for the host firmware to initiate the boot sequence. The prerequisite is that the AmdInitEntry API should get called only after the AmdInitReset is executed.

Over time, with the burden of a laborious open-source maintenance effort on AMD's part, the company decided to discontinue supporting the open-source AGESA implementation and focus on binary-based releases for customers.

Overview of Qualcomm's QTISECLIB and a Working Model on TF-A

Chapter 3's "Minimalistic Bootloader Design on the ARM Platform" section provided the detailed architectural overview of Trusted-Firmware (TF-A) to help you understand the different ARM exception levels and the responsibility of each bootloader operating in that exception level. This section will provide additional details about TF-A implementing the EL3 firmware using a closed source procedural binary (qtiseclib) for Qualcomm's Snapdragon 7c SoC platform initialization. Figure 5-8 describes the basic TF flow on any standard ARM platform.

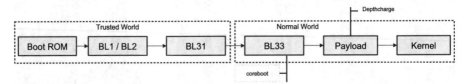

Figure 5-8.   *Generic TF-A boot flow*

The bootloader stages belonging to the trusted world are responsible for setting the required execution environment, setting up early and late architecture-specific initialization, platform-specific initialization prior to load, and executing the bootloader from the normal or non-trusted world. The code structure of the trusted firmware permits each bootloader stage to call into the SoC layer to perform a platform-specific implementation. Figure 5-9 shows the bootloader stage 1 entry function (bl1_main()) executed by the host CPU after a cold reset; it provides an opportunity to perform silicon initialization by ARM SoC vendors (bl1_platform_setup()) and additionally provides hooks to utilize any closed source procedure library implemented by SoC vendor to obscure platform initialization in the open-source.

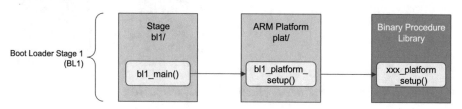

Figure 5-9. *BL1 performs platform initialization*

The later bootloader stages like BL31 are intended to perform the similar architecture initialization being done by BL1 as BL31 has a provision to override any previous initialization done by the BL1 stage. Therefore, the Qualcomm SoC platform has implemented QTISECLIB, a procedural library that works with the BL31 image to perform additional platform initialization using a close source implementation.

QTISECLIB (libqtisec.a) publishes a bunch of required APIs for performing platform initialization on the QC SoC platform, such as a CPU reset handler, system initialization for waking all CPUs (in a multicore environment, including the bootstrap processor and application processors), performing platform-specific initialization, and managing events using Power State Coordination Interface (PSCI) like system_off and suspend.

Figure 5-10 shows the platform initialization model using QTISECLIB on the QC SoC platform, where the platform initialization request triggered during the BL31 stage entry function (bl31_main()) is handled by QC platform initialization code utilizing qtiseclib_bl31_platform_setup() API from the libqtisec.a library.

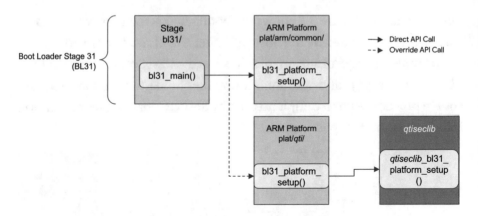

Figure 5-10. *BL31 performs platform initialization*

The hybrid firmware architecture implemented in the ARM SoC platform is developed using a flexible single operation API-based implementation which is more feature or function specific. Therefore, the caller can easily decouple the close source blob layer at compile time from the open source implementation and still be able to create the stable platform boot recipe.

Overview of Intel Firmware Support Package

The Intel Firmware Support Package (FSP) is a solution towards performing processor and chipset initialization using the binary platform initialization (PI) model. The foundation block of the FSP is based on the UEFI architecture (explained in Chapter 4). The glue layer is added on top to support an API that allows seamless integration of any standard boot firmware with the FSP without revealing the proprietary silicon initialization code for platform enabling. Figure 5-11 shows the seamless integration of FSP with a proprietary EDKII-based platform implementation or with open source coreboot.

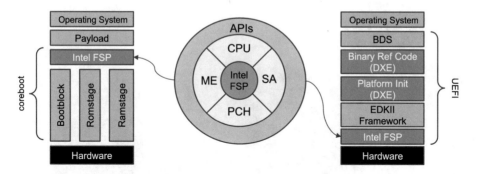

Figure 5-11. *Intel FSP usage model*

Compared to the other hybrid firmware architecture (as explained in earlier sections, implemented by AMD and Qualcomm), Intel's FSP design philosophy is partly different. With other SoC vendors, binary PI implementations running on the host CPU are developed with the principle of a procedural binary, meaning the binary blob gets linked as a library with the open source boot firmware and interface code allowing transferring the call into the respective APIs. On the contrary, the FSP is developed based on the UEFI design philosophy of having one or more firmware volumes (FVs), which further consists of executable modules as per the UEFI specification, as shown in Figure 5-12.

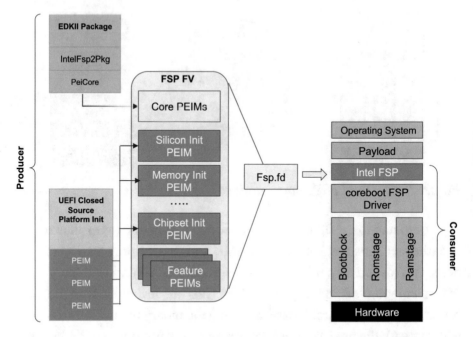

Figure 5-12. *Intel FSP producer/consumer model*

Figure 5-12 shows the Intel FSP producer and consumer model where EDKII, the open-source implementation of UEFI firmware, and UEFI closed source platform initialization modules are represented as FSP producer modules to build an FSP binary. In EDKII, there are two special FSP-related packages. One is IntelFsp2Pkg, which is used to implement underlying calling interface and another is PeiCore, which provides the foundation layer for dispatching of the PEIM (pre-EFI initialization modules) used to produce an FSP binary together with other EDKII silicon packages. Chapter 4 presented the required knowledge to understand the many different terminology inside FSP like hand-off blocks, firmware volumes, and firmware files.

Figure 5-13 illustrates the underhood calling convention implemented inside IntelFsp2Pkg. At the start of the program execution in the hybrid firmware architecture, both the bootloader and the FSP set the program stack to maintain its own execution flow independently. The FSP stack frame includes all general purpose registers, so that the FSP API can perform the SetJump/LongJump-like operation to switch the context between the original FSP API caller provided stack from the FSP's internal stack.

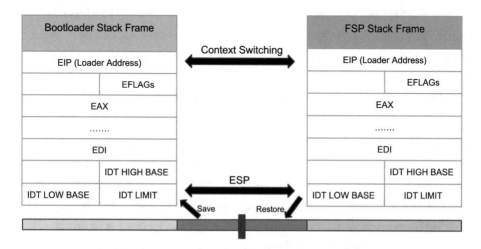

Figure 5-13. *IntelFsp2Pkg handles context switching*

The FSP architecture splits the stack and memory usages separately, meaning the stack is used for normal program execution and the memory is used to restore the context for a later stage to locate and use without reinitialization. Prior to the FSP 2.1 specification in 2018, the expectation for the bootloader is to maintain a separate stack for its own operation and for FSP, this might add an extra stack requirement on the bootloader side. To overcome this, with the FSP 2.1 specification, FSP recommends the bootloader provide a single stack with a size requirement of the maximum size for the FSP and the bootloader to execute.

Focusing back on Figure 5-12, the other side of the diagram represents the consumer of the FSP. Figure 5-12 describes the FSP boot flow where the operation performed by the FSP Producer is highlighted in gray and the platform code that integrates the FSP binary and calls into is the FSP Consumer layer is represented in green. Although the FSP External Architecture Specification (EAS) provides two different modes of operation for FSP as the API mode and the dispatch mode (introduced with FSP 2.1 to facilitate the EDKII bootloaders), this section will focus on the API mode to make it more relevant for users with an open-source bootloader with a non-EDKII background (refer to Chapter 1 in *Firmware Development* to understand the application of the FSP dispatch mode). The FSP EAS describes the five major APIs to finish the silicon initialization for the Intel SoC platform.

Figure 5-14 represents the evolution of FSP on the Intel platform in the last decade. The FSP 1.x specification from 2014 defines FSP APIs with a single monolithic FSP binary. Having a single monolithic FSP blob is acceptable if the targeted boot media is SPI NOR, where the entire flash region is memory mapped. With more embedded design scenarios with NVMe/NAND flash-based booting, where the flash part can't be mapped during the system power on by default, a stepwise approach needs to be adopted for platform initialization and that brings the requirement of splitting a single monolithic silicon initialization blob like FSP into multiple binaries.

- **Pre-memory initialization phase**: Immediately after the initial boot, it needs temporary memory (either system SRAM or CPU cache) to start the code execution.

- **Memory initialization phase**: The memory initialization code is loaded to the temporary memory by the prior boot stage.

- **Post-memory initialization phase**: The silicon initialization code is loaded into the system DRAM by the prior stage.

The FSP 2.0 specification introduces such flexibility in the design to support the boot media beyond just SPI NOR. Since then, the FSP supports multiple binary components and allows flexibility at the boot firmware to replace the proprietary blob implementation with open source native drivers.

FSP binaries	Description
FSP-T	**Entry point**: TempRamInit
	The FSP API is responsible for setting up the temporary memory (a.k.a. cache-as-RAM (CAR)) setup on x86 and preparing the execution environment.
	Starting with the FSP 2.0 specification, the integration of FSP-T is completely optional with coreboot. It relies on a native open source CAR implementation rather than a proprietary implementation using FSP.
FSP-M	**Entry point**: MemoryInit
	Entry point: TempRamExit
	MemoryInit is the most critical FSP API that sets up physical memory for the rest of the platform usage. It supports migration of program execution from temporary memory into physical memory. Typically, it's the first FSP API entry point that gets called by coreboot (romstage).
	The usage of the TempRamExit API is dependent over the execution of the TempRamInit API. If a platform uses FSP-T for temporary memory setup, then it needs to use the TempRamExit API to tear down the temporary memory. On an x86-based platform, the coreboot boot stage postcar is used to tear down the temporary memory.

(continued)

FSP binaries	Description
FSP-S	**Entry point**: SiliconInit
	Entry point: MultiPhaseSiInit
	Entry point: NotifyPhase
	FSP-S is divided into multiple entry and exit points. Typically, SiliconInit is responsible for performing the processor and chipset initialization (apart from memory controller).
	MultiPhaseSiInit is a newly added FSP API since the FSP 2.2 specification. It was introduced to perform any additional programming prior to display initialization.
	Additionally, FSP-S supports three notify phase callbacks
	1. Post PCI enumeration
	2. Ready to boot
	3. End of firmware
	to perform the silicon vendor-recommended lock configuration and final programming of the hardware control block prior to booting the payload/OS.

Figure 5-14 represents the journey of the Intel FSP specification and provides more granular APIs based on functionality. This provides better flexibility on the consumer side of the FSP to drop the unnecessary APIs if an alternative method has been implemented by the boot firmware. For example, coreboot used on Chrome AP firmware development never stitched with FSP-T blob. Lately, an alternative coreboot native driver is implemented to skip calling into the FSP-S Notify Phase APIs.

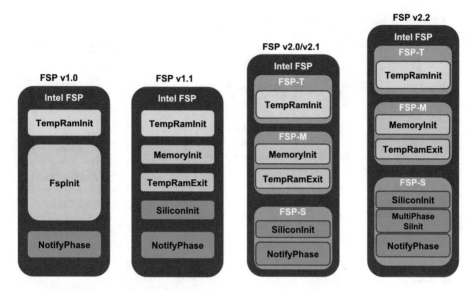

Figure 5-14. *Evolution of the Intel FSP specification*

According to the FSP EAS, the integrator of the FSP binary should well up to the below information:

- **FSP data structure**: The FSP_INFO_HEADER structure provides information about the FSP entry points, configuration block, and more. This information can be located in firmware section data, part of the first firmware file in the FSP firmware volume. Figure 5-15 shows the FSP_INFO_HEADER layout.

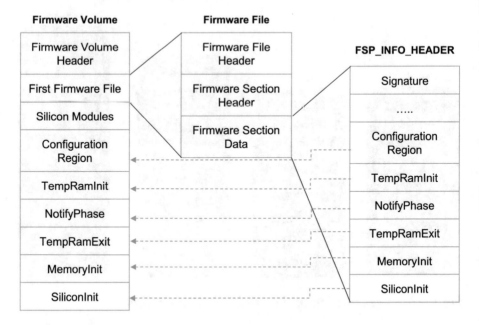

Figure 5-15. *FSP_INFO_HEADER layout implement in IntelFsp2Pkg*

In the FSP_INFO_HEADER, ImageBase is the pointer to the FSP binary base address and Configuration Region (CgfRegion) is a pointer to the configuration block inside each FSP component, as shown in Figure 5-16. The FSP header also consists of the five API entry points (TempRamInit, NotifyPhase, MemoryInit, TempRamExit, and Silicon Init). These entry points will be invoked by the boot firmware as highlighted in Figure 5-17. Each component of the FSP binary (i.e., FSP-T, FSP-M, and FSP-S) has its own FSP_INFO_HEADER, code and configuration data region.

- **Configuration data region**: The silicon initialization modules reside inside the FSP firmware volumes where the code block is responsible for performing the platform initialization. These code blocks typically act based on the policy information. In the UEFI firmware architecture, the policy information is what is given by the user and can be updated from the UEFI BIOS Setup Option. In the absence of the BIOS Setup Option like a user interface with all system firmware architecture, the configuration data region belonging to the FSP is used to pass the policy information to silicon modules for platform initialization, such as to specify the UART number for serial debugging, enable or disable the hardware interface, and more.

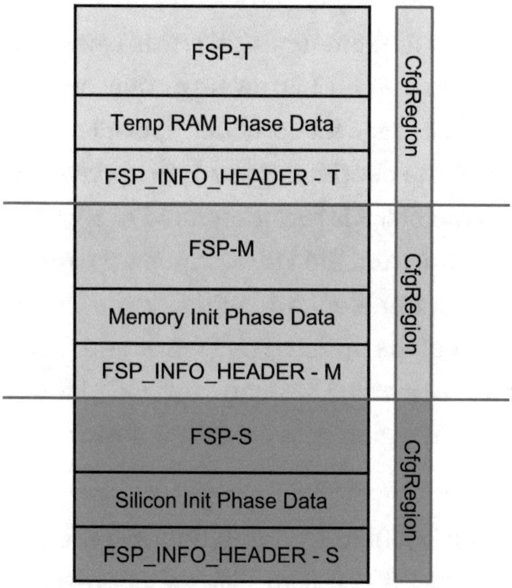

Figure 5-16. *FSP Component logical view*

Each FSP module (FSP-T, FSP-M, FSP-S) contains its own configurable data region which will be used by the consumer of the FSP during boot. This configuration region is a data structure known as updateable product data (UPD) and contains the default parameters for the FSP initialization.

The UPD parameters can be statically customized using a separate YAML-based open-source configuration utility known as the Config Editor (Refer to Chapter 2 of *Firmware Development* for more details). The UPD data can also be dynamically overridden by the bootloader at runtime. In most cases, the default configuration as part of the FSP configuration data region is the one taking effect during the platform initialization as a silicon policy unless overridden by the bootloader. The bootloader can decide to implement the override using BIOS Setup Page in the UEFI firmware or may need a direct source code change for coreboot-like open-source boot firmware. If the bootloader needs to update any of the UPD parameters, it is recommended to copy the whole UPD structure from the FSP component to memory, update the parameters, and initialize the UPD pointer to the address of the updated UPD structure. The FSP API will then use this data structure instead of the default configuration region data for the platform initialization.

Facts   A session presented by the author as part of the Open Source Firmware Conference 2021 called "*MicroPython-based interactive platform configuration for Coreboot*" can be a possible solution to provide a generic user interface to implement FSP UPD override seamlessly on x86 platforms.

- **Silicon initialization**: The main purpose of Intel's FSP is to develop an ecosystem with a binary-based silicon initialization model to avoid running into a complex silicon issue debugging and at the same time ensure meeting the TTM. The closed source nature of silicon code modules inside the FSP are developed according to the Intel external design specification (a.k.a. the EDS recommendation), such as memory initialization, processor and coprocessors bringing up code, and more. This piece of code only requires updating to support newer SoC design.

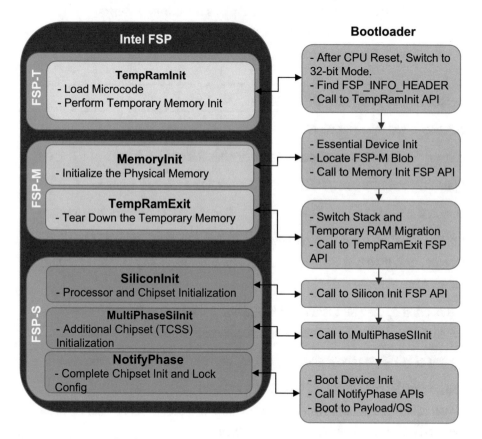

Figure 5-17. *Platform initialization boot flow using the FSP 2.2 specification*

Generic code modules typically come from open-source EDKII and are used for building the silicon and platform code blocks. Examples: PEI core, PCI bus

The platform code is developed based on the actual target hardware and the code pieces are mostly board-centric initialization. Examples: GPIO settings, ACPI table creation. Figure 5-17 highlights the communication between the bootloader and FSP using mandatory FSP APIs. This table presents the detailed coreboot boot flow using the FSP 2.2 specification binary.

---

coreboot boot flow with FSP 2.2 blobs

coreboot owns the reset vector.

coreboot contains the real mode reset vector handler code.

Optionally, coreboot can call FSP-T for CAR setup and create the stack.

coreboot fills in the required UPDs before calling FSP-M for memory initialization.

On exit of FSP-M, coreboot tears down the CAR and does the required silicon programming including filling up UPDs for FSP-S before calling FSP-S to initialize the chipset.

If supported by the FSP, the bootloader enables multi-phase silicon initialization by setting FSPS_ARCH_UPD.EnableMultiPhaseSiliconInit to a non-zero value.

On exit of FSP-S, coreboot performs PCI enumeration and resource allocation.

The bootloader calls the MultiPhaseSiInit() API with the EnumMultiPhaseGetNumberOfPhases parameter to discover the number of silicon initialization phases supported by the bootloader.

The bootloader must call the MultiPhaseSiInit() API with the EnumMultiPhaseExecutePhase parameter n times, where n is the number of phases returned previously. The bootloader may perform board-specific code in between each phase as needed.

Finally, coreboot calls the NotifyPhase API from the proper boot stage before handing over to payload.

- **FSP output**: The FSP architecture relies on the API-based platform initialization using a single binary solution that meets every platform's purpose. The only way to pass the specific information to FSP based on target hardware is by using UPDs. Post FSP done with silicon/hardware initialization, the FSP produces a series of data structures known as HOBs to pass the platform initialization information to the consumer of the FSP. The expectation from the master bootloader is to implement logic that parses those HOBs to consume the platform information. For example, the bootloader needs to parse the resource descriptor HOBs produced by FSP-M to understand the system memory map. The UEFI PI specification provides details about implementing the HOB.

Application of Hybrid Firmware Architecture

Figure 5-5 from the earlier section of this chapter outlined the applicability of the closed source firmware during platform bring up and also highlighted that it's not only limited to the firmware running on the host CPU. Figure 5-4 presents the current industry trend where the boot media holds firmware that must either run on the essential coprocessors or by the host processor to meet the platform initialization goal before handing off to the kernel. This section will demonstrate the application of hybrid firmware architecture on Intel SoC-based Chrome OS platform enabling. The section will help you understand the applicability of every closed-source binary blob that gets stitched to create the final boot recipe for the Intel SoC. For the last several years, booting using SPI NOR has been the de facto standard on the Chrome OS platform using Intel SoC. Typically, Intel's chipset supports multiple masters accessing the SPI flash. Due to the BoM configuration, the Chrome OS platform doesn't use GbE (Gigabit Ethernet) and uses a dedicated Chrome EC SPINOR, hence the SPI NOR layout can be further simplified as illustrated in Figure 5-18 for the Chrome OS platform.

Descriptor: A tiny binary file that holds pointers to the different flash regions like the BIOS region and CSE region. It defines the access control for the master accessing the other regions, various processor, and chipset hardware interface control knobs known as soft-strap.

CSE partition: A region that holds several boot critical and non-boot critical blobs expected to run by coprocessors to prepare the environment for bringing the host CPU out from the reset and loading the required firmware blob into a specific hardware controller (typically referred to as IP) where the host CPU doesn't have access to those hardware block physical register space. Figure 5-19 represents the mapping between Intel SoC SPI layout into the hybrid firmware architecture.

BIOS region (coreboot): The code block belonging to this region is executed by the host processor immediately after coming out from the reset. In the hybrid work model, the BIOS region is created after integrating one or more closed source binaries. Figure 5-19 shows the mapping between the Intel SoC SPI layout into the hybrid firmware architecture.

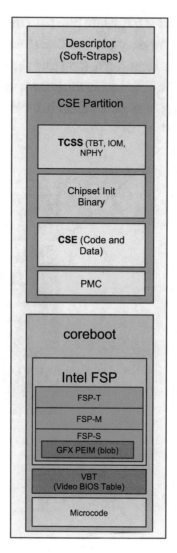

Figure 5-18. *Intel SoC SPI layout*

On the Intel SoC platform, the firmware belonging to the hybrid architecture can be split into three categories:

Closed source firmware *running on co-processors* are typically the ones considered as boot-critical firmware. The various microcontrollers residing deep in the SoC can access the SPI layout to retrieve and load the firmware into respective hardware blocks in the process of allowing CPU out from the reset. For example, the CSE (Intel's converged security engine) firmware block is required to load into the CSE hardware to apply the latest patch released by Intel to fix the known vulnerabilities. Similar logic also applies to other hardware blocks like PMC and PUNIT.

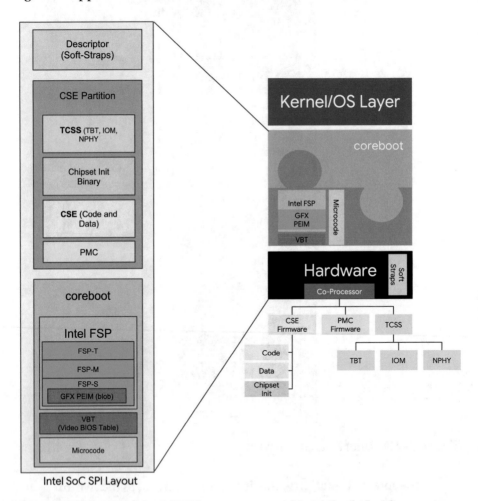

Figure 5-19. *Intel SoC SPI layout mapped into the hybrid work model*

Additionally, it contains non-boot critical firmware running on the co-processor, required to enable the specific SoC features. For example, the Type-C subsystem enablement process requires loading a set of firmware blobs into the specific IPs and performing register programming for initialization.

The host CPU initialization process requires execution of a few more closed source binaries on the host CPU, such as Intel's FSP silicon binary and associated configuration file to complete the platform initialization. See Figure 5-20.

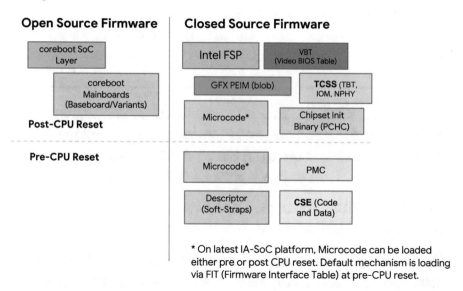

Figure 5-20. *Spectrum between open and closed source firmware on Intel SoC SPI layout*

On the Intel SoC platform, the open source firmware running on the host CPU is really limited. In the hybrid work model adopted in Chrome, the AP firmware development uses coreboot as the bootloader for calling into the silicon initialization APIs. The idea behind adopting open source firmware for the Chrome OS platform is to maintain the flexibility of using an open-source firmware native driver implementation instead of calling into the closed source APIs.

Figure 5-20 shows the spectrum of open and closed source firmware for IA SoC platform binaries in consideration of firmware operational mode between pre- and post-CPU reset.

This table shows the usage of closed source blobs during the pre-CPU reset flow.

Step 1: Pre-CPU reset flow

---

1. With the platform power-on reset, the first hardware block that comes out from reset is CSE (security controller on the Intel latest SoC platform) and the boot ROM code inside CSE will start the ignition of the pre-CPU reset process.

2. The CSE boot ROM will initialize the CSE SRAM to load the binary blobs from the SPI NOR into the SRAM and perform verification prior to execution.

3. The first patchable firmware copy that loads into the CSE SRAM is the CSE binary (includes code and data) to apply the latest patch firmware running on top of the boot ROM. CSE applies the updatable patch firmware to continue the operation further.

4. CSE releases the PMC controller out from the reset and loads the PMC patch firmware from SPI NOR into the CSE SRAM prior loading into the PMC hardware block. It's able to read and apply the PCH soft-strap configuration on the hardware.

5. CSE utilizes the shared SRAM to load the microcode (that combines the ucode for the CPU patch and pcode for the PUNIT patch).

(continued)

6. PMC instructs the north component to come out from reset by bringing PUNIT from reset and loading the pcode patch into the PUNIT.

7. PUNIT further brings the CPU from the reset and loads the ucode patch into the CPU. The CPU is now able to apply the CPU-related soft-strap configuration.

8. In the case of a SPI mapped memory-based SoC design, immediately after the CPU comes out from reset, it will start patching the reset-vector code and jumping into the first code piece of the host firmware.

Figure 5-21 pictorially represents the pre-CPU reset flow on the Intel SoC where the SPI NOR layout at the extreme right of the diagram is highlighted with a green circle indicating the applicability of the firmware blob as part of the pre-CPU reset flow involving various closed-source firmware binaries (descriptor, CSE, PMC, microcode) for the platform initialization.

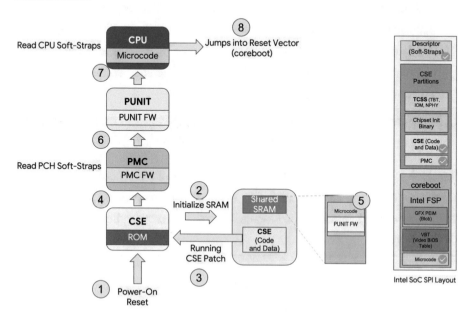

Figure 5-21. *Applicability of the hybrid firmware model during pre-CPU reset flow on Intel SoC platform*

After the CPU comes out from the reset and code block as part of the coreboot, the bootblock starts execution. Typically, on the Intel SoC platform, the CPU starts the operation in a memory-constant manner unless some future platform decides to overcome the memory constraints boot limitation by performing DRAM-based initialization using another auxiliary processor even at reset, like the methodology used on the AMD SoC platform by leveraging the PSP. The main purpose of Step 2 is to initialize some temporary memory to allow execution of the advanced boot stage. This table represents the stepwise pre-memory initialization process utilizing coreboot on the latest Intel SoC platform.

Step-2: Pre-memory initialization phase

---

1. Bootblock, the first coreboot boot phase, does the setting up of the temporary memory (CAR) for code execution.

2. It performs the early initialization of the hardware interface required for communication with the boot critical devices. For example, the TPM is required for the later boot phase so initialization of the I2C/GSPI interface is required prior to communication with TPM. Figure 5-22 provides a pictorial representation of a reference hardware block platform initialization.

3. The pre-memory boot phase is limited in size and operation so it's response is to decompress and load the next boot phase.

Note: FSP-T API, part of Intel's closed-source silicon initialization code FSP, is capable of performing the CAR setup. Due to bringing more openness in the platform initialization process, the Chrome AP firmware excludes the FSP-T from the SPI NOR layout.

Figure 5-22 pictorially represents the pre-memory initialization phase. At the starting of this phase, the hardware components that are readily available after the pre-CPU reset flow are highlighted in green (SPI flash mapped memory, CSE, BSP running the host-firmware). The hardware components colored gray still remain inactive or uninitialized and are waiting for their execution changes. The components colored in blue are getting initialized during this process. A special mention about the exclusion of the FSP-TempRamInit API while working with coreboot on the Chrome OS platform is highlighted in orange.

This phase of platform initialization runs using the BIOS/coreboot region, without any closed-source binary blob. coreboot code is used during this phase of platform initialization and is indicated in yellow to represent the work-in-progress operations.

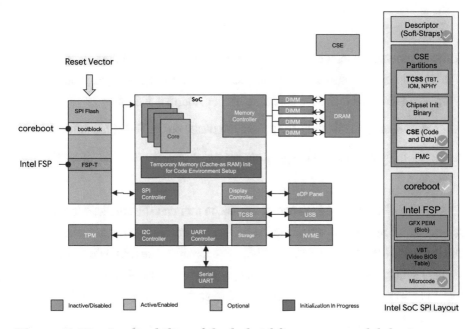

Figure 5-22. *Applicability of the hybrid firmware model during pre-memory initialization phase on the Intel SoC platform*

Romstage, the boot phase as part of the coreboot, is responsible for performing the physical memory initialization. This boot phase leverages the silicon initialization FSP-MemoryInit (a.k.a. FSP-M) API to call into the Memory Reference Code (MRC) code block for DRAM initialization. The only purpose of this phase is to allow the host firmware to migrate into the physical memory-based execution. This table represents the memory initialization steps utilizing the hybrid firmware architecture on the latest Intel SoC platform.

Step 3: Memory initialization phase

---

1. Romstage, the first coreboot module, runs part of the updatable BIOS region. It loads and executes the FSP-M binary blob part of the SPI NOR. Due to the memory-restricted nature of the boot, FSP-M also gets XIP.

2. The silicon vendor-provided closed-source code block runs as part of the FSP-M API and the primary task is to perform DRAM initialization.

3. The pre-memory boot phase is limited in size and operation so the response is to decompress and load the next boot phase. Figure 5-23 provides a pictorial representation of a reference hardware block platform initialization.

4. coreboot sets up the infrastructure (cbmem) based on the DRAM resources.

5. It perform the migration of the program execution environment into physical memory.

Note: The MRC code running as part of the silicon reference binary blobs is typically self-contained in terms of initializing the DRAM. The configuration information that is passed between coreboot to FSP-M API uses UPDs like SPD data and other memory settings. Refer to Chapter 7's "Adopting Hybrid Firmware Development" section to understand the detailed configuration parameters used for board initialization.

Figure 5-23 pictorially represents the memory initialization phase. At the start of this phase, the hardware components that are readily available after the pre-memory initialization phase are highlighted in green (host communication with I2C, SPI, UART, etc.). Hardware components colored gray still remain inactive or uninitialized and are waiting for their execution changes. The components that are colored in blue are getting initialized during this process. The memory controller(s) are getting initialized during this process and ensure the availability of DRAM-based resources for the advanced boot stage.

This phase of platform initialization runs using BIOS/coreboot region, with major contributions from the closed-source binary blob. coreboot code is used during this phase along with Intel FSP for platform initialization and is indicated in yellow to represent the work-in-progress operations.

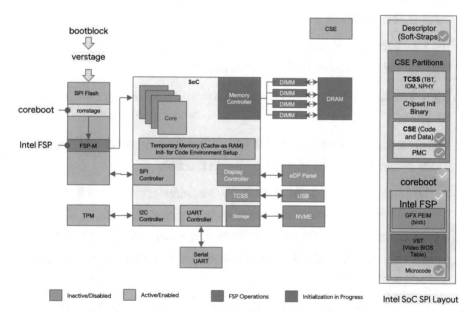

Figure 5-23. *Applicability of the hybrid firmware model during memory initialization phase on the Intel SoC platform*

This table lists the operation performed by the host firmware prior to handing over either payload/boot to an operating system. Typically, coreboot-like open-source boot firmware that inherently doesn't include the payload along with coreboot.rom is concerned about limiting the usage of silicon initialization code prior handing off to payload.

Step 4: Post-memory initialization phase

1. Ramstage, the coreboot module, is relocated into the DRAM and is responsible for post-memory init operation. Ramstage starts by performing the multiprocessor initialization using the open-source native driver in coreboot (developed using Intel's software developer manuals) to let all application processors come out from the reset.

2. The FSP-S binary blob gets integrated with coreboot to perform the silicon initialization. Figure 5-24 provides a pictorial representation of a reference hardware block platform initialization.

3. The vcoreboot stage locates and loads the FSP-S binary blob into the main memory. The FSP-SiliconInit API starts the execution.

4. FSP-S initiates remaining silicon initialization like graphics, storage, and type-c subsystems.

5. There is a specific dependency on the CSE to load the non-boot critical binaries for the silicon initialization prior to the FSP-S execution.

6. The CSE initiates loading of the TCSS firmwares (which combines the IOM, TBT/USB4, and PHY firmware) into the respective hardware block after CSE SRAM is used for performing the required verification prior to loading. The FSP-S API performs the required TCSS configuration based on the platform policy, like the USB port configuration.

7. Performing the high-speed IOs initialization by FSP-S depends on the required binary extraction from the CSE binary. For example, the chipset binary a.k.a. PCHC is extracted from the CSE partition and loaded into the physical layer.

8. The FSP-S relies on another PEIM module named Graphics PEIM (part of the FSP-S blob) for pre-OS display initialization. The configuration file required by the Graphics PEIM is known as video BIOS table (VBT) packed into the coreboot file system (cbfs) to specify the display end-point configuration, resolution, and such.

(continued)

Note: Silicon initialization modules running as part of the FSP-S binary blobs handle all the chipset and processor initialization. The configuration information that is passed between coreboot to FSP-S API uses UPDs like USB Over Current setting, pointers to the VBT in the memory, enables/disables certain hardware interfaces, and such. Refer to Chapter 7's "Adopting Hybrid Firmware Development" section to understand the detailed configuration parameters used for silicon initialization.

Figure 5-24 pictorially represents the post-memory initialization phase. At the start of this phase, the hardware components that are readily available after the memory initialization phase are highlighted in green (the memory controller is now out from reset and the physical memory is in use). There are no pending hardware component initializations after this stage. The components that are colored in blue get initialized during this process. The memory controller(s) get initialized during this process as highlighted by the table.

This phase of platform initialization runs using BIOS/coreboot region, with major contributions from the closed-source binary blob.

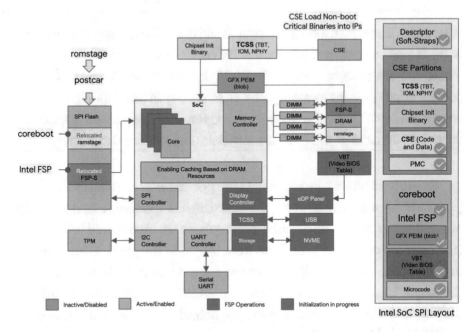

Figure 5-24. *Applicability of the hybrid firmware model during the post-memory initialization phase on the Intel SoC platform*

At the end of the ramstage operation, typically coreboot is done with the platform initialization. All binaries packaged to create the SPI layout image using the hybrid firmware model have now fulfilled their purposes and the entire SPI layout is marked in green.

Summary

This book has orchestrated the possible different types of firmware architecture used while designing the system firmware for the embedded system and this chapter was planned to specifically highlight the challenges that both silicon vendors and the open source community are seeing due to non-identical visions about the future platform enabling model. This chapter provided all essential and real-world platform enabling data that help to justify the need for adapting a hybrid firmware development model (with minimal closed source blobs and maximizing the platform enablement using open-source initiative firmware). Hybrid firmware architecture is the most used approach in modern firmware development to support restricted SoC platforms. Chrome AP firmware development is expected to see more openness towards platform enablement solutions but still adopt the hybrid model to balance out the business in front of certain limitations in the current open-sourcing approach from the SoC/hardware partners. All leading silicon vendors are committed to ensuring platform initialization using closed source ABI-based models. This ABI-based model is flexible for a single binary to get integrated even with non-EDKII bootloader to utilize the silicon reference code for TTM readiness. The hybrid work model helps ensure scalability by providing a single validated SoC binary across different OEMs/ODMs and expects the configuration based on target hardware needs. The understanding of the usefulness of each and every closed source blob during platform initialization on Intel SoC platform eventually serves the education purpose at the ODM sides and provides flexibility for the enablement partners to configure the underlying firmware layer as per the target platform needs.

There are several potential opportunities for improving the current hybrid work model:

- A potential analysis between the feature/functionality against the applicability on the platform might help to optimize the footprint for closed source binary. For example, separating out the debug functionality from the closed source based production blobs might help to further optimize the SPINOR footprint. Additionally, it might provide flexibility at the user hand to choose between the feature and its size and boot time implications even while working on a closed source binary.

- A single binary solution from the silicon vendor can't be optimized enough to meet every different product's needs. Hence, required a compilation flag or binary level utility to drop the unnecessary feature i.e., not applicable on the targeted hardware to gain the SPINOR size, improve the boot time, reduce the attack surface.

- It's a potential opportunity for the SoC vendors to engage with the open community early during the design phase to define an open-source roadmap that helps everyone align with the single goal of more openness in firmware development.

- The hybrid model demands a more flexible platform enabling utilities that define the openness in terms of configuring the hardware interface by eliminating the source code dependency. This would help to ensure more engagement with the cross-functional team involved in the platform enabling, like hardware engineers validating the hardware interface, collaborating with silicon validation, and ensuring firmware verification without code dependencies.

- Finally, the opportunity to increase code sharing between open- source and closed source firmware development using a static library model might be beneficial, such as a debug library on the hybrid model.

A deep study on the hybrid firmware architecture would help silicon vendors to define a better work model in the future for platform enabling. The expectation is to have zero or absolute essential binary blobs, which are reduced in size, easy to configure, and flexible enough to build using a software development kit (SDK), that would bring more code visibility in public. Additionally, it would allow users to build and integrate the essential binary blobs with pure open source boot firmware for creating the system firmware for the targeted embedded system.

CHAPTER 6

Payload

"Journey of a thousand miles begins with a single step."

—*Lao-tzu*

An aspiring journey towards booting an operating system starts with the platform reaching a payload. A payload is a separate firmware block that is architecture neutral and platform independent. It is responsible for understanding the system state, preparing lists of boot devices that are attached to the platform, looking for the boot manager (as per the priority) to load, and executing the operating system. Hence, it's also called an OS loader. A payload may also be responsible for providing the first sign of life indicator during a system firmware boot, as a payload can make use of both platform input and output devices to show boot progress at the display console or take some inputs (if required) to interact with the boot manager (to alter the boot priority). Some payloads are also capable of launching value-added services like pre-OS applications like diagnostics utilities and the updater package to update the full boot flash alongside the operating system at the end of a system firmware boot. The expectation is that the payload will pass control to the OS after the pre-OS application finishes execution. The entire system firmware functioning can be divided into two major categories: ensuring all required platform hardware is initialized and relevant system state information is gathered, and that this information is passed to the payload so that the system can initiate booting to an operating system. The payload is a unique piece of firmware that

S. Banik and V. Zimmer, *System Firmware*,
https://doi.org/10.1007/978-1-4842-7939-7_6

relies on the boot firmware to get the platform-centric information and is responsible for consuming services provided by the boot firmware during platform initialization while booting the platform to the operating system. Ideally, system firmware shouldn't bother about what payload is being used to boot as the operating system booting is the ultimate priority. Over time, device vendors have tied several value-add services with the payload, which makes it specific for certain operating systems. For example, the different boot modes supported by ChromeOS (i.e., Developer Mode, Recovery Mode, Normal Mode, and Legacy Mode) are associated with a specific payload called Depthcharge, and this can't be accomplished with other payloads. Figure 6-1 describes the current system firmware model, which provides flexibility so platform owners can choose the right payload for their targeted embedded systems.

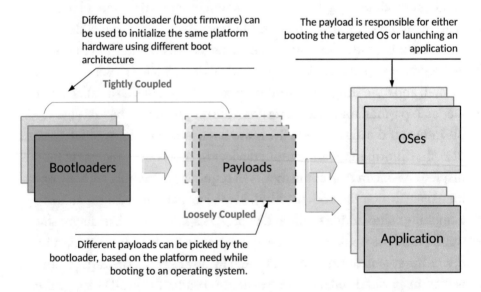

Figure 6-1. *Types of system firmware in context of the payload*

Typically, the system firmware implementations are divided into two types based on the presence of a payload:

Tightly coupled: The payload is an integral part of the system firmware and can't be detached or separated from the boot firmware. As a whole, the boot firmware and the payload are used to qualify as a system firmware and are used to boot the platform to the OS. Examples of system firmware that contain a payload within the system stack are UEFI and U-Boot.

Loosely Coupled: The payloads are self-sufficient in nature, meaning all required libraries for the payload to work are integrated in the payload binary image itself. The bootloader is free to choose any such payload from the available supported lists. The only information that is required to pass between the boot firmware to the payload is through the standard data structure. LinuxBoot and the Linux payload are examples of a payload that belongs to this category. The tightly coupled system firmware can even be used while booting the loosely coupled system firmware, such as the UEFI payload and the U-Boot payload.

This book is committed to providing all relevant information that you should have to build your own system firmware for targeted embedded systems. The payload is the last piece of the firmware block that completes the system firmware journey and lets the system boot to an OS. Hence, this chapter will provide the architecture overview of the boot flow of popular and open source friendly payloads and their interfaces while communicating with the lower-level bootloader and higher-level system software. Also, it will describe the value-add services provided by each payload to make it exclusive while booting to a dedicated operating system.

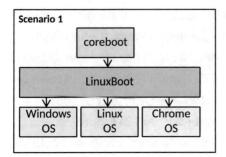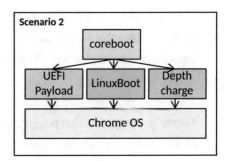

Figure 6-2. *Relationship between bootloader (coreboot) and payload*

Without understanding these details, it would be difficult for the system integrator to choose the correct payload for the system firmware, as the same payload is able to boot various operating systems or a single bootloader can work with different payloads while booting a fixed operating system, as described in Figure 6-2.

This chapter will focus on *loosely coupled* system firmware implementations where the bootloader doesn't mandate how the boot process should look; rather, it just ensures that the platform initialization does the hardware initialization and then passes control to the payload firmware block. For example, coreboot as boot firmware is flexible enough to integrate with different payloads while qualifying as system firmware. This chapter will discuss three popular payloads:

- **Depthcharge**: The payload for the ChromeOS platform is specifically designed to work with coreboot, which allows access to other libraries to have a securely booted Chrome OS.

- **UEFI Payload**: The Unified Extensible Firmware Interface (UEFI) payload is based on the open source implementation of UEFI known as TianoCore. It provides extensibility to the bootloader with the Extensible Firmware Interface (EFI) Shell and Test

Setup Engine (TSE) also known as Setup Page, allowing you modifying the priority of the boot media listed by the boot manager while booting the UEFI-aware OS. It's an integral part of the UEFI system firmware and the most widely used by all bootloaders for different OSes like Windows, Linux, and Android.

- **LinuxBoot**: The concept of LinuxBoot is to reduce the system firmware boundary and let the system boot using Linux as a payload. In this approach, the boot firmware loads the Linux kernel as the payload from the boot storage (typically SPI NOR) and runs the initramfs to find the OS from the possible boot media and boots to the OS.

There are other popular payloads such as SeaBIOS and GRUB2, which can be used with legacy bootloaders.

- **SeaBIOS**: SeaBIOS is an open source implementation of the x86 BIOS. It supports standard BIOS features and interfaces provided by the BIOS. Presently, SeaBIOS is either used as a payload for coreboot projects or is used inside an QEMU emulator.

- **GRUB2**: Grand Unified Bootloader 2 is the default open source boot loader and boot manager for Ubuntu. It is used to take control from the boot firmware, load itself, load the Linux Kernel into memory, and execute. GRUB2 has finished its job once the control reaches the kernel. It can also work with coreboot projects as a payload.

And, providing a conceptual overview of Universal Payload Layer (UPL), is used to solve the redundancy problem caused due to a single bootloader being required to provide dedicated interfaces while communicating with different payloads as shown in Figure 6-2 scenario 2.

Depthcharge

Depthcharge is the default payload for booting the CrOS (Chromium OS/ Chrome OS) platforms. From Haswell onwards, all Chrome OS devices use Depthcharge as a payload along with coreboot as the boot firmware, replacing U-Boot entirely, which makes the boot process lighter. The design principle of Depthcharge is thinner, simpler, and faster by doing the minimalistic job as a payload to securely boot to CrOS.

- **Thinner**: Compared to other payloads, Depthcharge does the minimum job and relies on the bootloader for doing PCI enumeration, enabling the device resources, and such. It provides a very basic CLI to allow minimal access to the CPU and chipset registers and memory for pre-OS-related operations like debugging and running commands.

- **Simpler**: The Depthcharge payload provides a simple architecture with very minimal communication with the bootloader and doesn't provide any runtime services for Chrome OS to use. Hence, the attack surface is less. The code structure is also simple, so it's easy to learn and maintain across different CrOS platforms.

- **Faster**: It has a reduced firmware boundary which allows faster loading time into memory and also fast execution time. As Depthcharge provides common drivers and architecture code, it also provides faster enabling time while porting a new board.

- **Secure**: The CrOS devices are very strict about the security model and ensuring that these devices aren't compromised. It implements a verified boot (vboot) layer that works with Depthcharge to make sure the device boots to a verified and secured operating system; otherwise, it triggers a recovery.

Depthcharge Architecture

Like other payloads, Depthcharge is loaded by the bootloader at the end of the platform initialization phase. It resides in the CBFS in an uncompressed format and is loaded into memory by the bootloader and then jumps into its main() function to start the execution.

It consists of several platform device drivers required to read the kernel partitions from the boot device, a display driver for drawing localized firmware screens, sound drivers for beeps (which is a CrOS accessibility requirement), and value-add services like Depthcharge Shell.

Depthcharge uses two libraries: libpayload to access generic drivers and retrieve information from the bootloader and verified boot (vboot) to ensure a secure boot. Figure 6-3 shows the architecture of Depthcharge.

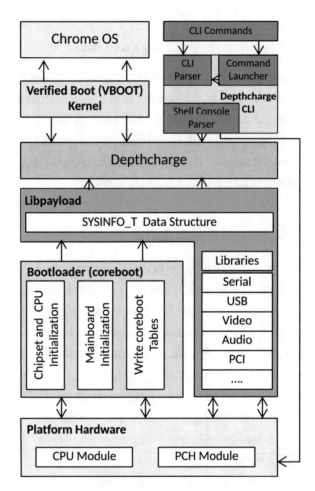

Figure 6-3. *Depthcharge architecture*

Bootloader

coreboot is the de facto bootloader for the Depthcharge payload and
is intended to make the boot flow simple. coreboot is responsible for
performing the entire hardware initialization and loading Depthcharge at
the end of ramstage using BS_PAYLOAD_LOAD and BS_PAYLOAD_BOOT
state machines. For Depthcharge to get loaded and executed in the proper
way, there are expectations from the underlying bootloaders including

- **Allocating and enabling device resources**: On x86
  platforms, devices sitting behind the PCI and/or
  PCIe buses require a special enumeration technique
  to detect the device presence, allocate resources
  dynamically, and enable access to device resources
  using memory and/or I/O access. Depthcharge, being
  lazy in device initialization (it doesn't perform generic
  PCI enumeration and relies on bootloader-enabling
  devices), expects that all device resources are readily
  available prior to control reaching the payload. Hence,
  the bootloader ensures device resources are enabled
  for those required to be operational in Depthcharge.

- **Preparing system memory layout**: coreboot is
  expected to load depthcharge.elf into the system
  memory, hence coreboot reserves memory ranges
  starting from TOLUD and marks the system-available
  memory base and limit for allowing Depthcharge
  to get loaded into the available system memory. It's
  done as part of the DRAM-based resource reservation
  process. For example, on x86 platforms, the Host Bridge
  resource allocation takes care of DRAM-based system
  memory layout creation.

- **Writing coreboot tables**: coreboot needs to create
  tables to pass the platform-centric information to the
  payload and to the loaded OS image. This information
  is something that can't be discovered by other means,
  like querying the platform hardware directly. Figure 6-4
  shows the coreboot tables, which are written into the
  available system memory with a table header that

includes the table signature LBIO, the table size in bytes, and the number of entries. Newer entries are added into the existing coreboot tables as per unique LB_TAGs.

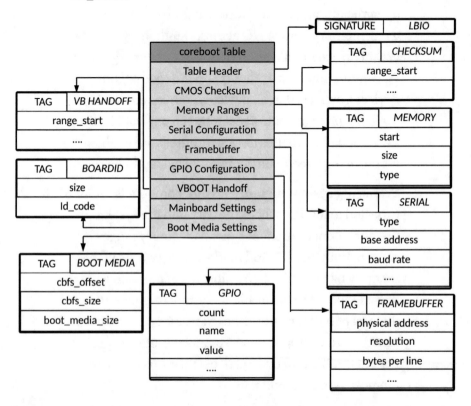

Figure 6-4. *coreboot tables to pass information to the payload*

This is the minimal configuration that a bootloader should provide to load Depthcharge as a payload and execute.

Libpayload

Libpayload is a small, static library distributed under a BSD license and intended to be used as a common function for coreboot payloads. It uses a ncurses-based (new curses) implementation to provide an API that allows it to communicate with payloads by passing parameters. This API is used to pass an argument from the caller (coreboot) to the payload using the API provided by the Libpayload. The calling application pushes on the stack (as per the table below) the number of elements in the array (argc), a pointer to the array (argv) and a magic number (0x12345678). The payload first checks stack offset 0x04 for the magic number. If it is not present, then the payload assumes that the caller did not pass any parameters (probably because it was a legacy application). Failure to check for the magic number could cause program failure too. After verifying the magic number successfully, the payload can collect the other two elements and process them accordingly.

Having Libpayload statically linked with Depthcharge helps to make the Depthcharge platform independent and architecture neutral where it doesn't need to access the low-level code for I/O, common functions, generic drivers, and such. The features provided by Libpayload include the following:

- A subset of libc functions, such as allocating or deallocating the resources malloc/free, functions for string operations like strcpy/strcat, console functions like printf/getchar/putchar.

- Various drivers for

- USB stack: HID, mass storage, hubs

- Serial consoles

- Display consoles

- CBMEM consoles

- NVRAM/CMOS access

- LZMA compression

- Storage drivers like SATA, eMMC, NVMe

Note   Libpayload has another feature called a permissive BSD license that allows for extracting data structures and content ordinarily found in GPL-licensed code like coreboot into other permissively licensed code bases, such as EDKII. This is how the UEFI Payload Package in EDKII initially curated this content.

- **Reads and parses the coreboot table:** At the C entry point of Libpayload, it gathers the system information using the lib_get_sysinfo() function. SYSINFO_T is a data structure that contains both architecture-independent and architecture-specific information that is required for the payload or going forward for CrOS. Figure 6-5 shows the parsing of the coreboot table between coreboot to Depthcharge using Libpayload.

- The sysinfo_t structure is created to store the information after parsing the coreboot table. The coreboot table works as an input for Libpayload and retrieves the maximum table entries from the coreboot table header. It parse the table entries to fill all relevant information into sysinfo_t structure based on the coreboot tag entry marked as CB_TAG_xxxx.

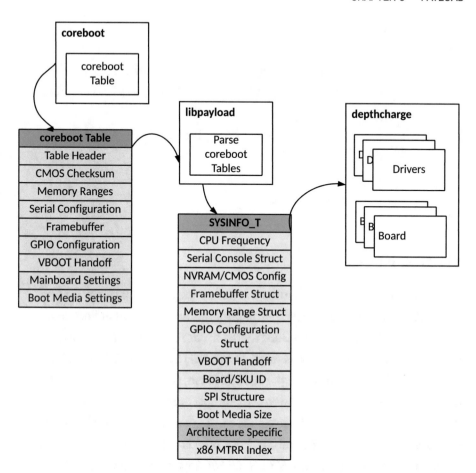

Figure 6-5. *coreboot tables to pass information to payload*

- All drivers and boards entries that are part of Depthcharge use the sysinfo_t structure to retrieve the required information to make the driver operational. For example, the SPI driver inside Depthcharge relies on SPI structure variables spi_flash.size, .spi_ flash.sector_size, and .spi_flash.erase_cmd as shown here:

```
SpiFlash *new_spi_flash(SpiOps *spi)
{
        uint32_t rom_size = lib_sysinfo.spi_flash.size;
        uint32_t sector_size = lib_sysinfo.spi_flash.
        sector_size;
        uint8_t erase_cmd = lib_sysinfo.spi_flash.
        erase_cmd;
        ...
        return flash;
}
```

Verified Boot

The verified boot (vboot) ensures a secure computing platform for end users. The security is kept inside the targeted hardware, also known as Root of Trust (RoT). Verified boot works on the principle that it enforces two sets of firmware blocks as Read-Only (RO) and Read-Write (RW).

The RO firmware block is part of SPI Flash, protected with hardware write protection, and is considered as the platform Root of Trust. Once the device RO firmware block is frozen, it can't get updated in the field. The verstage belonging to the coreboot boot flow is part of the RO firmware block to initiate the firmware Verified Boot flow using the verified boot library. The vboot layer uses public keys to verify other stages belong to the RW firmware block. See Figure 6-6.

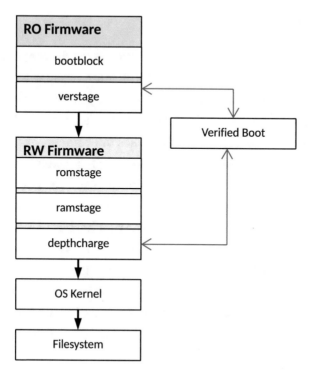

Figure 6-6. *Verified boot flow*

It ensures a secure platform by executing only signed code. The RO firmware verifies a signed RW firmware. (The RW firmware is an updatable copy present inside the SPI Flash.) The RW firmware is further used to verify the signed kernel using vboot handle prior to loading it into memory. Failure to verify the kernel partition would trigger the platform recovery.

Depthcharge communicates with the vboot library to ensure it can validate the kernel boot partition based on the CrOS boot modes: Verified Mode, Recovery Mode, Developer Mode, and Legacy Mode.

Kernel Verification

Depthcharge is the last executable firmware part of the RW firmware block that is responsible for performing the verification of the kernel prior to loading into memory. Depthcharge is able to detect the kernel from the boot device based on the CrOS boot mode. It uses the vboot library for this verification purpose. Depthcharge uses the *kernel subkey* to verify the kernel's keyblock, which contains the kernel data key. The *kernel data key* is further used to verify the kernel preamble and the kernel body. After that, the kernel image gets loaded into the memory and starts its execution. After the kernel has loaded, the root hash is passed to the kernel as command-line parameters. The kernel security hashes each block in the kernel image. The block hashes are combined and structured in a tree. The subsequent read blocks are hashed and checked against the tree. The hash tree is stored in the page cache. Figure 6-7 shows the relationship between Depthcharge and vboot while verifying the kernel partitions.

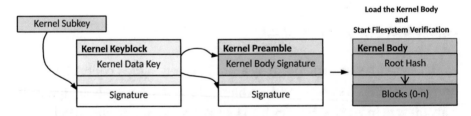

Figure 6-7. *Verifying the kernel partitions at Depthcharge*

Verified Boot also allows you to turn off the verification using the CrOS configuration tool named crossystem, which allows Depthcharge to boot to the CrOS kernel without any verification.

Handling Chrome OS Boot Modes

Chrome OS supports different boot modes that execute within Depthcharge and in context to verified boot (vboot). It allows Depthcharge to boot the operating system from different boot media (fixed or removable) with different security levels such as verified and unverified.

Verified Mode

Verified mode enforces complete verification at both the firmware level using VB_FIRMWARE and in the kernel scope using VB_KERNEL.

VB_FIRMWARE utilizes the Root of Trust burned inside the RO firmware and verifies the RW firmware during the firmware boot path. Similarly, Depthcharge verifies the VB_KERNEL either belongs to the RW-A or the RW-B partition in the fixed boot media. In this mode, the device tries to boot from the fixed boot media upon successful verification of the GPT. Figure 6-8 shows the verified mode high-level boot flow. Failure to verify the VB_FIRMWARE or VB_KERNEL block sets the boot mode to recovery. A device is only allowed to boot using Google-signed Chrome OS images in verified boot mode.

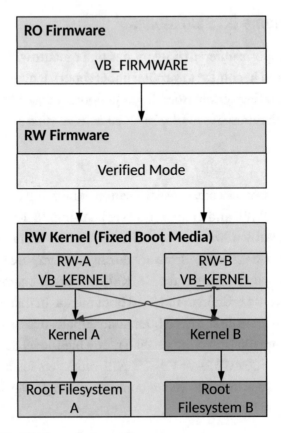

Figure 6-8. *Verified mode boot flow*

Recovery Mode

A device can enter into recovery mode if any of the below conditions are met:

- Failure to verify either the VB_FIRMWARE or the VB_ KERNEL image

- Hardware failure like a failure of the Platform Trusted Module a.k.a. TPM or the embedded controller (EC)

- End user pressing the special key sequences of ESC + REF + POWER (keyboard) or POWER + VOL-UP + VOL-DOWN (tablet)

The recovery mode allows the system to only boot using the RO firmware to the Google-signed Chrome OS image with a recovery key from the recovery media like a USB or SD card. Depthcharge renders the recovery firmware localized screen when the attached media doesn't have the valid recovery signed OS image present.

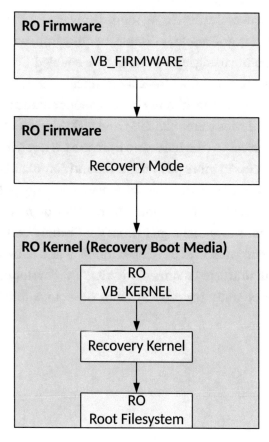

Figure 6-9. *Recovery mode boot flow*

Figure 6-9 shows the recovery mode high-level boot flow. The intention is to use the recovery mode to get the Chrome OS device back to the trusted state or switch to the developer mode.

Developer Mode

Developer mode is a special mode that provides freedom to end users to use the device to boot from internal or fixed storage, boot from removable or external storage, turn off the kernel verification, or boot from a legacy payload without voiding the warranty.

Depthcharge uses the developer mode firmware localized screen to warn users that the verification is disable, booting from external media is enabled, and booting using legacy payloads is enabled. To enter into this mode, users need to verify the physical presence via the recovery mode by pressing CTRL + D. Transitioning into developer mode from other modes will erase device states like TPM and disk. The intent of this mode is to allow more access to the hardware from the OS layer, like the root shell provides access to more powerful tools and commands to override the chipset registers or override the CrOS device security policies using the crossystem tool. Figure 6-10 shows the override of the verified boot policies, which allow Depthcharge to boot the Chrome OS from both fixed and removable media in developer mode. It also allows booting the Chrome OS in an untrusted manner. Additionally, developer mode allows booting to other operating systems by using the compatible payloads in legacy mode.

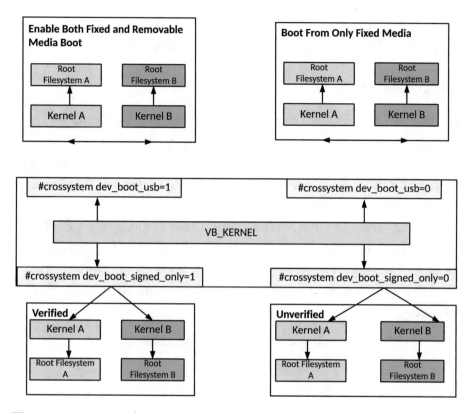

Figure 6-10. *Developer mode boot flow with security overrides*

Legacy Mode

Legacy mode allows the device to boot using an alternate OS upon launching a separate payload by pressing CTRL + L while Depthcharge is booting in developer mode. Transitioning into this mode is possible through a dedicated payload, residing in the RW_LEGACY region, known as the secondary payload. A device supporting this mode must enable crossystem configuration parameters as follows from developer mode:

```
#crossystem dev_boot_legacy=1
```

The latest devices use the UEFI payload as an alternative payload for booting the UEFI-aware OS or launching applications in this mode.

Depthcharge Shell

The Depthcharge shell is a preboot environment to access the native hardware to assist early development and easy debugging. The Depthcharge shell provides a serial-based interactive console for running the prebuilt commands instead of directly booting to the OS. Depthcharge kconfig CONFIG_CLI must be selected while enabling this interactive console. CONFIG_SYS_PROMPT kconfig is used to specify the console prompt name; the default is dpch. At the C entry point of Depthcharge, detect CLI kconfig is enabled and it launches the preboot environment. The Depthcharge shell provides several built-in commands that do the following:

- Allow access to memory and I/O addresses at different widths

- Scan the PCI/PCIe tree and access the PCI configuration space for devices

- Render various firmware localized screens on display

- Perform rudimentary tests on hardware controllers like memory and display

- Probe the storage devices and read blocks from the device

Compared to other payloads, Depthcharge provides less flexibility to allow running manufacturing tools, hardware independent debug, or running firmware validation test suites at pre-OS due to unavailability of the shell script and shell processor to allow running independent shell applications.

Depthcharge Boot Flow

Figure 6-11 describes the Depthcharge boot flow after coreboot has loaded the Depthcharge binary from the CBFS into the memory and the control jumps in the Depthcharge C entry point. Drivers and libraries that are part of Depthcharge are able to access the Libpayload drivers and libraries because it has been statically linked. During boot, Depthcharge communicates with the vboot library to verify the OS kernel. The detailed steps are as follows:

- At the C entry point, Depthcharge initializes serial consoles and the cbmem console and enables timestamps.

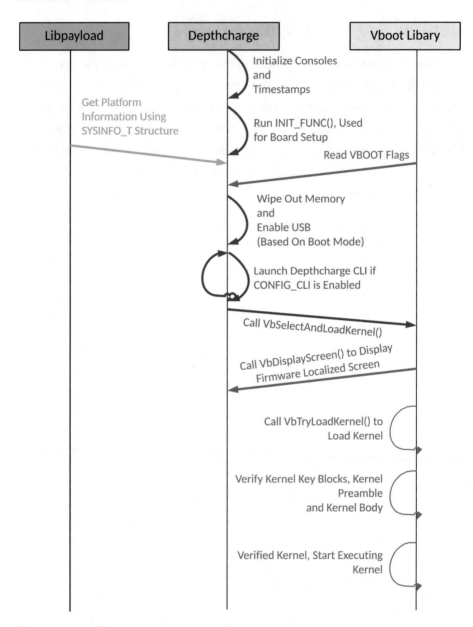

Figure 6-11. *Depthcharge boot flow*

- Run all initialization functions attached with the INIT_
  FUNC(func_name) macro (generic and mainboard
  specific) that are compiled in.

- Generic drivers and mainboard-specific code retrieve
  platform-centric information using sysinfo_t structure.

- Wipe memory and enable USB if necessary while
  booting in either developer or recovery mode, prior to
  executing vboot functions.

- Check if Depthcharge shell kconfig is enabled and
  needs to launch the pre-OS environment.

- Call vboot_select_and_load_kernel() to enter the
  vboot library, which decides the boot mode (i.e.,
  verified, recovery, developer, etc.).

- Draw firmware localized screen over the display
  console to notify the user about the boot mode.

- Based on the boot mode, get the kernel image from the
  block device, verify the kernel partition, load the kernel
  into memory, and jump to the kernel image.

Depthcharge Code Structure

Depthcharge tries to be as lazy as possible, so it only does the operation
that is requested during the board setup. It doesn't set up a device without
its being used. It focuses on booting to CrOS in a secured manner, so the
code structure is very basic and simple. Depthcharge code is distributed
under the GNU General Public License v2 (GPLv2) license to project
usage. This table provides the high-level overview of the Depthcharge code
structure.

Directory	Description
board	Contains board config settings, defined as defconfig. It's used to select the required generic drivers, specifying arch support, kernel format, and any other drivers required by the board setup.
src/ arch	This directory contains architecture-specific code.
src/ board	This directory holds the board-specific setup code. Each reference mainboard should have one entry here to provide the device lists required to boot to CrOS. All variants of the reference mainboard typically use the same Depthcharge target. For example, src/board/ reference_mainboard is enough to support all derivative designs of a reference mainboard.
src/ boot	This directory holds code that supports booting the kernel.
src/ diag	This directory holds code for measuring the device health state.
src/ debug	The serial console-based Depthcharge shell and its associated commands reside here.
src/ drivers	All types of drivers are used by Depthcharge for booting to the OS: generic drivers (bus, dma, flash, timer, video, and tpm) and SoC-specific drivers (soc, gpio, etc.).
src/net src/ netboot	This directory support the netboot feature using DHCP, TFTP.
src/ vboot	This directory holds the interface to communicate with vboot.

Value-Added Services

Apart from just booting to the operating system, Depthcharge also provides some value-added services on the Chrome platform like ensuring seamless firmware updates of platform-associated microcontrollers, like the EC and the USB-C Power Delivery (PD) controller on latest devices.

EC Software Sync

The Chrome OS platform has two dedicated SPI flashes, one for the system firmware that contains coreboot image, also known as the AP firmware, and another for the EC firmware. All Chrome firmware parts of the SPI flash have two regions: RO is write-protected and RW is updatable in the field. It's important to ensure that the AP firmware and the EC firmware remain compatible through field upgrades. The in-field firmware updater only updates the RW region on the AP SPI flash. The process that ensures the seamless sync between the updated AP firmware and the EC RW firmware is known as EC software sync. Figure 6-12 describes the EC software sync process in detail.

- The EC boots its RO firmware and powers on the AP.

- The AP boots its RO firmware.

- The AP verifies its RW firmware and jumps to it.

- The EC computes a hash of its RW firmware.

- The AP RW firmware contains a copy of the EC's RW firmware. At Depthcharge, the AP compares its hash with the EC's hash.

- If they differ, the AP gives the EC the correct RW firmware, which the EC writes to its flash.

- The EC jumps to its RW firmware.

411

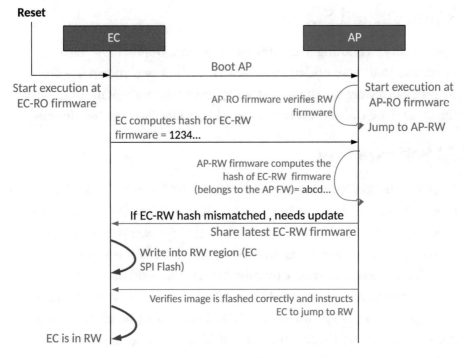

Figure 6-12. *EC software sync flow*

PD Firmware Update

Type-C Port Controller (TCPC) chips in Chrome OS devices are programmed with a firmware known as PD firmware. This firmware is field updatable. Depthcharge performs updates to the PD firmware as part of EC software sync. It requires configs that are enabled in Depthcharge:

- Depthcharge needs to identify the TCPC chip based on the EC-provided vendor id and product id of the chip. Then Depthcharge needs to build with all supported TCPC drivers that the platform supports, such as CONFIG_DRIVER_EC_ANX3429 to support the ANX3429 TCPC chip.

- CONFIG_CROS_EC_PROBE_AUX_FW_INFO is used to get information about the TCPC chip and invokes the appropriate TCPC chip driver to perform the firmware update.

The PD firmware update is performed after the EC's firmware is updated and has jumped to the RW section successfully. The updatable PD firmware image is part of the AP firmware RW-CBFS along with the PD firmware hash. The PD firmware hash includes firmware version information. At Depthcharge, the AP firmware requests the firmware version from the TCPC chip. If the firmware version returned by the TCPC chip differs from the firmware version built into the CBFS, the AP firmware triggers the PD firmware update. The PD firmware update progress is displayed using a Depthcharge firmware screen. Once the PD firmware update is complete, the EC will reboot to RO so that the TCPC chips are also reset.

UEFI Payload

The UEFI payload is based on the open source EDKII project to allow booting the UEFI OS or launching the UEFI value-added services. The UEFI specification defines interfaces for firmware to become modular (each module in EFI is defined using .inf) so that it can increase interoperability and provides an interface for the operating system to consume the firmware services. Loosely coupled system firmware follows a modular design approach where the bootloader focuses on the initializing hardware and separate firmware logic and the payload is responsible for the OS boot logic. This separation of platform initialization allows the bootloader to choose different payloads. The later boot logic of the UEFI-system firmware can be used as a payload to allow coreboot and Slim Bootloader-like non-UEFI bootloaders to even boot to an UEFI-aware OS or launch EFI applications, making use of UEFI services. It increases the scope of a bootloader beyond its specific target platform and/or operating system. The UEFI payload relies on the underlying boot firmware to perform the SoC and mainboard device initialization and the payload consumes the platform information, being architecture neutral and hardware independent as much as possible. Figure 6-13 emphasizes that UEFI payload doesn't dictate how the platform firmware is built. Also, it doesn't have any prerequisites to implement by the underlying boot firmware explicitly while loading the UEFI payload. Rather, the UEFI payload provides its services and interfaces independently, which allows an UEFI-aware OS to boot and consume the required services from the underlying system firmware.

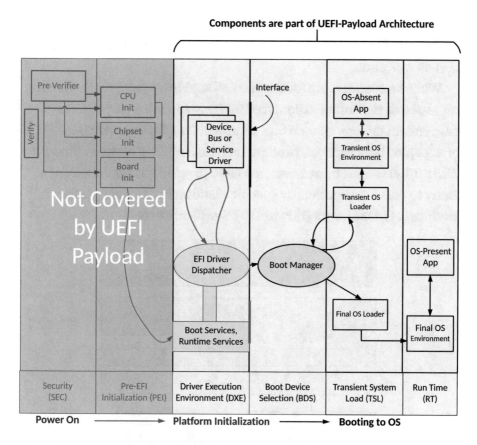

Figure 6-13. *Understanding the difference between UEFI-based system firmware and the UEFI payload*

UEFI Payload Architecture

Figure 6-13 shows the high-level architecture differences between the UEFI-based system firmware and the UEFI payload. They both use the same UEFI specification so the architecture implemented for the UEFI payload is derived from what was discussed earlier in Chapter 4's "UEFI Architecture" section. This section is going to provide the UEFI payload architecture overview and focus on how it is designed to interface with underlying boot firmware that may be a non-UEFI bootloader like coreboot and doesn't provide any UEFI-services or protocols as per the UEFI specification.

While bootloaders are focused on CPUs, chipsets, and motherboard-associated device initialization, the UEFI payload relies on platform-independent drivers: generic bus, controller and device drivers and services plus boot services, runtime services, and DXE services. Since the EDKII 201905 stable tag releases, the UEFI payload has implemented a library to parse the bootloader-specific platform information, called the Bootloader Parse Library (BlParseLib). See Figure 6-14.

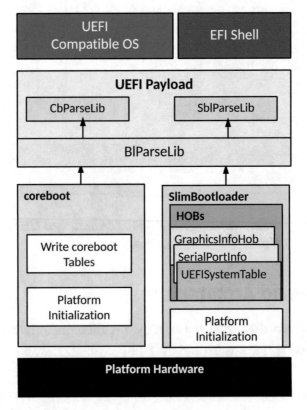

Figure 6-14. *UEFI payload architecture*

The platform-specific information like memory map information, framebuffer details, and console settings are retrieved by this library from the bootloader (based on how it's been implemented) to feed into the UEFI Payload in generic way, as specified by the PI specification. It gets the bootloader-specific information and builds HOBs for the UEFI payload modules to consume.

Facts   Prior to the EDKII 201905 stable release, the UEFI payload had two dedicated packages for supporting coreboot as boot firmware. CorebootModulePkg was used to parse the coreboot tables and feed the data into the EFI system table, and CorebootPayloadPkg contained firmware volumes that listed the modules required for the UEFI payload to boot to the OS. Later, UefiPayloadPkg replaced those two packages to make the UEFI payload implementation more scalable and generic.

Figure 6-14 describes the architecture of UEFI payload. This next section will cover the components that define the goal of booting to the UEFI OS using the UEFI payload and bootloaders like SBL and coreboot.

UEFI Payload Flash Layout

The UEFI payload is an independent firmware binary that is injected into coreboot CBFS as a payload to let coreboot provide a complete, open source UEFI environment. The UefiPayloadPkg inside EDKII lists the modules required to create the payload image. In the UEFI specification, the FDF file lists the modules that go into the UEFI flash layout. The UEFI payload firmware binary must contain all required libraries and dispatchers that will execute when the bootloader copies the binary from the SPI flash into the system memory. UefiPayload.fd is the flash layout

that holds other firmware volumes (FVs). A firmware volume is a collection
of DXE foundation, DXE and UEFI drivers, and the shell package.
Figure 6-15 shows the UEFI payload flash layout.

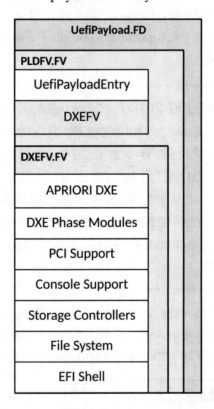

Figure 6-15. *UEFI payload flash layout*

It contains two firmware volumes:

1. PLDFV: The primary firmware volume that
   contains the first module of the UEFI payload
   as PayloadEntry, responsible for presenting the
   bootloader platform information as a UEFI standard
   for the other modules to consume; and a DXE
   firmware volume named DXEFV

2. DXEFV: Firmware volume that contains the a priori file for the UEFI infrastructure and bootloader support, DXE foundation, generic DXE drivers that produce DXE architecture protocols, generic bus drivers, host controller drivers, device drivers, file system driver, network driver, and value-added EFI shell.

After a successful build, the payload image (UEFIPAYLOAD.fd) will be generated inside the Build\UefiPayloadPkg directory.

Interface Between Bootloader and UEFI Payload

The UEFI-based system firmware implementation is divided into two specifications, where the PI specification specifies the communication between firmware modules to ensure all platform hardware is being initialized and passes that information to a later stage (DXE) to create services and populate interfaces for abstracting the underlying hardware from the high-level system software. The UEFI payload is a generic boot logic implementation of UEFI, so it can't dictate how the bootloader should pass the information to the UEFI payload. This leads to the requirement of having a unified interface between the bootloader and the UEFI payload for passing the bootloader platform information.

Bootloader

Different bootloaders have their own PI specifications and ways to create the interface for passing information to the payload, which can't be standardized. This section covers the interface used by coreboot and SBL to pass information to the payload as follows.

coreboot: As explained, the coreboot table is the way to pass control to a payload or OS. It is an extensible data structure that provides the information gathered by coreboot during the platform initialization phase.

The following code describes the coreboot table header and every entry in the boot environment list will correspond to a boot info record. Each record has a type to indicate what it is for.

```c
struct lb_header {
        uint8_t  signature[4]; /* LBIO */
        uint32_t header_bytes;
        uint32_t header_checksum;
        uint32_t table_bytes;
        uint32_t table_checksum;
        uint32_t table_entries;
};
```

Slim Bootloader: SBL produces HOB data structures to pass information about the platform like the memory map, graphics information, and serial settings as part of the SBL Stage 2 Phase, BuildExtraInfoHob(). It allows the UEFI payload to use the SBL without any platform porting.

```c
VOID *
EFIAPI
BuildExtraInfoHob (
  IN  STAGE2_PARAM                     *Stage2Param
  )
{
  // Update graphic info HOB
  PlatformUpdateHobInfo (&gEfiGraphicsInfoHobGuid, GfxInfoHob);

  // Update serial port hob
  PlatformUpdateHobInfo (&gLoaderSerialPortInfoGuid,
  SerialPortInfo);

  ....
}
```

BlParseLib

To allow the UEFI payload to be a generic payload, the payload implements the BlParseLib library based on the underlying bootloader type. The BlParseLib library is defined using the UefiPayloadPkg.DSC file as follows:

```
!if $(BOOTLOADER) == "COREBOOT"
  BlParseLib|UefiPayloadPkg/Library/CbParseLib/CbParseLib.inf
!else
  BlParseLib|UefiPayloadPkg/Library/SblParseLib/SblParseLib.inf
!endif
```

The UEFI payload entry point driver, UefiPayloadEntry.inf, includes the BlParseLib library to retrieve bootloader platform information using two separate library implementations:

CbParseLib: This library is used to retrieve coreboot table information and create a HOB structure. The table usually resides in memory around address 0x500 and has a library function to locate the coreboot table and parse the coreboot records, required by the UEFI payload with a given tag. Here is lists of coreboot records that the UEFI payload require for later stages:

coreboot record tag	Description
CB_TAG_MEMORY	To acquire the coreboot memory table
CB_TAG_SERIAL	Gets the serial port information
CB_TAG_ FRAMEBUFFER	Finds the video framebuffer information

The UEFI Payload retrieves the ACPI and SMBIOS tables from the coreboot memory table based on the table signature.

SblParseLib: Since SBL creates HOBs to pass the platform information for UEFI payload, the library function retrieves the HobList pointer for SBL to get all platform-specific HOBs. SblParseLib implements functions to retrieve the data from the SBL GUIDed HOB. Here is lists of HOBs that the UEFI payload require for its later stages:

GUIDed HOB	Description
gLoaderMemoryMapInfoGuid	To acquire the coreboot memory table
gUefiSystemTableInfoGuid	Gets the ACPI and SMBIOS tables from the bootloader
gUefiSerialPortInfoGuid	Finds the serial port information
gEfiGraphicsInfoHobGuid	Finds the video framebuffer information

The UEFI payload builds HOBs based on the information from BlParseLib.

UEFI Payload Boot Flow

The UEFI payload boot flow only focuses on creating the UEFI infrastructure and services so that it can reuse most of the UEFI specification and code for booting to a UEFI-aware OS or drop into the EFI shell. The major difference between UEFI-based system firmware and the UEFI payload is how the PI is implemented. The UEFI payload needs to make sure it retrieves platform information from the bootloader so that it can pass it in a more generic way to the DXE phase. Figure 6-16 describes the bootloader flow with the UEFI payload.

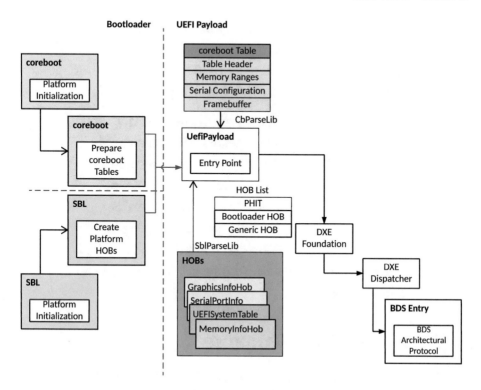

Figure 6-16. *Bootloader boot flow with the UEFI payload*

The detailed steps are as follows:

- At the C entry point of the UEFI payload, PayloadEntry builds a HOB based on information from the bootloader.

- It creates other generic HOBs required by DXE.

- It jumps into DXE core entry point, which loads the DXE foundation and DXE dispatches, which are responsible for discovering and executing DXE drivers as per the order in the Firmware Volume.

- Based on the DXE a priori, the dispatch bootloader support the DXE module, which reports MMIO/IO

423

resources, installs ACPI and SMBIOS tables into UEFI system table, and updates PCDs with information retrieved from the bootloader HOB like framebuffer for display (required for the Graphics Output Protocol).

- The UEFI payload produces the EFI boot services and EFI runtime services and a set of DXE architectural protocols. After the DXE dispatcher has executed all the DXE drivers, the BDS architecture protocol is discovered in the DXE phase and the control is transferred into the BDS entry point. The BDS phase terminates once the OS loader has created all required infrastructure for ensuring the successful loading of an operating system.

UEFI Payload Code Structure

The UEFI payload is part of the open source EDKII Project, which provides a modern, feature-rich payload environment for any bootloader. As a payload, it provides an extensible firmware interface (EFI) shell to bootloaders and allows for booting the UEFI OS. All UEFI payload content uses a BSD-2-Clause Plus Patent License. This table provides the high-level directory structure of the UEFI payload:

Directory	Description
UefiPayloadEntry	The first module in the UEFI payload flash layout, which contains the assembly entry point, sets up the stack and jumps into the C entry point, and performs operations mentioned in the "Boot Flow" section. The module type is SEC.

(continued)

Directory	Description
Library/ CbParseLib Library/ SblParseLib	The Bootloader Parse Library (BlParseLib) that holds the parsing logic to retrieve bootloader platform information
Library/ AcpiTimerLib Library/HobLib Library/ PciHostBridgeLib Library/ ResetSystemLib Library/...	Generic libraries for payload uses, such as create, find HOB, timer, reset platform, debug library, boot manager, host bridge, etc.
Include	Header files required by the payload, such as Coreboot.h to parse the coreboot table records
GraphicsOutputDxe	Implements a generic GOP driver
BlSupportDxe	DXE driver to report MMIO/IO resources and extract SMBIOS and ACPI tables from bootloader
ShellPkg	A value-added service, the shell application

To make the UEFI payload a generic payload, it needs to rely on the build parameter to know the bootloader type to specify which bootloader parsing library to use.

UEFI payload build command for an X64 build with a IA32 entry point

build -a IA32 -a X64 -p UefiPayloadPkg\UefiPayloadPkg.dsc -b *BuildType* -t *ToolChain* -D BOOTLOADER=*Bootloader*

BuildType: Support DEBUG, RELEASE, and NOOPT.

ToolChain is the EDK II build environment on the build host. For example: VS2015x86 toolchain.

Bootloader. Could be "SBL" for Slim Bootloader and "COREBOOT" for coreboot.

Value-Added Services

The EFI shell is a special EFI application as part of the UEFI payload and it provides an alternative to boot to the UEFI operating system. The EFI shell is a simple, interactive environment that provides access to hardware registers, memory, and I/O using in-built shell commands, allows batch scripting, loads EFI device drivers, executes independent EFI shell applications, and finally boots to an operating system. Figure 6-17 shows the EFI shell GUI with the device mapping table.

```
UEFI Interactive Shell v2.2
EDK II
UEFI v2.70 (EDK II, 0x00010000)
Mapping table
       FS0: Alias(s) :HD0a65535a1::BLK1:
             PciRoot(0x0)/Pci(0x17,0x0)/Sata(0x0,0xFFFF,0x0)/HD(1,MBR,0x00000000,0x
3F,0x31FC1)
       BLK0: Alias(s):
             PciRoot(0x0)/Pci(0x17,0x0)/Sata(0x0,0xFFFF,0x0)
       BLK2: Alias(s):
             PciRoot(0x0)/Pci(0x17,0x0)/Sata(0x1,0xFFFF,0x0)
Press ESC in 1 seconds to skip startup.nsh or any other key to continue.
Shell> _
```

Figure 6-17.   The EFI shell GUI

The EFI shell supports three types of commands as described in this table:

Type of command	Description
In-built commands	These commands are integrated with the EFI shell core image and are also called internal commands. These commands are useful for early development, debugging, and general-purpose management. Like any operating system command line interface, the EFI shell has a consistent command line format. The command should be the first argument, followed by options and parameters, all separated by spaces. For example: help, cp, date, cd, reset, ver, time, load, etc.
External commands	External commands are a set of shell applications. External commands are part of a file system, typically a storage device. Hence, prior to running them, users need to first create a mapping between a user-defined name and a device using the map internal command. They can execute those external commands under that file system.
Batch scripts	The EFI shell defines a scripting language. This language provides batch-script-only commands that allows execution of either internal or external commands in a loop, conditional operation of commands, data storage, and retrieval via environment variables. The scripting language makes the UEFI shell unique.

LinuxBoot

The LinuxBoot project aims to replace hidden, proprietary, vendor-supplied complex firmware drivers running on the computer with a Linux kernel and an initramfs. It's intended to not reinvent the wheel by implementing device drivers for firmware; rather, it saves development time by utilizing device drivers from the Linux kernel and reduces the firmware attack surface by removing almost all functionality that is not necessary to start the operating system. LinuxBoot is part of a system firmware image that resides in the SPI Flash. It is a combination of the Linux upstream kernel while the user-space initramfs image written with Go language for system booting is known as u-root. Due to its modularity and only performing operations required for system booting to the OS, LinuxBoot can be used as a generic cross-architecture and cross-platform portable payload with any traditional boot firmware. Although LinuxBoot has been demonstrated on consumer computers, recently the paradigm has shifted to modern servers as part of the open compute project. LinuxBoot along with minimal boot firmware provides following benefits over other system firmware:

- **Reliability**: Increases reliability in boot by replacing lightly-tested firmware drivers with mature, well-tested Linux drivers used across different computing scenarios like consumer electronics and supercomputing systems.

- **Security**: Reduces the firmware attack surface by removing the code density from the "Ring 0" bootloader. Brings the kernel into the Trusted Computing Boundary (TCB) along with firmware so that kernel security patches can apply to firmware as well.

- **Flexibility**: LinuxBoot is a generic payload and can be used with any bootloader solutions, like coreboot, U-Boot, OpenPower Abstraction Layer (OPAL), SBL, and Trusted Firmware (TF). Can boot multiple operating systems (Linux, Windows, Chrome, etc.).

- **Performance**: Provides improved boot time by reducing the redundant firmware drivers with the kernel (claimed 20x times faster). Integrating LinuxBoot as a payload solution also reduces the system firmware build time.

- **Customization**: Allows customization of the initrd runtime to support device driver needs as well as for custom executables.

LinuxBoot Architecture

The goal of LinuxBoot is to reduce the role of firmware to ensure only executing "bare-minimal" hardware initialization prior to booting into the Linux kernel using kexec.

LinuxBoot, to be a true generic payload, does not state how the "bare essentials" firmware prepares the hardware. It just relies on boot firmware to load the flash-based Linux kernel into memory. Then, the Linux kernel starts execution and runs a Go-based userland environment on the target hardware. The LinuxBoot consists of three components:

- Bootloader

- Linux kernel

- Initramfs

These components all make up one bundle and are stored in SPI flash. See Figure 6-18.

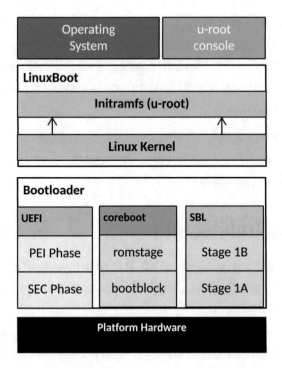

Figure 6-18. *Linux boot architecture*

Bootloader

Being a generic payload, LinuxBoot doesn't have much expectation from the underlying boot firmware except performing minimal hardware initialization like initializing the memory controller to have physical memory available to load the Linux kernel into memory. The bootloader also needs to prepare the system memory map and pass the information to the payload either using INT 15h or e820h interface in a legacy bootloader or UEFI-enabled bootloader to convey memory resources using GetMemoryMap() boot services. Any configurable data that needs to pass between a bootloader to the LinuxBoot payload uses the Linux kernel command line parameter (CONFIG_LINUX_COMMAND config on coreboot). For example, the Linux kernel part of LinuxBoot uses command line parameters to get the serial port information or get the IRQ routing table information on x86 systems.

```
CONFIG_LINUX_COMMAND_LINE="loglevel=7 apic=debug show_
lapic=all irqpoll idle=nomwait earlyprintk=ttyS0,115200n8
console=ttyS0,115200n8 pci=biosirq"
```

Typically, different bootloaders contain device drivers and utilities for advanced operations where fixing the bugs is a redundant task or can be a source of security issues, which can be replaced using Linux drivers and utilities part of LinuxBoot. Hence, LinuxBoot is aimed at replacing advanced bootloader stages like DXE onwards from UEFI, ramstage in coreboot, and Stage 2 in SBL with LinuxBoot payload.

Linux Kernel

LinuxBoot relies on the vendor-specific bootloader, which does the early CPU, chipset, and board component initialization part, and replaces the advanced bootloader phases of the boot process with a custom-built Linux kernel that acts like an OS loader, which finds the target kernel from the boot medium attached to the motherboard and invokes it via kexec. kexec, referred to as the currenting running Linux kernel, allows booting of a new kernel from the block device. This mechanism essentially skips the bootloader stage and platform initialization performed by the system firmware, and directly loads the new kernel into the main memory and starts executing it. Memory contexts of the old kernel will get overridden by the new kernel. Utilizing the power of the Linux kernel as a payload saves the additional code in the firmware used for the PCI bus enumeration, multiprocessor initialization, generic device initialization, and such.

LinuxBoot also limits the unnecessary use of a limited scripting language in the EFI shell; rather it utilizes the power of shell scripting that Linux provides for writing system initialization scripts.

LinuxBoot also provides the option to configure the Linux kernel using configuration files to limit its capabilities to what it is required to boot to an operating system, without bloating the size of system firmware with unused drivers. Developers can choose these config files, disable options, and discard features that are not needed in the LinuxBoot kernel. See Figure 6-19.

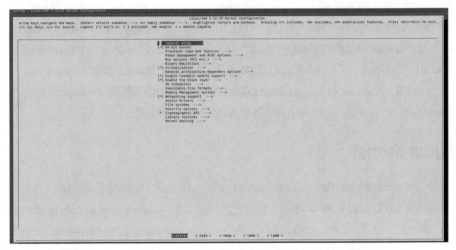

Figure 6-19. *Linux kernel configuration*

Examples: The developer to enable the CONFIG_SPI config to allow LinuxBoot to access the hardware SPI controller and SPI driver support in Linux kernel.

LinuxBoot supports different runtimes, sorts of services that can be used to ensure platform security prior loading the newer kernel from a block device or network into the memory. Heads firmware or Verified Boot or u-root works well with LinuxBoot as the initramfs.

The Linux kernel alone is not of much use when the system has booted to Linux; it needs a user space that provides boot and startup utilities. An initramfs file system provides that user space. LinuxBoot provides different options for user-space tools. u-root is the recommended solution for LinuxBoot as initramfs.

bzImage: As the Linux kernel matured, the size of the kernels generated by users grew beyond the limits imposed by some architectures, where the space available to store the compressed kernel code is limited.

The bzImage (big zImage) format was developed to overcome this limitation by cleverly splitting the kernel over discontinuous memory regions. The output LinuxBoot build process is a bzImage, which is stitched with a bootloader to create the system firmware. During boot, the bootloader loads the bzImage into memory and starts the kernel.

Initramfs (Initial RAM Filesystem)

Initramfs is the first root filesystem that the system has access to upon booting to the Linux kernel. The purpose of an initramfs is to mount the rootfs. The initramfs carries a complete set of directories that can be found after mounting the rootfs. Initramfs is the solution introduced in the Linux kernel 2.6 series. The key components inside the initramfs are

- A single CPIO archive, which is extracted into `rootfs` when the kernel boots up.

- After extracting, the kernel checks to see if rootfs contains a file named `init`, and, if found, mounts it as '/' and runs '/init'. The `init` program is typically a shell script that is responsible for locating and bringing the real root device (if any available) and setting up the system. If `rootfs` does not contain an `init` program after the CPIO archive is extracted, the kernel will fall through to the older code to locate and mount a root partition, then exec some variant of `/sbin/init` out of that.

There are different types of initramfs, and LinuxBoot is agnostic to what initramfs is used with the kernel.

- **u-root**: u-root is a tiny userland binary, written in the Go language, containing a set of programs and libraries that are used to interact with the kernel. It contains a toolset of standard Linux applications and commands. u-root can create initramfs in two different modes:

  - **Source-based mode**: It contains Go toolchain binaries and compiles the source code from the shell to create the initramfs binary as in the example below:

  Download the required package to create u-root

    1. go -u get github.com/u-root/u-root

    2. go -u get github.com/systemboot/
       systemboot/{uinit,localboot,netboot}

    3. go get -u github.com/u-root/u-root/xcmds/
       rush github.com/u-root/u-root/cmds/init
       github.com/u-root/u-root/cmds/{ls,cat,date}

  Build u-root

    ```
    ./u-root  -build=bb  core
    github.com/systemboot/systemboot/localboot
    github.com/systemboot/systemboot/netboot
    github.com/systemboot/systemboot/uinit
    ```

  - **Busybox (bb) mode**: This is similar to the busybox binary that comprises all the requested utilities.

    u-root is a complete solution to start the final operating system from the boot media by simply executing its kernel using kexec.

- **HEADS**: A secure runtime that can be used as the initramfs for LinuxBoot as well. This is a solution designed to be secure even when an attacker has physical access to the system. HEADS firmware utilizes the TPM-based trusted hardware to protect against the firmware attacks.

This section will only focus on u-root as an initramfs.

u-root

The initramfs provided by u-root implements the toolchain needed to securely boot the machine from either the network or localhost after performing the required verification, communicating with different internal boot-related components, and kexec-ing the next kernel. u-root is an embedded root file system sitting inside SPI slash as part of the system firmware image along with a Linux kernel. u-root is packaged as an LZMA-compressed initial RAM file system (initramfs) in cpio format. It is contained in a Linux compressed kernel image, also known as bzImage. The bootloader (for example, syslinux) or firmware (for example, coreboot) loads the bzImage into memory and starts it. The Linux kernel sets up a RAM-based root file system and unpacks the u-root file system into it. Unlike other root file systems, which consist of multiple binaries, u-root only contains five binaries: an init program and four Go-compiled binaries.

u-root is an open source project hosted on GitHub. The u-root image is built out of the u-root source code. The Linux kernel starts an init process during boot and it provides opportunity for u-root to start getting executed. The init process for u-root sets up the key directories (/etc, /proc, /dev, etc.), symlinks, and files. u-root provides flexibility to modify the init program based on the use cases:

- Typically, u-root takes 3 seconds to get to a shell, which might not meet the fast boot requirement of embedded systems like automotive. Hence, as an alternative, some programs can be precompiled into /bin.

- If the performance is not a critical indicator, then don't use any precompiled binaries or commands. A background thread in the init process can be used to build all the programs during boot.

- On a limited spaced system, once booted, a script can remove all precompiled binaries from /bin. Utilities or commands can be compiled based on-demand during boot.

u-root has a very simple init system, controlled by the --initcmd and --uinitcmd command-line flags.

- --initcmd: This command line is used to determine what /init is symlinked to.

- --uinitcmd: This command is run by the u-boot init after basic setup is done. If a uinit program is required, the user need to specify the name with arguments or the symlink target with an argument.

- After running the uinit, init will start a shell known as the u-root shell.

After setting up the rootfs, u-root needs to detect the boot kernel from the bootable media, hence it needs an OS loader. SystemBoot is a distribution for LinuxBoot to create a system firmware and boot loader. At present its been merged into u-root itself.

SystemBoot

SystemBoot is a set of OS loaders written in Go. The programs it includes are the following:

- **fbnetboot**: Used for a network boot, it uses DHCP and HTTP to get the Linux OS and uses kexec to run it.

- **localboot**: Used to find the local boot media (typically SATA, NVME, eMMC, etc.) and the bootable kernel to boot to OS.

systemboot is a wrapper around fbnetboot and localboot to perform an iterative operation to attempt to boot from a network or a local boot device. Use the -uinitcmd argument to the u-root build tool to make the boot program appear similar to the BDS phase of the UEFI-based system firmware.

Apart from these commands, there are commands like pxeboot and boot, which are part of u-root.

- pxeboot: Used for network boot, it uses DHCP and HTTP or TFTP to get a boot configuration, which can be parsed as PXELinux or iPXE configuration files to get a boot program.

- boot: Used to find the bootable kernel on a local disk, show a menu, and boot to the OS. It supports GRUB, syslinux, BootLoaderSpec and ESXi configurations.

All of these programs use kexec to boot.

fbnetboot

The fbnetboot client is responsible for configuring the network, downloading a boot program, and kexec-ing it.

Here is a fbnetboot operation in DHCP mode:

- Bring up the selected network interface (eth0 by default).

- Make a DHCPv6 transaction asking for the network configuration, DNS, and a boot file URL.

- Configure the interface based on the reply from DHCP.

- Extract the boot file URL from the DHCP reply and download it.

- kexec the downloaded boot program.

localboot

The localboot program is designed to find bootable kernels on storage attached to the motherboard and boot as per the boot order.

The localboot does the following:

- Looks for all the locally attached block devices

- Mounts the block device with supported file systems

- Looks for a GRUB configuration on each mounted partition, such as [localboot -grub -d]

- Looks for valid kernel configurations in each GRUB config, such as parsing a GRUB config /mnt/sdax/efi/ boot/grub.cfg

- Boots the newer kernel via kexec, based on the valid kernel/ramfs combination found above.

Figure 6-20 shows the complete system firmware that includes LinuxBoot as the payload.

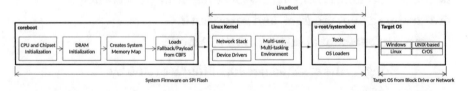

Figure 6-20. *coreboot system firmware boot flow with LinuxBoot*

LinuxBoot Boot Flow

This section provides the LinuxBoot boot process with UEFI boot firmware. A UEFI-compliant system firmware resides in the SPI flash. Upon power on reset, the security phase (SEC) and the pre-EFI initialization phase (PEI) start execution from temporary memory and are responsible for low-level platform hardware initialization, preparing the main memory. and creating system memory map. Typically, after these two stages, the remaining boot phases like DXE and BDS are executed from main memory, where various drivers are used to boot the system to the OS. This includes storage drivers, graphics drivers, and network drivers that are part of the boot firmware.

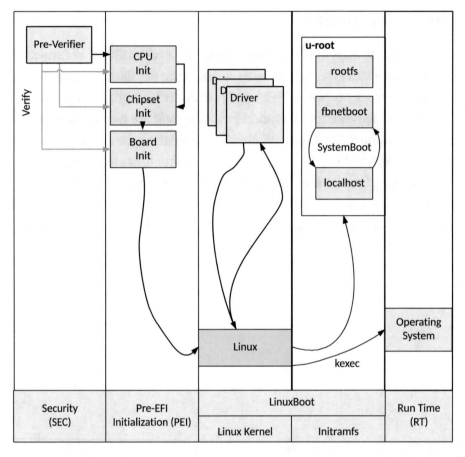

Figure 6-21. *Transitioning from UEFI Boot to LinuxBoot with UEFI*

LinuxBoot is intended to replace many driver execution environment (DXE) modules, particularly the network stack, file systems, and storage firmware drivers with Linux kernel; and the boot device selection (BDS) phase is replaced using Go userland-based initramfs to mount the rootfs and boot to the operating system using kexec from either network using netboot or platform block devices using localboot. Figure 6-21 shows the UEFI boot process with LinuxBoot as the payload.

In this boot flow, LinuxBoot starts as a replacement of the traditional DXE phase, resulting in most of the drivers not being loaded; instead, a Linux kernel is loaded as a driver. This brings several advantages:

- Running Linux at the earliest helps to reduce the attack surface by receiving regular security packers and bug fixes.

- The Linux kernel and associated application utilities provide a standardized and well-known programming environment for developers rather than learning UEFI capabilities.

- Since LinuxBoot runs after the first two boot phases of UEFI, it helps to reduce a large portion of SPI flash.

LinuxBoot Code Structure

LinuxBoot is a combination of a boot firmware, a Linux kernel, and an initramfs file with enough tools to kexec the rest of the system; except the first one, the others are part of a single LinuxBoot binary. This source code is scattered into different GitHub projects:

- **linuxboot/linuxboot**: The source code is distributed under a GPLv2 license to replace the platform firmware using Linux kernel.

- **u-root/u-root**: A fully Go userland for the Linux kernel. u-root is used to create a single binary rootfs containing a busy-box like set of tools written in Go. The source code is distributed under a BSD-3 Clause license.

This table shows the source code structure of LinuxBoot:

linuxboot/linuxboot	
Source directory	**Description**
/bin	Directory that contains various tools like create-ffs, create-fv, and extract-firmware to work on UEFI images
/boards	Specific targeted mainboard under a LinuxBoot project. Some of these mainboards are part of an open compute project, where DxeCore and SmmCore are replaced with the Linux kernel and initramfs as UEFI modules.
/dxe	These are small DXE modules that help bootstrap the LinuxBoot kernel.
/lib	A library used to parse GUIDs, generate EFI structs, etc.
Makefile	Required to build the LinuxBoot firmware image. This requires the vendor firmware image, a Linux kernel, and an initrd.cpio.xz file.

This table shows the source code structure of u-root:

u-root/u-root	
Source directory	**Description**
/cmds/boot	Go-based boot utilities like fbnetboot, localboot, pxeboot, and systemboot for booting to the Linux kernel
/cmds/core	Set of u-root source files for basic commands like cat, dd, go. etc. These tools are archived into a single package part of an initramfs.

(continued)

/pkg /tools	The /pkg and /tools directory are where binaries for various architecture/kernel combinations and compiler toolchain binaries reside.
/integration	Various VM based tests for core u-root functionality are present here: retrieving and kexec'ing Linux kernel, DHCP client tests, and uinit tests.
/examples	Provides an example of a writing uinit using Go
/configs	Provides kernel configuration files, generic and architecture specific
/docs	Documentation required to understand u-root

Value-Added Services

Every OS loader in modern system firmware has some sort of shell capability. A shell has built-in commands, commands that don't invoke another program while executing; rather, a shell is able to recognize them and execute, for example, a cd command. A shell may also support running scripts from a file. Scripts are usually a simple sequence of commands. These scripts are useful to define a program that is an alternative to creating a new shell command in the absence of shell source code. LinuxBoot provides a shell known as the u-root shell.

The u-root Shell

The U-root shell is a basic implementation of a shell that provides fundamental features like read commands using a Go scanner package. It can expand the command elements using the Go filepath package. And it allows running those commands either standalone or by running shell scripts. The u-root shell supports pipelines and IO redirection. It doesn't define its own scripting language; rather, it uses the Go compilers for commands and creates shell scripts.

This section describes the basic implementation of the u-root shell built-in commands. The shell built-ins are defined by a name and a function. The name is kept in a map and the map is searched for a command name before looking in the file system. An init() function is used to connect the built-in command to the map. It adds the name and function to the map. The init() function is special because it gets executed by Go when the program starts up. The following code provides an example of the init() function and the built-in time command.

Setting up the code for `time` built-in:

```
// Synopsis:
//      time CMD [ARG]...

// Package main is the 'root' of the package hierarchy for a
    program.
// This code is part of the main program, not another package,
// and is declared as package main.

package main
// A Go source file list all the packages on which it has
    a direct
// dependency.

import (
        "fmt"
        "os"
        "os/exec"
        "time"
)

// init() is an optional function. If init () is present
    in a file,
// the Go compiler and runtime arrange for it to be called at
// program startup. It is therefore like a constructor.
```

```go
func init() {
    addBuiltIn("time", runtime)
}
```

Actual "runtime" function that provides time in the u-root shell:

```go
func printTime(label string, t time.Duration) {
    fmt.Fprintf(os.Stderr, "%s %.03f\n", label, t.Seconds())
}

func runtime(c *Command) error {
    var err error
    start := time.Now()
    if len(c.argv) > 0 {
        c.cmd = c.argv[0]
        c.argv = c.argv[1:]
        c.args = c.args[1:]
        // If we are in a builtin, then the lookup fails.
        // The result of the failed lookup remains in
        // c.Cmd and will make the start fail. We have to make
        // a new Cmd.
        ...
        err = runit(c)
    }
    realTime := time.Since(start)
    printTime("real", realTime)
    if c.ProcessState != nil {
        printTime("user", c.ProcessState.UserTime())
        printTime("sys", c.ProcessState.SystemTime())
    }
    return err
}
```

During the LinuxBoot boot process, the init() function of the u-root.go determines what /init is symlinked to and also checks symlink targets and arguments for /bin/uinit. After running a uinit, init will start a shell determined by the -defaultsh. The following code provides a snapshot of the u-root shell running on QEMU x86_64 after the /init is successful.

```
cpio -ivt /tmp/initramfs.linux_amd64.cpio
# ...
# lrwxrwxrwx   0 root     root              9 Nov 30  2018 init
-> bbin/init

qemu-system-x86_64 -kernel $KERNEL -initrd /tmp/initramfs.
linux_amd64.cpio -nographic -append "console=ttyS0"
# ...
# 2018/06/05 23:53:26 Welcome to u-root
#                                          _
#   _    _      _ __   __  | |_
#  | | | | |__| '_/ _ \ / _ \ |  _|
#  | |_| |__| | | ( ) | ( ) | | |_
#   \_,_|    |_| \_/ \__/ \_|
#
# ~/>
```

At the u-root entry, if it fails to do proper init because of some initialization failure, then the shell will start without a proper init as shown in this example:

```
cpio -ivt /tmp/initramfs.linux_amd64.cpio
# ...
# lrwxrwxrwx   0 root     root              9 Nov
30  2018 init ->

qemu-system-x86_64 -kernel $KERNEL -initrd /tmp/initramfs.
linux_amd64.cpio -nographic -append "console=ttyS0"
```

```
# ...
# failed to put myself in foreground: ioctl: inappropriate
ioctl for device
# ~/>
```

Universal Payload Layer (UPL)

The definition of system firmware has evolved based on industry requirements over the last few years. The silicon vendor decides what should be the system firmware used on the target hardware built using the specific silicon vendor-provided CPU or SoC. But with the increasing demands of new features and the evolution of specific market needs (for example,: automotive expects a system to boot to the kernel UI within 800ms after power-on, and a compliance guideline for an infotainment system with a display is to show "splash" screen within one second of bootup to allow user interaction within two seconds of bootup), a system firmware specification designed for a server might not hold for automotive use case. Hence, in the modern era of computing, device manufacturers are looking for more custom solutions when building their system firmware. For the same reason, all modern system firmware provides flexibility to pick the bootloader that does the platform initialization and the OS loader responsible for managing the boot logic separately. If you take an example of designing system firmware for automotive systems, the device manufacturer can choose to have Slim Bootloader for hardware initialization and LinuxBoot as a payload to bring the early Linux kernel for ease of configuration. Similarly, the mix and match between other boot firmwares and payloads are possible while booting the system to an OS.

But the fundamental problem in these cases is the lack of a standard interface that can be used on the bootloader side to pass the platform initialization information to any payload seamlessly. Earlier sections of this chapter highlighted the architecture of different popular payloads. Every OS loader has its own way to get platform initialization information from the underlying boot firmware:

- **Depthcharge**: Depthcharge uses a SYSINFO table as part of a static library known as Libpayload to retrieve the platform-centric information that can't be retrieved directly from the platform hardware. Libpayload, being a static library part of coreboot, parses the coreboot table to fill that information into the SYSINFO table.

- UEFI Payload: The UEFI payload relies on a static library, selected based on the compile time flag to choose the right parsing library to retrieve bootloader platform information. BlParseLib is the interface that looks into CbParseLib to parse the coreboot table for coreboot bootloader or use SblParseLib for parsing HOBs for the SBL bootloader. UEFI payload intends to create HOBs using this bootloader platform information and pass it to the DXE Foundation.

  This condition will be more complicated with the increasing number of bootloaders to support like u-boot or OPAL firmware.

- **LinuxBoot**: LinuxBoot doesn't expect much information from the bootloader as it is capable of performing the redundant initialization like PCI enumeration and display initialization being done by the bootloader but still relies on DRAM-based system memory map. Hence, it introduces redundancy in the payload code structure when it claims to have support for all possible market leading bootloaders.

Now, let's take a look at the boot firmware side and understand the various interfaces that a boot firmware provides.

- **coreboot**: coreboot, being the non-UEFI bootloader, passes the platform information to downstream users (payloads and/or operating systems) using coreboot tables. The coreboot table is located in the memory address at lower memory range 0x500, and when the coreboot table is moved into the higher memory address, it keeps a single sub table in lower memory, which points to the real coreboot table.

  Apart from the platform initialization information, coreboot uses legacy INT 15h and e820h to pass the memory map to the operating system. Also, coreboot publishes tables for industry standard interfaces like Advanced Configuration and Power Interface (ACPI) and System Management BIOS (SMBIOS) or architecture-specific data structures like device trees for ARM to the OS as well.

- **UEFI**: During the PEI phase of the UEFI boot process, all platform-required information is created as HOBs. This includes information like describing the physical system memory, boot-strap processor (BSP) stack information, and information regarding the firmware devices and firmware volumes. The start of all these HOBs is the Phase Handoff Information Table (PHIT) HOB. At the end of the PEI phase, the DXE IPL PPI passes the HOB list from PEI to the DXE Foundation to retrieve the platform boot information and create a system memory layout for creating UEFI service tables, preparing the lists of DXE modules to begin dispatch, and such.

The UEFI-based system firmware relies on UEFI interfaces like protocols to pass the information about display framebuffers, input devices, and UEFI device paths to find the OS loader inside the boot media to boot to an OS.

Apart from these, UEFI also creates OS interfaces such as ACPI tables, SMBIOS tables, and UEFI runtime services as per the specification.

- **Slim Bootloader**: SBL supports a loosely coupled payload, so to pass the platform initialization information, it creates HOB data structures and provides the HOB list pointer to the payloads. SBL also meets specifications for creating OS interfaces like ACPI tables, SMBIOS tables, and such.

The comparative analysis between various boot firmwares helps to understand that all boot firmwares are good to implement the interfaces required to pass information to an operating system, whether it's a system memory map, a runtime interface like a ACPI table, or a UEFI-aware operating system that expects runtime services. Bootloaders implement OS interfaces properly because there are specifications or standards and to qualify the product for productization, the system firmware vendor needs to ensure it is meeting those specifications. When it comes to system firmware, there is no standard specification to define the interfaces between boot firmware and payloads. Over the last few years, there has been lots of innovation in the system firmware area and this space is rapidly growing. It's high time to think about enforcing a standard so that a smooth handshake can happen between boot firmware (bootloader) and OS loader. This will help the industry to scale the system firmware more efficiently than ever as the mix and match between bootloader and payload solutions can be seamless. This specification defines an interface between a bootloader (responsible for platform initialization) and an OS loader (responsible for booting to an OS), called the Universal Payload Layer (UPL). Figure 6-22 describes the UPL Interface in detail.

Figure 6-22. *Universal Payload Layer design*

This specification is used to describe a unified method (described in the "Universal Payload Interface" section below) to pass the platform initialization information to the payload phase. It includes how to pass parameters to a payload, the required format, the payload image format, boot mode, stack usage, etc. The intention for this specification includes the following:

- Make all the payloads generic without implementing any bootloader-specific libraries to parse the platform information table at the payloader side.

- The bootloader passes platform information in a more flexible, well-defined, industry standard format so that any bootloader can understand it without any additional parsing algorithm.

- This will eventually increase the interoperability between spec-compliant bootloaders and spec-compliant payloads.

Universal Payload Image Format

A payload is a separate firmware binary that resides into the same SPI flash where the bootloader resides. Being the primary boot firmware, it's the responsibility of the bootloader to locate the payload image into the SPI flash (either into the firmware volume or cbfs) and then hash, verify, load, and finally execute it. Due to the fact that different payloads are using their own image format like Portable Executable (PE), Executable and Linkable Format (ELF), Firmware Volume (FV), and RAW, it is challenging for the bootloader to identify and support all these different payloader image types.

The Universal Payload specification addresses this concern by adopting a unified payload image format to facilitate the payload loading process. *This specification recommends reusing an existing format like ELF as the common universal payload image format.* The ELF format is flexible, extensible, and cross-platform. It supports different endiannesses and address sizes, so it does not exclude any particular CPU or instruction set architecture. Many different operating systems on many different hardware platforms have adopted this format.

A platform that supports more than one payload has a secondary payload as part of the system firmware, such as the CrOS platform. The secondary payload also resides in the same firmware file system along with the primary payload, creating a problem for bootloaders to differentiate a payload that supports a universal payload layer from a regular payload. As the handshaking method between these two payloads are different, it might be unable to detect a universal payload and might cause a system hang while transferring control to the payload. To solve this problem, the following section provides additional information as part of new defined ELF section, as per the Universal Payload Specification.

Universal Payload Image Information Section

The Universal Payload Image Information Section is a section inside the ELF image to specify that the payload image adheres to Universal Payload Specification. It's a mandatory section inside an ELF image to retrieve payload-specific information like payload version, payload ID, and such prior to handing off control to the payload during the boot process. The Universal Payload Information Section must include

- Section name defined as ".upld_info"

- Section aligned at 4-byte boundary within the ELF image

- Must contain a UNIVERSAL_PAYLOAD_INFO structure within this section:

UNIVERSAL_PAYLOAD_INFO structure

Offset	Size (in bytes)	Description
0	4	*Signature*: 'PLDH' is the identifier for the universal payload info.
4	4	*HeaderLength*: Length of the structure in bytes
8	2	*SpecRevision*: Indicates the revision of this specification: Bit 7:0 - Minor Version Bit 15:8 - Major Version
10	2	*Reserved*

(continued)

UNIVERSAL_PAYLOAD_INFO structure

Offset	Size (in bytes)	Description
12	4	*Revision:* Indicates the version of the payload binary: Bit 7:0 - Build Number Bit 15:8 - Revision Bit 23:16 - Minor Version Bit 31:24 - Major Version
16	4	*Attribute:* Bit field indicator of the payload image type: Bit 0: Release Build, Bit 1: Debug Build. Others are reserved.
20	4	*Capability:* Indicates the various capabilities of the payload image, example: Bit 0: Support SMM rebase.
24	16	*ProducerId:* A NULL-terminated OEM-supplied string to specify the vendors
40	16	*ImageId:* A NULL-terminated ASCII string that identifies the payload name

Universal Payload Support Extra Image Section

A payload might need an extra image to proceed to the boot flow. For example, a UEFI payload might need additional FV images or a Linux payload might need an additional InitRd image. To meet such requirements, it is expected that the bootloader will pass the additional payload information while transferring control to the payload so that the payload can consume these images later.

The Universal Payload Specification defines an optional section for extra images. If this section exists during boot, the bootloader can retrieve such information and create extra images into HOBs to pass the information to the single universal payload ELF image.

The Universal Payload Extra Section must include

- A unique section name, defined as ".upld.*". Here "*" can be any ASCII string that is referred to as full section name; the length should be less than 16 bytes.

- The section is 4KB-page aligned.

- This section contains the RAW extra image data.

Universal Payload Interface

The Universal Payload Interface is what the bootloader creates based on the platform information it gathers and passes on to the OS loader while transferring control. This proposed interface would replace the need to have proprietary tables and equivalent parsing logic in the payloader code to understand these critical pieces of information. Typically, this information contains system memory information and memory ranges, information about ACPI and SMBIOS tables, device tree structures, and passes to the payload using a series of HOBs.

If the information is already present in industry-defined specifications like ACPI, SMBIOS, or device trees, then payload can parse it to get the required information. For the platform specification information that is not defined in the standard tables, the bootloader should build multiple HOBs and pass a HOB list pointer to the payload. The prototype of payload entry point with universal payload layer (UPL) is defined as:

```
typedef
VOID
(*PAYLOAD_ENTRY) (
  EFI_HOB_HANDOFF_INFO_TABLE *HobList
);
```

Here is detailed HOB list that the bootloader needs to create to transfer the platform initialization data from the bootloader to payloads:

HOB types	Description
Phase Handoff Info Table(PHIT) HOB	The bootloader reports the general state information through the HOB following the EFI_HOB_HANDOFF_INFO_TABLE format.
CPU HOB	The bootloader reports the processor information to the payload through the HOB following EFI_HOB_CPU; it contains the address space and I/O space capabilities of the processor.
Resource Descriptor HOB	The bootloader reports the system resources through the HOB following the EFI_HOB_RESOURCE_DESCRIPTOR format.
	For example, memory resources found by the bootloader report using resource type EFI_RESOURCE_SYSTEM_MEMORY, and reserved memory used by the bootloader is reported using resource type EFI_RESOURCE_MEMORY_RESERVED.
	I/O and MMIO resources use resource type EFI_RESOURCE_IO and EFI_RESOURCE_MEMORY_MAPPED_IO to report using HOB.
Memory Allocation HOB	The bootloader reports the memory usages that exist outside the HOB list through the HOB following the EFI_HOB_MEMORY_ALLOCATION format.
Boot-Strap Processor (BSP) Stack Memory Allocation HOB	The bootloader reports the initial stack prepared for payload through the HOB following the EFI_HOB_MEMORY_ALLOCATION_STACK format.

(continued)

HOB types	Description
Memory Allocation Module HOB	The bootloader reports the payload memory location and entry point through the HOB following the EFI_HOB_MEMORY_ALLOCATION_MODULE format.
Graphics Information HOB	The payload relying on the bootloader to initialize the graphics device, so it expects the bootloader to report graphics-related information like graphics mode, framebuffer, resolution, etc. through EFI_PEI_GRAPHICS_INFO_HOB and EFI_PEI_GRAPHICS_DEVICE_INFO_HOB.
ACPI Table HOB	The bootloader passes ACPI table information using GUIDed type HOB, EFI_HOB_GUID_TYPE, so that the payload can get the platform information from the ACPI table. The HOB data structure contains pointers to the ACPI RSDP table.
SMBIOS Table HOB	The bootloader might pass SMBIOS tables to the payload using GUIDed type HOB. SmBiosEntryPoint points to the SMBIOS table.
Device Tree HOB	The bootloader might pass device tree to the payload using the HOB structure. DeviceTreeAddress points to the device tree entry point.
Serial Information HOB	Rather having back-and-forth calls between the bootloader and payload to make use of bootloader serial debug port library, the bootloader should pass serial debug port information to the payload. It includes information like UseMmio, which indicates type of serial port memory mapped or I/O mapped; RegisterStride, which indicates the number of bytes between registers; a DWORD field for BaudRate; and RegisterBase to specify base address of serial port registers in MMIO or I/O space.

Implementation of Universal Payload Layer

This section provides the implementation of the Universal Payload Specification using the coreboot bootloader with the UEFI universal payload image booting on a x86-based platform. Typically, coreboot supports a wide range of payloads to integrate with it. The bootloader performs the following operations before transferring control to the payload:

- Initializes the processor and chipset using vendor-specific silicon implementation

- The memory controller is initialized, and the system memory layout is created.

- All logical processors are out of reset, initialized, and are patched with microcode.

- Performs PCI enumeration and device resource (IO, MMIO space) allocation

- Initializes the graphics controller

Additionally, coreboot builds platform initialization information in the form of HOBs at ramstage. The following code shows the implementation details of bootloader building HOBs for a payload:

```
/* It will build HOBs based on information from bootloaders.*/
void *build_payload_hobs (void)
{
  EFI_HOB_HANDOFF_INFO_TABLE     *HobTable;
  void                                          *HobBase;
  struct lb_header                              *header;
  EFI_RESOURCE_ATTRIBUTE_TYPE    ResourceAttribute;
```

```
header    = (struct lb_header *)cbmem_find(CBMEM_ID_CBTABLE);
HobBase   = cbmem_add(CBMEM_ID_HOB_POINTER, 0x4000);
HobTable = HobTableInit(HobBase, 0x4000, HobBase, (u8 *)
HobBase + 0x40000);

build_gfx_info_hob (header);
build_serial_hob (header);
build_memory_hobs (header);
// Hard code for now
BuildCpuHob (36, 16);
build_acpi_hob ();
build_smbios_hob ();

// Report Local APIC range
ResourceAttribute = EFI_RESOURCE_ATTRIBUTE_PRESENT
|\          EFI_RESOURCE_ATTRIBUTE_INITIALIZED |\
EFI_RESOURCE_ATTRIBUTE_UNCACHEABLE |\ EFI_RESOURCE_
ATTRIBUTE_TESTED;
BuildResourceDescriptorHob (EFI_RESOURCE_MEMORY_MAPPED_IO,
ResourceAttribute, 0xFEC80000, SIZE_512KB);
BuildMemoryAllocationHob ( 0xFEC80000, SIZE_512KB,
EfiMemoryMappedIO);

return HobTable;
}
```

Typically, coreboot calls into the payload entry point with a pointer to coreboot tables as an argument. With coreboot adhering to the Universal Payload Specification, it passes the HOB lists pointer while calling the universal payload image as follows:

```
#if CONFIG(UNIVERSAL_PAYLOAD_LAYER)
/* Pass Hoblist pointer to universal payload image. */
```

```
prog_set_entry(payload, (void *)entry, build_payload_hobs ());
#else
/* Pass cbtables to payload if architecture desires it. */
prog_set_entry(payload, (void *)entry, cbmem_find(CBMEM_ID_
CBTABLE));
#endif
```

This unified bootloader interface passes the information while calling the universal payload entry point and eventually helps to optimize the redundant bootloader-specific code at the payloader side, and the payload firmware may qualify as a real generic OS loader. In an earlier section, Figure 6-16 described the bootloader flow with the UEFI Payload; now Figure 6-23 shows an optimized boot flow while using the universal payload layer between the bootloader and the UEFI payload.

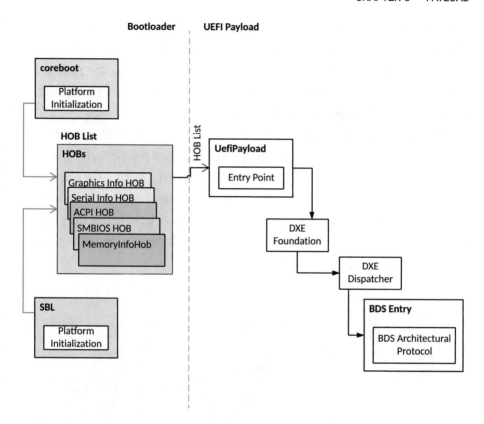

Figure 6-23. *Bootloader flow using UPL with a universal UEFI payload mage*

Summary

This chapter provided architectural details on industry-leading payload firmware. Modern system firmware provides more modularity and flexibility to choose between the platform initialization firmware (the bootloader) and the firmware for later stages, which only deals with OS loading magic (the payload). Without having detailed knowledge of the payloader architecture and its operational model, code structure, and interfaces to pass information between bootloader and payload and any special value-added services, it's unfeasible for developers to choose the right payload firmware for the targeted operating system. Additionally, this chapter provided the relationship between target hardware, the payload, and final operating system to boot. Without considering these details, it's impractical to design a system firmware.

Typically, payload is the last stage prior loading an operating system, hence any platform centric security, and interface to pass information to underlying hardware can be obliged by the payload. Figure 6-24 offers a comparison between all possible payloads and associated libraries to show that all payload firmwares do the same job as an OS loader, but they have their own specification which you need to consider while choosing either one of them for target embedded systems.

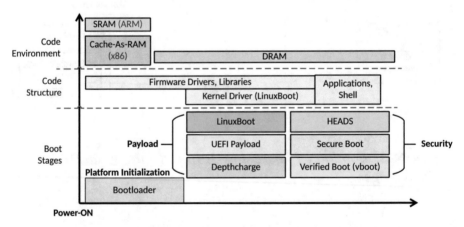

Figure 6-24. *Comparison between payload firmwares*

Additionally, this chapter highlighted the problem of not having a unified interface for passing the platform initialization information to a payload without duplicating effort at both bootloader and payload firmware. Having a proper interface specification such as Universal Payload would help the bootloader to do less generic operations and only focus on silicon initialization.

Chapter 4 provided an architecture overview of system firmware in the case of a loosely coupled system firmware, which allows you to choose the payload as per your orchestration This chapter covered the required knowledge on payloader architecture that can be used to complete the system firmware journey and begin the journey towards high-level system firmware. Chapter 7 covers studies using some of these payload solutions integrated with bootloader to address unique platform requirements.

CHAPTER 7

Case Studies

"If you're not doing some things that are crazy, then you're doing the wrong things."

—Larry Page

To support system firmware architecture migration, understanding the various firmware architecture differences is important. In fact, such learning can help you make the right decisions that need to be made for the betterment of the product. In this book, we have discussed various system firmware architectures and their offerings, so it should become easier to make such decisions correctly when required. Some of those decisions are related to platform-specific features, such as should system firmware designed to use the extra cores that are available? Can system firmware use a payload that is more accepted as an OS but still eligible to boot another operating system? Do you choose to change the infrastructure and tools to save the platform Bill-of-Materials (BoM) cost? For all these questions, one very important consideration point is meeting the real hardware requirements.

Let's leverage the concepts described in this book with real-world applications that can be demonstrated on real hardware. Two such system firmware frameworks, namely coreboot and UEFI EDKII, are covered in great detail in this chapter. We choose coreboot on more occasions for several reasons: it is popular in the open source community, it is freely available, and it represents a simple firmware architecture using the

© Subrata Banik and Vincent Zimmer 2022
S. Banik and V. Zimmer, *System Firmware*,
https://doi.org/10.1007/978-1-4842-7939-7_7

more popular C language. This gives a student of computer science and engineering an opportunity to access, read, and modify system firmware source code without running into any licensing issues.

We have also covered UEFI in great detail due to its popularity among production systems. The majority of modern computing devices are still running UEFI as system firmware, not only in personal computers, but also in data centers and IoT devices as well. We will demonstrate a case study using closed source system firmware as well to understand the design and implementation with a different philosophy from coreboot, like open source system firmware.

In addition, we briefly discuss other firmware ingredients that are also in scope of system firmware such as payload, including LinuxBoot, which has also defined its own market space in recent times and shows great prospects to get used in more product segments in the future than its present operational scope.

Finally, we provide a real-world example of a product development cycle that combines both closed and open source firmware development, typically referred to as a hybrid firmware development mode in this book. This solution is more applicable for x86 platforms where the expectation is to ensure all pieces of the firmware are open source, but still can accept binary blobs for initializing the auxiliary processor and silicon reference code.

This chapter offers a case study of various system firmware work and some forward-looking initiatives in the firmware space described in another book by the same authors named *Firmware Development: A Guide to Specialized Systemic Knowledge* (see Chapter 6). All these case studies are made based on different ARM and x86 processor-based platforms.

Reduce FW Booting Time Using Multi-Threaded Environment

This case study is a further extension of some future-looking system firmware aspects described in *Firmware Development: A Guide to Specialized Systemic Knowledge,* as part of the "Designing Multithreaded System Firmware" section in Chapter 6.

In the modern world, where usage of IoT devices (like automotive and navigation devices and home appliance devices) and client devices are rapidly increasing, performance is a key measure. Users expect to see the device operational as soon as they switch it on. It's also a fact that all modern day CPUs are multi-core processors in nature where more than one core is available and these logical processors are equally capable of running tasks in parallel to the BSP if the required resources are provided. But due to the legacy system firmware design where basic platform initialization has been handled by BSPs in a single-threaded environment without being bothered about the modern CPU architecture with more logical processors.

Over time, due to an increase in complexity of computers, software updates, and more I/O subsystems needed inside SoC or CPU architecture, the hardware abstraction layer of the system firmware can't maintain its legacy. It must operate differently, sometimes a little smarter than the traditional system firmware design. This means that system firmware should adopt some good learning from operating systems and become a little complicated in its operation to meet the customer expectation for better user expcrience with faster boot to the OS, thereby providing an instant-on experience.

The assumption of modern platform design is that the underlying system firmware or boot firmware should not be aware of many advanced SoC or CPU features, such as the multicore environment or heterogeneous CPU architecture while booting to the OS. And these underlying hardware capacities like multicore or heterogeneous CPUs can "only" be exercised in the

OS/kernel layer and no scope beneath that layer. Hence initialization of I/Os, which are independent in nature in terms of resources from each other, still need to go through a sequential order during the firmware initialization phase.

This case study will nullify such assumptions by making use of such key offerings of the CPU architecture in a pre-OS environment as needed to perform the system firmware boot process efficiently.

1. This art proposes identifying key contexts for concurrency with methods for concurrency and synchronization between boot firmware and other platform initialization entities for faster boot flow.

   a. It's possible to bring more than one logical processor out of reset to run an operation concurrently based on the boot mode like a firmware update.

   b. It can perform basic hardware initialization without being dependent on DRAM initialization (as on typical x86 platform, physical memory is not available on reset; the exception is the latest AMD SoCs in x86 CPU architecture) in low power mode or S5 charging to make a shorter firmware boundary when booting to an OS is not a concern anymore.

2. Utilizing the power and performance efficiency of a heterogeneous CPU architecture on boot scenarios.

   a. Example: A firmware update which is exclusive case that can't perform at OS layer and today's system firmware is performing the traditional chipset/CPU initialization along with FW update without being innovative in firmware design to utilize the heterogenous CPUs to optimize the boot task even if running on heterogeneous processor like Apple A1x chip or Intel Lakefield on client segment.

3. More efficient usage of efficient CPUs and not only encompassing the default boot processor.

Rather than executing the entire platform initialization in sequential order, all the independent resource initializations could have been done in parallel using other available cores to utilize the multi-core architecture, where all possible logical processors except the boot strap one remain in dormant states during the entire system firmware phase. While the industry is talks about advancement, progress in technology and new discoveries are being made by bringing more cores to increase the processing capabilities. The best high- and mid-entry segment CPUs are claiming to introduce more cores and hyperthreading but are still lagging in exploring those capabilities in the system firmware boundary when required to improve the boot performance to quality for instant system boot.

This case study will describe how platform booting time can be opportunistically optimized by executing independent initialization of I/Os over parallel threads during the system firmware phase. It also demonstrates the boot time improvement by performing early initialization of storage devices over logical processors, so that the payload can directly perform the required read operations from the block device and boot to the OS without performing the read, followed by the load operation in the payload to boot to the OS.

This section will focus on demonstrating the work on the open source firmware development approach using Open Source BIOS (alias coreboot) on an Intel-based Chrome platform.

Before entering into the detailed case study section, let's go over some terminology that is going to be used repeatedly.

coreboot

coreboot, formerly known as LinuxBIOS, is a software project aimed at replacing proprietary firmware (the BIOS or UEFI) found in most computers with a lightweight firmware designed to perform only the minimum number of tasks necessary to boot the platform. coreboot is also known as open source BIOS.

Bootstrap Processor

In a multicore CPU design, at reset, only a single CPU core comes out of reset and is able to execute the instructions as part of the platform initialization process. In a boot firmware design prospective, this core is known as BSP.

Application Processor

In multicore CPU design, all other logical processors except the BSP are known as application processors (APs). Typically, during boot, all APs remain in the dormant stage unless BSP is able to take those APs out of reset and allocate the resources to perform the operations independently.

Multithreading

Multithreading is the ability of a CPU to execute multiple processes concurrently. In the multicore platform, it is the responsibility of the BSP to perform multiprocessor initialization to bring APs out from reset. In a multiprocessor environment, each processor can perform independent execution of assigned tasks.

Figure 7-1 provides the high-level difference between tasks performed in a single-threaded environment where same resources being accessed over different processes results in idolant time. In a multithreaded environment, the resources are shared across available logical processors such that those logical processors can perform the assigned tasks independently and concurrently along with the BSP. If the thread synchronization is taken care of and ensures no resource conflict while performing parallel tasks using APs, then this method can be used to optimize the boot firmware task significantly to reduce the overall system firmware boot time and improve the system firmware update experience.

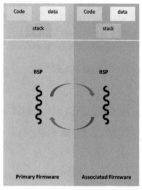
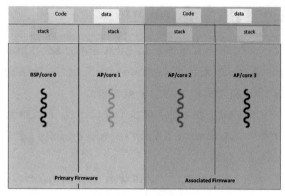

Single-Threaded Process   Multithreaded Process

Figure 7-1. *Resource utilization differences between single and multithreaded processes*

ChromeOS

Chromium OS is an open-source project that aims to build an operating system that provides a fast, simple, and more secure computing experience for people who spend most of their time on the Web.

Crosh

This is the homepage/documentation for the crosh, the Chromium OS shell. If you're on a CrOS device right now, you should be able to launch crosh by hitting Ctrl+Alt+T.

Depthcharge

The official payload for the ChromeOS projects. Depthcharge is responsible for performing the ChromeOS-specific operations required prior to boot to OS and also act as bootloader for ChromeOS.

Goal and Motivation

Today coreboot is not only limited to enabling Chrome devices like chromebooks. It has grown its adoptability among other end user products, IoT, or even on servers.

On Chrome platforms, booting to the OS is a key measuring element. Right now, there is a strict requirement of booting to the OS in less than one second.

It is important to note that the complexity in platform design increases generation over generation with the introduction of newer I/O subsystems that could be discrete (graphic cards, storage) and plug and play (TBT, USB4, storage). These I/O subsystems along with larger addressable memory ranges consume more time for their initialization. The existing legacy BIOS model lacks an advanced methodology that can be used to balance the additional load in the boot process along with the effective usage of system resources of newer platforms. Additionally, with the introduction of the SoC design that comprehends independent IPs provides an opportunity to improve system response time by running IP initialization in parallel.

Additionally, in servers with 99.999% availability means 5 minutes and 15 seconds or less of downtime in a year, so fast reboot is a key figure of merit. For example, if the server cannot be online constantly, it should reboot as quickly as possible. Given the potential terabytes of memory to initialize and ECC syndromes to set, there are embarrassingly parallel opportunities.

Implementation Schema

For end users, after pressing the power button to something showing on the screen of the devices where the user can interact is typically known as platform bootup time. It mostly comprises the system firmware initializing the underlying CPU and chipset time till the first line of kernel is fetched from bootable media plus the OS booting time (until the login prompt or UI).

Figure 7-2 illustrates a platform booting scenario where the total booting time of the device until it reaches the login prompt is ~3 seconds. Figure 7-2 helps to further deduce that time to understand the underlying breakup of the entire platform boot time; within that, the pre-OS or boot firmware takes around ~1.4 seconds, and the rest of the platform booting time is the time that kernel (OS) boots, which is also around to ~1.6 seconds.

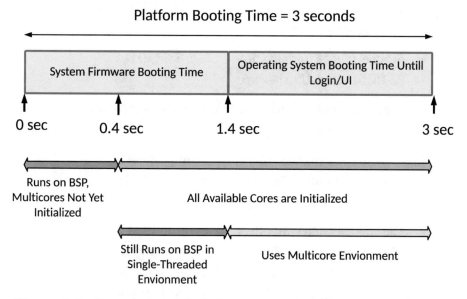

Figure 7-2. *Boot time analysis between system firmware and OS*

As the scope of this exercise is to reduce the system firmware boot time and get within 1 sec, let's start focusing on the breakdown of the system firmware boot time. Due to memory constraints in nature of the x86 reset architecture, at reset not all logical processors are available hence within this 1.4 seconds of firmware booting time, let's say, after around ~400 milliseconds of system boot, typically after DRAM being initialized the BSP would perform the multiprocessor initialization and in that process,

BSP will bring rest of the CPU cores (APs) into active state. Irrespective of whether more than one logical processor is out of reset, traditionally, boot firmware continues to operate in a single threaded environment, to run all chipset initialization, authenticating other associated firmware and loading prior execution works on the BSP (bootstrap processor, single core) alone. See Figure 7-2.

The case study here is to implement a scheduler that uses the multi-core environment even in the pre-OS phase instead of just running the entire system firmware execution only using the BSP, although the rest of cores are up. Here are examples of independent I/O initialization over multiprocessor environment:

- Storage device initialization: NVME, SSD, EMMC, SATA, SD card, USB storage

- Input and output device initialization: USB keyboard, graphics device

- Initialization of platform security components: Platform Module (TPM) discrete solution, locking down specific chipset registers

- Communicating with other microcontrollers as part of the boot process: Supporting EC sync, a special communication to ensure EC firmware is running the latest firmware and switches to the RW section rather than remain in the RO firmware block in the entire boot.

In this proposal, we will demonstrate a savings of around ~300-400 milliseconds of platform booting time if we could follow the system firmware design principle shown in Figure 7-3.

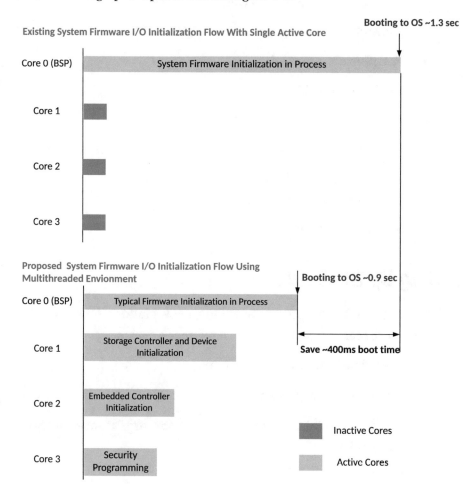

Figure 7-3. *Comparison between existing and proposed system firmware boot flow*

This case study demonstrated using an Intel SoC-based Chrome device. Here are the reference hardware and firmware details:

- **CPU**: Intel Core m3-7Y30 CPU (x86 CPU)

- **Number of cores**: Quad Core CPU @2.6GHz

- **Peripherals attached**:

  - Boot using SPI NOR

  - Output: Display over eDP

  - Boot Device: EMMC device

  - Other devices like connectivity, embedded controller, TPM, audio

- **System firmware**: coreboot 4.11

Setting Up the Board

This section describes the process of adding a new platform ("board") to the existing firmware project, based on a reference design.

- **Download coreboot source code**

1. Clone the latest coreboot code:

```
$ git clone https://review.coreboot.org/a/coreboot.git
cd coreboot
git submodule update --init --checkout
```

2. Place the associated blobs in appropriate locations.

Note   Consider the fact that the ucode and ME kit for Kaby Lake SoC are available externally. Additionally, after product launch, FSP binaries and required headers are available externally at 3rdparty/fsp/KabylakeFspBinPkg/.

- Building coreboot for the board

1. Build the toolchain:

   ```
   CPUS=$(nproc--ignore=1) make  crossgcc-i386  iasl
   ```

2. Create coreboot .config.

   The default options for this board should result in a fully working image:

   ```
   # echo "CONFIG_VENDOR_GOOGLE=y" > .config
   # echo "CONFIG_BOARD_GOOGLE_SORAKA=y" >> .config
   ```

3. Build the image:

   ```
   $ make # the image is generated as build/coreboot.rom
   ```

- **Flashing coreboot**

Use the following mechanism to flash final coreboot.rom image on the board.

Flashing mechanism on Chromebooks are via servo using flashrom utility:

```
$ dut-control spi2_vref:pp3300 spi2_buf_en:on
spi2_buf_on_flex_en:on warm_reset:on
$ sudo flashrom -n -p ft2232_spi:type=servo-v2 -w <bios_image>
$ dut-control spi2_vref:off spi2_buf_en:off
spi2_buf_on_flex_en:off warm_reset:off
```

Boot Time Measurement with existing System Firmware Design

Upon flashing the coreboot image on the targeted board, the system will start booting and will reach the Chrome OS logic screen, as shown in Figure 7-4.

Figure 7-4. *ChromeOS user login screen*

After logging in as a user into ChromeOS, press CTRL + ALT + T to launch crosh shell (command prompt/terminal), as shown in Figure 7-5.

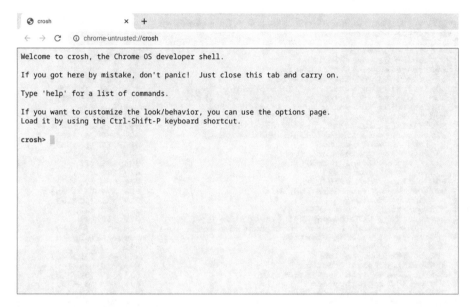

Figure 7-5. *Crosh shell*

Type the advance command cbmem -t at crosh to list the detailed
firmware booting time, as shown in Figure 7-6.

```
[?25h[?0c[01;31mlocalhost[01;34m ~ #[00m cbmem -t
49 entries total:

     0:1st timestamp                                         10,820
     5:start of verified boot                                32,324 (21,504)
   503:starting to initialize TPM                            32,741 (417)
   504:finished TPM initialization                          201,927 (169,185)
   505:starting to verify keyblock/preamble (RSA)           203,052 (1,124)
   506:finished verifying keyblock/preamble (RSA)           222,671 (19,619)
   507:starting to verify body (load+SHA2+RSA)              222,674 (2)
   508:finished loading body (ignore for x86)              349,293 (126,619)
   509:finished calculating body hash (SHA2)                367,342 (18,048)
   510:finished verifying body signature (RSA)              370,788 (3,446)
     6:end of verified boot                                 423,851 (53,063)
    13:starting to load romstage                            424,150 (298)
    14:finished loading romstage                            424,158 (7)
     1:start of rom stage                                   424,202 (43)
   950:calling FspMemoryInit                                426,596 (2,393)
   951:returning from FspMemoryInit                         515,534 (88,938)
     4:end of romstage                                      524,952 (9,418)
     8:starting to load ramstage                            525,082 (129)
    15:starting LZMA decompress (ignore for x86)            525,085 (2)
    16:finished LZMA decompress (ignore for x86)            549,916 (24,830)
     9:finished loading ramstage                            550,075 (159)
    10:start of ramstage                                    550,453 (377)
    30:device enumeration                                   590,061 (39,608)
   954:calling FspSiliconInit                               591,276 (1,214)
   955:returning from FspSiliconInit                        621,686 (30,410)
    40:device configuration                                 625,741 (4,055)
   956:calling FspNotify(AfterPciEnumeration)               642,390 (16,648)
   957:returning from FspNotify(AfterPciEnumeration)        642,582 (192)
    50:device enable                                        642,692 (109)
    60:device initialization                                650,599 (7,907)
    70:device setup done                                    697,840 (47,241)
    75:cbmem post                                           698,442 (602)
    80:write tables                                         715,331 (16,889)
    85:finalize chips                                       726,147 (10,816)
    90:load payload                                         735,942 (9,794)
    15:starting LZMA decompress (ignore for x86)            736,358 (416)
    16:finished LZMA decompress (ignore for x86)            789,885 (53,527)
   958:calling FspNotify(ReadyToBoot)                       792,030 (2,144)
   959:returning from FspNotify(ReadyToBoot)                809,527 (17,497)
   960:calling FspNotify(EndOfFirmware)                     809,581 (53)
   961:returning from FspNotify(EndOfFirmware)              811,735 (2,153)
    99:selfboot jump                                        812,109 (374)
  1000:depthcharge start                                    812,131 (21)
  1002:RO vboot init                                        815,929 (3,798)
  1020:vboot select&load kernel                             815,929 (0)
  1030:finished EC verification                             841,044 (25,115)
  1040:finished storage device initialization             1,141,229 (300,184)
  1050:finished reading kernel from disk                   1,280,169 (138,940)
  1100:finished vboot kernel verification                  1,381,173 (101,003)
  1101:jumping to kernel                                    1,382,692 (1,519)

Total Time: 1,371,850
```

Figure 7-6. *coreboot booting time (in reboot scenario) until
starting kernel*

Now let's analyze the system firmware boot performance data as shown in Figure 7-6. Listing the boot performance data in descending order showed the most time consuming entries are **1040** and **1050**.

```
1040:finished storage device initialization  1,81,229 (300,184)
```

```
1050:finished reading kernel from disk       1,280,169 (138,940)
```

These two entries together took around 440ms of total firmware boot time. So, close to ~32% of the entire platform booting time is consumed by storage initialization and reading the first partition of the kernel from the storage drive alone.

Detailed Implementation

This section will describe the implementation schema in detail to save an additional ~440ms of firmware booting time as discussed in prior sections.

Earlier chapters provided the architecture details of coreboot and its roles and responsibilities. Refer to Figure 4-16 for the coreboot boot flow architecture. Primarily it has two major components:

- **coreboot**: Does the entire chipset, CPU initialization, PCI resource enumeration, and runtime table creation

- **Payload (Depthcharge)**: Payload for Chrome OS to initialize the storage subsystem and read the OS partition from storage device to boot to the OS

In the existing model, this entire firmware initialization takes place using the BSP. Although right after DRAM is initialized and firmware has switched its context from temporary memory to physical memory, at very early "ramstage", coreboot will perform CPU initialization to bring all application processors (AP) out from reset. Since then till booting to OS, those APs are available but in dormant state.

The detailed boot performance time data is shown in Figure 7-7.

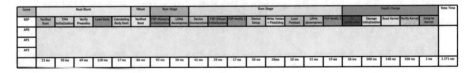

Figure 7-7. *CPU core view from boot task lists*

All the required boot firmware operations are over the BSP, and other APs typically don't perform any operations during the boot process.

In the coreboot build and boot process, the payload is treated as a separate binary and the only communication that exists between coreboot and the payload stage is SYSINFO table. The idea is to provide the required information that the payload would like to have about the underlying hardware and platform, such as serial port number, base address of serial port, system memory range, video framebuffer for user interaction, SPI NOR layout, board details, boot media details like size, coreboot file system details like base and size, and any product related data as VPD (vital product data). See Figure 7-8.

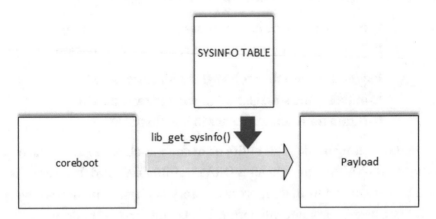

Figure 7-8. *Static information passed to the payload from coreboot*

Refer to https://github.com/coreboot/coreboot/blob/master/payloads/libpayload/include/sysinfo.h for the entire SYSINFO_T structure.

In this proposal, we are trying to pull in several payload-related features like initializing storage controllers and storage devices into coreboot's context to ensure concurrency in firmware boot. Concurrency in firmware boot is ensured by ramstage like the advanced boot stage by reading kernel boot partitions to save sequential read time in the payload. All these mundane device initializations are being executed by the application processors in parallel to the BSP, where the BSP is ensuring generic firmware programming and other chipset initialization tasks.

Here's a detailed boot performance breakdown with the proposed model.

Cores	Boot Block					VBoot	Ram Stage			Ram Stage								Depth Charge			Total Time
	Verified Boot	TPM Initialization	Verify Preamble	Load Body	Calculating Body Hash	Verified Boot	FSP-Memory Initialization	LZMA decompress	Device Enumeration	FSP-Silicon Initialization	FSP-Notify 1	Device Setup	Write Tables + Finalizing Chip	Load Payload	LZMA decompress	FSP Notify 2	AC verification	Read Kernel	Verify Kernel	Jump to Kernel	
BSP																					
AP0									Storage Initialization					Update the SYSINFO structure							
AP1																					
AP2																					
	23 ms	30 ms	69 ms	128 ms	17 ms	86 ms	92 ms	50 ms	43 ms	29 ms	17 ms	30 ms	28ms	10 ms	55 ms	19 ms	26 ms	50 ms	108 ms	2 ms	1.07 sec

If you compare the modified flow with the existing one, you will see that AP0 (Logical Processor 0) is running additional storage initialization that was supposed to be a payload activity in the earlier design and the BSP is still executing its primary job of chipset initialization. So, tasks 1040 and 1050 are now pulled into AP0 concurrently.

In this process we could save additional ~400ms of booting time. There could be still some possibility to optimize this work as other cores like AP1 and AP2 are still in the dormant stage and free to execute any independent initialization as per requirement.

As mentioned above, in this proposal, we had to make some changes in the existing coreboot and Depthcharge working model. The following sections list the specific code changes to achieve this target.

Changes in Boot Firmware - coreboot

In existing models on the x86 architecture, most of the advanced chipset initialization is handled by boot stage runs post-DRAM initialization being done, hence ramstage is where majority of chipset initializations are getting executed. The job responsibilities of ramstage are the following.

CPU multi-processor initialization: coreboot is responsible for making multi-processor initialization as per Intel Software Developer Manuals (SDM) guideline to take all possible APs out from reset. coreboot has basic infrastructure to perform specific function execution over all APs or a single AP based on APIC ID.

PCI enumeration: Additionally, ramstage is also responsible for making resource allocation and enabling those resources for PCI devices. As Depthcharge is a lazy payload that doesn't have the ability to perform the resource enabling hence, this is the must-have step for the payload to ensure access of various boot devices and associated devices if any.

Hand-off to payload: Depthcharge being the specific payload for chrome devices, it looks for coreboot to know certain information about the platform. Any information that coreboot would like to pass to Depthcharge will be in the form of a sysinfo table, as explained in Figure 7-8.

In order to make early storage controller and device initialization (SDHC controller and eMMC device) a part of ramstage using multi-threaded environment, here is the list of changes that made it possible:

Add the API to let APs perform operations in parallel to BSP: Typically, coreboot has support to perform a single operation iteratively on multiple cores, but the idea here is to create a scheduler so that independent tasks can be assigned to a logical processor based on APIC ID.

Create a common eMMC IP initialization block: This block will perform eMMC storage controller and device initialization over an application processor specified by the APIC ID. It's prescribed to start eMMC initialization as early as possible after the application processors are available to execute any operation. Hence in this block, we are focusing on three major tasks:

- Assign a fixed MMIO base address for the eMMC PCH controller to perform additional device-related operations over the MMIO space

- Initialize the SDHC controller

- Initialize the media as in the card device

Make a fixed BAR assignment for the eMMC controller during PCI enumeration: Since the PCI enumeration will continue over BSP and in same time we will have eMMC controller and device initialization over AP (based on the APIC ID), it's important to ensure the MMIO base address for the eMMC controller remains unchanged during PCI enumeration as well.

Pass the SDHC controller and media information to the payload: So far its payload to make storage controller initialization, so it never looks for such data from coreboot, but in order to make eMMC early initialization over APs to save boot time, it's also important to let the payload know that eMMC device is readily available to continue booting to the OS. Hence required to create additional controller and media structure into the SYSINFO table to pass from coreboot to payload.

Create new structure variables inside the SYSINFO table as follows:

- **To pass information about the SDHCI host:** The primary information that goes from coreboot to the payload to notify the payload whether to perform storage device initialization as part of the payload or just use the additional structure for the MMC controller and MMC media device. If the `.initialized` variable is set to 1, it means coreboot has already done the initialization and the payload can parse the remaining host controller information:

```
#define CB_TAG_SDHCI_HOST 0x0034
struct cb_sdhci_host_info {
    uint32_t tag;
    uint32_t size;
    int initialized;
    unsigned quirks;
    unsigned host_caps;
    unsigned version;
    unsigned clock;
    unsigned clock_f_min;
    unsigned clock_f_max;
    unsigned clock_base;
    int removable;
    unsigned voltages;
    unsigned dma64;
};
```

- **To pass information about the MMC controller and MMC media device:** An additional structure to populate information about the controller and device like operating frequency, bus width, and voltage for the host controller and device capacity, vendor identification, and size for the MMC card device:

```
#define CB_TAG_MMC_MEDIA 0x0035          #define CB_TAG_MMC_CTRLR 0x0036
struct cb_mmc_media_info {               struct cb_mmc_ctrlr_info {
       uint32_t tag;                            uint32_t tag;
       uint32_t size;                           uint32_t size;
       uint32_t caps;                           uint32_t voltages;
       uint32_t version;                        uint32_t f_min;
       uint32_t read_bl_len;                    uint32_t f_max;
       uint32_t write_bl_len;                   uint32_t bus_width;
       uint64_t capacity;                       uint32_t bus_hz;
       int high_capacity;                       uint32_t caps;
       uint32_t tran_speed;                     uint32_t b_max;
       uint32_t erase_size;                     uint32_t timing;
       uint32_t trim_mult;                      uint32_t hardcoded_voltage;
       uint32_t ocr;                     };
       uint16_t rca;
       uint32_t scr[2];
       uint32_t csd[4];
       uint32_t cid[4];
       uint32_t op_cond_response;
};
```

Changes in Payload - Depthcharge

In the existing model, Depthcharge is where storage controller and media device initializations take place.

Storage controller initialization: It requires to provide details about the underlying hardware controller to which the block device is attached. For example: eMMC card device is attached to the eMMC controller PCI bus: device: function and required operational mode as HS400/HS200.

Storage media initialization: Additionally, it performs the required initialization of storage media devices (here eMMC) to know the number of blocks, section, and size information.

Boot from media to OS: Once the controller and device have been initialized, it just reads the block from the eMMC device to boot to the OS.

As the storage controller and media devices have already been initialized by coreboot during ramstage over APs, the boot firmware can pass the design choice information to the payload as follows:

Skip SDHC and media initialization: Create a skip method by using struct cb_sdhci_host_info.initialized = 1 to let Depthcharge know that device is ready to use.

Provide device configuration: As part of the sysinfo table, coreboot is now able to pass required information about the controller and devices to the payload using `struct cb_mmc_media_info` and `struct cb_mmc_ctrlr_info` so that it can read the kernel partition directly from the block device without bothering about reinitialization.

Final Boot-Time Measurement

Finally we are ready to create the new coreboot.rom that includes the required coreboot and Depthcharge changes.

Let the system boot to the crosh shell after flashing the new binary. Run the `cbmem -t` command from the shell to capture the boot performance time, as shown in Figure 7-9.

```
[?25h[?0c[01;31mlocalhost[01;34m ~ #[00m cbmem -t
49 entries total:

    0:1st timestamp                                      10,820
    5:start of verified boot                             32,324 (21,504)
  503:starting to initialize TPM                         32,741 (417)
  504:finished TPM initialization                        201,927 (169,185)
  505:starting to verify keyblock/preamble (RSA)         203,052 (1,124)
  506:finished verifying keyblock/preamble (RSA)         222,671 (19,619)
  507:starting to verify body (load+SHA2+RSA)            222,674 (2)
  508:finished loading body (ignore for x86)             349,293 (126,619)
  509:finished calculating body hash (SHA2)              367,342 (18,048)
  510:finished verifying body signature (RSA)            370,788 (3,446)
    6:end of verified boot                               423,851 (53,063)
   13:starting to load romstage                          424,150 (298)
   14:finished loading romstage                          424,158 (7)
    1:start of rom stage                                 424,202 (43)
  950:calling FspMemoryInit                              426,596 (2,393)
  951:returning from FspMemoryInit                       515,534 (88,938)
    4:end of romstage                                    524,952 (9,418)
    8:starting to load ramstage                          525,082 (129)
   15:starting LZMA decompress (ignore for x86)          525,085 (2)
   16:finished LZMA decompress (ignore for x86)          549,916 (24,830)
    9:finished loading ramstage                          550,075 (159)
   10:start of ramstage                                  550,453 (377)
   30:device enumeration                                 590,061 (39,608)
  954:calling FspSiliconInit                             591,276 (1,214)
  955:returning from FspSiliconInit                      621,686 (30,410)
   40:device configuration                               625,741 (4,055)
  956:calling FspNotify(AfterPciEnumeration)             642,390 (16,648)
  957:returning from FspNotify(AfterPciEnumeration)      642,582 (192)
   50:device enable                                      642,692 (109)|
   60:device initialization                              650,599 (7,907)
   70:device setup done                                  697,840 (47,241)
   75:cbmem post                                         698,442 (602)
   80:write tables                                       715,331 (16,889)
   85:finalize chips                                     726,147 (10,816)
   90:load payload                                       735,942 (9,794)
   15:starting LZMA decompress (ignore for x86)          736,358 (416)
   16:finished LZMA decompress (ignore for x86)          789,885 (53,527)
  958:calling FspNotify(ReadyToBoot)                     792,030 (2,144)
  959:returning from FspNotify(ReadyToBoot)              809,527 (17,497)
  960:calling FspNotify(EndOfFirmware)                   809,581 (53)
  961:returning from FspNotify(EndOfFirmware)            811,735 (2,153)
   99:selfboot jump                                      812,109 (374)
 1000:depthcharge start                                  812,131 (21)
 1002:RO vboot init                                      815,929 (3,798)
 1020:vboot select&load kernel                           815,929 (0)
 1030:finished EC verification                           841,044 (25,115)
 1040:finished storage device initialization             844,228 (3,184)
 1050:finished reading kernel from disk                  875,168 (30,940)
 1100:finished vboot kernel verification                 976,171 (101,003)
 1101:jumping to kernel                                  977,690 (1,519)

Total Time: 966,870
```

Figure 7-9. *Final coreboot booting time (in reboot scenario) until starting the kernel*

Now let's analyze the system firmware boot performance data as shown in Figure 7-8. It saves around ~440ms of firmware booting time in this process. In specific details, boot performance data for task id 1040 and 1050 are now optimized as follows:

```
1040:finished storage device initialization    844, 228 (3,184)

1050:finished reading kernel from disk          875, 168 (30,940)
```

Firmware Boot Time Optimization for Capsule Update

This responsiveness is even important on UEFI machines during an update. For example, any parallelization during the UEFI capsule update process (more details can be found at the reference section by Intel Corporation presented during FOSDEM, slide 10) can improve the user experience. This is because the capsule update process entails reboots and suspends the user from being able to do useful work with their device during the process. This use case is in addition to the value of responsiveness for any system restart, too, as the user expectation of electronic devices continues toward an "instant on" perception of the hardware.

Firmware Boot Time Optimization Conclusion

Platform booting time is a critical performance indicator for modern computing devices. This case study describes how to optimize platform firmware booting time by performing independent I/O initialization using multi-threaded environments. Although we have demonstrated this concept using coreboot, this concept is equally relevant for the UEFI BIOS as well due to the bottleneck of mundane speed device initialization sequentially during boot. We also discussed the possibility of extending this support over remaining APs in order to further optimize the boot time.

Supporting New CPU Architecture Migration with UEFI

This case study is a further extension of some future-looking system firmware aspects described in *Firmware Development: A Guide to Specialized Systemic Knowledge,* Chapter 6 as part of the "Innovation in Hardware Design" section.

The earlier section highlighted that system firmware being innovative and simple also depends on underlying hardware and SoC design. If underlying CPU architecture and board design is able to nullify the unnecessary complexity in the reset process, then the system firmware can also get rid of inheriting undue complications, which involves adding unrequired stages in the boot process.

The scope of this work is to explain and show the real use case scenario to help you understand how to design system firmware differently for each SoC without encompassing the traditional system firmware design. See Figure 7-10.

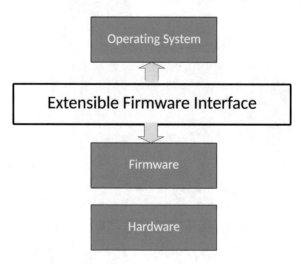

Figure 7-10. *UEFI in the system software stack*

We are going to use the Open Source EDK2-based system firmware development approach for this case study section. It is widely known that UEFI is one of the market-leading firmware technologies used across various CPU architectures like ARM, IA32, X64, and RISC V with greater modularity and portability.

UEFI describes an interface between the OS and the platform firmware as per Figure 7-10.

An OS that intends to run on the platform must be compatible with the supported processor specifications and able to boot on a variety of system designs without further platform or OS customization. The definition is also supportive of any platform innovation like the introduction of new features and functionality that could enhance the platform capability without impacting the OS boot scenarios. See Figure 7-11.

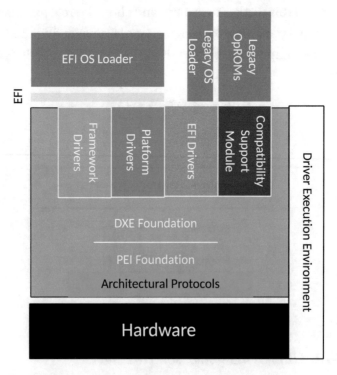

Figure 7-11. *UEFI system architecture*

UEFI comes with an inherent solid foundation of code written in C along with an array of device drivers and debugging tools for various platforms which are architecture neutral. Thus, successive generations of products based on CISC and/or RISC CPU architecture can leverage the pre-boot software investment from previous generations while isolating any required changes to the EFI drivers.

As mentioned in the UEFI system architecture section as part of this book, various boot stages in the UEFI architecture perform hardware initialization as per underlying hardware requirements.

Before going into further details, let's understand few keywords in details as they are going to use repeatedly.

CISC: Complex Instruction Set Computer Architecture. The idea here is that a single instruction can perform a number of low-level operations like a load from memory, an arithmetic operation, or store or read from memory, so multiple steps can be accommodated using a single instruction.

RISC: Reduced Instruction Set Computer Architecture. The idea here is to use simple commands that can be divided into several instructions but operate within a single clock cycle.

Reset vector: A 32-bit address where the CPU will start fetching the instruction post CPU reset. This address can be different between CISC and RISC architectures and in most cases, this address is patchable using monitor code.

Monitor code: A tiny firmware block that resides in permanent non-volatile memory typically referred to as ROM. Mostly used to verify the basic hardware interface at reset without complex or high-level system firmware.

U-Boot: Refer as Universal Boot Loader, mostly used on embedded devices as a first stage bootloader with basic command line support. It can be further used as second stage bootloader to boot to an OS from a block device or used as underlying firmware for developing high-level system firmware like coreboot, UEFI or SBL, without flashing the SPI NOR several times; rather, you can use simple load and go commands to run system firmware on top of U-Boot. See Figure 7-12.

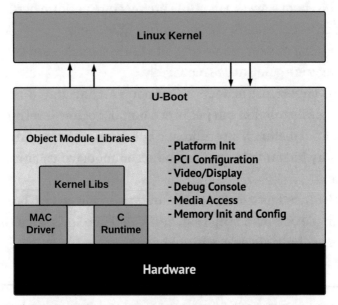

Figure 7-12. *U-Boot system architecture*

Embedded Bootloader (EBL): A tiny version of the EFI shell, mostly designed for embedded devices to run basic hardware and firmware checklists and further load a kernel image.

Refer to these sections for typical UEFI SoC-independent boot architecture:

- **SEC (security) phase:**

  - A phase that is designed to run without decompression

  - Reset vector patched at 0th address

  - C stack setup using available SRAM

  - Jump into PEI core

- **PEI phase**: Pre-EFI initialization phase

  - Performs early chipset initialization

  - Typically compressed in flash and needs decompression

  - Started before memory initialized

  - Executes directly from SRAM mapped memory

  - Performs DRAM initialization

  - Reads chipset registers to know the boot mode to skip certain chipset initialization on resume

  - Dispatches PEI modules

  - PEI modules communicate using PPI (PEI to PEI interface)

  - Finally, jumps into DXE core (Figure 7-13)

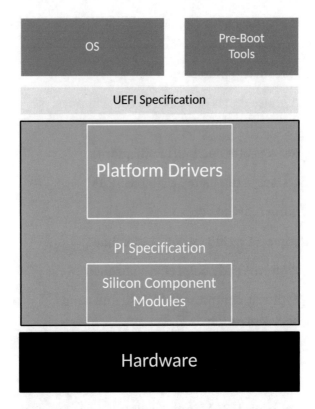

Figure 7-13. *PEI phase internals*

- **DXE phase:** Driver execution environment phase

  - Executes out of physical memory

  - Typically compressed in SPI NOR and loaded into main memory and runs after decompression

  - Several DXE drivers for non-enumerable hardware

    - CPU: Init, exceptions, MMU

    - Timer, RTC, platform reset

- Non-volatile data store for UEFI variables

- UEFI status code for debug and error code

- **BDS phase**: Boot dev select phase

  - Launches all UEFI drivers as applicable using bus architecture

  - Locates boot critical devices to boot to OS bootloader

This case study is going to nullify the legacy assumption made in Figure 7-11 with the de facto UEFI-based system firmware architecture for an evaluation board created using a new RISC-based CPU architecture.

Goal and Motivation

The de facto standard for booting the evaluation or education board is typically u-boot for booting into Linux OS. Due to the fact that platform initialization done by a default boot loader in an embedded system (u-boot in our scenario) contains the least modular, least architecture and most custom components. Basic implementation done by the u-boot bootloader contains only a "barebones" implementation of tools like platform diagnostics, flash updates, and other libraries that are rarely usable on future platforms and require higher maintenance. EFI/UEFI serves a very important purpose, which is future upgradability and maintainability as compared to u-boot-based embedded systems.

- The aim is to develop EFI-aware system firmware for a new CPU architecture with rich features of initializing and configuring all peripherals during POST, EBL, and graphical setup engine support.

- Learning how to add support for new CPU architecture in the EDKII build environment for choosing the target compiler and assembler tools.

- Demonstrating system firmware development with a SoC design where physical memory is initialized at reset, thus the modularity in the EFI architecture is used to reduce the conventional boot operation

- As per the study, based on the required functionality to enable the evaluation board, the UEFI ROM image size is expected to be much less compared to the u-boot ROM image size.

- UEFI has a driver-based architecture and developers can create each module independently. The UEFI framework is strongly scalable and provides a set of value-added features that can be added without modifying the existing implementation.

Implementation Schema

Figure 7-14 provides the high-level boot operational model of a hypothetical (illustrated for educational purpose as part of this chapter) RISC-based SoC architecture referred as ELIXIR in this case study. ELIXIR has its own design innovation where it has pre-initialized memory (SRAM) available at reset to innovate in firmware operation as well.

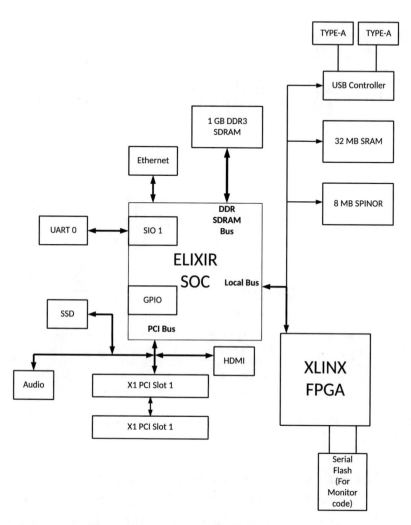

Figure 7-14. *High-level SoC-hardware design*

DRAM is also available in CACHE ENABLE mode for system firmware to use immediately at CPU reset. Figure 7-14 illustrates the high level hardware design architecture.

The ELIXIR processor ensures that preinitialized memory is available at reset, so it doesn't need to set up temporary memory for the early boot sequence. This helps to redesign the system firmware boot operational model opportunistically as in Figure 7-15.

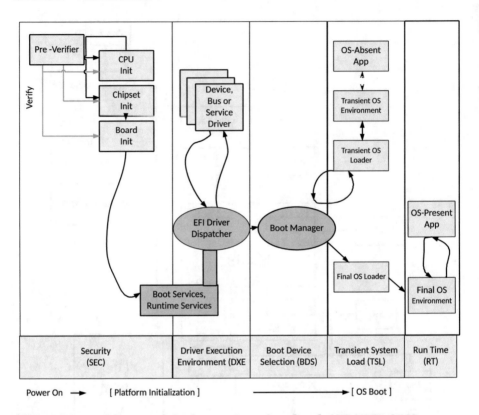

Figure 7-15. *Phases of the boot pperation for the ELIXIR CPU architecture*

On ARM or x86 architectures, the SEC phase begins with power-on and includes the steps that are required to find and authenticate the PEI Foundation prior to launching it. But in the case of the ELIXIR architecture, both the SEC and PEI phases are combined to perform specific initial configuration routines for the processor, chipset, and motherboard and create the HOBs.

In the traditional UEFI reset architecture, the PEI phase operation consists of invoking the PEI Foundation, dispatching all PEIMs in an orderly manner, creating HOBs for passing system state information to the next phase, and discovering and invoking the next phase. Memory discovery is an important architectural event during the PEI phase. The PEI Foundation switches PEI stack usage from temporary RAM to permanent system memory.

But in the case of the ELIXIR architecture, there is no need for a dedicated PEI phase because memory is available in the initial stage itself. Having a dedicated stage is costly for many reasons for system firmware design architecture.

- Firstly, creating stages like PEI requires additional PEI foundations and modules, which would anyway consume the SPI NOR.

- Secondly, additional stages force an incremental effort to locate the stage, hash the entire binary, verify and load it into memory, and execute it.

For space and time boundary constraints, it's better to avoid an additional stage unless absolutely required.

The rest of the UEFI phases remain as is with required functionality to perform the bare minimal hardware initialization and finally launch EBL or the graphics setup page or launch Linux OS as per applicability.

This case study is made on an evaluation board with hypothetical RISC-based CPU design where the memory is preinitialized at reset. Here are the reference hardware and firmware details:

- **CPU**: RISC-based 32-bit processor

- **Number of cores**: Dual Core CPU @1GHz.

- **Peripherals attached**:

  - Boot using SPI NOR 8MB

  - Output: Display over HDMI

  - Boot Device: SSD

  - Debugging-aid: UART

- Memory: 32MB SRAM and 1GB DRR3 SDRAM

- 2 x1 PCI Slot

- Audio controller and Codec

- 10/100 Phy Ethernet

- 2 Type-A USB port

- **System firmware**: EFI (UEFI Specification 2.9)

Setting Up the Code Base

EDKII is the open source firmware development vehicle that has an enhanced build environment compared to its predecessor, EDKI. EDKII is flexible enough to choose the compiler and assembler tools. It also has a provision to add support for building any new SoC architecture.

Here we will discuss adding support for new SoC architecture into EDKII tool chain and set up the flash layout for ELIXIR.

The compiler for the ELIXIR processor is based on the Linux operating system. EDKII already has support for IA32, IA64, IPF, and ARM processors. The EDKII framework has a set of build configuration tools to provide a flexible build process.

- **BUILD environment**:

  - Setting environment variables:

The first variable to be set is WORKSPACE. This variable points to the root directory of an EDKII directory tree. More than one development tree can exist, and this environment variable is used to identify the current working directory tree.

Another environment variable to be set is EDK_TOOLS_PATH. It points to the directory containing the Bin directory for the BaseTools directory.

  - Setting ELIXIR tools chain in the EDKII build environment:

The compiler to build the source is copied to the proper directory. (e.g., /root/tools/$COMPILER_NAME)

- GenFw changes:

GenFw tools have to be changed to support ELIXIR ELF files. This tool is used to generate UEFI Firmware image files based on component or module types listed in the INF files from the PE/PE32+/COFF images generated by the third-party tool chains. Current GenFw only supports i386 and ARM CPUs; to make GenFw support new a CPU architecture, BaseTools/Source/C/GenFw.c must be changed to add the ELIXIR CPU type in the ELF header.

- Add a new tool chain:

A new tool chain has to be added for the new processor type. conf\ tools_def.txt is the file that provides a variable mapping of compiler tool chains and flags.

The ELIXIR tool chain is added in this file:

```
*_ELIXIRGCC_ARM_ASLCC_PATH         = DEF(ELIXIR_TOOLS)/
                                     elixir-linux-gcc

*_ELIXIRGCC_ARM_ASLDLINK_PATH      = DEF(ELIXIR_TOOLS)/
                                     elixir-linux-ld

*_ELIXIRGCC_ARM_ASLPP_PATH         = DEF(ELIXIR_TOOLS)/
                                     elixir-linux-gcc

*_ELIXIRGCC_ARM_CC_PATH            = DEF(ELIXIR_TOOLS)/
                                     elixir-linux-gcc

*_ELIXIRGCC_ARM_SLINK_PATH         = DEF(ELIXIR_TOOLS)/
                                     elixir-linux-ar

*_ELIXIRGCC_ARM_DLINK_PATH         = DEF(ELIXIR_TOOLS)/
                                     elixir-linux-ld

*_ELIXIRGCC_ARM_ASM_PATH           = DEF(ELIXIR_TOOLS)/
                                     elixir-linux-as
```

```
*_ELIXIRGCC_ARM_PP_PATH                = DEF(ELIXIR_TOOLS)/
                                         elixir-linux-gcc
*_ELIXIRGCC_ARM_VFRPP_PATH             = DEF(ELIXIR_TOOLS)/
                                         elixir-linux-gcc
```

- Defining rules:

The Build_rule.txt file provides rules to specify how individual modules are compiled and linked. The tools and flags specified in the tools_def.txt file (and the optional BuildOptions in the INF and/or DSC files) are used with the templates in this file to generate makefiles.

Rules have to be defined for the new architecture "ELIXIR".

```
< Command.ELIXIRGCC>
             "$(SLINK)" $(SLINK_FLAGS) ${dst} $(OBJECT_FILES)
<Command.ELIXIRGCC>
        "$(DLINK)" -o ${dst} $(DLINK_FLAGS)  $(DLINK_SPATH)
        $(STATIC_LIBRARY_FILES)  $(DLINK2_FLAGS)
```

- Change the EDKII source code format from DOSs to UNIX.

All EDKII source files are written in the DOS format, which uses "\n\r" to change lines, but the Linux compiler only supports the Linux format, which uses "\n" to change lines. Before building EDK2 source code, all source code must be changed to the DOS format.

```
Run " find . —name "*.[ch]" —print |xargs dos2unix"
```

- Add underlying assembly code.

Most EDKII source code has been written in C, but there's still some CPU-related code written in assembly; that code must be changed to support the new CPU architecture.

- Rewrite assembly code to support the new CPU architecture.

    - Set up the build environment in the build script.

In Linux, the default GNU build toolchain can be used (e.g., /usr/bin/ gcc, /usr/bin/as, /usr/bin/link), but to use custom GNU build tools, the Linux path environment variable must be changed:

```
In ./ElixirPkg/build.sh add (e.g)
ELIXIR_PATH=/root/tools//lib/gcc-lib/
ELIXIR_PATH=$ELIXIR_PATH:/root/tools/$COMPILER_NAME/bin/
ELIXIR_PATH=$ELIXIR_PATH:/root/tools/$COMPILER_NAME/lib/
 export PATH=$ELIXIR_PATH:$PATH:
In ./ElixirPkg/build.sh set TARGET_TOOLS to ELIXIRGCC.
```

- Run build script and build the target.

Run build.sh to build target files and generate the .ROM image.

- **FirmwareILayout:**

In UEFI terminology, a ROM image that is stored into SPI NOR is known as firmware device image or .FD. As mentioned, the FD consists of one or more Firmware Volumes (FVs).

Figure 7-16 provides the firmware layout for the target evaluation hardware, where only required modules are combined into a firmware volume to create the final firmware device. As the CPU architecture already has physical memory initialized at reset, the boot firmware design doesn't need to have PEI-associated modules and drivers. This helps to create a simple firmware device layout as shown here. The FD consists of two firmware volumes, FV_Main and FV_MainCompact. FV_Main consists of all DXE drivers, and FV_Main_Compact consists of SEC drivers and the compressed form of all DXE drivers.

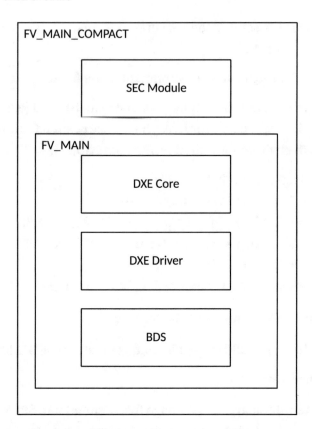

Figure 7-16. *Firmware device design*

Detailed Implementation

This section provides the detailed implementation of the system firmware for the evaluation hardware. The expectation is that you can understand the drivers, protocols, and service requirements as applicable to the underlying hardware. Additionally, consider the feature set that the system firmware would like to provide to the end users for developing their own advanced features like audio and video drivers or utilities to diagnose the hardware.

Boot operational phases are

- SEC (security) phase

- DXE (driver execution environment) phase

- BDS (boot device select) phase

- TSL (transient system load) phase

- RT (run time) phase

Details on the SEC Phase

- 1GB pre-initialized physical memory at reset. Starting from DDR bank 0x4000_0000 to 0x8000_0000.

- As pre-reset SPI NOR is already mapped to DDR bank

- Reset vector mapped at 0x4000_0000 (patched using monitor code)

- As per Figure 7-16, the SEC module is packed uncompressed so after setting up the required stack based on available physical memory, the SEC phase will start executing on its own.

- Figure 7-17 provides a system memory map, which typically gets created at the end of the PEI phase but here due to memory availability, system firmware creates the memory layout even in the SEC phase itself.

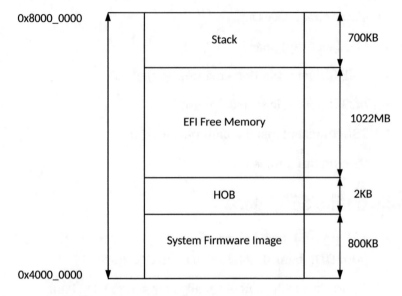

0x8000_0000

Stack — 700KB

EFI Free Memory — 1022MB

HOB — 2KB

System Firmware Image — 800KB

0x4000_0000

Figure 7-17. *EFI system memory map*

- Prepare the HOB list.

- Initialize the UART controller for serial messages. The serial console is also used for early debugging.

- There is no PEI phase in this project due to the RISC-based processor where memory will be by default initialized. All the necessary initializations are done in the SEC phase. See Figure 7-18.

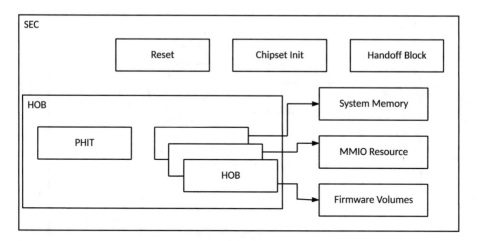

Figure 7-18. *SEC phase boot operation*

Details on the DXE Phase

- DXE drivers are compressed so SEC phases need to uncompress and load into memory prior execution.

- Figure 7-19 illustrate the boot operational model for this stage, where DXE dispatches several DXE and EFI drivers and publishes required services used in later stages

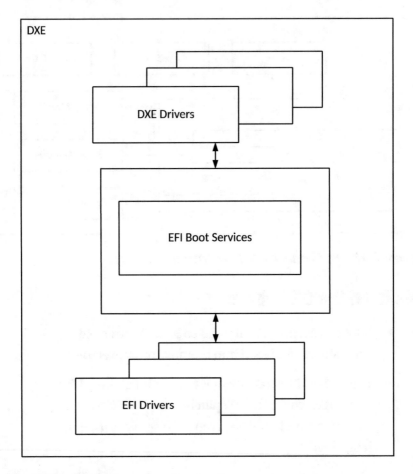

Figure 7-19. *DXE phase boot operation*

- **Protocols published by DXE drivers:**

  - EFI_FIRMWARE_VOLUME_BLOCK_PROTOCOL

  - EFI_DEVICE_PATH_PROTOCOL

  - EFI_SERIAL_IO_PROTOCOL

  - EFI_TIMER_ARCH_PROTOCOL

  - EFI_SIMPLE_TEXT_OUTPUT_PROTOCOL

- EFI_HII_CONFIG_ROUTING_PROTOCOL

- EFI_HII_CONFIG_ACCESS_PROTOCOL

- EFI_HII_DATABASE_PROTOCOL

- SPI flash library:

  - Base library to perform read, write, erase, and apply protection for SPI NOR

  - System firmware would also be designed to keep a configuration region mapped to SPI flash for storing UEFI variable services for allowing configuration of SoC interface and hardware capabilities using the graphics setup engine.

- **Serial IO library**: Used to initialize the UART over the Super IO interface

- **Timer library**: Configures the on-chip programmable timers and enables the timer

- **XHCI host controller and USB bus driver**:

  - Implemented as EFI driver

  - Installs host controller protocol for USB devices

  - Enumerates all USB ports to detect the device presence and assign unique numbers to the device available in ports

  - Establishes bus communication with the XHCI controller

  - Installs USB BUS IO protocol for further communication

- Supports both high and low speed device communication with XHCI controller using BUS and HOST protocols

- **Device drivers for USB keyboard, Mice, and mass storage:**

  - Implemented as EFI driver

  - USB keyboard will install SimpleTextIn Protocol.

  - Installs SimplePointer protocol for USB mice

  - USB mass storage will publish BLOCK IO protocol

  - USB mass storage and keyboards will be working in setup where all USB can be worked at EBL

- **IDE BUS driver and SATA controller:**

  - Implemented as EFI driver

  - Responsible for communicating with the SATA controller and initializing the channels and getting the info.

  - IDE bus will install the IDE Bus Init Protocol for further communication

  - SATA devices will be detected at both setup and EBL

- **FileSystem driver:**

  - USB mass storage and SATA in IDE mode will provide the features to boot to respective media, in order to support the bootable media file system driver that needs to be implemented.

- MBR partition supported

- The file system only supported the English language.

- **Network stack and PXE:**

  - Implemented as EFI driver

  - Implements IP4 network stack based on all standard network protocols

  - Creates a small client/server communication and establishes the connection in order to support diskless boot

  - Features supported in both setup and EBL

- **PCI Driver:**

  - Implemented as DXE driver

  - Reads the PCI config for PCI devices, say VGA and SATA

  - Fills the PCI I/O structure and publishes the PCI I/O protocol for communication to PCI devices

Details on BDS, TSL, and RT Phases

- **BDS (boot device selection) phase:**

  - In BDS phase, it will find out the CONSOLE IN devices, CONSOLE OUT devices, and First Boot device, and try to load the OS image from that device.

  - All the UEFI drivers have been connected in this phase via ConnectController.

- On failure to boot from the first boot device, it enters into the next boot device until the last boot device on the list.

- In the absence of all bootable devices, it boots to default EBL from the flash part.

- **EBL:**

  - Embedded boot loader(EBL) which is a CLI-based environment almost similar to an EFI shell.

  - A set of commands like Memmap and HOB need to be implemented .

  - A special set of commands called "loads" and "go" are required to replace the u-boot on such evaluation boards to allow developers to create their own firmware and/or drivers.

  - Upgrade the BIOS utility.

- **Setup customization:**

  - Rich and configurable utility available after POST for modifying the hardware interface and capabilities.

  - Enable or disable a few peripheral components.

  - Boot to Inbuilt EBL.

- **TSL (transient system load) phase:**

  - It will load the OS from a bootable device.

  - As the target is to boot the Linux kernel, thus RamDisk and bzImage are two necessary binary images in the process to load the Linux kernel for this evaluation board.

  - The kernel partition would mount the partitions and create the basic file system where at the minimum level "ls" would show the primary file systems under root (/).

- **RT (run time) phase:**

  - Although the control has been transferred to OS, still a set of runtime services will be available, which are provided during the system firmware lifespan to access several features: RTC time (set time/get time), timers, and variable services to access NVRAM variables.

Figure 7-20 illustrates the boot operational model for this stage.

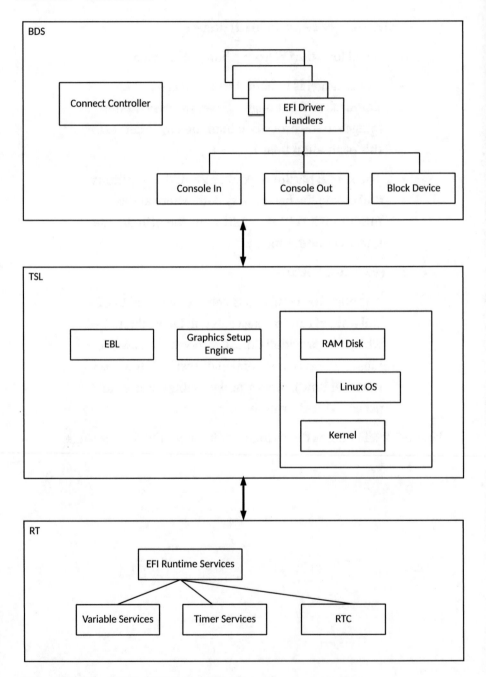

Figure 7-20. *BDS, TSL, and RT phase boot operations*

Porting a New CPU Architecture (Elixir) Conclusion

System firmware is meant to provide the abstraction of the hardware layer to the OS like advanced system software and provide the basic initialization of hardware. The system firmware architecture shouldn't create a bottleneck for designing such thinner firmware to solves the basic purpose of booting the platform to the OS. This case study was done on an evaluation board with a RISC CPU architecture so that you can see how to add support for the new SoC architecture or associated compiler and tools into a UEFI-like advanced system firmware in a step-by-step approach. Also, you can specify all the required infrastructure changes to design system firmware where innovation in SoC/hardware design would nullify the legacy assumption of UEFI-like system firmware boot operation design as well.

Reducing the System Firmware Boundary with LinuxBoot

This case study is a further extension of some future-looking system firmware aspects described in *Firmware Development: A Guide to Specialized Systemic Knowledge* as part of the "Designing LITE Firmware" section in Chapter 6.

Over time, several components of system firmware have grown out of their traditional boundaries to support complex features, which makes system firmware pretended more like an operating system than bare minimum block to initialize the underlying hardware. The idea here is to remove those complex layers from the system firmware and design a more simplistic and open source friendly firmware for embedded systems.

Typically, in the system firmware design, the payload and its loader stage (example: DXE, BDS in UEFI and romstage, Depthcharge in coreboot) are designed to perform operations that require specific device drivers and utilities, which need regular maintenance for newer SoC or platform design to ensure they're not getting out of service. Also, there might be cases where these drivers are actually backported from kernel layers so any bug fixes at the source driver in the kernel might need attention for the maintainer to port them back into these specific firmware layers as well. This back-and-forth exercise might result in bugs or an unmaintained code base in the long run, which can be an additional problem and also a security concern.

The LinuxBoot project with LITE firmware design principle is the answer to avoid having specific proprietary, closed source, vendor-specific, kernel backported drivers into the firmware layer.

We are going to use an open source firmware development approach as coreboot for silicon and platform initialization and LinuxBoot as the replacement for the payload to demonstrate this work done on an IA-based evaluation board, with UP Squared Atom with 2GB memory and 32GB eMMC.

The idea here is to create a thinner footprint for system firmware and bring the power of the Linux kernel into the firmware trusted computing boundary to bring back the trust in a more generic and standard way across different boot firmware while booting to a Linux or equivalent OS. See Figure 7-21.

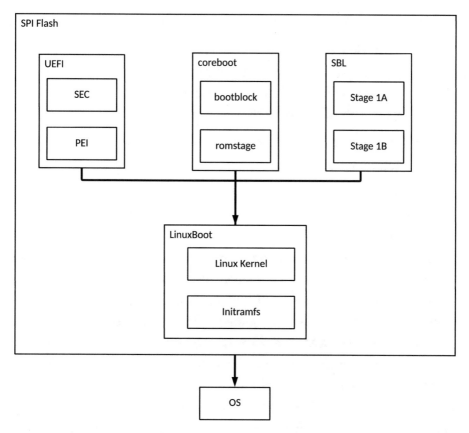

Figure 7-21. *LinuxBoot principal with different boot firmware (BIOS)*

Before going to further details, let's understand some terminology:

LinuxBoot: Originally, LinuxBoot was intended to be a firmware for modern servers to replace specific firmware functionality like the UEFI DXE phase with a Linux kernel and runtime. But with growing demands in both client and IoT computing machines, LinuxBoot is now a unified solution for all computing machines.

LinuxBoot is consists of two major components:

1. **Linux kernel**: One can specify the required upstream Linux kernel version while creating a LinuxBoot image. Example: 5.11.2 is the latest version as of February 2021.

2. Initramfs: In the context of LinuxBoot, it's also referred to as u-root.

Linux kernel: LinuxBoot is intended as a replacement of payload and advanced stages in a system firmware design where LinuxBoot is located on SPI NOR and can be used to boot the Linux-equivalent OS from a block device or over a network. LinuxBoot is not designed to be a runtime kernel. While generating the LinuxBoot image, one could use the menuconfig option to select the required device drivers and feature sets prior to generating the LinuxBoot kernel; some patches are needed.

Initramfs (initial RAM filesystem): The initramfs is a root file system that is needed by Linux to get boot and startup utilities. The initramfs is embedded within the LinuxBoot image, which resides in the system firmware image located in SPI NOR itself. There are many ways to create initramfs. LinuxBoot uses u-root to create initramfs. The initramfs is a set of directories packed into a single cpio archive. The Linux kernel part of the LinuxBoot image checks the presence of the initramfs and unpacks it, mount sit as '/', and executes '/init'.

bzImage: As the Linux kernel matures, the size of the kernel also grows beyond the limits imposed by some architectures, where the space available to store the compressed kernel code is limited.

The bzImage (big zImage) format was developed to overcome this limitation by cleverly splitting the kernel over discontinuous memory regions.

The bzImage was compressed using the zlib algorithm from Linux version 2.6.30 onwards, which introduced more algorithms. Although there is the popular misconception that the *bz-* prefix means that bzip2 compression is used (the bzip2 package is often distributed with tools prefixed with "bz-", such as bzless, bzcat, etc.), this is not the case. See Figure 7-22.

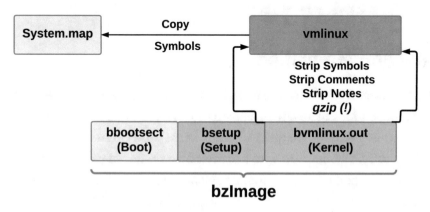

Figure 7-22. *Anatomy of bzImage*

u-root: u-root is a part of initramfs in LinuxBoot and serves as an embedded root file system sitting inside SPI NOR as part of system firmware image. u-root is written in Go, a modern and high-level language for improved security. u-root is packaged as an LZMA-compressed initial RAM file system (initramfs) in cpio format. It is contained in a Linux compressed kernel image, also known as bzImage. The bootloader (for example, syslinux) or firmware (for example, coreboot) loads the bzImage into memory and starts it. The Linux kernel sets up a RAM-based root file system and unpacks the u-root file system into it.

SystemBoot: Part of LinuxBoot distribution package, it typically works as a bootloader to find the OS from possible boot media and boot to OS. It is based on u-root and provided with the following programs:

- **netboot**: Use for network boot, it uses DHCP and HTTP to get the Linux OS and use kexec to run it.

- **localboot**: Used to find the local boot media, typically SATA, NVME, eMMC, etc. and bootable kernel to boot to the OS.

- **uinit**: A utility around netboot and localboot to perform iterative operations to attempt to boot from a network or local boot device.

Goal and Motivation

The goal here is to reduce the complexity in system firmware design and get rid of complex firmware drivers in the payload or its loading stages and replace them with the maturity of Linux kernel and OS runtime services.

Typically, all boot firmware has their own preferred payload solutions and implementations inside those payloads are not unified, so a bigger portion of system firmware development is relying on adding new SoC or platform support into a payload to ensure booting to the OS. Also, many firmware drivers implement specific solutions to enable certain use case scenarios. For example, the Google Chrome platform has a requirement of implementing a boot beep solution to notify users in the absence of valid OS partitions, and this implementation is in the Depthcharge payload, which needs regular maintenance and requires porting for new platform support. Having a Linux kernel equivalent solution sitting in SPI flash and getting control prior to booting the OS to allow loading audio firmware into controllers and using audio codecs to generate boot beep in a more generic way.

The Linux kernel as part of LinuxBoot architecture is an unmodified kernel along with the user-space initramfs created using Go tools for system booting. It provides high modularity and is widely shareable across different SoC or architecture.

Implementation Schema

This case study demonstrates the migration of an existing system firmware development using open source coreboot and the Depthcharge payload booting to ChromeOS on an Apollo lake-based UP square evaluation platform by replacing the Depthcharge payload with more generic LinuxBoot implementation.

The scope of booting various Linux and equivalent OSes is limited with Depthcharge-like specific bootloaders. Also, the idea here is to reduce the system firmware boundary by eliminating proprietary firmware drivers and let the Linux boot kernel take care of OS-like features.

Figure 7-23 provides a high-level hardware block diagram for the UP square board with an Atom processor.

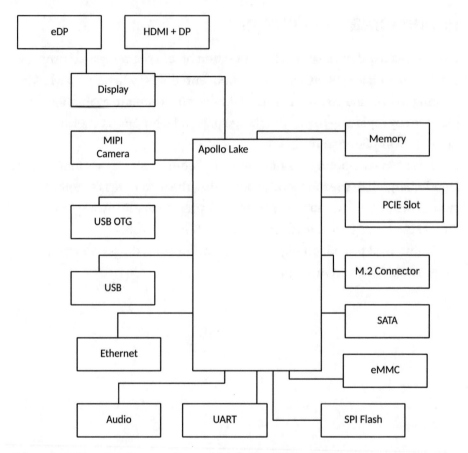

Figure 7-23. *UP Square board high-level block diagram*

Refer to Figure 7-24 to understand the existing system firmware boot operational flow on the UP Square board with coreboot and Depthcharge.

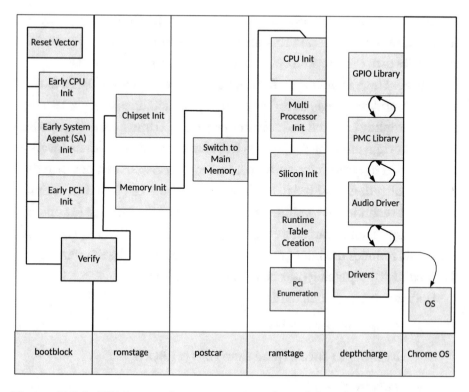

Figure 7-24. *UP Square boot operational model with ChromeOS stack*

Here we are going to discuss the migration to LinuxBoot with coreboot. After hitting the reset vector, the CPU will start executing instructions from bootblock, the first boot stage in coreboot, responsible for doing early CPU, System Agents (SA), and PCH initialization to get basic hardware initialization for ease of development and debugging. Verified boot is an optional layer that can be used to verify upcoming stages prior to loading into memory for execution. romstage is very similar to the PEI phase in the UEFI architecture where the focus is to initialize the memory and migrate the whole system firmware execution from temporary memory to physical memory. After this ramstage performs various advanced CPU and chipset initialization followed by PCI enumeration, then the Depthcharge payload stage begins where several firmware drivers perform OS-like operations and finally pick the Chrome OS from boot media to boot to the OS.

The goal here is not to modify the mandatory and early phases like bootblock and romstage, as the roles and responsibilities of these two stages are tightly coupled with the underlying CPU and board. If LinuxBoot could start right after the memory is initialized and the system firmware has switched its context into physical memory, coreboot can perform the basic initialization required to fetch LinuxBoot from SPI flash into memory and start execution. By loading LinuxBoot right after romstage (or postcar, i.e., the stage prior to ramstage), by replacing ramstage and Depthcharge, it not only reduces the boot boundary but also reduces the SPI flash size significantly by replacing those large firmware blocks.

Here are the reference hardware and firmware details:

- **CPU**: Intel Atom E3940

- **Number of cores**: Quad Core CPU @1.8GHz

- **Peripherals attached**:

  - Boot using SPI NOR

  - Output: Display over eDP, HDMI

  - Boot device: SATA, eMMC

  - Debugging-aid: UART

  - Memory: 2GB LPDDR4

  - mPCIe slot

  - I2S audio controller and Codec

  - 2 GbeLAN

  - 2 Type-A USB 3.0

- **System Firmware**: coreboot and LinuxBoot

Setting Up the Board

This section describes the process of building the UP squared board with coreboot and a LinuxBoot payload.

- **Download coreboot source code:**

1. Clone the latest coreboot code:

   ```
   $ git clone https://review.coreboot.org/a/coreboot.git
   cd coreboot

   git submodule update --init --checkout
   ```

2. Place associated blobs in appropriate locations

Note   Consider the fact that ucode and the ME kit for Apollo Lake SoC are downloadable externally. FSP binaries and required headers are also available externally at `3rdparty/fsp/ApolloLakeFspBinPkg/`.

- **Download the LinuxBoot source code and building image:**

  - **Create initramfs**

1. Download the Go package:

   ```
   curl -O https://storage.googleapis.com/
   golang/go1.11.8.linux-amd64.tar.gz
   ```

Note   Download the package after knowing the latest version, supported HOST machine mode, 32-bit or 64-bit, Windows or Linux, etc.

---

2. Decompress the downloaded Go package:

    ```
    tar -xvf go1.11.1.linux-amd64.tar.gz
    ```

3. Move the package into /usr/local and modify the permission:

    ```
    sudo chown -R root:root ./go
    sudo mv go /usr/local
    ```

4. Update the PATH and GOPATH:

    ```
    export GOPATH=$HOME/go
    export PATH=$PATH:/usr/local/go/bin:$GOPATH/bin
    ```

5. Download the required package to create u-root:

    ```
    go  -u get github.com/u-root/u-root
    go  -u get github.com/systemboot/systemboot/
    {uinit,localboot,netboot}
    go  get  -u  github.com/u-root/u-root/xcmds/rush
    github.com/u-root/u-root/cmds/init github.com/u-root/
    u-root/cmds/{ls,cat,date}
    ```

6. Build u-root:

    ```
    ./u-root  -build=bb  core
    github.com/systemboot/systemboot/localboot
    github.com/systemboot/systemboot/netboot
    github.com/systemboot/systemboot/uinit
    ```

7. At this stage, initramfs.linux_amd64.cpio would be locate inside the /tmp directory.

Note   The initramfs will be located in /tmp/ based on $platform and $arch.

---

8. Use XZ compression as required:

```
xz  -C  crc32  --lzma2=dict=512KiB
/tmp/initramfs.linux_amd64.cpio
```

9. After compression, the compressed image would be located into the same /tmp directory in the .xz format.

- **Creating LinuxBoot payload**

1. Download the kernel:

```
wget https://mirrors.edge.kernel.org/pub/linux/kernel/
v5.x/linux-5.11.3.tar.xz
```

2. Decompress the kernel:

```
tar Jxf linux-5.11.3.tar.xz
```

3. Copy the config, update Initramfs path to point at the initramfs created using previously mentioned steps:

```
make menuconfig
```

4. Update the Initramfs path:

```
CONFIG_BLK_DEV_INITRD=y
CONFIG_INITRAMFS_SOURCE="/tmp/initramfs.linux_amd64.
cpio.xz"
CONFIG_RD_XZ=y
```

5. Update the command line parameter if required:

```
CONFIG_CMDLINE="earlyprintk=serial,ttyS0,57600
console=ttyS0,57600"
```

- Save and exit.

- Make.

6. Finally, **bzImage** will get created in the arch/$ARCH/ boot/ directory.

- **Build coreboot for "Squared" board**

1. Build toolchain:

```
CPUS=$(nproc--ignore=1) make  crossgcc-i386  iasl
```

2. Create coreboot .config.

   The default options for this board should result in a fully working image:

```
# echo "CONFIG_VENDOR_UP=y" > .config
# echo "CONFIG_BOARD_UP_SQUARED=y" >> .config
```

3. Select LinuxBoot payload with cmd line if required:

```
CONFIG_PAYLOAD_LINUX=y
CONFIG_PAYLOAD_FILE= <PATH of bzImage>
CONFIG_LINUX_INITRD=""
CONFIG_PAYLOAD_OPTIONS=""
CONFIG_LINUX_COMMAND_LINE="loglevel=7 panic=0
earlyprintk=ttyS0,115200n8 console=ttyS0,115200n8"
```

4. Build image:

```
$ make # the image is generated as build/coreboot.rom
```

- **Flash coreboot**

Follow this mechanism to flash final coreboot.rom image on the UP Squared board. The flashing mechanism uses the flashrom utility.

```
$    flashrom -p <PROGRAMMER> -w build/coreboot.rom
```

Detailed Implementation

To adhere to the principle of designing LITE firmware for all computing machines, this case study is focused on replacing complex kernel-redundant functionality like the netboot driver, block device drivers, audio drivers, and GPIO driver with newer SoC and platform in the firmware space with a Linux kernel and userspace. The reason this idea is more scalable is because we are going to use the upstream Linux kernel, which already has support for any new SoC from CPU vendors and generic a driver implementation like block device, netboot, and audio.

This is migrating a project development from coreboot with a specific payload (Depthcharge) experience to use LinuxBoot so that the underlying platform can run any flavor of the Linux runtime kernel without any system firmware modification.

Here are the changes required to achieve this goal.

Step 1: Replace Depthcharge with the LinuxBoot payload

Depthcharge being the official payload used to boot the CrOS (Chrome/Chromium OS) contains many vendor specific firmware drivers, lacking in runtime configuration to a great extent in comparison to Tianocore or LinuxBoot payload. Depthcharge being independent binary in Chrome stack, results in redundant chipset initialization, requiring additional patches to enable support for new SoC and board. Depthcharge is another firmware block without any OS-level intelligence so it basically increases the redundancy in the system firmware boot process on embedded systems where boot time is critical and flash space is precious.

Figure 7-25 shows the migration in the system boot process, where the items highlighted in yellow are components that are either reduced or replaced with LinuxBoot.

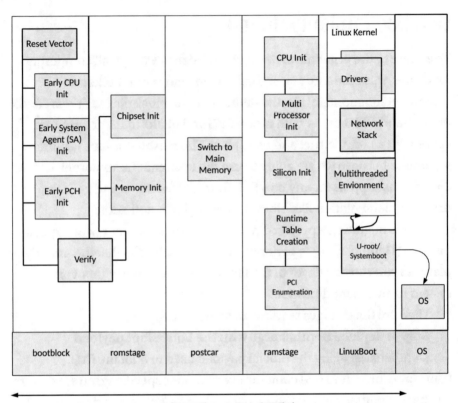

Figure 7-25. *UP Square modified flow with LinuxBoot to boot any OS*

LinuxBoot being part of the system firmware image resides in SPI flash that replaces redundant OS like functionality with a Linux kernel. This migration will also help to nullify the limitation of "only" being able to boot to ChromeOS and not the other flavors of Linux like Yocto, Ubuntu, or even Microsoft Windows.

In this case study, we created a LinuxBoot image with 5.2.9 Linux Kernel and initramfs with u-root/systemboot to try booting to the OS from SATA boot media.

At the end of ramstage, when the boot state machine is done with the execution of all available boot states, it loads the LinuxBoot payload from cbfs and executes it. The control will transfer to the Linux kernel and the user can verify the same using the sample log:

```
Jumping to boot code at 0x00040000(0x5bab8000)
CPU0: stack: 0x5bf49000 - 0x5bf4d000, lowest used address
0x5bf4a81c, stack used: 10212 bytes
Linux version 5.2.9 (gcc version 8.4.1 20200928 (Red Hat
8.4.1-1) (GCC)) #3 SMP Thu Feb 25 08:57:15 PST 2021
Command line: loglevel=7 earlyprintk=ttyS0,115200n8
console=ttyS0,115200n8
```

The Linux kernel will perform the early parsing of system firmware provided system memory map, ACPI tables, PCI enumeration, and multiprocessor initialization and wait for the init process. All Linux systems start an init process on boot and in the case of LinuxBoot, it's u-root. The init for u-root sets up some basic directories, symlinks and files. User can verify the execution of u-root when the /init process starts:

```
Run /init as init process
2018/06/05 23:52:47 Welcome to u-root!
```

Systemboot, a part of u-root, will now start running the uinit program to find the bootable OS either using netboot or localboot to boot to the OS. Systemboot also has its shell prompt for debugging any boot-related issues. Users need to press CTRL-C within 5 seconds to drop into the shell.

Once localboot is able to read the bootable partition and use Kexec, systemboot will attempt to boot to the OS.

```
Decompressing Linux... Parsing ELF... Performing
relocations... done.
Booting the kernel.
[    0.000000] Linux version 5.11.0-rc7 (Chromium OS
11.0_pre387436_p20200403-r4 clang version 11.0.0 (/var/
cache/chromeos-cache/distfiles/host/egit-src/llvm-project
c47f971694be0159ffddfee8a75ae515eba9839), LLD 11.0.0 (/var/
cache/chromeos-cache/distfiles/host/egit-src/llvm-project
c47f971694be0159ffddfee8a75ae515eba9839)) #52 SMP PREEMPT Mon
Mar 1 11:23:00 IST 2021

Developer Console

To return to the browser, press:

  [ Ctrl ] and [ Alt ] and [ <- ]  (F1)

To use this console, the developer mode switch must be engaged.
Doing so will destroy any saved data on the system.

In developer mode, it is possible to
- login and sudo as user 'chronos'
- require a password for sudo and login(*)
- disable power management behavior (screen dimming):
  sudo initctl stop powerd
- install your own operating system image!
```

* To set a password for 'chronos', run the following as root:

chromeos-setdevpasswd

If you are having trouble booting a self-signed kernel, you may need to enable USB booting. To do so, run the following as root:

enable_dev_usb_boot

Have fun and send patches!

localhost login:

Step 2: Remove "redundant" firmware operations from ramstage

Figure 7-26 shows the reduced ramstage where it deletes or replaces many firmware drivers or modules as LinuxBoot is capable of doing those operations without any firmware driver.

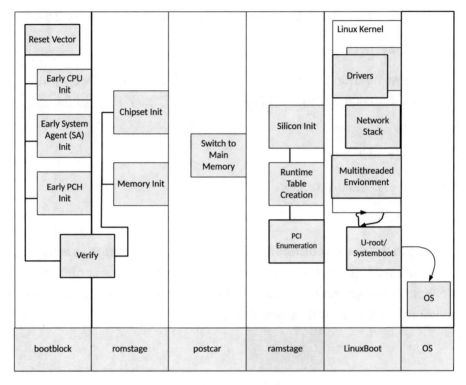

Figure 7-26. *Boot operational model with reduced ramstage*

Step 3: RomPayload: Booting LinuxBoot from Romstage

The most desirable thing is to remove the entire ramstage, as now with the Step 2 approach, the ramstage with the reduced firmware drivers has become really thin and operations getting performed now inside ramstage can further pull into any earlier stage like romstage or postcar without needing a dedicated stage like ramstage. Now, the earlier boot stage will operate as a stage to load the LinuxBoot payload, so it can easily be renamed as just "payloader stage" depending on which state (either romstage or payload) is used to boot the LinuxBoot payload.

Note   The *oreboot* boot architecture doesn't have a stage like ramstage for performing advanced chipset programming including loading the payload. The stage that is responsible for loading the payload is known as the payloader stage. This is the direct influence based on the proof of concept being performed using LITE firmware in the coreboot community and also presented as part of Open Source Firmware Conference (OSFC) 2019 (`https://2019.osfc.io/talks/coreboot-lite-rampayload-and-linuxboot.html`).

As mentioned in *Firmware Development: A Guide to Specialized Systemic Knowledge* in Chapter 6 in the "LITE Firmware Design Principle" section, that early payloader stage can additionally perform platform-specific minimum SoC and hardware initialization and creation of system memory layout based on physical memory required to load the payload.

Figure 7-27 shows the benefits of using the LinuxBoot solution where

- The Linux kernel helps to remove redundant firmware initialization code blocks.

- It makes system firmware simple with SoC and platform-specific initialization rather than acting more as an operating system.

- It help to reduce platform boot time.

- It reduces the firmware boundary by removing the ramstage-like boot stage in coreboot and similarly it's possible to remove DXE in UEFI as well.

- It provides a Go-based userland that is able to bring up any user preferred kernel on the machine.

- It brings back the entire Linux ecosystem as part of
  SPI NOR where traditional firmware applications,
  debugging, and diagnosis can now be replaced using
  cross-architecture and cross-platform portable Linux
  applications.

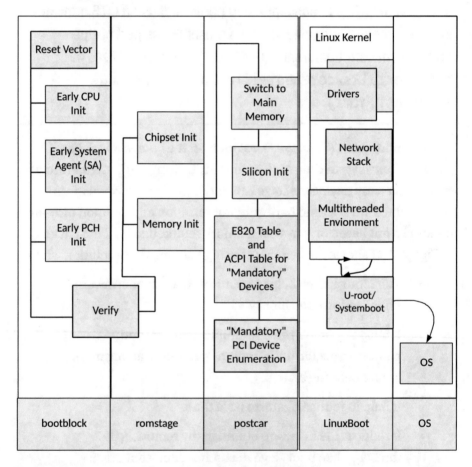

Figure 7-27. *LinuxBoot payload is loading from postcar on a x86 platform*

LinuxBoot Conclusion

This case study has shown a path forward to design system firmware with more a scalable and universal payload that can be used to boot various OS as needed. Also, it shares a working model between coreboot and LinuxBoot using a LITE firmware design principle in order to make a reduced system firmware boundary with improved responsiveness.

You can view this work as an opportunity to create such a solution even in production firmware to improve productivity, where a driver is written once and used across various system firmwares. Examples: coreboot, u-boot, SBL, UEFI, ARM trusted firmware, OPAL without any additional cost.

Adopting a Hybrid Firmware Development Model

This case study is a real-life application of a proposed work model described in Chapter 5 as part of the hybrid work model to balance the system firmware development ecosystem between an open source and closed source approach.

As a theme of this book to cover the all possible system firmware development approaches using an open source firmware development model, it's also a commitment to cover the challenges that the industry is seeing in this migration of firmware or software development approach from traditional closed source practices to more open-source-friendly methods. Firmware is an integral part of system hardware and is designed to abstract the underlying hardware to its upper layer system software like OSes and/or applications, so it poses challenges to SoC vendors, hardware designers, and device manufacturers to provide the required documentation and reference source code for CPU, memory, chipset, and IO initialization. Although the real desire to have an entire product development using an open source approach is not only limited to firmware development, but also the SoC design specification, hardware schematics, and layout availability in public repository.

There are some ongoing initiatives as part of Open Compute Project (OCP) which aims to reinvent product development with an open source vision for improved efficiency, flexibility, and scalability. Unfortunately, at the present time, the majority of computing devices that we are evidencing in our daily life belong to such a category where not all SoC vendors are ready to adopt such open product development models due to multiple reasons:

- **Comparative threat model**: Many SoC or CPU design companies invest in their R&D to innovate features that can really be the product differentiator.

- **Protecting intellectual property (IP)**: Many times for the first generation of a product, it's really tough to disclose a key feature without protecting the IP part wisely.

- **Lack of understanding of open source development**: In many companies or organizations, the definition of open source development is not clear and the default assumption is that any source development or hardware design inside a corporate boundary is typically considered as a candidate for closed source without a real assessment of the possibility of becoming a part of an open source project.

Traditionally, SoC vendors share reference code or an early platform bring up kit as part of a licensing agreement among a small enabling group known as Independent BIOS Vendors (IBV). This closed source enabling model prohibits a non-corporate person like a grad school student or a freelancer without a proper contract with a SoC vendor from learn the tricks to bring a new platform or gain the required knowledge on system firmware development.

In Chapter 5, we discussed in detail the possible way to avoid such problems by introducing a model that we call the hybrid firmware development model.

Presently, on x86 CPU architecture, the proprietary SoC initialization code is distributed as part of a binary package along with required data files to integrate with compliant boot firmware to create a system firmware that can perform required CPU, chipset, and IO initialization along with other platform-related features prior booting to OS.

The idea here is to make users understand the hybrid firmware development model and integration process so that they can apply this knowledge on their platform to configure the required knobs while bringing up the platform.

For this demonstration, we are going to use coreboot with a closed source binary provided by SoC vendors on an Intel powered Kaby Lake-based reference platform.

Before going to further details, here are some keywords.

FSP: The Firmware Support Package is a kit released by SoC vendors that includes binary file(s), an integration guide, tools, and header(s). FSP is a specification designed with a standard API interface to perform silicon initialization and provide information back to the boot firmware in the form of standard output structure. Figure 7-28 provides package information about FSP.

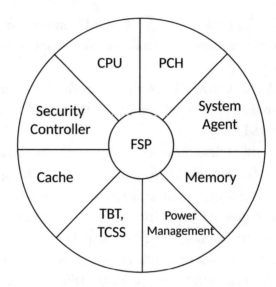

Figure 7-28. *FSP binary package overview*

UPD: The FSP module may have one or more configurable data regions. This configuration region is a data structure known as Updatable Product Data (UPD).

BCT: The Binary Configuration Tool is used to configure the UPD statically. The Config Editor is the typical replacement of the BCT as it supports changing FSP configuration settings directly from the interface without a need to modify the source code.

HOB: Typically, the FSP is created with an EFI specification where HOBs are the standard way to pass information between one boot phase an another (between PEI to DXE). In this hybrid model, FSP produces HOBs and passes them to the boot firmware to know various SoC, memory, chipset, and feature-related information.

Goal and Motivation

The goal here is to understand the hybrid work model and integration process, which is important knowledge for you to create your own system firmware while working on the x86-based platform. This work is done in such a way that you can understand the entire ecosystem involved in bringing up a new platform using SoC vendor-provided FSP-like blobs.

One of the key motivations for a hybrid work model is the adaptation of the latest chipset development using the Open Source Firmware development model, where limited closed source blobs are still allowed. Due to increasing customer demands, it has been seen that a platform power on (PO) until product final shipment time has been drastically reduced in the last few years. It's challenging for the ecosystem partners to be active at the same pace as SoC vendors to meet such aggressive product timelines by adhering to so many SoC recommendations as part of silicon specification, BIOS writer's Guide (BWG), and such. Also, at the same time, they need to protect the IP to mitigate the comparative threat model in product design. To answer to such opens, on the x86 based platform, silicon initialization code is now provided in the form of a royalty-free binary with standard APIs to integrate with a wide range of boot firmware solutions such as coreboot, SBL, and UEFI.

Platform owners can now almost be assured about silicon validation coverage with FSP-like pre-validated silicon code and they just need to focus on the platform bring up activity by knowing the configuration parameters using the silicon capabilities.

Implementation Schema

This case study demonstrates the real-world x86-based platform porting using a hybrid work model where coreboot is used as a boot firmware along with Intel FSP for performing the silicon recommended programming in configurable fashion.

Prior to the invention of FSP-like scalable IP encapsulated binary models, the platform bring up activity was a complicated affair. Figure 7-29 explains the traditional platform enabling model without FSP.

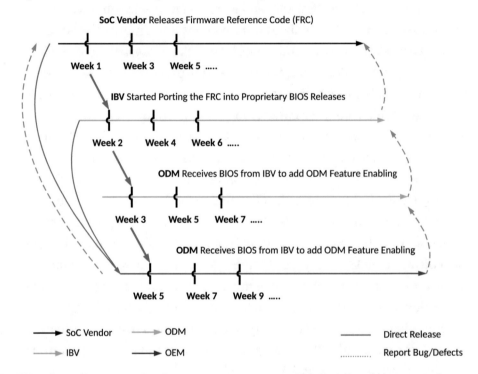

Figure 7-29. *Supply chain management of IA BIOS reference code*

This traditional model was lacking in many ways. In the first place, this model incurred unavoidable delays in the enabling process with so many manual process at specific sites like IBVs and ODM/OEMs, which increased the chances of human errors like missing implementations of certain SoC recommendation steps in the platform BIOS resulting in unexpected behavior, potential security holes, and such.

In order to avoid such duplication and ensure a wider audience with more pre-validated silicon code in the form of FSP for faster integration with any boot firmware, even non-UEFI compliment ones like coreboot. FSP being the passive silicon initialization code, relies a lot on the boot firmware for its calling opportunities and prior to that, it's also critical to ensure all prerequisites are being met.

Figure 7-30 provides a system architecture overview of a hybrid firmware development model where coreboot and FSP are an integral part of hardware initialization process after ensuring the following:

- Protect the SoC-developed new hardware IP and associated code in open source.

- Maintain a balance in the product development cycle with majority of open source and very minimum usage of blobs with partial and potential open source candidate configuration parameters to allow configuring the hardware interfaces using closed source blobs.

- Minimize the development cost among partners.

- Ensure Time To Market (TTM) with higher confidence.

- Increase reliability and flexibility in the process.

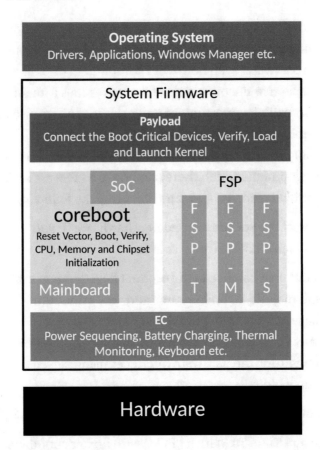

Figure 7-30. System architecture overview in Hybrid FW model

On the x86 platform, such reliability and flexibility has been ensured by several entities, as shown in Figure 7-31.

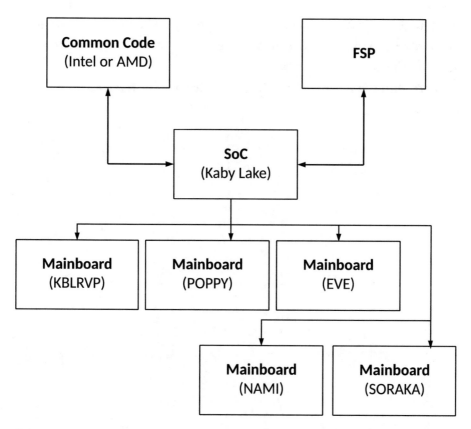

Figure 7-31. *Hybrid model that brings scalability, reliability, and flexibility*

By utilizing the "Common Code" layer, which is designed to bring the reliability in open source firmware development along with the FSP layer to abstract the silicon programming for faster enabling of the platform results minimum development cost while bringing a new platform eventually improves scalability.

As part of the case study implementation section, you will learn to port a new x86-based platform using FSP and coreboot, and you'll see the maximum configurable parameters can be touched while bringing the new platform based on hardware schematics. You can prepare such configurable parameters based on your underlying hardware and pass them into FSP either in the form of static configuration or dynamic to initialize the hardware interface.

Let's start the porting of the sample mainboard as referred in Figure 7-32.

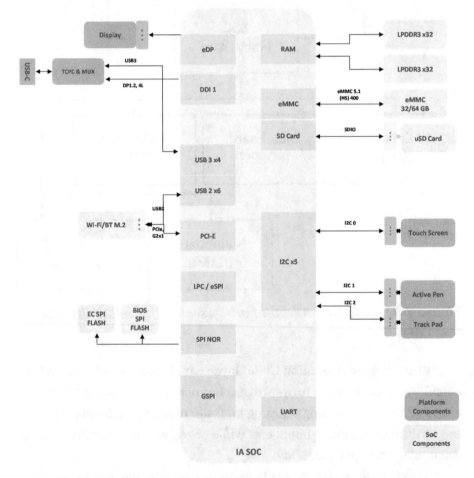

Figure 7-32. *Kaby Lake-based sample mainboard block diagram*

Here are the reference hardware and firmware details:

- **CPU**: Intel 7th Generation Intel Core™ i3 Processors - i3-7100E

- **Number of cores:** Quad Core CPU @2.90GHz

- Peripherals attached:

  - Dual Channel Hynix 4GB LPDDR3 Memory Down solution

  - PCH UART2 for serial debug

  - USB device configuration

  - Two Type-A USB 2.0 at Port 6 and 8

  - One Type-C at USB Port 0

  - Bluetooth connected at USB 2.0 Port 3

  - One Type-A USB 3.0 at Port 2

- LPSS device configuration

  - I2C0-2 Enable

  - GSPI0 Enable

  - UART2 Enable

- Storage device configuration

  - EMMC Enable in HS400 mode

  - SD controller Enable

- Connectivity device configuration

  - WIFI PCIE device at Root Port 9 with ClkSrc 2

System Firmware: coreboot and Intel Kaby Lake FSP (specification 2.0)

Setting Up the Board

This section describes the process of building the Kaby Lake-based new board with coreboot and Intel FSP.

- **Download Coreboot Source Code**

1. Clone latest coreboot code:

```
$ git clone https://review.coreboot.org/a/coreboot.git
$ cd coreboot
$ git submodule update --init --checkout
```

2. Place associated blobs in appropriate locations

Note   Consider the fact that all essential pre-x86 reset blobs are distributed using Intel release portal a.k.a. RDC (Resource and Design Center) link at `www.intel.in/content/www/in/en/design/resource-design-center.html`. In this scenario, either download the ucode and CSME external package for Kaby Lake SoC from the RDC portal or decompress the IFWI (Intel Firmware Image a.k.a. the final BIOS ROM) image from an existing device. The latter one is the most widely used model for the open source developers community working on Intel SoC platforms.

- **Download FSP binary and associated files**

  After the SoC product launch, SoC vendor representatives normally upload the required FSP kit into the `https://github.com/intel/FSP` external repository for open source system firmware development activities without being bottlenecked to corporate accounts.

1. Clone the latest FSP repository:

    ```
    $ gh repo clone intel/FSP
    ```

2. Switch to the Kaby Lake FSP directory:

    ```
    $ cd KabylakeFspBinPkg
    ```

This package contains the official release for Kaby Lake FSP as below:

Directory structure	Contains
Docs	Repository to keep all documentation required to understand the FSP release cadence, ingredients inside FSP, dependent binaries like ucode, ME, VBT (Video BIOS Table), and the FSP integration guide to know the recommended settings for the BIOS while creating system firmware in the hybrid model
Include	All FSP binary-dependent header files are part of this directory. • FspUpd.h => As master header • FsptUpd.h => Configuration block for FSP-T • FspmUpd.h => Configuration block for FSP-M • FspsUpd.h => Configuration block for FSP-S • MemInfoHob.h => To parse FSP provided Mem Information Hob Similarly, other headers to parse various FSP populated data structures like SMBIOS Processor Information HOB, Cache Information HOB, etc. The number of headers inside the Include directory might differ in different SoC FSP releases.

Directory structure	Contains
SampleCode/ Vbt	As FSP is responsible for performing the display initialization using the SoC-integrated display controller, the files inside this directory provide the configuration (vbt.bin) and boot setting file (vbt.bsf) to modify the display end-point devices as per platform design.
FSP Binary	The FSP specification is derived from the EFI specification so it follows the output binary in the form of Firmware Device (.FD). Fsp.fd is the final FSP binary, which internally might consist of one or more associated binaries as per the FSP specification.

3. Split the FSP binary.

    FSP is a standard specification that uses API
    interfaces to control its execution in order to provide
    modularity. The FSP binary can be divided into a
    number of API interfaces using available tools as
    part of the FSP repository.

Directory structure	Contains
FSP/Tools	SplitFspBin.py is the tool part of open source Edk2 release repository (Edk2/IntelFsp2Pkg/Tools) also checked into the FSP release database and is responsible for splitting Fsp.fd into multiple sub-binaries.

Here is the command to use for this split operation:

```
$ python FSP/Tools/SplitFspBin.py split -f FSP/
KabylakeFspBinPkg/Fsp.fd
```

The output of SplitFspBin.py is three smaller binaries:

- Fsp_T.fd

- Fsp_M.fd

- Fsp_S.fd

4. Place FSP binaries and headers into coreboot code

   After creating those required FSP binary files and associated headers, let's keep these files in their designated directories prior to building the mainboard.

   Typically, CONFIG_FSP_HEADER_PATH Kconfig is used to point to the path where FSP headers are located. There could be multiple options to update the FSP header path.

1. Use open source FSP repository directly as `3rdparty/fsp/KabylakeFspBinPkg/Include/`.

2. Use the coreboot internal "vendorcode" repository that also contains FSP header path as `vendor code/intel/fsp/fsp2_0/SkyKabyLake`.

Note   Typically, after FSP headers are available in an external GitHub, there is a practice to remove the headers from the internal repository to avoid duplication.

---

3. Update the .config file to point to FSP header
    Kconfig at any location from site-local as well.

Mainboard users also need to select CONFIG_ADD_FSP_BINARIES
Kconfig to add FSP binaries as required:

FSP Binary	Kconfig	Path
FSP-T	CONFIG_FSP_T_FILE	If SoC users decide to use FSP-T, then they need to provide PATH for Fsp_T.fd.
FSP-M	CONFIG_FSP_M_FILE	Mandatory FSP stage so users must provide PATH for Fsp_M.fd
FSP-S	CONFIG_FSP_S_FILE	Mandatory FSP stage so users must provide PATH for Fsp_S.fd

At this stage, users are now ready to select the required mainboard
Kconfig to start the coreboot build and generate final coreboot.rom to flash
on target hardware. The only missing piece in this system firmware hybrid
model that remains unknown to users is the knowledge of configuring the
FSP based on the underlying hardware. You will learn about that in the
detailed implementation section.

Detailed Implementation

This section will provide the step-by-step approach for porting a
mainboard in a hybrid system firmware development model where users
might not have source code or the silicon reference code but have a deep
knowledge of required configuration knobs, would will help achieve the
platform being up activity with ease, which is also aligns with the goal of
FSP being introduced by SoC vendors.

Figure 7-33 shows the methodology behind creating the mainboard in
the hybrid work model.

- The SoC vendor (here Intel) develops initial firmware code for new SoC.

    - In this case study, we are going to use Intel Kaby Lake, so SoC as `soc/intel/skylake`.

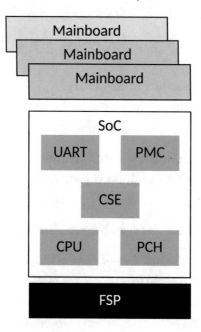

Figure 7-33. *coreboot code structure in the hybrid model*

Note   Kaby Lake is the successor for Skylake SoC and both SoCs are using the same code block as "skylake."

- Additionally, it provides support for the first reference platform typically referred to as a Customer Reference Board (CRB) with the same SoC in upstream.

    - Example: Reference platform as "Kaby Lake RVP" (`src/mainboard/intel/kblrvp`)

- This initial SoC code and support for reference platforms helps device manufacturers (ODMs/OEMs) to design based on a reference design and make use of mainboard sample code.

  - Example: Multiple OEM designs are derived out of baseboard as "poppy" (`src/mainboard/google/poppy`).

Step 1: Create a mainboard directory

To port a new mainboard using the FSP specification, first you need to create a mainboard directory inside a specific $VENDOR directory.

- Example: `../coreboot/src/mainboard/$VENDOR`. In this case, the new mainboard would locate into the `intel` directory since Intel is the vendor.

  - `../coreboot/src/mainboard/intel`

Let's refer to the mainboard as ***$BOARD*** in this example where Figure 7-34 explains the code tree structure used for development.

This entire mainboard structure can be further categorized into several smaller buckets based on its usage towards initializing the SoC and platform components.

In the scope of this case study, we are going to limit ourselves to FSP related mainboard changes alone.

Here are FSP v2.0 related mainboard changes from Figure 7-34:

- `mainboard/intel/$BOARD/Kconfig`

- `mainboard/intel/$BOARD/romstage.c`

- `mainboard/intel/$BOARD/ramstage.c`

- `mainboard/intel/$BOARD/devicetree.cb`

A firmware developer in a hybrid development model only needs to bother with four files!

```
$BOARD/
|-- acpi
|   |-- dptf.asl
|   |-- ec.asl
|   `-- superio.asl
|-- board_info.txt
|-- bootblock.c
|-- chromeos.c
|-- chromeos.fmd
|-- data.vbt
|-- devicetree.cb
|-- dsdt.asl
|-- ec.c
|-- ec.h
|-- gma-mainboard.ads
|-- gpio.h
|-- Kconfig
|-- Kconfig.name
|-- mainboard.c
|-- Makefile.inc
|-- romstage.c
|-- smihandler.c
`-- spd
    |-- empty.spd.hex
    |-- hynix_dimm_H9CCNNN8GTALAR.spd.hex
    |-- hynix_dimm_H9CCNNNBJTALAR.spd.hex
    |-- hynix_dimm_H9CCNNNCLTMLAR.spd.hex
    |-- Makefile.inc
    |-- samsung_dimm_K4E6E304EB.spd.hex
    |-- samsung_dimm_K4E8E324EB.spd.hex
    |-- samsung_dimm_K4EBE304EB.spd.hex
    |-- spd.c
    `-- spd.h
```

Figure 7-34. *Tree structure of a sample mainboard with FSP spec 2.0*

Step 2: Configuring SoC capabilities as per target hardware

The purpose of the FSP binary is to abstract the underlying hardware capabilities and provide configuration options as part of UPD to enable/disable the required hardware interface.

As part of FSP specific 2.0, FSP has three major entry and exit points which work based on UPD variables. Each FSP blob and supported header has a dedicated configuration data region to let SoC or mainboard users configure the hardware interface.

From the coreboot side, these UPDs can be classified into two parts:

- UPDs need to be configured from SoC directories (i.e., `soc/intel/skylake`)

- Mainboard to configure FSP UPDs (i.e., `mainboard/intel/kblrvp`)

We're assuming there is already an underlying SoC directory as "Kaby Lake" (using Sky Lake). So the focus would be only at mainboard side porting with FSP v2.0.

Step 2.a: Enable the FSP v2.0 specification for the mainboard

Mainboard users can select the supported FSP specification in the mainboard directory. This information is part of FSP integration guide shared externally using `https://github.com/intel/FSP/tree/master/KabylakeFspBinPkg/Docs`.

```
config BOARD_SPECIFIC_OPTIONS
        def_bool y
        select MAINBOARD_USES_FSP2_0
```

This enabling is done as part of the `mainboard/intel/$BOARD/Kconfig` file.

Step 2.b : Configure FSP-T related UPDs

In general, FSP-T is designed to perform temporary memory (CAR) setting up, which is part of SoC-related initialization and not many configuration options are available for mainboard users.

FSP-T mainboard configurable UPD	Description
PcdSerialIoUartDebugEnable	If SoC users are relying on FSP-T to perform UART initialization rather than native coreboot code
PcdSerialIoUartNumber	Mainboard users provide the Serial IO UART number for debug. CONFIG_UART_FOR_CONSOLE is assigned into this UPD.

There could be multiple methods to get a serial console enabled for debugging on a mainboard based on the hardware design:

- **Using legacy UART**: In the hardware design, CPU UART is routed using legacy UART 0 (IO port 0x3f8) or UART 1 (IO port 0x2f8).

- **Using PCH UART**: Modern hardware expects a low power debug interface hence utilizing PCH UART capabilities. In this example, the underlying hardware uses the PCH LPSS (Low Power Sub System) UART 0 controller for Serial IO.

- **Using UART over Super IO**: In some cases, hardware designers consider Super IO chips for enabling various legacy devices together using the CPU interface to minimize the cost.

Step 2.c: Configure FSP-M related UPDs

As the name suggests, FSP-M is primarily responsible for performing the DRAM initialization and providing the system memory map after curving out resources required for various traditional ranges like SMM, display, CPU, and PCH related features.

Memory-related configurations are like 3-way communication between *SoC vendors* as Memory controller is being part of SoC, *Memory vendors* as board design will use a memory card belonging to specific memory technology and finally the *firmware developer* who gathers all these relevant information together to perform the required memory initialization. The Memory initialization process is a series of training algorithms designed as part of Memory Reference Code (MRC). Previously as part of the platform enabling model, memory vendors used to provide the memory reference code in form of binary blobs and expected system firmware to integrate and launch it as part of the memory initialization process. But presently, the MRC being part of Silicon reference code aka. FSP and designed to work seamlessly with all possible memory technology supported by the target SoC design based on an easy configuration interface.

Memory devices can be attached differently based on the board design and depending on that boot firmware needs to provide the memory configuration parameter to FSP for initializing the target memory device.

There are two possible solutions that are applied while designing the computing machines:

- **Socketed memory**: A motherboard design has a memory slot or socket for inserting the memory card into the computer. Most desktop computers with DDR type memory technology use this type of hardware design. The benefit of this design solution is that users can easily replace the existing DIMM with higher capacity based on usage. In the majority of cases, these memory modules are equipped with SPD (Serial Presence Detect) which is accessible using SMBUS or I2C interface to read information about memory modules.

In this operational mode, system firmware supports complete automation while reading memory module information over SMBUS based on slave address.

- **Soldered memory**: Typically, on laptops or smartphones where device manufacturers don't support the upgrade of the memory system after purchase, use this kind of hardware design where DIMMs are soldered down directly on the motherboard. In the majority of these cases, devices don't support reading SPD information on the fly; rather, system firmware is equipped with relevant memory module information and passes it to FSP for initialization process. This type of hardware design is also referred to as Memory Down RAM.

  In this operational mode, system firmware engineers are expected to get a static SPD data file from the memory vendor as per the DIMM part number.

In our example here, the board design has a dual channel Hynix 4GB LPDDR3 memory down solution, so we expect to get the exact SPD hex data file from the memory vendor.

This table provide a description of the generic SPD hex data file.

Byte	Description
0	SPD device size – SPD bytes used 128/SPD bytes total 256 (for LPDDR3) – SPD bytes used 384/SPD bytes total 512 (for LPDDR4)
1	SPD revision (of JEDEC spec) – 0x11 (Revision 1.1) – 020 (Revision 2.0)
2	DRAM device type – 0x0B (for DDR3) – 0x10 (for LPDDR4) – 0x11 (for LPDDR4x) – 0xF1 (for LPDDR3)
3	Module type
4	SDRAM density and canks
5	SDRAM addressing
6	Module nominal voltage
7	SDRAM width
8	SDRAM bus width
9-35	Module timing parameters, CAS latency
36-116	Reserved
117-175	Module manufacturer information and specific data
176-255	Open for customer usage
256-319	Hybrid memory architecture-specific parameters (not for LPDDR3)
320-383	Module supplier's data (not for LPDDR3)

Apart from SPD information, here is the complete list of FSP-M UPDs that boot firmware might need to configure based on board design:

FSP-M mainboard memory configurable UPD	Description	Programmable value
MemorySpdDataLen	SPD data length	0x100:256 Bytes, 0x200:512 Bytes
MemorySpdPtr00	Memory SPD Pointer Channel 0 Dimm 0	Memory vendor to provide the SPD data (as explained in earlier section)
MemorySpdPtr10	Memory SPD Pointer Channel 1 Dimm 0	Assign MemorySpdPtrXX UPD:
MemorySpdPtr01	Memory SPD Pointer Channel 0 Dimm 1	mem_cfg->MemorySpdPtr00 = mainboard_get_spd_data(); /* Function to read static SPD hex data from CBFS */
MemorySpdPtr11	Memory SPD Pointer Channel 1 Dimm 1	
		mem_cfg->MemorySpdPtr10 = mem_cfg->MemorySpdPtr00; Similarly apply on other SPD pointer UPDs as well.
SpdAddressTable[0]	Specify SPD address table for CH0D0/CH0D1/ CH1D0&CH1D1.	0xA0 SPD address is a 7-bit address and BIT 0 is for read/write. 0 for Read and 1 for Write operation.
SpdAddressTable[1]	For socketed memory design, specify the SMBUS address to read SPD from SPD EEPROM.	0xA2
SpdAddressTable[2]		0xA3
SpdAddressTable[3]		0xA4

(continued)

FSP-M mainboard memory configurable UPD	Description	Programmable value
DqPinsInterleaved	Dqs Pins Interleaved Setting	Interleaving mode of DQ/DQS pins - depends on board routing
DqByteMapCh0[12] DqByteMapCh1[12]	Dq byte mapping between CPU and DRAM, Channel 0/1	The representation of this UPD as [No. of Channel] [Iteration].
		Example: No. of Channel is 2 and Iteration is 12
		This UPD represent which PI clocks are getting used by what LPDDR DQ Bytes (from CPU side)
		DQByteMap[0] - ClkDQByteMap: − If clock is per rank, program to [0xFF, 0xFF] − If clock is shared by 2 ranks, program to [0xFF, 0] or [0, 0xFF] − If clock is shared by 2 ranks but does not go to all bytes, Entry[i] defines which DQ bytes Group i services
		DQByteMap[1] - CmdNDQByteMap: − [0] is CmdN/CAA and [1] is CmdN/CAB DQByteMap[2] - CmdSDQByteMap: − [0] is CmdS/CAA and [1] is CmdS/CAB

(*continued*)

FSP-M mainboard memory configurable UPD	Description	Programmable value
		DQByteMap[3] - CkeDQByteMap : — 0] is CKE /CAA and [1] is CKE / CAB, For DDR, DQByteMap [3:1] = [0xFF, 0]
		DQByteMap[4] - CtlDQByteMap : Always program to [0xFF, 0] since we have 1 CTL / rank
		DQByteMap[5] - CmdVDQByteMap: Always program to [0xFF, 0] since we have 1 CA Vref
DqsMapCpu2DramCh0 DqsMapCpu2DramCh1	Set Dqs mapping relationship between CPU and DRAM, Channel 0	The representation of this UPD as [No. of Channel] [MAX_BYTES]. Example: No. of Channel is 2 and Max Bytes is 8
		This UPD represent LPDDR3 Map from CPU DQS pins to SDRAM DQS pins
Rcomp (Resistive Compensation) Resistor	Indicates RcompResistor settings	Assign Rcomp resistor UPD based on Kaby Lake SoC example: const u16 rcomp_resistor[] = { 200, 81, 162 }; memcpy(&mem_cfg->RcompResistor, rcomp_resistor, sizeof(rcomp_resistor));

(*continued*)

FSP-M mainboard memory configurable UPD	Description	Programmable value
RcompTarget	RcompTarget settings	Assign Rcomp resistor UPD based on Kaby Lake SoC example: const u16 rcomp_target[] = { 100, 40, 40, 23, 40 }; memcpy(&mem_cfg->RcompTarget, rcomp_target, sizeof(rcomp_target));
SaGv	System Agent dynamic frequency support and when enabled memory will be training at two different frequencies	Board-dependent settings, typically set as "Enable" unless any board-related issues operate at higher frequency or enable dynamic switching 0:Disabled, 1:FixedLow, 2:FixedHigh, 3:Enabled

This list provides almost all memory-related configuration options that can be set based on target hardware schematics. With a memory-related UPD override from the boot firmware, it's expected that MRC code as part of FSP will be able to train the memory successfully. Upon physical memory being available, FSP creates the system memory map with a set of ranges being reserved based on additional input parameters:

FSP-M mainboard device configurable UPD	Description	Programmable value
PcieRpEnableMask	Enable PCIE Root Ports	Although it's the boot firmware's responsibility of doing the PCIE enumeration, FSP would like to understand the PCIE Root Ports (RP) being enabled in the early boot process to read the attached endpoint device to know the maximum resource limit to curve out such memory if it's required. Example: discrete graphics devices attached to x8 PCH or CPU slot.
		Typically this UPD is assigned after parsing the PCI tree "ON" device tag as part of the devicetree.cb file.
PcdSerialIoUartNumber	Select SerialIo Uart Controller for debug	It's an additional responsibility of FSP-M to perform initialization of Serial IO UART due to the fact that FSP-T is optional.
		Mainboard users provide the Serial IO UART number for debug. CONFIG_UART_FOR_CONSOLE is getting assigned into this UPD.

With this, the system firmware in hybrid mode is almost ready to pass the FSP-M stage seamlessly. This board configuration is done as part of the following files:

- `mainboard/intel/$BOARD/romstage.c`

- `mainboard/intel/$BOARD/devicetree.cb`

Step 2.d: Configure FSP-S related UPDs

The remaining platform initialization (CPU feature initialization, chipset registers and IO interfaces) are programmed as part of FSP-S API being called from the boot firmware. As the CPU is capable of enabling the same hardware controller using different an interface and relying on the underlying hardware to design with a single interface (for example, the audio controller can configure using HDA link, non-HDA I2S interface, or modern soundwire), it's the hardware design which enables a single interface and responsibility of the system firmware to initialize the audio controller in the desire mode.

FSP-S being the replacement for the silicon reference code to enable/ disable the hardware interface as per hardware design requirement with easy to configure UPDs.

In this case study, we are using a reference schematic where a number of IOs are attached with PCH. Hence, FSP-S is not only responsible to make these devices functional but also to disable the unused hardware interfaces for better power number during the active idle scenarios.

Let's start with the USB device configuration as per reference schematics.

Controller	Device	Endpoints
XHCI	USB	Two Type-A USB 2.0 at Port 6 and 8
		One Type-C at USB Port 0
		Bluetooth connected at USB2.0 Port 3
		1 Type-C USB 3.0 at Port 2

The underlying SoC has 10 USB 2.0 ports and 4 USB 3.0 ports, out of that only the listed above USB endpoints are exposed to the platform layer hence system firmware is responsible for enabling these endpoint devices and exposing the same capabilities to upper layer system software as well.

Typically, the USB configuration in system firmware has multiple operations in it:

1. **Ensure the USB Over Current (OC) Programming**: As per board schematics, there is an OC PIN associated with every USB port and it is the responsibility of the silicon reference code to ensure the OC PIN is getting program correctly to avoid damaging any USB ports or associated device to it.

2. **Disable the unused USB ports**: Turn off the port power for unused USB ports.

3. **Runtime interface**: Provide information about the USB port like location on board and the types of USB device being connected to the kernel USB driver for runtime managing the port power.

At present FSP-S is responsible for all sorts of boot services related to communication with IP components using applicable UPD.

FSP-S mainboard USB configurable UPD	Description	Programmable value
PortUsb20Enable PortUsb30Enable	Enable USB2/USB3 ports. One byte for each port, byte0 for port0, byte1 for port1, and so on.	coreboot USB device configuration as part of devicetree.cb takes care of enabling the used port going through USB OC programming.
		And any USB port that doesn't have a device is tagged as USBx_PORT_ EMPTY, where x= 2 or 3 based on the USB port, so the respective port index will be set to 0.
Usb20verCurrentPin Usb30verCurrentPin	Describe the specific overcurrent pin number of USB 2.0/3.0 Port N	Based on hardware design, the number of the OC PIN count can be used here in this example:
		For USB 2.0 device:
| | | ```
# Type-C Port 1
register "usb2_ports[0]"
= "USB2_PORT_LONG(OC0)"

# Empty
register "usb2_ports[1]"
= "USB2_PORT_EMPTY"

# Bluetooth
register "usb2_ports[2]"
= "USB2_PORT_MID(OC_SKIP)"

# Type-A
register "usb2_ports[6]" =
"USB2_PORT_MID(OC2)"
``` |

(continued)
```

FSP-S mainboard USB configurable UPD	Description	Programmable value
| | | ```
# Type-A
register "usb2_ports[8]" = "USB2_PORT_MID(OC2)"
``` |
| | | For USB 3.0 device: |
| | | ```
# Type-C Port 1
register "usb3_ports[0]" = "USB3_PORT_DEFAULT(OC0)"
``` |
| | | ```
# Empty
register "usb3_ports[1]" = "USB3_PORT_EMPTY"
``` |
| | | ```
# Type-A Port
register "usb3_ports[2]" = "USB3_PORT_DEFAULT(OC2)"
``` |
| | | ```
# Empty
register "usb3_ports[3]" = "USB3_PORT_EMPTY"
``` |

Similarly, here is the LPSS device configuration as per reference schematics:

Controller	Device	Endpoints
LPSS	I2C	3 I2C devices in PCI mode
	GSPI	1 GSPI device in PCI mode
	UART	Only UART2 enable in PCI mode
```

Platform devices like touch screens, trackpads, styluses, TPM chips, and the kernel debug interface relying on LPSS controllers. These devices can be configured into different modes based on the usage mode in system firmware or OS. Here is list of different operating mode in general that can be used for any LPSS device configuration as applicable:

Disable: The device is not required in the boot phase or after booting to the OS so make use of sideband interface to disable that device. Note: Once the device is disable as part of FSP initialization it can't be enabled without modifying the system firmware.

PCI mode: The device being configured to this mode is accessible using PCI configuration read/write operations while in the pre-boot phase and also after booting to the OS.

ACPI mode: Mostly used for higher level system software; in this mode, the device is mapped to system memory and put into lower power mode unless the kernel driver again brings back the device.

Hidden mode: The device is not completely disable but hidden from PCI bus by padding the PCI device Device ID (DID)and Vendor ID (VID) so that any high-level software or driver can't access the device unless it knows the Base Address Register (BAR) value for accessing the device register's space.

SkipInit mode: The device is already initialized by the boot firmware and users don't want to disturb the hardware initialization; rather they want FSP to use the device as is if required. In this mode, FSP is not initializing the device prior to use.

FSP-S mainboard LPSS configurable UPD	Description	Programmable value

SeriaIIoI2cMode SeriaIIoSpiMode SeriaIIoUartMode	Enable SeriaIIo I2C/SPI/ UART device mode
	
	Depending on these values, FSP would configure the LPSS device into the desired mode.
	
	0: Disabled, 1: PCI mode, 2: Acpi mode, 3: Hidden mode
	
	For UART, there is another special mode called SkipInit.
		In devicetree.cb, LPSS device configuration being taken care:
		`register "SerialIoDevMode"`
		`= "{`
		`[PchSerialIoIndexI2C0]  =`
		`PchSerialIoPci,`
		`[PchSerialIoIndexI2C1]  =`
		`PchSerialIoPci,`
		`[PchSerialIoIndexI2C2]  =`
		`PchSerialIoPci,`
		`[PchSerialIoIndexSpi0]  =`
		`PchSerialIoPci,`
		`[PchSerialIoIndexUart0] =`
		`PchSerialIoPci,`
		`[PchSerialIoIndexUart1] =`
		`PchSerialIoDisabled,`
		`[PchSerialIoIndexUart2] =`
		`PchSerialIoSkipInit, }"`

Apart from this, there are other I/O devices attached to the motherboard that also need to be configured as per schematics hence this list is useful for overriding the UPD as applicable as per the underlying hardware.

FSP-S mainboard device configurable UPD	Description	Programmable value
ScsEmmcEnabled	Enable eMMC Controller	Enable eMMC controller as part of devicetree.cb configuration block: `register "ScsEmmcEnabled" = "1"`
ScsEmmcHs400Enabled	Enable eMMC in HS400 mode and perform the DLL tuning	`register "ScsEmmcHs400Enabled" = "1"`
ScsSdCardEnabled	Enable SdCard controller	`register "ScsSdCardEnabled" = "1"`
PcieRpClkReqSupport	Enable PCIe Root Port CLKREQ Support	This information can be retrieved from hardware schematics as in Figure 33. Each byte represents each PCIe root port.
PcieRpClkReqNumber	Configure root port CLKREQ number if CLKREQ is supported	Each value in the array can be between 0-6. This information can be retrieved from hardware schematics as in Figure 33.
PcieRpClkSrcNumber	Configure CLKSRC number	This CLKSRC number can be either a PEG CLKSRC (0x40 onwards) or PCH CLKSRC (between 0-6) or LAN CLKSRC (0x70) or unused as 0xFF.

For any endpoint device like WLAN, SSD, NVME, Discrete cards are attached to the PCIe root port, users need to gather the required root port numbers, CLKSRC and CLKREQ details to feed into FSP for endpoint device initialization. See Figure 7-35.

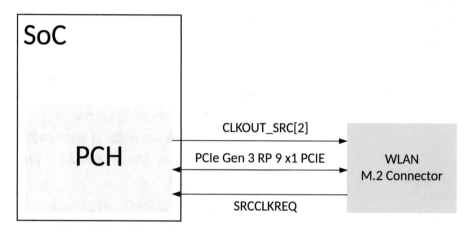

Figure 7-35. *Example of WLAN device attached to PCIe x1 slot*

Note   The BIOS to program CLKREQ as Native GPIO function to use these pins as CLKREQ.

Apart from this list, there can be other useful UPDs as additional devices are attached to the motherboard.

FSP-S mainboard device configurable UPD	Description	Programmable value
GraphicsConfigPtr	Graphics configuration pointer to VBT	Video BIOS Table (VBT) being part of FSP external GitHub needs additional configuration based on the motherboard display endpoint device attached.
		BIOS to get VBT from CBFS and update this UPD to let FSP allow programming the onboard display controller.
		`params->GraphicsConfigPtr = (u32) vbt_get();`
SataEnable	Enable SATA controller if the board has provision for M.2 slot for SATA or direct SATA port	Enable SATA port and configure the operating mode either as AHCI or RAID mode.

At the exit of FSP-S and as control gets back into the boot firmware, all required hardware interfaces are configured as per target hardware. Now the BIOS performs the PCI enumeration and resource allocation, followed by the creation of a runtime system memory map table for OS consumption as part of E820 table, ACPI tables, SMBIOS tables, and tables required for payload to pass the boot critical information. coreboot calls NotifyPhase (a subphase of FSP-S for any additional SoC recommended lockdown and configuration typically independent of board config) prior handing over to the payload.

Hybrid Firmware Development Model Conclusion

This case study provided a vision of the future system firmware scope using widely used CPU architectures where the hybrid model is already being adapted by leading SoC suppliers for various product segments, such as AMD and Intel for their latest products. Due to the wider acceptance of this model, this case study is different from the other case studies presented in this chapter earlier because it provides the real platform enabling knowledge that you can apply directly while working on your product without much deviation.

Summary

This chapter provided extensive case studies with a thorough exercise in analyzing the real-time requirements of various computing machines with different application scope like evaluation engineering board, laptops, and servers on a wide range of CPU architecture like x86 and ARM-based system solutions.

These case studies are performed across various system firmware frameworks like coreboot, UEFI, LinuxBoot, and FSP in order to demonstrate that there is no need to stick with a specific firmware design while supporting architecture migration or exploring an out-of-box design approach in system firmware which eventually nullifies the legacy assumptions.

Adaptive multithreaded in a pre-boot environment is the future of system firmware based on various use case limitations and scope of improvement in modern computing systems.

Innovation in CPU architecture and platform design really helps to reduce the firmware boundary, and this migration is also reflective to any system firmware architecture.

The legacy of system firmware is being continued even in the modern era where OSes are quite powerful enough to understand the underlying hardware or able to communicate with native hardware directly. This migration in system firmware architecture is a much needed step towards designing LITE firmware.

Finally, in this competitive world where the open source firmware model is also looking to find its permanent place in the mainstream of firmware development across widely used CPU architecture based products, the hybrid firmware development model is the answer towards such adaptability questions.

The results shown from these case studies are optimistic that most stringent real-time platform requirements can be addressed by open source firmware solutions with ease. Thus, the open source firmware solution can apply on any CPU architecture with a vision to design system firmware with flexibility and reduced boundary to boot to the OS. The open source firmware development with an FSP-like minimum binary model is positioned to meet and potentially extend the support even on latest chipsets from CPU vendors where the entire specification is not open source friendly yet.

Correction to: Starter

Correction to:

Chapter 1 in Subrata Banik and Vincent Zimmer, *System Firmware*
https://doi.org/10.1007/978-1-4842-7939-7_1

The title of this chapter has been changed from Introduction to Starter
after the initial publication.

The updated original version of the chapter can be found at
https://doi.org/10.1007/978-1-4842-7939-7_1

© Subrata Banik and Vincent Zimmer 2023
S. Banik and V. Zimmer, *System Firmware*,
https://doi.org/10.1007/978-1-4842-7939-7_8

APPENDIX A

Postcodes

Postcodes are a sign of life on embedded systems. A postcode is typically a small number that designates where in the startup of the firmware or its "power on self test" the firmware has last reached. Typically, all embedded devices are flashed with released versions of system firmware, which means postcodes are the only possible way to detect any failures. Depending on the endpoint, postcodes could be either 1 or 2 bytes in width. Each system firmware uses its own implementation of postcodes to report device boot state. Tables A-1 and A-2 list the postcodes used in the FSP specification and Table A-3 lists coreboot as the boot firmware. Table A-4 lists postcodes when coreboot and FSP work in hybrid mode.

© Subrata Banik and Vincent Zimmer 2022
S. Banik and V. Zimmer, *System Firmware*,
https://doi.org/10.1007/978-1-4842-7939-7

Table A-1. *Generic FSP Postcodes*

FSP API: TempRamInit

Postcode	Description
0x0000	TempRamInit API Entry
0x007F	TempRamInit API Exit

FSP API: FspMemoryInit

0xD800	FspMemoryInit API Entry
0xD87F	FspMemoryInit API Exit
0xDC00	Pre-Mem Entry
0xDC7F	Pre-Mem Exit

FSP API: TempRamExit

0xB800	TempRamExit API Entry
0xB87F	TempRamExit API Exit

FSP API: FspSiliconInit

0x9800	FspSiliconInit API Entry
0x987F	FspSiliconInit API Exit
0x9C00	Post-Mem Entry
0x9C7F	Post-Mem Exit

FSP API: NotifyPhase

0x6800	NotifyPhase API Entry
0x687F	NotifyPhase API Exit

Table A-2. *Platform-Specific FSP Postcodes (Subject to Change)*

Postcode	Description
0xDA00	Pre-Mem SaInit Entry
0xDA01	DeviceConfigurePreMem Start
0xDA06	Programming SA BARs
0xDA08	Install SA HOBs
0xDA10	Initializing DMI
0xDA50	Initializing Graphics
0xDB00	PCH API Entry
0x9A00	Post-Mem SaInit Entry
0x9A01	DeviceConfigure Start
0x9A03	Initializing Pei Display
0x9A05	CallPpiAndFillFrameBuffer
0x9A06	GraphicsPpiInit
0x9A07	GraphicsPpiGetMode
0x9A61	Set BIOS_RESET_CPL to indicate all configurations complete
0x9A63	GraphicsPmInit Start
0x9B01 - 0x980D	Post-Mem Device Configuration
0x9B40	Post-Mem OnEndOfPEI Entry
0x9B4F	Post-Mem OnEndOfPEI Exit

Table A-3. *coreboot Generic Postcodes*

Postcode	Description
0x01	Reset Vector jumps into correct code segment
0x10	Entry into protected mode
0x11	Prior ramstage is loaded into memory (decompressed if compressed before copying)
0x12	Represents the end of romstage (ramstage is copied into memory and about to jump there)
0x13	Entry into ramstage
0x34	Pre-memory init preparation start
0x36	Pre-memory init preparation end
0x39	Console is initialized and is ready to use
0x40	Console boot message has successfully transmitted
0x60	Prior enabling the cache
0x6e	Pre call to ramstage main() function
0x6f	Starting of ramstage (represents ramstage has loaded and executed successfully)
0x70	Boot State Machine: Before device probe
0x71	Boot State Machine: Initialize chips
0x72	Boot State Machine: Start device enumeration
0x73	Boot State Machine: Device resource allocation
0x74	Boot State Machine: Device enable
0x75	Boot State Machine: Device initialization
0x76	Boot State Machine: Device probe

(continued)

Table A-3. (*continued*)

Postcode	Description
0x77	Boot State Machine: OS resume check
0x78	Boot State Machine: OS resume
0x79	Boot State Machine: Write tables
0x7a	Boot State Machine: Load payload
0x7b	Boot State Machine: Boot payload
0x96	Indicates entry into ACPI _PTS control method
0x97	Indicates entry into ACPI _WAK control method
0xe1	Invalid or corrupt CBFS
0xe4	Hardware initialization failure
0xe5	TPM state or failure during communication
0xee	Entry into dead code (function that shouldn't have returned)
0xef	Resume from suspend failure
0xf3	Jumping to payload
0xfd	Successfully able to resume from suspend
0xfe	Successfully able to boot to OS
0xff	Error code attached with boot stage or payload

Table A-4. *coreboot Postcodes with FSP in Hybrid Mode*

0x88	Prior calling FSP Notify phase (End of Firmware)
0x89	After calling FSP Notify phase (End of Firmware)
0x90	Before calling FSP TempRamInit
0x91	Before calling FSP TempRamExit
0x92	Before calling FSP Memory Init
0x93	Before calling FSP Silicon Init
0x94	Before calling FSP Notify phase (after PCI enumeration)
0x95	Before calling FSP Notify phase (ready to boot)
0x98	After calling FSP Memory Init
0x99	After calling FSP Silicon Init
0xa0	Before calling FSP Multiphase Silicon Init
0xa1	After calling FSP Multiphase Silicon Init

APPENDIX B

Data Types

In the type-based system programming language that is used for system firmware development, such as C, a data type represents the attribute of the data. Every bootloader has its own way to tell the compiler how they intended to use the data. Each bootloader implements its own data types, so developers need to have an understanding of the different data types used by popular open source bootloaders, such as EFI/UEFI or coreboot, while working on architecture migration from closed source firmware projects. Tables B-1 and B-3 provide a high-level overview of the most common data types and modifiers in system firmware development. Table B-2 lists unique EFI data types. When adding new compiler support using these bootloaders, developers should be aware of which file to locate, such as the file ProcessorBind.h in EDKII to add UEFI data types and stdint.h in a coreboot project to add compiler-specific data types. These data types can be used to build more complex data structures.

© Subrata Banik and Vincent Zimmer 2022
S. Banik and V. Zimmer, *System Firmware*,
https://doi.org/10.1007/978-1-4842-7939-7

Table B-1. *Common EFI and coreboot Data Types*

EFI Mnemonic	coreboot Mnemonic	Description
BOOLEAN	bool	Logical Boolean Size: 1-byte Possible Values: 1 for TRUE/true, 0 for FALSE/false
INT8	int8_t	Signed 1-byte value Min Value: 0x80 Max Value: 0x7F
UINT8	uint8_t	Unsigned 1-byte value Max Value: 0xFF
INT16	int16_t	Signed 2-byte value Min Value: 0x8000 Max Value: 0x7FFF
UINT16	uint16_t	Unsigned 2-byte value Max Value: 0xFFFF
INT32	int32_t	Signed 4-byte value Min Value: 0x8000_0000 Max Value: 0x7FFF_FFFF
UINT32	uint32_t	Unsigned 4-byte value Max Value: 0xFFFF_FFFF
INT64	int64_t	Signed 8-byte value Min Value: 0x80000000_00000000 Max Value: 0x7FFFFFFF_FFFFFFFF
UINT64	uint64_t	Unsigned 8-byte value Max Value: 0xFFFFFFFF_FFFFFFFF

(*continued*)

Table B-1. (*continued*)

EFI Mnemonic	coreboot Mnemonic	Description
INTN	intmax_t	Signed n-byte value n = 4 bytes on 32-bit and 8 bytes on 64-bit operations
UINTN	uintmax_t	Unsigned n-byte value n = 4 bytes on 32-bit and 8 bytes on 64-bit operations
CHAR8	char	1-byte character
VOID	void	Undeclared type When used in a function, referred as no return value has the return type as void. Similarly no argument value in function calls uses void argument. Using pointers represents the address of an object, which can be cast into any other data type.
Enumerated Type (Enum)		Elements inside an enum are a signed value

Table B-2. *Unique EFI Data Types*

EFI Mnemonic	Description
EFI_GUID	128-bit number that represents a global unique identifier. Any ppi, protocol, device, instance, and image defined in UEFI should be associated with an EFI_GUID type.
EFI_STATUS	Represents an EFI status code in INTN type. This could be a combination of success, failure, warning, and device states.

Table B-3. *Common EFI and coreboot Modifiers*

EFI Mnemonic	Coreboot	Description
CONST	DEVTREE_ CONST	This modifier associated with a data type makes the data *read only*. This allows the compiler to enable optimization to generate more efficient code.
STATIC	MAYBE_ STATIC_ NONZERO	Having a local scope while defined in a function and defined as a variable increases its scope to lifetime while the program is running.
VOLATILE	volatile	Defines a variable as volatile and tells the compiler that it's exempt from optimization because the value of the variable may change without any action being taken as part of the code. This data type should be used on variables accessing the hardware device.

Glossary

ACPI	Advanced Configuration and Power Interface
AL	After Life; in the context of this book, any runtime service that is part of system firmware is referred to as AL.
ALU	Arithmetic-logic unit; a part of the CPU that performs arithmetic and logical operations on the operands. It is divided into two units, an arithmetic unit (AU) and a logic unit (LU).
AMBA	Advanced Microcontroller Bus Architecture
AP	Application processor; typically, in a multicore environment, any other processor cores apart from the powered-on default processor are referred to as application processors. Also, in embedded systems, application processors are referred to as the core that runs the bootstrap program.
APCB	AMD PSP Control Block
ARM	Advanced RISC Machine, formerly known as Acorn RISC machine
ASL	ACPI source language
BAR(s)	Base Address Register(s); typically used to access the device address space that is behind the host bus
BIOS	Basic input/output system; in the context of this book, the bootloader, boot firmware, and payload are all part of the BIOS, which does the basic hardware initialization and boot to OS.
BIU	Bus Interface Unit

© Subrata Banik and Vincent Zimmer 2022
S. Banik and V. Zimmer, *System Firmware*,
https://doi.org/10.1007/978-1-4842-7939-7

BLx	Boot Loader stages as part of Trusted Firmware; examples are BL1, BL2, and BL3x
BSP	Boot Strap Processor, which comes out from the power-on reset and handles the platform initialization
CBFS	CBFS is a scheme for managing independent blocks of data as part of ROM. Though not a true filesystem, the style and concepts are similar to the coreboot filesystem.
CCD	Closed Case Debugging
CISC	Complex instruction set computer architecture; the idea here is that a single instruction can perform a number of low-level operations like a load from memory or an arithmetic operation that also stores or reads from memory, hence multiple steps can be accommodated using a single instruction.
coreboot	An open sourced, extended firmware platform that delivers a lightning fast and secure boot experience on embedded systems
CPU	Central processing unit
CSE	Intel® Converged Security Engine
CU	Control unit, a component of the CPU that directs operations within the processor
DCI	Intel® Direct Connect Interface
Depthcharge	Depthcharge is responsible for performing the Chrome OS-specific operations required prior to boot to OS and also act as bootloader for Chrome OS
DMI	Direct Media Interface, a proprietary link between the northbridge and southbridge on a computer motherboard
DSP	Digital signal processors
e820	A legacy mechanism to pass the memory map from boot firmware to the operating system
eNEM	enhanced NEM (No-Evict Mode)
EBC	EFI Byte Code

FSP	Firmware Support Package, a specification designed with standard API interface to perform silicon initialization and provide information back to the boot firmware
GCC	GNU Compiler Collection
GUID	Globally unique identifier, a unique identifier used in UEFI-based firmware is specified by a GUID
HOB(s)	Hand-off blocks; define a way to pass information between different phases of types of boot firmware
Hybrid	The term *hybrid* is used in the context of this book to define a firmware development model that allows open-source firmware development using limited SoC vendor provided blobs, such as coreboot. A coreboot firmware project accepts minimal boot critical SoC blobs integrated as part of the ROM image.
ICH	I/O controller hub; managed data communication between the CPU and motherboard components
IDE	An integrated development environment is used for software development.
IMD	In-memory database; an IMD resides in the cbmem region for creating a dynamic cbmem infrastructure
IRQ	Interrupt request
ISA	Instruction Set Architecture, also used in bus specification as Industry Standard Architecture
LinuxBoot	LinuxBoot was intended to be a firmware for modern servers that replaces specific firmware functionality like the UEFI DXE phase with a Linux kernel and runtime.
MCH	Intel® Memory Controller Hub
MIPS	Microprocessor without interlocked pipeline stages, a part of the RISC family
MMU	Memory management unit, responsible for translating all CPU virtual addresses into physical addresses and additionally controlling memory accesses

Multithreading	An environment that allows all possible processor cores to operate at same time using dedicated code and data stack without any coherency and resource conflicts
NEM	No-eviction mode
Payload	A separate firmware block that is responsible for booting to the kernel
PCH	Peripheral Controller Hub, the next generation to ICH that controls certain data paths and support functions used in conjunction with CPUs
PCI	Peripheral Component Interconnect
PCIe	Peripheral Component Interconnect Express
Product Development Phase	Typically, an embedded system goes through several phases starting from schematics design to the product reaching shelves. These stages are categories between Proto, Engineering Validation Test (EVT), Design Validation Test (DVT), Production Validation Test (PVT), and Mass Production (MP).
PSP	AMD Platform Security Processor, used to provide the trusted execution environment
Reset Vector	A 32-bit address where the CPU will start fetching the instruction post CPU reset. This address can be different between CISC and RISC architectures, and in most cases, this address is patchable using monitor code.
RISC	Reduced instruction set computer architecture; the idea here is to use simple commands that can be divided into several instructions but operate within a single clock cycle.

RISC-V   An open source instruction set architecture based on the RISC family

SA   System agent, traditionally known as *uncore*. Defined as a part of a microprocessor that is not in the core but still closely connected to the core to achieve high performance.

SBL   Slim Bootloader

SIMD   Single instruction multiple data

SPARC   Scalable Processor Architecture is a family member of RISC, originally developed by Sun Microsystems.

TF   Trusted Firmware, formerly known as ARM Trusted Firmware

Tianocore   An open source implementation of UEFI. In some cases, it's used as a payload with other bootloaders, such as coreboot and SBL.

TLB   Translation lookaside buffer, contains a translated entry for the virtual address and the access control logic to determine the access if permitted

TOLUD   Top of lower usable DRAM

TOM   Top of memory

TOUUD   Top of upper usable DRAM

TSEG   Top of the main memory segment; this region is used to specify the amount of memory space required while operating in System Management Mode (SMM).

UEFI   Unified Extensible Firmware Interface

U-root   Universal root, an open source project hosted on GitHub

UPD   Updatable product data, a data structure that holds configuration regions being part of FSP binary

x86   A family member of CISC. x86 is typically used to refer to the 8086 processor family.

Reference

Websites

Coredna. *What is Open Source Software?,* Comparing Open Source Software vs Closed Source Software (Introduction): `www.coredna.com/blogs/comparing-open-closed-source-software`

Christian. *Open-source-firmware-why-should-we-support-it,* Alternatives for the Basic Input Output System for server or client devices (Introduction): `https://hackernoon.com/open-source-firmware-why-should-we-support-it-xqdy3bjg`

Abhishek Pande. *ARM Processor Modes,* Understanding the ARM Processor Operational Modes (Chapter 2): `www.slideshare.net/abhi165/arm-modes`

John Catsoulis. *Designing Embedded Hardware,* Explore a preview version of Designing Embedded Hardware (Chapter 2): `www.oreilly.com/library/view/designing-embedded-hardware/0596007558/ch01.html`

GeeksforGeeks. *I/O Interface (Interrupt and DMA Mode),* Understanding the method that is used to transfer information between internal storage and external I/O devices is known as I/O interface (Chapter 2): `www.geeksforgeeks.org/io-interface-interrupt-dma-mode/`

Deep Raj Bhujel. *Functional Block Diagram of 8086 microprocessor,* A simple overview of 8086 microprocessor (Chapter 2): `https://deeprajbhujel.blogspot.com/2015/12/functional-block-diagram-of-8086.html`

REFERENCE

Intel Corporation. *Intel 64 and IA-32 Architectures Software Developer Manuals,* These manuals describe the architecture and programming environment of the Intel 64 and IA-32 architectures (Chapter 2): www.intel.com/content/www/us/en/developer/articles/technical/intel-sdm.html

Alex Dzyoba. *Basic X86 interrupts,* Knowledge to initiallze x86 interrupts (Chapter 2): https://alex.dzyoba.com/blog/os-interrupts/

ARM Limited. *Trusted Firmware Open Governance Project,* The reference implementation of Secure world software for Arm architectures (Chapter 3): https://developer.arm.com/tools-and-software/open-source-software/firmware/trusted-firmware

Chromium OS. *ARM Trusted Firmware Design,* Understanding ARM Trusted Firmware (Chapter 3): https://chromium.googlesource.com/external/github.com/ARM-software/arm-trusted-firmware/+/v0.4-rc1/docs/firmware-design.md

Brett Daniel. *Giant List of Intel's Advanced Technologies,* Intel's processors are equipped with a multitude of technologies that can improve the overall performance of your rugged server or workstation (Chapter 3): www.trentonsystems.com/blog/giant-list-intel-advanced-technologies

Science Direct. *Reset Vector,* By enabling the reset Vector-Catch feature and resetting the system (Chapter 3): www.sciencedirect.com/topics/engineering/reset-vector

Coreboot GitHub. *Starting from scratch,* This document to guide about how to build coreboot (Chapter 4): https://doc.coreboot.org/tutorial/part1.html

TrustedFirmware.org. *Trusted Firmware-A Documentation,* Trusted Firmware-A (TF-A) provides a reference implementation of secure world software for Arm SoCs (Chapter 4: https://trustedfirmware-a.readthedocs.io/en/latest/

Slim Bootloader. *Slim Bootloader Project Documentation*, Slim Bootloader Open Source Project (version 1.0) documentation! (Chapter 4): `https://slimbootloader.github.io/index.html`

PhoenixTS. *UEFI-vs-Legacy-BIOS*, UEFI vs Legacy BIOS Booting: What's the Difference? (Chapter 4): `https://phoenixts.com/blog/uefi-vs-legacy-bios/`

David Morelo. *Coreboot Versus UEFI*, High level difference between coreboot and UEFI (Chapter 4): `https://linuxhint.com/coreboot-vs-uefi/`

Universal Scalable Firmware. *Linux Payload*, To build a basic Linux payload conforming to universal payload standard (Chapter 6): `https://github.com/UniversalScalableFirmware/linuxpayload`

Universal Scalable Firmware. *Welcome to the Universal Scalable Firmware project*, Universal Scalable Firmware Specification (Chapter 6): `https://github.com/UniversalScalableFirmware`

Tianocore. *UEFI Payload for Coreboot Project*, Understanding Tianocore UefiPayloadPkg (Chapter 6): `https://github.com/tianocore/tianocore.github.io/wiki/Coreboot_UEFI_payload`

Chromium OS Document. *USB Type-C PD Firmware*, Understanding firmware update for TCPC chips (Chapter 6): `https://chromium.googlesource.com/chromiumos/docs/+/master/pd_firmware_update.md`

LWN.net. *LinuxBoot: Linux as firmware*, Application for Linux as Firmware (Chapter 6 and Chapter 7): `https://lwn.net/Articles/748586/`

Coreboot GitHub. *Starting from scratch*, This document to guide about how to build coreboot (Chapter 7): `https://doc.coreboot.org/tutorial/part1.html`

Lowrisc. *Open source silicon*, Open silicon makes it easier to create derivative designs and reduces time to market, while significantly lowering the barriers to producing an SoC design (Chapter 7): `www.lowrisc.org/`

Subrata Banik and Barnali Sarkar, Intel Corporation. *Reduce-firmware-booting-time-whitepaper*, Open Source Firmware Development Reduce

Firmware Booting Time Using Multi-Threaded Environment (Chapter 7): www.intel.com/content/dam/www/public/us/en/documents/ white-papers/reduce-firmware-booting-time-whitepaper.pdf

FOSDEM, Intel Corporation. *Capsule Update and LVFS Improving System Firmware Update* (Chapter 7): https://archive.fosdem. org/2020/schedule/event/firmware_culisfu/attachments/ slides/3709/export/events/attachments/firmware_culisfu/ slides/3709/FOSDEM_2020_Intel_Capsule_Update.pdf

References for the Chapter 1

Books

[B-1] Jiming Sun, Vincent Zimmer, Marc Jones, Stefan Reinauer, *Embedded Firmware Solutions*, Apress 2015.

[B-2] Vincent Zimmer, Michael Rothman, Suresh Marisetty, *Beyond BIOS: Developing with the Unified Extensible Firmware Interface, 3rd edition*, DeG, 2017.

[B-3] Vincent Zimmer, Michael Rothman, Robert Hale, *UEFI: From Reset Vector to Operating System*, in Chapter 3 of Hardware-Dependent Software, Springer, 2009.

[B-4] Sunil Cheruvu, Anil Kumar, Ned Smith, David M. Wheeler, *Demystifying Internet of Things Security*, Apress, 2020.

Conferences, Journals, and Papers

[P-1] David Weston, *"Hardening With Hardware"*, in BlueHat 2018 https://github.com/microsoft/MSRC-Security-Research/blob/ master/presentations/2018_01_BlueHatIL/BlueHatIL18_Weston_ Hardening_With_Hardware.pdf

[P-2] David Weston, "*Advanced Windows Security*", in Platform Security Summit 2019, www.platformsecuritysummit.com/2019/speaker/weston/

[P-3] Eclypsium, "*Anatomy of a Firmware Attack*", 2019, https://eclypsium.com/2019/12/20/anatomy-of-a-firmware-attack/

[P-4] Eclypsium, "*FISMA compliance firmware security best practices*", 2019, https://eclypsium.com/2019/05/13/fisma-compliance-firmware-security-best-practices/

[P-5] NIST, "*Hardware-Enabled Security for Server Platforms*", in NIST whitepaper, 2020, available at https://nvlpubs.nist.gov/nistpubs/CSWP/NIST.CSWP.04282020-draft.pdf

Specifications and Guidelines

[S-1] UEFI Organization, "*UEFI Specification*", 2019, available at www.uefi.org/

[S-2] UEFI Organization, "*UEFI Platform Initialization Specification*", 2019, available at www.uefi.org/

[S-3] UEFI Organization, "*ACPI Specification*", 2019, available at www.uefi.org/

[S-4] PCI-SIG, "*PCI Express Base Specification*", 2019, https://pcisig.com/

[S-5] CXL Org, "*Compute Express Link Specification*", 2019, www.computeexpresslink.org/

Websites

Tianocore. *What is TianoCore?*, TianoCore, the community supporting an open source implementation of the Unified Extensible Firmware Interface (UEFI): www.tianocore.org/

Coreboot. *Fast, secure and flexible OpenSource firmware,* an open source project that provides auditability and maximum control over technology: `www.coreboot.org/`

Linuxboot. *Linux as Firmware,* LinuxBoot is a firmware for modern servers that replaces specific firmware functionality like the UEFI DXE phase with a Linux kernel and runtime: `www.linuxboot.org`

Slim Booloader. *Slim Bootloader Project Documentation*, Welcome to Slim Bootloader Open Source Project (version 1.0) documentation!: `https://slimbootloader.github.io/`

U-Boot. *Das U-Boot -- the Universal Boot Loader,* Welcome to the Wiki area for cooperating on U-Boot development. `www.denx.de/wiki/U-Boot`

Intel. *Intel Firmware Support Package (FSP)*, Intel Firmware Support Package (Intel FSP) provides key programming information for initializing Intel silicon and can be easily integrated into a boot loader of the developer's choice: `www.intel.com/FSP`

GitHub. *Sound Open Firmware (SOF)*, Sound Open Firmware is an open source community that provides an open source audio DSP firmware and SDK for audio or signal processing on modern DSPs: `https://github.com/thesofproject`

GitHub. *Open Baseboard Management Controller (openbmc),* OpenBMC is a Linux distribution for management controllers used in devices such as servers, top of rack switches or RAID appliances. `https://github.com/openbmc/openbmc`

GitHub. *Open Power*, A place to collaborate on OpenPOWER firmware related projects: `https://github.com/open-power`

IBM. Technical Reference for developing BIOS for IBM PC/AT Platform: `http://bitsavers.informatik.uni-stuttgart.de/pdf/ibm/pc/at/6183355_PC_AT_Technical_Reference_Mar86.pdf`

References for Chapter 5

ACPI. *Advanced Configuration and Power Interface,* version 6.0, www.uefi.org

BSF. *Boot Setting File (BSF) Specification,* https://firmware.intel.com/sites/default/files/BSF_1_0.pdf

EDK2. *UEFI Developer Kit,* www.tianocore.org

EDKII specification. *A set of specifications describe EDKII DEC/INF/DSC/FDF file format, as well as EDKII BUILD.* http://tianocore.sourceforge.net/wiki/EDK_II_Specifications

FSP EAS. *FSP External Architecture Specification,* www.intel.com/content/www/us/en/embedded/software/fsp/fsp-architecture-spec-v2.html

FSP Consumer. Yao, Zimmer, Rangarajan, Ma, Estrada, Mudusuru, *A_Tour_Beyond_BIOS_Using_the_Intel_Firmware_Support_Package_with_the_EFI_Developer_Kit_II_(FSP2.0),* https://github.com/tianocore/tianocore.github.io/wiki/EDK-II-white-papers

UEFI Book. Zimmer, et al, *Beyond BIOS: Developing with the Unified Extensible Firmware Interface,* 2nd edition, Intel Press, January 2011

UEFI Overview. Zimmer, Rothman, Hale, "UEFI: From Reset Vector to Operating System," Chapter 3 of *Hardware-Dependent Software,* Springer, 2009.

UEFI PI Specification. *UEFI Platform Initialization (PI) Specifications, volumes 1-5, Version 1.4,* www.uefi.org

Index

A

ACPI BIOS
  DSDT, 139
  post-OS boot, 139
  pre-OS boot, 139
ACPI fixed hardware/
      register, 135–137
ACPI namespace, 138
ACPI platform firmware, *see*
      ACPI BIOS
ACPI Source Language (ASL),
      139–141, 195
ACPI specification, 133, 135, 139,
      191, 302
ADD assembly instruction, 51
Address bus, 64, 66, 67, 84, 106, 108
Advanced Configuration and
      Power Interface (ACPI),
      32, 33, 133
  components, 134, 135
  hardware/register
    ACPI-compliant hardware
        platform, 135
    fixed, 135–137
    generic, 137
    programming model, 135
  OSPM enabling interface, 133

platform firmware, 139–141
software specification, 134
system description
      tables, 137–139
system power states, 141, 142
Advanced Power Management
      (APM), 23, 33, 134
Advanced programmable interrupt
      controller (APIC), 92,
      94, 96, 187
Advanced RISC Machines
      (ARM), 100
Advanced technology (AT), 120
Advanced vector extensions
      (AVX), 77
After Life (AL), 153, 195, 246
ALU operations instructions, 52
Always On Processor (AOP), 333
AMBA High-Speed Bus (AHB), 132
AMBA Peripheral Bus
      (APB), 65, 133
AMD Generic Encapsulated
      Software Architecture
      (AGESA), 321, 351–354
AmdInitEntry, 353, 354
AMD Opteron, 321
Analytical Engine, 47

© Subrata Banik and Vincent Zimmer 2022
S. Banik and V. Zimmer, *System Firmware*,
https://doi.org/10.1007/978-1-4842-7939-7

B

S